Ideology and Inquisition

MARTIN AUSTIN NESVIG

Ideology and Inquisition

THE WORLD OF THE CENSORS IN
EARLY MEXICO

Yale University Press
New Haven &
London

Published with assistance from the income of the Frederick John Kingsbury
Memorial Fund.

Set in Sabon type by Keystone Typesetting, Inc.
Printed in the United States of America by Sheridan Books.

Library of Congress Cataloging-in-Publication Data
Nesvig, Martin Austin, 1968–
Ideology and inquisition : the world of the censors in early Mexico / Martin
Austin Nesvig.
p. cm.
Includes bibliographical references and index.
ISBN 978-0-300-14040-8 (pbk. : alk. paper) 1. Inquisition — Mexico.
2. Censorship — Religious aspects — Catholic Church. 3. Censorship —
Mexico. I. Title.
BX1740.M6N47 2009
272'.20972 — dc22

2008054919

A catalogue record for this book is available from the British Library.

This paper meets the requirements of ANSI/NISO Z39.48-1992 (Permanence of
Paper).

10 9 8 7 6 5 4 3 2 1

For my parents

Contents

Acknowledgments

As in all projects like this one, one accumulates a good deal of debt from a wide range of people, institutions, and patrons. This book began nebulously as an investigation into the book trade and developed into a study of the ideology and mentality of censors. The result became less and less about the way the laity read books and more and more about the justification for restricting those books. When I formed it as a dissertation at Yale it was a pleasure being a student of Stuart Schwartz, whose wit and erudition remain ever impressive and who trained me in the vast and sprawling scholarship of the Iberian Atlantic and colonial world. Gil Joseph was a constant supporter and mentor and took on the chore of reading a colonialist and intellectual historian's work with characteristic generosity. Carlos Eire's keen sense for the subtleties of religious thought and deeply human sympathies continue to astonish me, even if my agnostic doubts continue. Paul Vanderwood has been a kind of vicarious mentor and terrific friend over the years, providing feedback and support (on many levels) all the while. Jim Muldoon lent the expertise of his medievalist eye and offered valuable feedback on the manuscript. Finally, I would like to thank the anonymous reviewers for Yale University Press, who provided scrutiny, close criticism, and suggestions that I hope have helped make this a better book. Likewise, had it not been for the support of Chris Rogers at Yale University Press this book would not have come to fruition; I want to thank him for his support as well as Laura Davulis for her help in the production process and Lawrence Kenney for his tremendous copyediting.

I received the social and intellectual support from many peers throughout the germination and completion of this project, and I wish to thank Alison Bruey, John Chuchiak, Alejandro Cortazar, Ryan Crew, Raphael Folsom, Íñigo García-Bryce, Sandra González Camacho, Pedro Guibovich, Dan Gutiér-rez, Renzo Honores, Kimberly Hossain, Emily Michelson, Claudia Montero, Jeremy Mumford, Matt O'Hara, Darren Provost, Jessica Stites-Mor, Zeb Tor-torici, Javier Villa-Flores, Nicole Von Germeten, and Eddie Wright-Rios. I want to thank especially Tatiana Seijas for her support in general and in par-ticular in the final stages of preparing the manuscript, as I scrambled to put together citations and gather permissions for images. In the broader Latin Americanist community many (senior) scholars have been generous with their time in offering advice, criticism, and reactions to this project: Linda Arnold, Sylvia Arrom, Dave and Sasha Cook, Susan Deeds, Bob Ferry, LuAnn Homza, Lyman Johnson, Kris Lane, Asunción Lavrin, Sonya Lipsett-Rivera, René Millar Carvacho, Cynthia Radding, Clara Inés Ramírez, Susan Ramírez, Terry Rugeley, Barry Sell, Gretchen Starr-LeBeau, Víctor Uribe, Ronaldo Vainfas, Pamela Voekel, and Eric Van Young.

Finally, I want to thank my parents for their enduring support through all these years. They were the first to teach me the value of education. And of course Paty for reminding me of why I love Mexico.

Members of the archival community, far and wide, have been especially gracious in allowing me access to their collections and materials. Father Sal-vador Treviño, S.J., has been a wonderful friend and sounding board over the years and was helpful, many years ago, in helping me to gain access to the Jesuits' Kino Library. I would like to extend my thanks to the staffs of the Archivo General de la Nación in Mexico, the Archivo del Convento de San Esteban, Salamanca, and the Archivo de la Universidad de Salamanca; to the staff of the British Library for their prompt response to requests for photo-copies of Melchor Cano's attack on the Jesuits; and to the Archivio Segreto Vaticano for providing a photocopy of Francisco Peña's unpublished censor-ship manual and to Emily Michelson for tracking down the photocopy for me while she was living in Rome. Likewise, the staffs of many libraries, not least that of Yale's Sterling Library, extended their every courtesy and access: the Beinecke Rare Book and Manuscript Library, the Biblioteca del Antiguo Col-egio de San Nicolás de Hidalgo in Morelia (where I felt every bit the part as I pored over Luis de Páramo's history of the Inquisition in the choir loft of the former Jesuit church), the Biblioteca Eusebio Kino, the Biblioteca Nacional de Chile, the Biblioteca Nacional de España, the Biblioteca Nacional de México, the Centro de Estudios de Historia de México, Condumex, and the John Carter Brown Library.

Several individuals and institutions were generous in allowing the reproduction of images: the Beinecke, the John Carter Brown Library, and the Archivo General de la Nación of Mexico. Portions of chapter 7 appeared as part of an article, " 'Heretical Plagues' and Censorship Cordons: Colonial Mexico and the Trans-Atlantic Book Trade" in *Church History* 75 (2006): 1–37.

Since coming to the Department of History at the University of Miami in 2005, I have been fortunate to work with a collegial and active group of scholars who have provided me with support and feedback. In addition to my colleagues in general, I want to thank Guido Ruggiero, Richard Godbeer, and Mary Lindemann for their helpful suggestions on the process of producing one's first monograph.

In addition to these collegial and social acknowledgments, I owe a debt of gratitude to various organizations that helped fund this project through many stages: the Yale Center for Latin American and Iberian Studies, the Department of History of Yale University, the Andrew W. Mellon Foundation, the Fulbright Commission, the Program for Cultural Cooperation between Spain's Ministry of Education, Culture, and Sports and United States Universities, a Hewlett Latin American Travel Grant, Henry Hart Rice Research Fellowship and John F. Enders Research Fellowship from the Yale Council on Latin American and Iberian Studies, the Beinecke, a Whiting Fellowship in the Humanities, and the University of Miami with Max Orowitz Awards in the Humanities and General Research and Scholarship Awards. Finally, Dean Michael Halleran and Senior Associate Dean Perri Lee Roberts of UM's College of Arts and Sciences generously granted a subvention for this book.

Note on Orthography and Names

In most cases I have included in the notes the original Latin quotations from the canonists' and theologians' discussions in as complete a form as is reasonable, given the frequent prolixity of these writers. I have preserved the idiosyncrasies of the late medieval and early modern Latin prose without changing it, with the exception of standardizing the spelling of the *Directorium Inquisitorum*. I have also modernized the spelling of Eimeric, as this seems to be the standardized modern Catalan spelling, though the variant spellings Eymeric, Eymerich, and Eimerich are found. I have otherwise also modernized medieval and early modern Latin proper names. Thus Gundissalvum becomes Gonzalo, Didacus and Jacobo become Diego, and so on. I have done the same with Latinized place-names, especially as they appear in publications, since they are listed in the locative case. Matriti (which means "in Madrid") becomes Madrid for a publication site, along with numerous other cities like Compluti (Alcalá or Madrid) and Venetiae (Venice). I have also Anglicized readily recognizable non-English place-names, such as Antwerp (instead of Amberes), Seville (instead of Sevilla), and Rome (instead of Roma).

Early modern Spanish orthography, the grammarian Antonio de Nebrija's notoriety notwithstanding, varied considerably in the early modern period. Letters like b, u, and v were often interchangeable, leading to multiple variant spellings like *cibdad* (*ciudad*) for "city," *a beces* (*a veces*) for "at times," to say nothing of the many auxiliary verbs in Spanish with the letter *b* (*haver,* in place of *haber; huuo,* in place of *hubo*). The same was true of the letters *ç, s,* and *z* and *x* and *j.* Thus one finds *muger* instead of *mujer* for "woman"; Suárez is found as Xuárez; González is found as Gonçález and Gonsález. A silent *h* is often found, and in other cases a silent *h* common today was absent. As a general rule I have modernized and standardized words with variant spellings, though I have left the original orthography in transcription. I have added accents where none existed in archival sources for grammatical consistency.

There is a growing debate among historical linguists, philologists, and ethnohistorians over the proper accentuation and spelling of various Indian language words, especially place-names, in Mexico. Nahuatl conventions are such that the penultimate syllable is stressed. The Hispanicization effort thus entered physical accent marks to change the pronunciation to final syllable pronunciation for hundreds of place-names to make their pronunciation more palatable to the Spanish ear. Virtually all Nahuatl place-names in Mexico that end in *-tlan* or *-an* have a diacritic over the final *a,* though this is, strictly speaking, incorrect. For example, the Nahuatl pronunciation of the capital, Tenochtitlan, should be pronounced thus even according to Spanish grammatical conventions, but the Hispanicized Tenochtitlán is often heard. Some have been moving toward the original Nahuatl pronunciation. However, it seems unlikely that certain place-names — for example, Michoacán, Mazatlán, and Culiacán — will ever return to the true Nahuatl pronunciation. Nevertheless, in places where it seems appropriate I have stuck with the non-Hispanicized diacritics and implied pronunciation, as in Tenochtitlan.

Unless otherwise specified all translations in this book are mine.

Introduction

Horace observed that "a word once uttered can never be recalled."[1] In 1552 the jurist Diego de Simancas — a member of the General Council of the Spanish Inquisition, bishop of Ciudad Rodrigo, hater and prosecutor of the archbishop of Toledo, Bartolomé Carranza — stole this line from Horace and concluded that "books of heretics must be sent to the fire . . . because they can endure for centuries and infect those that come after their publication. And while the voices of heretics can only fill a city, books can pass from region to region, from kingdom to kingdom."[2] Simancas expressed a centuries-old tradition in Catholic thought that associated heresy with abomination, sedition, and cancer. While the ultimate origins of heresy were often thought to be pride or the perversion of scripture, no one doubted that heresy was an infection. Jerome expressed this view, later codified in the Canon Law, the 1140 *Decretum:* "Heretics must be removed from the Church so that they do not infect the faithful with their contagion because putrescent meat must be cast out. The mangy sheep must be repelled from the flock and destroyed, so that it does not corrupt and putrefy the entire household, flock and body."[3]

Conquered in the context of growing religious reform and revolt in Spain, Mexico would provide fodder for the theorization of heresy as a "creeping evil." Mexico was seen as doctrinally isolated and a potentially unspoiled new Catholic kingdom, and the concerns about heresy related to the circulation of books and ideas were at the forefront of inquisitional debates about censorship there. Likewise, the question of Spanish men and women living in a transplanted Hispanic Catholic world of doctrine and culture manifested itself in questions about how to regulate ideas, tongues, and libraries through a supposedly universalist ideology (Catholicism) in a culturally specific region (the Indies). On the ideological frontlines of this debate were the censors of the Mexican Inquisition.

This book is about the world of the censor and the intellectual and cultural formation of his ideology. I examine the theory on which the inquisitional censorship apparatus was based and the subsequent application (or misapplication) of that theory in practice. In order to show just how censorship was viewed by the Church, the Crown, and the Crown's ministers, I include a discussion of the underlying theory of censorship that will elucidate the seriousness with which the censorship project was undertaken. The procedure of censorship occupies the other part of this study — the quotidian means by which the social control of ideas was implemented. Who were the censors? What made them think and operate the way they did? How did they come to the conclusions they made? On what did they base their decisions?

The conceptualization of censorship was deeply divided. From inquisitional manuals to the everyday debates within the confines of the Holy Office, the censors disagreed over many of the fundamental questions surrounding censorship. What was heresy? What was blasphemy? Could the Inquisition even claim jurisdiction over blasphemy? What books deserved censure? How did one go about finding a heretic? Could people be heretics if they had only had a heretical thought but never expressed it out loud? On these questions and many related ones, broad and significant disagreements emerged within the Hispanic Catholic world, reflecting less hegemony than discord and giving the lie to the presumption that the Catholic world quashed any substantive debate about political power, censorship, and, indeed, about the Inquisition itself.

While the censorship of books was the central concern of the Index of Prohibited Books, the process by which both books and ideas were regulated, censored, and controlled was the same. The Inquisition held jurisdiction over any sin-crimes (that is, violations of the Catholic doctrine, which were at once sins and crimes within the Inquisitional court) against the Catholic faith, and it did not distinguish between written heresy in a book and spoken heresy in the confines of a bar, home, convent, or pulpit. Thus the process of determining the nature of suspect statements was itself a subject of debate and deliberation — known as *calificación,* or review.

The inquisitional manual emerged in the thirteenth century to clarify the competing visions of inquisitional theory and censorship law, and by the sixteenth century it had developed into a form of high theory and practical advice. Such manuals contained interpretations of canon law, definitions of heresy, the logic for condemning heresy, and the need for such censorship. Censors were called as expert witnesses in inquisitional trials of both books and ideas. In the case of both Spain and Mexico, inquisitors called on theologians, often university professors or well-placed members of the mendicant orders or the Jesuits, to review the content of suspect ideas. The recommendations of the theologians concerning the orthodoxy of any given statement were influential pieces of an inquisitional trial, given that inquisitors, while not compelled to do so, rarely rejected the advice of theologians on the content of doctrinal issues.

While censors relied on the ostensibly universal definitions of Catholic doctrine, they came up squarely against the cultural exigencies of Mexico. Spanish men, who heavily outnumbered Spanish women among the Spaniards who came to Mexico in the sixteenth century, quickly adopted many cultural habits of Indians, surrounded as they were by their Indian domestic servants, lovers, and cooks. Chocolate, for example, a popular pre-Hispanic drink, underwent changes but was adopted as a stimulant by Spaniards. Theologians asked if it was a food or a drink. If it was only a drink, could one consume it before Mass without incurring penalty for having broken the ecclesiastical fast? Thus the official court historian of the Americas, Antonio de León Pinela, debated the issue in a treatise on the subject from 1636.[4] Peyote is a hallucinogen used by many Indians in religious ceremonies and by Spaniards as a divination device. Could it be rightfully consumed? The Mexican Inquisition banned its use in 1620, but within a year the Augustinian censor Martín Vergara asked if exceptions could be made to the ban if someone ate it for medicinal purposes.[5] How would Spanish priests preach the Gospel to the Indians — most of whom did not know Spanish, let alone Latin — with Latin Bibles? Could the ban on vernacular translations of the Bible promulgated in 1559 be overlooked in the interest of conversion? The infamous missionary Diego de Landa lobbied the Mexican Inquisition to overlook the prohibition on vernacular scripture in the interests of converting the Indians.[6] If a man was married to a woman in Spain and took a mistress in Mexico, did he violate the sacrament of marriage and therefore incur the penalty of heresy? All of these were questions that the inquisitors faced and on which they consulted their theologian-censors to help reconcile the global aspirations of universal doctrine with the cultural specificity of a new world, a new Church, and a new society.

But even if Mexico offered a unique context, the censors were schooled in a lengthy tradition of theological disputation as well as continuity in inquisitional law, theory, and practice. Simultaneously, they were living proof that

Figure 1. This image comes from a history of the Church in the Hispanic Americas (1649). From as early as the mid-sixteenth century indigenous symbols began to be incorporated into Spanish seals and coats of arms. The coat of arms pictured here is that of Mexico City. In the center are traditional symbols for Castile and León. Surrounding them are nopal cactus leaves, as a way of demonstrating the uniquely American identity of Mexico-Tenochtitlan. The Nahuatl word for the ancient capital means, loosely, in the place of the nopal cactus. Courtesy of John Carter Brown Library

the concerns about heresy as a "creeping evil" were more than the medieval minutiae of Innocent III or Boniface VIII. For example, in 1560 the dean of the Oaxaca cathedral chapter as inquisitor ordinary prosecuted the settler Arnaldo de Piamonte for blasphemy. The inquisitor called three Dominicans as censors to review the case—Pedro de la Peña, provincial of his order, Alonso de Sotomayor, lector in theology in Oaxaca, and Bernardo Albuquerque, bishop-elect of Oaxaca, prior of the Dominican house in Oaxaca, and himself inquisitor ordinary in 1563.[7] The Dominicans offered their review, concluding that Piamonte was guilty of heresy and "bad-sounding words." And while they offered no specific recommendations about punishment, they did offer a standard line about the dangers of heresy as a virus and Mexico as a pure land. They argued that Piamonte "should be punished very severely for his scandalous statements . . . especially considering that they were said in a new land, among people new in the faith and in such dangerous times."[8]

In addition to regulating everyday speech, the censors agreed that books which expressed heresy needed to be banned and destroyed. Likewise, given their view that the non-Latinized laity could not be expected to come to the correct exegetical conclusions from their reading of scripture, they generally agreed that translation of the Bible into the vernacular was a recipe for new heresies. The strictness of these views clashed with social reality on more than a few occasions. In 1572 the first large-scale purge of books took place in Mexico. Yet during this purge it was revealed that even the *Audiencia* (high court) judge Vasco de Puga possessed a banned copy of the Gospels in Spanish.[9] The Franciscans had also defied the Index in nearly all of their friaries' libraries, possessing prohibited books by Erasmus and John Wild (Johann Ferus). The Index may have arrived and its enforcer may have been empowered to see it obeyed, but many were loath to agree to its provisions.

The Index was the expression and culmination of the horror with which censors viewed heretical ideas expressed in print. And people have grown accustomed to assuming that the Index was a dreaded weapon of intellectual terror. Yet late in 1585 the inquisitors in Mexico City still had not received a copy of the new Index (1583).[10] Their deputies in most of Mexico never saw an Index. Some censors never liked the Dominicans of Salamanca, who fashioned the Index of 1583, in any case and were perfectly happy to ignore many of the prohibitions it made.

The overall picture is one of what William Christian Jr. calls the inherent entropy and decentralization of early modern Hispanic Catholicism.[11] But it is also a question of supposed universal theory and truths—the Doctrine—coming up against customary law and local tradition. If the Inquisition was based on eternal precepts, it also had to contend with the social and cultural

context in which it operated and which, like it or not, the censors and inquisitors had to consider in their daily decisions.

My book offers a reconsideration of inquisitional censorship in the Spanish
imperial world and colonial Mexico from methodological and thematic per-
spectives. Methodologically, the book combines traditional sources of intellectual history — printed discourse and treatises — with archival documentation
from within the confines of the Holy Office. Thematically, I reverse the investigative focus from those who were affected by the Inquisition to those who
fashioned and created it. The result is a book that examines the inner workings
and debates about the ideological justification for censorship from the point of
view of the censors themselves.

There is a venerable historiographic tradition associated largely with Spanish and Latin American historians who have labored intensely to show the
complexity of the many local Spanish Inquisitions as human institutions of
considerable ideological and social diversity, but very little of that scholarship
has focused on the ideological or sociological development of the censors
themselves.[12] Other studies have focused on the legal development of the
Inquisition or the jurisprudential context of its emergence.[13] Old conceptions
of the Spanish Inquisition as an integral part of the Black Legend portrayed the
Inquisition as an authoritarian and monochromatic institution bent on enforcing reactionary Catholicism. Henry Charles Lea saw the Inquisition as an
implacable force for obscurantism and repression.[14] This model has been challenged considerably, and even if there remains support for the Black Legend,
the assumption that the Inquisition was an undifferentiated tool of terror has
tended to be mitigated by the efforts of cultural historians. Henry Kamen and
Edward Peters were particularly influential in the English-speaking world for
revising this image, while an industry of Spanish and Latin American scholars
has consistently challenged the image of the Inquisition as ideologically uniform through various methodological and thematic examinations of the internal workings of the Inquisition and its sociological composition.[15] A good deal
of recent scholarship has focused on the social and cultural histories of peoples
and groups affected by inquisitional activities: folk healers, sodomites, black
African slaves, marginalized women, and people of mixed ethnicities.[16] The
scholarly investigations of Jews and *conversos* (Jews converted to Christianity), *alumbrados* (members of a spiritual sect which emphasized inner spirituality), and witchcraft have remained strong and vibrant subfields of Inquisition studies as well as valuable contributions to the newer tendency toward
cultural history.[17]

It is now a relatively accepted view that colonial rule and society were more
complex and interactive and less rigid than was once proposed. The Inquisi-

tion is seen as one of the principal bureaucratic instruments of Spanish colonial rule, and the colonial Iberian world is now seen as possessing a considerable degree of flexibility in adapting to local conditions. The additions to our understanding of colonial society and rule provided by social historians, ethnohistorians, and subaltern studies have emphasized the agency of peoples of formerly marginalized historiographic interest, of the back-and-forth nature of colonial power. That said, scholars remain relatively unsure of the nature of Catholic ideology which formed the basis for the justification of censorship. Accordingly, my conclusions about the Inquisition as being contingent on multiple competing interpretations of ideology add to the body of literature on the fluid nature of colonial or viceregal society.[18]

This book thus specifically examines the jurists and theologians who crafted inquisitional law and theory, put the Index into practice, and debated heresy in the secret confines of the inquisitional court. Some studies, like those by Roberto López Vela and Virgilio Pinto Crespo, have studied the censors and their collective ideologies, but in general little scholarly attention has been given to the censors as a group. In the Mexican context, they remain a shadowy group given the absence of sustained investigation (one exception is some brief work by María Águeda Méndez on Sor Juana's confessor, the Jesuit censor Antonio Núñez de Miranda).[19] Another strand of scholarship has focused on the legislative and legal developments of book censorship in global and often spectacularly wide-ranging fashion, as in the works of Jesús Martínez Bujanda, María Luisa López-Vidriero, Peter Cátedra, and Fermín de los Reyes Gómez.[20] Pedro Guibovich and Ángel Alcalá have examined the relationships between censors, inquisitional mentality, and book censorship more broadly.[21] In addition to excellent work on book censorship in broad terms, there is scholarship by Margarita Peña, Ángel Alcalá, Georges Baudot, and María Águeda Méndez on the content of texts, manuscripts, and books targeted by the censorship apparatus of various Inquisitions.[22] Other scholars have focused on the development of a history of literary taste and literary mentality in the context of censorship efforts, as in the studies of the transatlantic book trade and the *bibliothèque bleue* (popular, inexpensive, mass-produced books of early modern France).[23] Various intellectual and cultural histories of censorship have focused on the ways in which intellectual trends and thinkers were suppressed or attacked by the Inquisition, as noted in the extensive scholarship on Erasmianism, humanism, Lutheranism, and Calvinism.[24]

Influenced by the *Annales* or the emergent North American social history of the 1960s and 1970s, there is also a good deal of excellent social history of the Inquisition, tending toward a "total history" of the Inquisition: from the inquisitors to the accused, to the social, economic, and political structures of the

Inquisition itself, and to the overall effect of the Inquisition on society.[26] In this tradition, broadly speaking, can be counted the work of Solange Alberro, René Millar Carvacho, Jaime Contreras, Ricardo García Cárcel, and Richard Greenleaf.[27] Some social historical traditions have associated the Inquisition with social control of ideas. Bartolomé Bennassar, José Antonio Maravall, and Jaime Contreras, among others, argue that the Inquisition was an instrument of political hegemony.[25] One can also note large-scale projects like the comprehensive three-volume *Historia de la Inquisición en España y América,* under the direction of Joaquín Pérez Villanueva and Bartolomé Escandell Bonet. Such studies offer a global perspective on the Inquisition—narrative, topical, and social—while they do not specifically address censorship as the central theme.[28] Numerous other scholars have added depth and nuance to the modern understanding of the Inquisition with histories of local Inquisitions in regions like the Basque Lands, Valencia, Toledo, rural Castile, Catalonia, Sardinia, Sicily, Venezuela, Santo Domingo, Guatemala, the Azores, and Pernambuco. Many of these studies follow the general trend of total social histories of the Inquisition and add breadth to the field as a whole.[29]

In contrast to broad social histories, some classic works, like Emmanuel LeRoy Ladurie's *Montaillou* and Carlo Ginzburg's *The Cheese and the Worms,* offer microhistorical discussions and analyses of the mentalities of the subjects of inquisitional scrutiny and prosecution.[30] In addition to cultural histories of the Inquisition and its targets, there is a confluence with broader trends of cultural history associated with the work of Roger Chartier and Robert Darnton, which has tended to examine the cultural management of ideas rather than the content of the ideas themselves.[31] The works of Solange Alberro—for example, her landmark study of the Inquisition as well as her histories of cultural mentality, like *Del gachupín al criollo* and *El águila y la cruz*—offer detailed cultural as well as institutional histories of the Inquisition and religious mores in colonial Mexico.[32] While Alberro offers some vignettes on the internal development of the Inquisition, her principal aim is to demonstrate the effect the Inquisition had on Mexican society and culture writ large.

Overall these various approaches to the history of the Inquisition and censorship have tended to focus either on internal institutional development or on the external social effects of the Holy Office. In the former, individuals and humans tend to be flattened or erased, whereas in the latter, the institution is viewed as a totalizing, undifferentiated monolith. My book shows that while the institution of the Inquisition had a unique development, very human concerns, like ideological motive, jealousies, and personal ambition, as well as human actors affected that development. While little work has been done on the formation of censors as agents of the inquisitional project, there is some excellent work on the ideological history of the inquisitors which offers thematic suggestions for the work I offer here. Adriano Prosperi's various works, such as *Tribunali della coscienza,* and Virgilio Pinto Crespo's *Inquisición y control ideológico en la España del siglo XVI,* remain standards in this genre.[33] In addition to Prosperi, others have offered discussions of career paths and ideological formation of inquisitors, as in the work of Laurent Albaret and Ángel de Prado Moura.[34] Andrea Errera offers analysis of the development of inquisitional logic and criminal procedure in *Processus in causa fidei.*[35] Peter Godman's study of the role of the Jesuit Robert Bellarmine in the Roman Inquisition's censorship office has shown the complexity of ideological battles within the confines of the Holy Office.[36] Juan Antonio Alejandre García and María Jesús Torquemada have produced a discussion on the prosecution of propositions (heretical oral statements) in Seville, work which complements Torquemada's work on the problems of enforcing inquisitional controls on the book trade in port cities in Spain.[37] Taking cues from these scholars — and rather than focus exclusively on book censorship and circulation — I have taken a more expansive view of censorship as censure, since the censors and jurists never themselves divided the two categories in any epistemological sense. Prosperi, for one, has suggested that in order to understand the Inquisition and the ways in which inquisitors and censors conceptualized their roles, one must examine the "arsenals of the inquisitors": the canon law, medieval and early modern theology, and inquisitional manuals on which their collective ideology was based.[38] Yet even within this supposed uniform body of scholarship there were dramatic debates and disagreements about what constituted heresy, about the nature of religious authority and power, and about the scope of the Inquisition itself.

Methodologically, I offer an assessment of both the ideology (formal thought and works by specific philosophers, jurists, and theologians) and the mentality (social attitudes, informal thought structures, social mores) of the censors, to use Michel Vovelle's terminology.[39] On this level archival documents — the calificaciones and the trial records — function as a source for the study of collective doctrinal mentalities. This adds to the study of the more formal ideology of censorship as found in published treatises. Excellent studies that may offer the same conclusions as mine regarding the malleability and mitigated nature of inquisitional authority and colonial rule have tended to arrive at this conclusion from the opposite side of the investigational window. By offering a view from the other side, my work complements an increasingly complex field of study.

The temporal framework for the book is both early modern Spain and viceregal Mexico. In European terms, I examine the late medieval and early modern philosophical foundations of the ideology of censorship, beginning with the emergent conceptualization of Inquisition in the late twelfth century. In Mexico, I begin with the establishment there of local, noncentralized inquisitional authorities beginning in the 1520s, after the fall of the Mexica empire and its capital Tenochtitlan to Hernán Cortés in 1521. These inquisitors operated under the various and often competing privileges of diocesan powers, missionary privilege, authority delegated from the papacy or the general Spanish Inquisition itself. In November 1571 a central tribunal of the Inquisition was established in Mexico. A steady institutionalization followed, and along with this came the professional specialization of censors. In the first decades of the seventeenth century the role of the theologian-censor was increasingly important, given the dominance of the inquisitor's office by jurists. By the end of the 1630s the activity of censorship and the Inquisition in Mexico reached a nadir. I have chosen to end at this point to emphasize the variant possibilities of inquisitional censorship. Accordingly, my book traces a full cycle of inquisitional trends over a century-long period: missionary, sporadic Inquisitions of the 1520s; apostolic Inquisitions in central Mexico and diocesan Inquisitions in the provinces from the 1530s to the 1560s; centralization and intensely active periods of prosecution and censorship in the last decades of the sixteenth century; and a steady decline through the first four decades of the 1600s capped by the global conflicts of 1640 in which Spain lost Portugal but retained Catalonia. By the 1620s the Mexican Inquisition was plagued by massive floods in Mexico City as well as by dramatically declining revenues, circumstances that led to its lowest levels of activity in over a century. The flooding in Mexico City led to consideration of moving the viceregal capital as well as to evacuations. Lack of revenues led to widespread corruption.[40] And in the 1650s the inquisitor don Pedro Medina Rico conducted a royal inspection of the Mexican Inquisition, throwing into question all trials from 1640 to 1657.[41] The year 1640 was thus a critical end point for inquisitional — as well as royal — political activity. It also marks the beginning of a new era for the Mexican Holy Office as well as the end of the cycle on which this book focuses.

In the process of examining the relationship between inquisitional authority, as derived from theology and canon law, and the host culture and cultural practices in Mexico in which Spanish legal and ecclesiastical power operated, one comes up squarely against the issue of the law — is it immutable or is it culturally contingent? In the period I examine, the question of the relationship between law as universal and law as customary bedeviled censors and inquisitors almost constantly. The Jesuit philosopher Francisco Suárez outlined the derivation of human law — tangible and exercised by human actors — as the attempt to make divine precepts human.[42] This was the ostensible goal of canon law, on which the medieval and early modern Spanish Inquisitions were based.

The question of the relationship between doctrine and custom is a venerable theme of *derecho indiano* (Spanish law applied to the specific social world of the Indies) and of legal history in general. The Inquisition, in the Mexican context, is a classic dilemma for this field, since the Inquisition was presumptively an institution with universal aims and doctrines, but the Mexican Inquisition operated, as did the Inquisitions in Spain, in very specific cultural contexts. Even given these universalist aspirations, censors and inquisitors in Mexico often understood their charge in customary terms.

Legal historians have considered the extent to which early modern legal culture and the law were shaped by culture — in other words, even religious law derived, to a great extent, from custom.[43] For Víctor Tau Anzoátegui, the distinction between doctrine and custom is an illusion. In his estimation, "the complex American juridical order is integrated principally with three sources: the law, custom, and the doctrine of authors. These sources did not operate in a uniform or exclusive manner, nor did they respond to an established hierarchy."[44] Rather, law and custom operated together in the process by which law and doctrine were adapted to local conditions. Even Boniface VIII once remarked that a "subsequent general law does not abrogate a prior contrary particular and reasonable custom, without a specific derogation."[45] Custom itself was viewed by many as having the same force as positive law, or legislation. Doctine was the theoretical discussion by theologians and jurists — like Simancas — of the meaning of the law, and while it did not carry the compulsive quality of legislation — from the papacy or the Crown — it could carry the same force in the everyday practice of Church law, the Inquisition, and censorship. This meant that in the Mexican context censors were constantly dealing with the shifting boundaries and utility of custom and law, doctrine and legislation, and between "planned, associational" coercion and organic growth of cultural systems to fashion customary law. Consuetidinary interpretations of law fit especially well with the Jesuit vision of situational ethics and fluid theology.[46] For the Dominicans, who saw the Inquisition as an immutable edifice of protection against universal error, such customary and organic visions of law must have been nothing short of horrifying.

One is left with two seemingly irreconcilable visions of law and culture. One approach could study only the content of the law and the doctrine of its glossators and trace neat intellectual lines from thinker to thinker and from legislation to legislation; the other sees that same content as fashioned exclusively by social factors. But the ideological culture of the Inquisition was manifold, drawing on the relatively static quality of positive law in conjunction with doctrinal interpretation and customary concerns. In some cases the censors viewed their position in rigid terms — Lutheran heresy, for example, was linked to social dissolution. But in other cases, such as eating meat on Fridays or engaging in folk medicine, some censors were inclined to interpret such actions within cultural contexts. In many instances, those accused of superstition in frontier areas of Mexico were ignored because of more pressing concerns in the capital, political intrigues, or the perceived moral and soterio-logical dangers of Calvinist corsairs plying the gulf coast.

In order to make sense of the ways in which censors and inquisitors under-stood their assigned role as defenders of supposed Catholic universalism, part I of this book examines the ideological origins of censorship as an intrinsic component of the Inquisition. Chapter I offers a long-term view of the de-velopment of the emergent medieval and Iberian Inquisitions as expressions of ideology which was centuries in development from the early patristic Church and through the mature medieval Church. Chapter 2 analyzes medieval and early modern jurisprudence and theology as the foundation on which the Inquisition was based and by which it justified its censorship project. Prior to the invention of the printing press, the distinction between censorship of spo-ken and written words carried less significance than it did in the modern world. In the legal and doctrinal development of the Inquisition, the issue of heresy was linked inextricably to censorship. By the sixteenth century a well-developed body of inquisitional manuals emerged. These manuals offered censors their principal ideological arsenals on which they drew to justify the censorship project. Within these manuals as well as in speculative discussions by theorists, one finds agreement on the need to censor some books but broad disagreements over issues like papal authority, the nature of heresy itself, the causes of heresy, and the specifics of which kind of knowledge — legal or theological — was best suited to regulate ideas.

Chapter 3 focuses more specifically on the procedure of censure and inquisi-tional prosecution. In particular, there were deep disagreements about the nature of heresy and how it should be punished. Such disagreements led inev-itably to debates about power and authority. Specifically, if jurists and theolo-gians could not agree on fundamental issues like whose authority (pope or General Council, theology or law) was superior, questions about the nature of the control the inquisitional office exercised automatically arose.

The first disagreement concerned the question of judges. Should inquisitors, who had substantial power, be jurists or theologians? In the medieval period, most inquisitors were Dominican friars and theologians. In the early stages of the modern Spanish and Mexican inquisitions, this was also the case. But by the mid-sixteenth century this began to change, and ultimately lawyers came to dominate the inquisitorial office. The change had profound social and political effects, since theologians as a group lost power in the shift toward a more legally minded Inquisition.

Second, the question of expert advisors in the inquisitional process surfaced. There was a lengthy tradition in medieval theory that Inquisitions should be balanced. In other words, if the inquisitors were theologians, they should call on lawyers for advice and vice versa. As the various Hispanic Inquisitions came under the control of jurists, it was expected that expert theologians — i.e., the censors themselves — would be consulted on questions of doctrine. But the issue was one of power. Were the expert opinions of censors to be binding or advisory? There were vast divergences of opinion over this point, and in the end the view that the vote of the censors was to be nonbinding prevailed. This signaled a further deterioration in the authority of theologians in the context of a modernizing Inquisition. But this shift from theologian-inquisitor to jurist-inquisitor also reflected the rise of a specific professional and administrative group of censors on which the Inquisition would rely to define heresy, to make decisions concerning censorship, and to delegate the disputation of Catholic dogma.

Part 2 of this book discusses the ways in which the ideology of censorship was put into everyday practice in Mexico. Chapter 4 examines the deep trans-Atlantic connections inherent in both the ideological and administrative development of the Mexican Holy Office. Such connections were manifested most explicitly in the dominance of Salamanca — both the university and the Dominican house San Esteban — where most of the earliest inquisitors, jurists and censors of the Mexican Inquisition were trained in the cradle of Spanish Dominican theology. This chapter also prefaces the customary shifts in the Mexican Inquisition as it came to be more dominated by the criollo elite. Chapter 5 deals with the censorship debate within the context of the various local Inquisitions operating in Mexico prior to the establishment of one central Holy Office in 1571. In these various Inquisitions, the presence and power of friars were notable. Trials for heresy and heterodox ideas were decided not only by inquisitor judges, but also by the expert theological advice given by censors. These internal debates about the faith and doctrine demonstrate that the Inquisition was an active, if secret, location of political and theological debate. In 1569 the supreme ruling body of Spanish American holdings after the Crown, the Council of the Indies, voted to reorganize colonial administration on various levels, including the establishment of two central Inquisitions: one in Mexico and one in Lima (both physically founded in 1571). This effectively ended the claims to jurisdiction of no fewer than nine individual Inquisitions in Mexico.

The newly appointed inquisitor general of Mexico was not a theologian or a friar, like his medieval or early Mexican predecessors, but a canon lawyer, reflecting the consolidation of power in the hands of jurists and lawyers and shifting the theologians to the margins as nonvoting advisors. The substance of chapter 6 relies on the deliberations on doctrine within the Holy Office of Mexico, deliberations that reflected divisions within both the colonial (and Spanish) Church and Catholic thought. Among the debates that the censors took up were the frequent rejection of marriage as a preferable sexual state; interior versus exterior spirituality; the Eucharist; papal authority; Erasmianism; and the translation of scripture into Indian languages.

Chapter 7 examines the shifting characteristics of the Mexican Inquisition in its efforts to regulate doctrine and behavior in the period from 1590 to 1640. From the end of the sixteenth century up to 1640, however, the Mexican Inquisition saw a steady decline in its prosecutorial activity as a whole. The decline in severity in censure and regulation of the doctrine in this period was not exclusively the result of external causes like floods and underfunding. From the 1590s through the 1630s censure and inquisitional investigation of heterodoxy came to be influenced in particular by Jesuit censors. Their relatively liberal view of circumstantial morality and free will would result in fewer convictions and less severity of punishment for heresy, blasphemy, and general heterodoxy. Many of the same kinds of ideas or statements made in the crucial formative period of the 1570s and 1580s would later be viewed in a less severe light, given the scrutiny of Jesuit censors whose influence in this period would shape the ways in which the Inquisition in Mexico understood its charge as defender of the faith.

Part 3 of this book discusses two topical issues surrounding the sociopolitical worlds of the Mexican censors. Chapter 8 outlines the collective biography of the inquisitors, censors, legal *consultores,* and deputies (*comisarios*) of the Mexican Inquisition. The focus is on the censors, but I place their identity as a political-intellectual caste within the context of other functionaries of the Inquisition to show their changing position within the court as well as in society in general. Before the establishment of the Holy Office in Mexico in 1571, theologians were among the most powerful men in Mexico: they were judges of diocesan Inquisitions, archbishops, and inquisitors general. After 1571 the role of theologians and friars changed markedly, since they ceased to operate as judges and were relegated to an advisory role.

The theologians and friars who exercised authority as inquisitors prior to 1571 came from prominent families of Spain, and they were highly educated and highly motivated missionaries who came to Mexico to promote Catholicism. In the early years even of the 1570s Inquisition, the censors were often among the administrative upper class, as bishops, university professors, and high-ranking members of their orders. By 1640 the censors lacked the zealous bearing and high education of their predecessors. Instead, they were more likely to be ne'er-do-wells placed in the Inquisition as a form of horizontal clan growth in colonial society. Even though the mendicant and regular clergy began to exercise less control over the Church as a whole in Mexico, the censors as a group remained almost exclusively regular clergy: Franciscans, Dominicans, Augustinians, and Jesuits.

In chapter 9 I expand on the discussion of heresy as an ideological cancer and place this theory in the context of a debate on the transportation of books and the implementation of the Index of Prohibited Books. The application of book censorship and the rigorous prohibition of the Index were anything but uniform in Mexico. The enforcement of the Index was instead ad hoc and inconsistent; rather, its enforcement depended heavily on personal idiosyncrasy, took place within the deep cultural unpopularity of many aspects of the Index, and was regulated by comisarios who were not always scrupulous in their attention to detail. In the face of the lax enforcement of the details of the Index, a flood of prohibited books entered Mexico through Veracruz, the only legally approved port for international commerce in Mexico. In most rural areas of Mexico, evidence shows, the Index itself was not physically available. Even in cities, where regulation would normally have been more effective, the Index depended on individuals who were often more interested in gambling, brothels, and silk suits than in censorship.

From an intensely ideological religious crusade of the thirteenth century, the Inquisition emerged as an institution aimed squarely at censure. The same could be said of the early decades of its activity in Mexico. But while the ideology at the root of the inquisitional apparatus of censure and thought control was based in this zealous idealism, the realities of everyday life and social custom would never be far beyond the gaze of the censors. That ideological foundation and its resulting cultural adaptation in the context of early Mexico form the basis of the discussion in this book.

PART I

Theories of Inquisitional Authority

Longue Durée *Concerns*

The ideological and jurisprudential origins of the concept of an Inquisition date in many ways to the patristic Church, though the formal development of the Inquisition as a specially delegated tribunal had specific origins in the thirteenth century. As early as the third century, patristic thinkers like Tertullian were writing extensively on questions of the doctrine and the need to create a coherent orthodoxy. Augustine, Ambrose, and Jerome were the most noted polemicists of the patristic Church, promoting an orthodox doctrine as it related to various heresies — that is, the rejection of an officially established article of truth — and heterodox sects. Additionally, even though bishops had customary rights to regulate the doctrine, to excommunicate heretics, and to receive them back into the fold, throughout the late classic period it would fall to plenary Church councils to determine orthodox dogma and to condemn the various heresies competing in the early Church.[1]

Among the most pressing debates in the early Church were competing visions of the soul, the Trinity, the nature of Christ's humanity and divinity, monotheism, and canonical definitions of scripture. Many of these issues were resolved in a series of councils held by the early Church. The Nicene Council in 325 established the orthodoxy of the Trinity, in which Christ as coeternal was fixed as official doctrine. Nicene also settled various other questions surrounding the creed and monotheism. Later councils would establish the orthodoxy of various other points of Christian dogma and metaphysics. Acting in effect as an Inquisition, these councils issued edicts against heretics. Heretics, their leaders, and their works were condemned by the formal Church as anathema and were thenceforth excluded from the Church. Likewise, the secular state, in the form of the Roman empire, began to codify rules and punishments for heretics. The Imperial Constitution of 387 condemned the Manichean leaders to death and banned their books. The Theodosian Code of 407 condemned heresy as treason, and the Justinian law codes, the *Digest* (533), further codified the condemnation of heresy.

Augustine and others argued extensively against many of the various heresies of the late fourth and early fifth centuries that would resurface in the censors' mind in the medieval and early modern eras. The Pelagians formed a group which believed that by exercising free will and acting as a good Christian one could obtain salvation — a heresy that was condemned as rejecting the power of grace. Donatists believed that mortal sin invalidated the efficacy of the sacraments, arguing that a priest in a state of mortal sin could not effectively administer the Eucharist. This was condemned as an attack on the mysteries of the Mass and the Eucharist and on the efficacy of the sacraments. Manicheans viewed the world as dualistic and often thought the material universe was the dominion of Satan. Considering the Devil a coequal but evil god amounted to a rejection of monotheism. In all these cases, the debates tended to be limited to a group of scholar-priests and were decided by Church councils.[2]

The trend of speculative debate about heresy and its proper regulation and punishment developed throughout the medieval period. For example, in 1022 King Robert of France had thirteen clerics burned alive in Orleans for heresy. Queen Constance struck out the eye of Stephen, her former confessor, as the group of heretics to be immolated was being led out of the church where they had disputed with bishops. By the twelfth century various monks, like the Benedictines and Cistercians, had begun to organize disputations on theology. Simultaneously, cathedral chapters began to establish schools. In this context the debate over heresy and orthodoxy took on new meaning, since it was now not specifically restricted to conciliar debates. Bernard of Clairvaux was one such monk who disputed with heretics, attempting to convince them to recant their theological conclusions; he was instrumental in the condemnation of Peter of Abelard. The story of Héloïse and Abelard is well known, but it was in the context of ad hoc councils called to determine the quality of theological propositions — Abelard was condemned in such a council in 1140 at Sens — that the disputation of heretics took place.[3]

By the end of the twelfth century, the nature of disputing, punishing, and censuring heresy had undergone a transformation. In 1184 Lucius III issued his bull *Ad abolendam* at a council in Verona, codifying the right of bishops to investigate and punish heresy. It also allowed for the relaxation, or conveyance, of condemned heretics to the secular authorities for execution since clergy were barred from administering capital punishment. *Ad abolendam* was thus instrumental both in solidifying the right of bishops to act as ordinary inquisitors and in releasing condemned heretics to the secular authorities for execution.[4]

A second trend of the twelfth century had profound implications for the legal and theoretic development of the eventual Inquisition and the speculation on censorship: the resurgence of law as a form of study. Under the emerging university structure in Bologna, the study of Roman law and the application of Roman legal methodology to Church law led to the development of canon law as a specific genre of jurisprudence. Long associated with Gratian and others at Bologna, this innovation prefigured the codification of Church law. The first such law code, the *Decretum*, was published in 1140.[5] A combination of patristic writings, medieval commentary, glosses by Gratian, papal legislation, and conciliar decrees, the *Decretum* systematized Church law and was the first legal manual to deal with heresy. The *Decretum* included lengthy discussions of heresy, its causes, maladies, and evil effects.

At the end of the twelfth century came the breaking point between the old system of regulating heresy and the new system of Inquisition. Lothar of Segni — a Roman aristocrat whose uncle (Clement III), nephew (Gregory IX) and great-nephew (Alexander IV) were also upper-class Romans and popes — became Innocent III in 1198, widely regarded as the most powerful of the medieval popes.[6] Innocent III was the catalyst for the formation of the Holy Office as well as the most brilliant theorist of heresy among the late twelfth- and thirteenth-century popes involved in the establishment and development of the Inquisition. In 1199 he called on clergy and bishops to eradicate heresy and to prevent the encroachments of heresy into the "pure" lands of the Church. At the same time a quasi- or neo-Manichean heresy was spreading across southern France and Aragon. The Cathars rejected the authority of the Church and its sacraments and saw the material universe as the product of the devil. They rejected the Old Testament as having been written by Satan. Domingo de Guzmán was born in this climate in 1171 of old Spanish aristocratic lineage. He became a canon regular of Osma and accompanied his bishop to southern France to dispute with the Cathar heretics. He was at the forefront of both the old and new methods of attacking heretics. As a canon regular Domingo de Guzmán would go into towns with the express purpose of preaching to the heretics in an attempt to convince them to see the error of their ways and to recant and be accepted back into the Mother Church.[7]

Domingo de Guzmán, like Innocent III, was really an ideological founder of the Inquisition, conceiving and organizing a mendicant order — the Order of Preachers — whose stated intention was the training of preachers to go out and bring heretics back to the Church. Honorius III confirmed the order in 1216, and thus the foundation of the inquisitional apparatus was set. Simultaneously, Innocent III was battling on numerous fronts — diplomatic, political, theological, and, eventually, military — against the Cathars of southern France and Aragon. When frustrations boiled over, Innocent III called for a crusade, what came to be known as the Albigensian Crusade, to exterminate the "heretical pestilence."[8] Finally, in 1215, the year of his death, Innocent III convoked the IV Lateran Council. Among its innovations were the establishment of annual confession as a requirement of all Christians and a call to eradicate heresy.[9]

In 1216 the newly founded Dominican order grew rapidly, attracting some of the most brilliant minds of the thirteenth century, notably Thomas Aquinas. Within two decades it became a vibrant intellectual force. So zealous were these new defenders of the faith that they earned a less-than-flattering title that punned on their Latin name: Dominicani was split into two words, *domini cani,* meaning "dogs of the Pope [or Lord]." In the 1220s there were rumblings about the establishing of some kind of centralized tribunal to deal with the continuing Cathar and Waldensian heresies. Bishops were engaged in this activity, but increasing pressure was put on the papacy to create specially delegated judges of the faith — *inquisitores* (Latin for "investigators") — whose power would be unimpeachable and who would be specifically delegated to deal with heresy. The argument was that bishops, even though traditionally empowered to investigate and punish heresy, had too many other duties and that specially delegated inquisitors were necessary to stamp out the "heretical menace."

In 1230 Gregory IX commissioned the master general of the Dominicans, Raymond of Peñafort, to compile a new body of canon law — the *Decretales* — to centralize the relevant papal and conciliar legislation enacted since the *Decretum* of 1140. Gregory IX then invoked the specific legal concept of inquisitor in the bull *Ille humani generis* (1231) and appointed the first official inquisitors in Germany, the Dominicans Conrad of Marburg and Conrad of Tors — but so great were the procedural abuses of Marburg that he was murdered in 1233. In *Declinante iam mundi* (1232), Gregory IX called on the archbishop of Tarragona to proceed against heretics, noting that Dominican friars were also so deputized in Aragon, thus establishing the first Inquisition in Iberia. Peñafort finished the *Decretales* in 1234, and Gregory distributed the law book to universities. In the same year he commissioned the Dominicans as inquisitors in France. The Council of Tarragona of 1242 further cemented the Dominican presence in Aragonese Inquisitions. In 1249 Innocent IV specifically called on the Dominicans to take up inquisitional powers in Aragon, and in 1254 he made the Dominicans the proprietary inquisitors of Aragon — their control would last until the 1470s.[10]

Urban IV solidified the claims of the Dominicans as the attack dogs of the pope. In 1262 he issued *Prae cunctis,* which effectively dismissed the power of the diocesan courts to proceed against heresy in Aragon.[11] Even though this was a heavy setback to the diocesan authorities in Aragon, Urban IV enjoined the Dominican inquisitors to heed their advice when passing judgment. Such an enjoinder found its way into inquisitional practice in Spain and Mexico; when sentence was passed in an inquisitional court an ordinary assigned by the (arch)bishop was given the opportunity to cast a vote. Urban IV also conceded various privileges to the Dominican inquisitors, including immunity from inquisitional prosecutions and the ability to absolve any other Dominican from ecclesiastical censure.[12] Twelve hundred sixty-two was a banner year for Dominican privilege and the high-water mark of the expansion of the Inquisition as a particularly Dominican, papally delegated court.

These first decades of the Inquisition were a period of intense centralization of inquisitional powers, of fervent and often abusive inquisitional activities, and of the increasing confluence of papal authority, canon law, and the Dominican order as the ideological bulwarks of inquisitional censure and attack on heresy. The thirteenth century thus witnessed the steady erosion of the prerogatives of bishops as inquisitors ordinary in areas where the papacy delegated the Dominicans as inquisitors, especially in southern France, Lombardy, and Aragon. The Dominican Peter of Verona is a good example of the zealous early formation of Dominican inquisitors. Innocent IV appointed him inquisitor of Lombardy in 1251, and within a year he was murdered by people who saw him and the Dominicans as annoying do-gooders and serious political rivals in areas where Cathars were often aided by wealthy aristocrats and princes. The murder occurred on April 6, 1252, when a group of disgruntled locals assaulted fray Peter and an assassin hired by Cathars hacked his skull open with a sword. It is rumored that Peter, before he was stabbed through the heart and died, dipped his hands in his blood and wrote, "Credo en unum Deum" (I believe in one God) in the dirt. He was canonized by Innocent IV in 1253, less than a year after his martyrdom, making him the most hastily canonized saint in history.[13] He became the patron saint of the Inquisition and the eponymous patron of the confraternity of the Inquisition.[14]

In December 1294, in an election swirling with charges of fraud, Boniface VIII ascended to the papacy. An enigmatic and controversial man, Boniface was charged by his enemies in France with being a *debauché* and a sodomite who had an unhealthy (though hardly uncommon) habit of depucelating adolescent boys. In his nine-year papacy, Boniface VIII would prove himself a champion of papal supremacy and universal dominion, expanding the bailiwick of the Inquisition and overseeing the redaction and publication of a new volume of canon law, the *Sextus*. Boniface's most controversial bull, *Unam sanctam* (1302), would claim for the papacy and for himself complete spiritual jurisdiction (via Inquisition) over Christians as well as the right to depose wicked rulers when the pope saw fit. Responding to concerns about the jurisdiction of inquisitors in the bull *Per hoc*, Boniface reasoned that ordinary (diocesan) authorities were not stripped of their authority to proceed against heresy, but that inquisitors and bishops were empowered to proceed together or separately. When there was some disagreement over who held proper jurisdiction, the pope was to be consulted.[15]

After the death of Boniface VIII in 1303, the papacy was moved to Avignon, where it remained from 1305 to 1378. In the subsequent great schism, which lasted from 1378 to 1415, rival papal courts were established at Avignon and Rome, and numerous legal battles followed into the mid-fifteenth century. Ostensibly, the issue was resolved when the warring factions — who disagreed as to whether a council could compel a pope or vice versa — agreed to the election of Martin V in 1415 during the Council of Constance (1414–18), during which the attendees witnessed the execution by fire of the "schismatic dog" John Hus. Hus had called the papacy a sink of dissolution and Rome the home of the very Beast Himself, Satan.[16] But the debate over conciliar authority remained essentially unresolved, even if the immolation of Hus symbolized the reintegration of the papacy. The controversy would continue in various forms for the next century. Juan de Torquemada, a Dominican and the uncle of the first inquisitor general of Spain, the considerably more infamous Tomás de Torquemada (also a Dominican), was the staunchest supporter in the fifteenth century of papal supremacy above conciliar power.[17] Eventually a council in Rome was convened in 1445 to resolve the competing claims, but with little definitive appeal for either side.[18]

Through the thirteenth and fourteenth centuries, jurisdictional claims continued to overlap, a state of affairs that ultimately led to the development of inquisitional manuals and theoretical discussions. The Dominicans continued to solidify claims to their role as the specially charged defenders of the faith. Since the Inquisition was the property of the Dominicans in Aragon, its most famous inquisitor, Nicolau Eimeric, would assert the office periodically from 1357 until his death in 1399.[19]

The Inquisition solidified its basic procedure in the thirteenth and fourteenth centuries. Eimeric and Bernard Gui, a French inquisitor of the four-teenth century (Gui was the model for the villainous inquisitor in the film *The Name of the Rose*), provided the earliest manuals about the basic methods of inquisitional prosecution; the early Spanish inquisitors, like Tomás de Tor-quemada, drew on Eimeric and Gui to compile instructions on procedure and methodology for their regional inquisitors and deputies.[20] The inquisitor (or his deputy, the comisario) would read the edict of the faith in a prominent public place, like the cathedral church or major local church. The edict of the faith enjoined the faithful to denounce any heresy or doctrinal error of which they were aware within a period of grace, usually about thirty days. This included self-denunciation, and there were provisions for lesser sentences for voluntary confessions. Once someone had been denounced, an investigatory phase began in which the inquisitors interviewed those involved. When the inquisitor felt that an arrest was warranted, those accused were jailed and then interviewed. They were not told of the charges but were asked to reveal their consciences. The prosecutor would present his case to the inquisitor, and, in theory, a defense attorney would assist the accused. If the inquisitor felt that the accused was not forthcoming, and if the person was of sound body, then torture might be ordered, though many inquisitors, notably Jacques Fournier in Languedoc, eschewed torture in place of extensive psychological brinks-manship.[21] Confessions under torture were not allowed as evidence unless ratified after torture, but torture could be ordered again.[22]

Once the investigatory phase ended, in the medieval period the inquisitor passed judgment and sentence. In the modern period, theological advisors were consulted on points of doctrine. Eventually, the inquisitor would pass judgment and sentence, which ranged from the obligatory wearing of a *sanbenito* (a sackcloth smock with a yellow cross as a mark of one's conviction for heresy), exile, fines, whipping and public humiliations in an *auto de fe* (public sentenc-ing of heretics), or relaxation to the secular arm for execution at the stake. Execution on the bonfire remains one of the most powerful visual symbols of the ostensible evil of the Inquisition, though the numbers of those executed have been both grossly distorted as well as deliberately used as fodder for anti-Spanish and anti-Catholic propaganda. During the modern Spanish Inquisi-tions from 1540 to 1700, 1.8 percent of those convicted were executed in person on the bonfire, totaling fewer than one thousand individuals.[23]

In the Iberian peninsula, the only Inquisition with consistently delegated authority was that of Aragon. Valencian jurists successfully lobbied for an Inquisition independent of the Aragonese Dominicans in 1393, but Castile never had a medieval Inquisition delegated from Rome. Beginning in 1442 Castilian bishops appointed inquisitors, but this action derived on the old customary privileges of ordinary jurisdiction, codified in *Ad abolendam*, and Castile never saw an Inquisition delegated from Rome prior to the 1470s.[24] This was the context for the emergence of a specifically national Inquisition in Spain and later in Mexico. There is considerable debate about the emergence of the national Spanish Inquisition in the 1470s. Benzion Netanyahu argues that at its core the national Spanish Inquisition was established out of broad-based anti-Semitism.[25] There appears to be a good deal of evidence for this argument. There were widespread anti-Semitic pogroms in Castile in 1391 and in Toledo in 1449 amidst the Christian *reconquista* of Iberia as well as increasing obsession over Old Christian lineage and "purity of blood." But it is also clear that the emergent national Inquisition was part of a growing sense of Castilian identity, conservative Dominican theology, and increasing obsession with orthodoxy.

In any case, by the 1470s the Crowns of Castile and Aragon, united by the marriage of Ferdinand and Isabel, extracted a series of privileges from the papacy to establish a national Inquisition under the control and aegis of the Crown.[26] In 1478 Sixtus IV issued *Exigit sincerae devotionis affectus,* authorizing the Spanish Crown to appoint its own inquisitors. The first national Inquisition in Spain thus claimed, in theory, jurisdiction over all the lands under the unified Castilian-Aragonese crowns. The Dominicans, who were the proprietary owners of the inquisitional office in Aragon, did not, however, succumb easily. The first inquisitors—the Dominicans Miguel de Morillo and Juan de San Martín—arrived in Seville in November 1480, but their legal abuses were legendary and they were deposed.[27] In 1483 the Dominican Tomás de Torquemada was made the first inquisitor general of Spain.

After the establishment of a national Spanish Inquisition there was a steady institutionalization of the Holy Office on various fronts. The first decades of the tribunal were marked by a move from an administratively decentralized to a heavily bureaucratized Inquisition. The first inquisitors in the 1470s and early 1480s, like their medieval predecessors, were itinerant and did not have a specific physical home. After the appointment of Torquemada in 1483 as the first inquisitor general of the Spanish Inquisition, this began to change. The tribunal would soon come to be run under the auspices of a General Council (also known as the Suprema) which would eventually be fixed in Madrid. While in theory the inquisitors of Spain, and then Mexico, drew their power from the pope, the Spanish Crown appointed an inquisitor general who became the principal administrative officer of the General Spanish Inquisition as well as of the Suprema. The inquisitor general or the Crown appointed the inquisitors to the council and the inquisitors of the local tribunals. By the early sixteenth century the Spanish Inquisition was a vertically administered conciliar system of governance. At the top ruled the Suprema and the inquisitor general, which in turn appointed inquisitors to the satellite tribunals in places like Toledo, Valencia, Badajoz, Seville, Galicia, Sicily, and Mexico.[28]

This new national Inquisition would come to play an important role in the religious politics of the late fifteenth and sixteenth centuries, as the principal engine behind an apparatus intended to root out conversos and heretics and to censure ideas and books. In 1492, with the united Spanish Crown's defeat of the last Moorish stronghold in Granada, there was renewed enthusiasm for nascent nationalist programs. By royal edict all Jews in the Spanish kingdoms were ordered to convert to Christianity or leave the Spanish lands. The resulting exodus of the Sephardim and widespread forced conversions led the Spanish Inquisition to focus in subsequent years on prosecuting conversos who were suspected of having reverted to Judaism. But by the 1520s the Spanish Inquisition would come to focus its efforts increasingly on Lutheranism, Erasmianism, and Catholic humanism within the Church.

During the first decades of the Spanish Inquisition the office of inquisitor general fell to high-ranking clerics, both mendicant and diocesan, many of whom also held high-profile sees. Diego de Deza, who succeeded Torquemada in 1499, was also a Dominican. He was, in turn, succeeded by the Franciscan humanist Francisco Ximénez de Cisneros, archbishop of Toledo, in 1507. After Ximénez's tenure, which ended in 1517, the Inquisition began to confront issues of reform from within the Church. Erasmus had promoted a stripped-down and simplified Christianity and inner spirituality, which at first attracted many supporters, including Charles V. The goals of humanism—a return to ancient patristic teachings, a rejection of medieval scholasticism, an emphasis on the Bible, and the promotion of the translation of the Bible into the vernacular—also had considerable support in the 1520s and 1530s.[29]

The Inquisition as an institution and through its personalities increasingly became an instrument of the counterreform tendencies, which opposed Catholic Reform and humanism. The Spanish Inquisition sponsored investigations into the orthodoxy of Erasmus's work in 1527, and the inquisitors general increasingly were allied with conservative forces at Salamanca. There remained considerable support for humanism and for Erasmus, even at the debate in 1527.[30] But by the time Fernando de Valdés became inquisitor general in 1547 the tide had turned. The Inquisition was now largely allied with conservative (or reactionary) forces at Salamanca. Among Valdés's principal advisors and censors was the successor to Francisco Vitoria in the prime chair of theology at the University of Salamanca, the Dominican Melchor Cano, who proved to be the most forceful of the reactionaries of his day, pursuing Erasmians, *alumbrados* (enlightened people), Ignatius of Loyola, and humanists as part of a broad counter-reformation program. As the most vocal enemy of the Jesuits of his day and as a reliable proponent of counterreform, Cano held considerable sway as the Suprema's and Valdés's principal theological advisor in the 1550s.[31] Together Valdés and Cano would be instrumental in attacks on various reformers, and this tendency would have its denouement in the arrest and seventeen-year-trial of the archbishop of Toledo, Bartolomé Carranza. Carranza had been a member of the reform faction within the Dominican order that included Luis de Granada, the author of the sixteenth-century's greatest best-seller, the *Libro de oración y meditación,* and Felipe de Meneses.[32] Carranza, however, had made an enemy in Cano, whom he had surpassed in the ecclesiastical hierarchy, and Cano would make him pay by playing an instrumental role in the arrest, incarceration, and prosecution of Carranza by Valdés and his trusted jurist, Diego de Simancas.[33] This was the high point of the counterreform movement in Spain, in which a moderate humanist reformer was pilloried for his support of various reforms being considered within the Catholic world.

Among the reforms Carranza had supported—which no doubt were a thinly veiled attack on Valdés, who was an absentee archbishop of Seville—was the move to punish the widespread practice of bishops of holding sees while not being present in their diocese. The Council of Trent (1546–63) considered a wide range of reform proposals, and one of those it upheld was the principle that bishops must not absent themselves from their dioceses. As was so often the case in debates over heresy and inquisitional power, jurisdiction and the relationship between bishops and inquisitors was central, and the Carranza trial was a case in point.

In addition to its general move toward being a supporter of counterreform, the Inquisition began in the 1550s to formalize its power as an apparatus of book censorship. Valdés oversaw and promulgated the first Index of Prohibited Books, issued in 1554 and in corrected and expanded form in 1559. The Index of 1559 would formalize the ban on various known heretics' works, like those of Martin Luther and John Calvin, as well as of various suspect Catholic works, including several by Erasmus and the *Libro de oración y meditación* of Luis de Granada; the *Libro de oración* would not be approved for circulation until it was corrected and reissued in 1561. The later Index also made official the prohibition on vernacular translations of the Bible and on vernacular books of hours, extremely popular prayer books. Under the auspices of Inquisitor General Gaspar de Quiroga, and largely fashioned by conservative Dominicans in Salamanca in the 1570s, a massive Index was issued in 1583. Subsequent Indexes were issued in 1612 by Inquisitor General Bernardo de Sandoval y Rojas and in 1632 by Inquisitor General Antonio de Zapata.

Overall, from its early medieval beginnings to the early modern period the Inquisition would undergo radical administrative changes. From inquisitors who were Dominican friars acting in ad hoc cases to a national Inquisition under the patronage of the united Spanish Crown, the Inquisition would move from its medieval roots to a modern setting in which the censure of ideas was linked inextricably to that of books. But behind the Index and behind the workings of the inquisitors from their earliest days in the 1220s through the end of the sixteenth century, there were constant debates about the nature of the Inquisition and the need to provide a theological and jurisprudential explanation for its functioning. The underpinnings and the ideological reasoning behind this apparatus form the discussion of the following two chapters.

Medieval and Early Modern Precedents

The theory of censorship and of ecclesiastical censure cannot be separated from the theorization of heresy, Inquisition, and ecclesiology. To order an Inquisition was to censure, and censorship of books was only an extension of the fundamental concept and justification of the Inquisition, which was to stamp out heresy. In the collective mentality of inquisitors and censors, two principal metaphors expressed the dangers of heresy, heretical ideas, and the need for censorship: cancer and pearls before swine. With virtually no exception, theologians, jurists and inquisitional theorists viewed heresy as a virus — indeed, a cancer, a spreading evil which threatened to undermine the Church and, by extension, society. Simancas expressed it thus: "By heresies, the true and Catholic faith and religion are undermined, souls and bodies are ruined, tumults and seditions arise, the public peace is perturbed, and even the entire basis of the Christian Republic is corrupted and extinguished."[1] Like mushrooms, heresies would sprout in the fertile, dark lands of heretics, and like cancer, heresy would eat away at the Catholic faith and the Christian republic. Simancas may have given inquisitional theory some of its most memorable metaphors — he called heretics fat cows, vessels of evil, and wicked panthers who deserved more than mere physical death — but he expressed a tradition centuries old which made explicit connections between heresy, its potential to metastasize, and the responsibility of inquisitors to stamp it out.

If Simancas expressed the viral theory of heresy and the need to excise it, Matthew 7:6 expressed (and was used in turn by censors) the hierarchic vision of knowledge central to the regulation and control of ideas: "Do not give what is holy to dogs, nor cast your pearls before swine, lest they trample them underfoot, and turn and tear you to pieces." Aquinas would give the best known explanation of this hierarchy in the thirteenth century, when he concluded that, given the general ignorance of humanity, public disputation (and, implicitly, by extension, publication) must be closely regulated. Why? Proverbs 23:9 offered exegetes fodder for this contention: "Speak not for the fool's hearing; he will despise the wisdom of your words." Thus legend has it that Domingo de Guzmán, instead of specifically disputing with heretics in Languedoc, offered books to a fire. According to the story, the Cathars and Domingo de Guzmán both would offer their books to the fire: the books of the Cathars were consumed in flames, while those of the Catholics rose above the fire and were saved.

In the thirteenth and fourteenth centuries there were only manuscripts, not printed books, but the connections between the removal of heresy and the removal of heretical ideas — by extirpation, conversion, or the burning of books or heretics — were inextricable. Censorship was in every way the handmaid of the Inquisition. When the Inquisition was established in Mexico in the 1520s and formalized into one tribunal in 1571, the control of the book trade, the regulation of the doctrine, and the protection of a supposedly new and potentially pure Catholic land were all of a piece: corsairs who threatened the coast of Mexico also threatened the faith with their English Bibles. The English Crown's slave trader in the Caribbean, John Hawkins, was thus more than a mere freebooter — he and his English sailors were also potential heretical spores in the fertile missionary land of Mexico, bringing their vernacular Bibles, their iconoclastic hatred for the saints, and their evil disregard for the pope.[2]

Luis de Páramo, a Castilian inquisitor of Sicily (then part of the Spanish empire), explained the metaphysical logic of the Inquisition in the preface to his history *De origine et progressv officii sanctae inquisitionis* (On the Origin and Development of the Holy Office of the Inquisition) (1598): "The Holy Offices of the Inquisition annihilated the heretical plagues, since we should not allow the heretics, even in silence, to advance. Likewise we call on all kingdoms, republics, nations, regions, towns and cities to use this salubrious remedy to remove such a dangerous malady."[3] Páramo was especially fond of the disease metaphor. In a section titled "On the success of the Holy Office in precluding numerous calamities," he related the nightmarish demise of various heretics. Nestor, condemned in the Synod of Ephesius of 429, died only after worms had devoured his tongue. For his role in opposing the Council of Florence (presumably for supporting the conciliarists of Basel), Marcus Ephesius suffered so heavily from colic that he "hurled ordure from his mouth."[4] According to Páramo a host of sinister afflictions cursed Calvin in his last four years on earth: cholic, arthritis, kidney stones, hemorrhoids, fevers, migraines, phlegm, bloody vomit, and last but certainly not least a swarm of lice scurrying over his entire body.[5] These were the natural results of the heretical plague manifested in terrestrial suffering, presaging the torments awaiting the enemies of the faith in Hell itself.

Because heresy was seen as an infection borne along the vector of individuals and books, prohibiting the dissemination of heretical books was a linchpin of efforts of medieval and early modern Catholic authorities in their ideological war against the so-called heretical plagues. The fear of the spreading, creeping evil of heresy lay at the heart of the mechanical logic of Inquisition. In addition to metaphysical conceptions of heretical plagues, Innocent III offered the most vigorous and sophisticated arguments on the dangers of heresy to a papal state and a universal Church. In *Vergentis* Innocent III identified heresy with the crime of *laesae maiestatis* (treason).[6] Thus the connection of Church unity with the theorization of heresy was manifested in a bull that would give inquisitors the power to argue that heresy was not only a crime of the faith but also a crime against monarch, state, and society in general. Innocent argued that heresy was equal to cancer that "creeps more easily in stealth and in the open spreads its iniquitous poison."[7] He called heretics wolves among the flock of Christ, foxes in the vineyard of the Lord, and brutish dogs that did not deserve to bark — metaphors used three centuries later by Leo X when he condemned Luther.[8] Thus in the bull *Exurge Domine,* Leo X drew on Psalm 73: "Rise up O Lord and judge your cause . . . incline your ears to our prayers, for foxes seeking to destroy your vineyard have surged forth. . . . A wild boar is loose in your forest and is determined to exterminate and devour it."[9] It was no accident that the seal of the Inquisition bore the motto from the same Psalm: "Exurge Domine et judica causam tuam." The logical conclusion was that heretics and their defenders, aiders, and abettors all must be either brought back into the fold or extirpated. In the case of Innocent III, the final response was to initiate the Albigensian Crusade.

Innocent III did not stop at the association of heresy with poison but continued in a separate bull with a discussion on the dangers of allowing the laity to preach, prefacing future censorship efforts by outlining the need to regulate doctrinal dispute. In his bull incorporated in chapter 12 of the *Decretales'* section on heresy, *Cum ex iniuncto,* he argued that "laymen may not preach, nor may they make secret assemblies, nor censure priests."[10] In the context of the Waldensian movement — those who, like the Cathars, pronounced poverty the only legitimate physical state for salvation but, unlike Francis of Assisi, did not accept any overtures from the papacy — Innocent's argument here provided virtually seamless connections with his discussion of the concept of the flock and the believers and the need to protect them expressed in *Vergentis.* The "iniquitous poison" of heresy could deceive the simple just as it could "seduce others more astute."[11] Four centuries later, inquisitors would be bedeviled in Michoacán in western Mexico by unordained self-proclaimed holy men wandering the rural villages, by others preaching that the world would end soon and that only friars would remain faithful to the Church and thus be able to help others achieve salvation, and by men impersonating priests by preaching openly.[12]

Innocent III would decide that in the context of Waldensian wandering holy men only those who were properly ready to understand the more esoteric mysteries of the faith should be instructed in them, just as Augustine argued in his *De cathechizandis rudibus* (On Catechizing the Unlearned), relying on Paul's message that "as infants in Christ I fed you with milk, not solid food" to begin the journey of doctrinal comprehension.[13] Innocent warned thus of the potential distension of the metaphorical spiritual stomach if one still an infant in the faith was given too many complex concepts on which to ruminate, for "the profundity of holy scripture is such that not only the simple and illiterate, but even the learned and prudent sometimes lack the intelligence to investigate it."[14]

If the mysteries of the faith and scripture were so profound, then who could have charge of their explanation and preaching? Innocent turned to Paul's Letter to the Romans for a classic formulation of the Catholic hierarchy of knowledge: *Nolite sapere plus quam oportet sapere* — a line that, as Luis Gil Fernández writes, might have been the slogan for the "lawyers and theologians [of the Inquisition] who shared a similar medieval conception of knowledge" that was inherently distrustful of the non-Latinized laity.[15] The explanation of each according to his gifts was buttressed both by Romans 12 as well as by a general corporeal figuration of the Church and its believers: at the head was the pope, directing the various limbs and organs. Therefore, when a *mestizo,* or a person of mixed Spanish and Indian ancestry, named Alonso de Montúfar (no relation to the archbishop-inquisitor of the same name) was discovered to have impersonated priests and celebrated various sacraments like marriage, confession, and the Mass itself in several Indian villages in Michoacán in 1565, inquisitorial officials were especially appalled at this usurpation of clerical prerogatives and of epistemological hierarchies. Accordingly, the diocesan Inquisition in Michoacán sentenced the mestizo with full rigor of the law: to be paraded in an auto de fe and receive two hundred lashes in every town where he imitated a priest. Thereafter he was exiled to four years of galley slavery.[16]

Whereas the papal legislation concerning heresy would variously and serially examine questions of doctrinal debate and censorship, the task of centralizing the various sources and discussions of these topics fell to the inquisitional manual writers. The medieval and early modern period in Spain saw a proliferation of formal treatises on heresy, the Inquisition, and censorship. Practitioners of theology and canon law, while officially separated by profession, tended to borrow from each other's fields. The fruit of this high-end theoretical discussion was the inquisitor's manual, a specific type of treatise written by and for inquisitional authorities on procedure, jurisdiction, and philosophy of ecclesiastical prosecution of heresy. Francisco Tomás y Valiente sees an "intentional confusion between the political and the religious which always constituted the theoretical nucleus and institutional support" of the Holy Office as a symbolic entity of the ancien régime.[17] In this frontier between Church and state, sacred and prosaic, the inquisitional manual offers a laboratory of the interface of theology with law.

The production of inquisitional manuals and treatises may appear at first glance to be a highly abstruse field of scholastic endeavor, one in which canonists and theologians famously split hairs over inane topics. But consider the situation of the average inquisitional functionary of the late medieval or early modern period: he lacked centralized archives and extensive cataloguing systems. The problem of physical tools for the operation of censorship and Inquisition was no small anomaly in a system that was supposedly an efficient soul-crushing menace.

The practice of redacting rules for procedure, arguments for the inquiry and punishment of heresy, and theological reasoning for the Inquisition began in the thirteenth century. Antoine Dondaine shows how the earliest treatises dealt primarily with the theological question of heresy and not specifically with the Inquisition, as in Alain de Lille's *Summa quadripartia* (Four-Part Summary) c. 1190–95, the *Opusculum contra hereticos* (Against Heretics) probably written by Durand of Huesca (himself a reformed Cathar) around 1210, and the *Explicatio super officio inquisitionis* (Discussion on the Office of the Inquisition).[18] Later, more formulaic treatises appear, like the *Doctrina de modo procedendi contra hereticos* (Doctrine of the Method of Prosecuting Heretics) around 1278.[19]

It was not until the fourteenth century, however, that formal treatises on inquisitional procedure and theory began to appear. One of the earliest inquisitors' manuals was Gui's *Practica inquisitionis haeretica pravitate* (Practice of the Inquisition against Heretical Depravity) of the early fourteenth century. Based in part on the *De auctoritate et forma inquisitionis* (On the Authority and Form of the Inquisition) of the 1280s, Gui's *Practica* compiled a set of rules and procedural standards as well as a section on how to discover various types of heresies.[20] The instructions for regional inquisitors and officials of the Spanish Holy Office were based on manuscript versions of treatises on inquisitional practice, law, and theory. Tomás de Torquemada drew up instructions in turn appended by those who followed him, notably the inquisitors Diego de Deza and Fernando de Valdés.[21] In addition to formal instructions, canon law treatises were composed by a variety of authors for an erudite audience of canonists, inquisitors, inquisitional prosecutors, and censors. Besides the instructions promulgated by Torquemada, Deza, and Valdés, which were in Spanish and intended for easy legibility and clarity, inquisitional treatises were influential in the Hispanic world of the sixteenth and seventeenth centuries as templates of the highest theory of inquisitional authority.[22] The earlier treatises (like those by Gui and Lille), however, did not seem to have particular currency among Spanish inquisitional officials.

The most commonly used and most influential manual among Spanish and Mexican inquisitional authorities was written later, in the 1370s, by Eimeric —this was the *Directorium Inquisitorum* (The Inquisitors' Manual). Eimeric was a controversial character even in his own day. He was a supporter of the Avignon papacy and a frequent attacker of a group of spiritualists in Catalonia led by Ramon Llull. Born in Girona in 1320 Eimeric joined the Dominican order as a youth, was educated at Toulouse and Paris, and returned to Catalonia, eventually becoming inquisitor general of Aragon in 1357. Even though he was inquisitor general, Eimeric's attacks on Llull and his imbroglios with King Peter IV of Aragon (Eimeric had supported a rebellion of the diocese of Tarragona against the Aragonese Crown) led him eventually to seek exile in Avignon in 1376, where he completed the *Directorium*. He returned to Catalonia and had succeeded in having the works of Llull banned, which infuriated Peter IV, who ordered the Dominican drowned. The sentence was commuted by the intercession of the queen of Sicily on Eimeric's behalf. Eimeric lived the rest of his life sometimes battling and sometimes enjoying the support of the regal authorities in Aragon, but even the mighty Inquisition was not necessarily a match for the power of the Crown.[23]

In the medieval period the concept of an Inquisition remained a locally designated operation, ad hoc and geographically specific, unlike the universalism of the later central Spanish Inquisition. Even though the Dominican order placed higher emphasis on study of the canon law than other orders, friars were usually not formally trained in canon law as jurists even if they had studied canon law in addition to their central focus of theology. The result is that amidst the generally Dominican-run Inquisitions, the friar-inquisitors lacked a formal manual or guide on questions of Inquisition law, procedure, punishment, and auxiliary functionaries.[24]

Encyclopedic in scope, the *Directorium* was a critical edition of various sources: patristic theology, canon law, Aquinas, papal legislation, and commentaries on the canon law as well as Eimeric's own commentaries on doctrine and procedure. In part 1 of the *Directorium,* Eimeric compiled papal legislation pertaining to heresy and the Inquisition as well as sections of Augustine on various articles of the faith and the Church. Part 2 compiles more papal legislation that had been incorporated in the canon law in the various stages after the *Decretum* in the *Decretales, Sextus, Clementines,* and *Extravagantes.* Eimeric included further papal decrees, though never incorporated into the formal canon law, for the various privileges that they had conferred on inquisitors — and Dominicans in particular — as special deputies of the papacy. In addition to the content of canon law, Eimeric included the standard glosses on the sections of the canon law pertaining to heresy and the Inquisition. In Eimeric's first contribution from his own pen he added to part 2 "fifty-eight questions on heretical depravity pertaining to the office of the Inquisition." While Eimeric answered many of these questions by simply quoting various proof texts, in some places Eimeric offered his own discussions. Finally, part 3 dealt with the practice of the Inquisition and includes, in addition to explanations on that practice, "one-hundred thirty-one questions on the practice of the office of the Inquisition."

In view of the lack of the printing press, the importance of the *Directorium* was immense. Hitherto inquisitors (or bishops insisting on the ordinary jurisdiction of the diocese to prosecute religious error) had had to rely on ecclesiastical archives, conventual or monastic libraries, or their personal collections for the texts that explained the law of the Inquisition and the theory of heresy. For example, a friar might be able to draw on his order's library for a reliable edition of the *Decretum* or the *Decretales,* and most Dominican houses by the 1370s had copies of Aquinas's works. But such works were not always centralized, and one could not assume that all of the requisite texts dealing with the Inquisition and heresy would be found in a single repository. In centralizing all of the material relevant to inquisitional theory and practice, Eimeric single-handedly revolutionized the way inquisitors could work by providing them with a one-volume-serves-all manual. The inquisitor was at this point freed of the need to take several dozen books from a library shelf (or not find all the necessary volumes) and instead could rely on a single, comprehensive volume. Moreover, with the *Directorium* literally in hand, an inquisitor could take along with him all the relevant legal information he might need while on his peripatetic investigations that often took him to remote mountain villages and across unpopulated plains.

By the fifteenth century, theorization of heresy became more formalized, and the manual as a specific genre began to emerge. Juan de Torquemada's *Summa de ecclesia* (Summary of the Church) (1450), Gonsalvo Villadiego's *Tractatus contra hereticam pravitatem* (Treatise against Heretical Depravity) (1483), as well as dictionary-style catalogues of heresies — all began to vie for influence by the 1480s. It was not until the sixteenth century, however, that the inquisitional manual as a synthetic type of study gained momentum. There arose a need to put the broad inquisitorial scholarship of the thirteenth, fourteenth, and fifteenth centuries into summary, comprehensive form. This effort, unlike the production of the canon law, was undertaken not by the papacy but by various sixteenth-century scholars, ranging from theologians like Alfonso de Castro to jurists like Francisco Peña.[25]

Andrea Errera explains the dynamic emergence in the sixteenth century of synthetic and theoretical discussions of inquisitional law and procedure as "the continuous experiment of technique and methodology . . . to try to arrive at, as much as possible, a rational and coherent description of the structure of the inquisitional procedure."[26] This "experiment" consisted of three basic phases: (1) a period dominated by Spaniards and focused on essentially Spanish concerns, from the 1480s to 1542; (2) the emergence of a transnational, more universal inquisitional manual from 1542 to 1578; and (3) a period lasting from 1578 into the early seventeenth century dominated by the editorial and commentary efforts of Peña.

The phase beginning in the late fifteenth century emerged in the context of two important events: the development of the printing press and the establishment of the national Spanish Inquisition. In this context manuals on inquisitional theory and practice were written primarily by Spaniards and addressed mostly local concerns. Villadiego was a jurist trained at Salamanca and eventually a judge of the Roman Rota, which in the fifteenth century was a kind of supreme appellate court for the diocese of Rome and the Church in general. His *Tractatus,* dedicated to Ferdinand, was printed first in 1483 in Rome.[27] Though a jurist, Villadiego copied liberally from Aquinas's *Summa,* emphasizing the intersection of theology and law in this kind of treatise. An anonymous inquisitor of Valencia wrote the *Repertorium Inquisitorum haereticae pravitatis* (Handbook of Inquisitors of Heretical Depravity) in 1494, and the *Directorium* of Eimeric was printed in Seville in 1500 and again in Barcelona in 1503 in lost editions considered by contemporaries to be of especially poor quality and riddled with errors.[28]

Straddling the first, Spanish-dominated phase and second, international phase came the works of the Franciscan Castro. Born in Zamora in 1495, he began his university studies around 1507, probably at Alcalá. Shortly thereafter, in 1510, he took the Franciscan habit in Salamanca, where he spent a considerable amount of his illustrious career. By 1515 he held a chair of theology at Alcalá and subsequently was master of theology in the Franciscan house at Salamanca. He became an intimate of Charles V, who made him his confessor as well as royal advisor. In 1526 he traveled to Assis as a delegate to the Franciscan general chapter meeting and thereafter returned to Alcalá to resume his university studies from 1528 to 1532. By 1535 he had made Salamanca his permanent home and received a licenciate in theology from the University of Salamanca. In 1545 and 1547, he attended the Council of Trent as Philip II's theologian. In 1548 he was named *definidor* of his Franciscan province and in 1551 was made superior of the Salamanca Franciscan house. He was nominated to the see of Compostela in 1557 but fell ill and died on February 4, 1558, before having taken possession of the diocese.[29]

Castro was a prolific, wide-ranging writer. Being a trusted servant of the Crown, he was charged with defending the marriage of Catherine of Aragon to Henry VIII, though his *Memoria sobre la validez del matrimonio de Catalina de Aragón con Enrique VIII* (Report on the Validity of the Marriage of Catherine of Aragon with Henry VIII) in his capacity as royal advisor to Charles V has been lost. His *Aduersus omnes haereses* (Against All Heresies), published in 1534 in Paris, was his debut as a serious theorist of law and theology; the treatise went through twenty editions between 1534 and 1568, making it the all-time most widely printed inquisitional treatise. His *De justa haereticorum punitione* (On the Just Punishment of Heretics) was a much more serious treatise — *Aduersus omnes haereses* being essentially an encyclopedia — and was first printed in 1547 and solidified his reputation as a formidable theorist. Additionally, Castro wrote a lengthy discussion of penal law, *De potestate legis poenalis* (On the Power of the Penal Law), further expanding his intellectual range.[30] By contrast, other treatises, like Gui's *Practica*, were ignored by printers in the early modern period and fell into general disuse.[31] A stand-alone section of the *De iusta haereticorum punitione* as a treatise on witchcraft and superstition may have been published independently in 1568 in Lyon. We know that Castro was aware of the inquisitional investigations into witchcraft in northern Spain in the 1520s and commented on them in *Aduersus omnes haereses,* and he dedicates a considerable section of the *De iusta haereticorum punitione* to such a discussion, but references to a treatise *De sortilegiis et maleficiis eorumque punitione* (On Superstitions and Spells and Their Punishment) come from twentieth-century scholars. The work does not appear in the most comprehensive bibliography of works on the Inquisition, compiled by Emil van der Vekene. Neither was the work referenced contemporaneously nor did it appear in the Madrid compilation of Castro's complete works in 1773, leaving one to speculate as to whether such a work was ever produced and, if so, why it did not survive.[32]

Castro was one of the few theologians to produce an influential inquisitional manual after the medieval period. Like many of his contemporary theologians, Castro was little enamored of canon lawyers. His acid wit took aim at the tendency of canonists to pour on an overabundance of proof texts. He accused them of intellectual vanity in lieu of erudition, remarking in *De potestate legis poenalis* that "citation of canons and laws and doctors of the Church is so frequent and prolix that it only serves the ostentation of memory rather than better interpretation or greater comprehension, generates distaste for reading the laws, and often merely confuses their memory."[33]

In 1542 the papacy formally established a central Roman tribunal of the Inquisition, replacing the centuries-old tradition of local, delegated inquisitional authorities in Italy. In the wake of this new tribunal, Italian canonists joined their Spanish colleagues in producing inquisitional treatises, though the appeal of Italian commentators was weak in Spain and Mexico. Bernard Comensis's *Lucerna Inquisitorum* (Lantern, or Guide, of the Inquisitors) and the *Opus quod iudiciale Inquisitorum dicitur* (The Inquisitors' Law Book, As It is Called) by the deputy general of the Roman Holy Office, Umberto Locati, were among the treatises used most commonly by Italian inquisitors. The most influential Spanish jurist to produce an inquisitional treatise in this phase was Simancas. His *De catholicis institutionibus* was so lengthy and complex that he redacted it into a much smaller form as an *Enchiridion* (Guide), making it more effective as a manual. The original *De catholicis institutionibus*, however, remained a monumental, if vitriolic, work of legal scholarship. Given its emphasis on procedure and rules, Simancas's work was intended almost exclusively for other jurist-inquisitors, whereas more theoretically inspired works, like Castro's *De justa haereticorum punitione*, had broader appeal given its more universal, theoretical discussions of heresy in general.

The third phase of manual writing began with the first critical printed edition of Eimeric's *Directorium* by Peña. During the 1570s he produced his best-known and most influential work — editing and giving extensive commentary on Eimeric's *Directorium*. Peña pored through the papal and regional inquisitional archives and the private library of Giulio Antonio Santori, the cardinal-inquisitor, to produce a critical edition. Though born and raised in childhood in Aragon, Peña spent his entire adult life in Italy. He began his studies at Valencia and continued at Bologna, where he earned doctorates in both theology and canon law, and then removed to Rome, where he came to play an

F. ALFONSI

DE CASTRO ZA=
MORENSI ORDINIS MINORVM

regularis obseruantiæ, Almæ prouinciæ sancti Iaco-
bi, aduersus omnes hæreses Libri
quatuordecim.

OPVS HOC NVNC DENVO AB AVTO-

re ipso recognitum est, & multis ab eo locis supra omnes ante
æditiones auctum atcp locupletatum. Omnia autem ad-
ditamenta huiusmodi notis ✱ signata sunt. Vt autem cognoscas librum hunc plus habere in
recessu q̃ sit in fronte promissum, lege
nuncupatoriam autoris
epistolam.

FESTINA LENTE

Coloniæ ex officina Melchioris Novesiani.
M. D. XLIX.

Figure 2. Published originally in 1543, this is the title page from Alfonso de Castro's "corrected
and amplified" edition published in Cologne in 1549. Courtesy of Beinecke Rare Book and
Manuscript Library, Yale University

DIRECTORIVM
INQVISITORVM
F. NICOLAI EYMERICI
Ordinis Prædicatorum, *a le zoo. anos fez 336 flonz*.

CVM COMMENTARIIS FRANCISCI PEGÑAE
Sacræ Theologiæ ac Iuris Vtriufque Doctoris.

*IN HAC POSTREMA DITIONE ITERVM EMENDATVM
& auctum, & multis litteris Apoftolicis locupletatum,*

ACCESSIT HÆRESVM, RERVM ET VERBORVM
multiplex, & copiofiffimus Index.

AD S. D. N. GREGORIVM XIII. PONT. MAX.

VENETIIS,
Apud Marcum Antonium Zalterium. MDXCV.

Figure 3. Title page of the Venice edition of Nicolau Eimeric's manual (1595). This edition also included the *Litterae apostolicae* collected and edited by Franicsco Peña. Courtesy of Beinecke Rare Book and Manuscript Library, Yale University

important role, though to his bitter distaste he worked ever in the shadow of his rival, the Jesuit Bellarmine. Peña was by profession a jurist, known in Rome for his spirited defense of papal supremacy, and was commissioned by the papacy to compile a modern, critical edition of the canon law.[34] He was a vigorous opponent of the Jesuits, and the historian Peter Godman called him the "toughest censor in the Roman Curia."[35] He was appointed consultor to the Congregation of the Index in Rome as early as 1587.[36] Simultaneously, he was judge and later dean of the Roman Rota. While eventually the Rota would be concerned primarily with marriage annulments, in the sixteenth century it adjudicated a variety of cases. For example, Peña acted while he was dean (auditor) on the tribunal to verify the martyrdom of six Franciscan missionaries in Japan.[37] Though he was never elevated to cardinal, Peña possessed impressive political clout in the Roman world of censorship.[38]

Peña was also an active historian, archivist, and paleographer. In 1575 he wrote *De poenis haereticorum* (On the Punishment of Heretics) and in 1578 a manual on correcting potentially heretical legal treatises, "De expurgandis iuris consultorum libris abolendisque falsis eorum dogmatibus" (On Expurgating the Books of Jurisconsults and on Abolishing Any of Their False Dogmas), which has remained unpublished.[39] During the 1570s he produced a collection of papal archival material relating to the Inquisition as a tool for inquisitional officials — *Litterae apostolicae diversorum Romanorum Pontificium pro officio sanctissimae Inquisitionis* (Apostolic Statements of Various Roman Pontiffs in Favor of the Office of the Most Holy Inquisition).[40]

The editorial skills of Peña notwithstanding, the breadth of erudition in his commentaries solidified his reputation as one of the finest canonists of his day. While Peña's editorial energies and commentaries came to dominate the discussions of heresy and inquisitional procedure in the final decades of the seventeenth century, virtually no new scholarship on the theory or procedure of the Inquisition emerged. By the seventeenth century the need for readily usable and easily readable manuals generated the redactions of the important inquisitional manual writers and theorists, often titled "flores," or "flowers," meaning the best and most useful sections. Summaries of the *Directorium* and Peña's commentaries were among the most popular. The anonymous *Excerpta e libro cui titulus Directorium Inquisitorum* (Excepts from the Book Titled the Inquisitors' Manual) (1601) as well as the *Flores Directorii Inquisitorum* (Flowers of the Inquisitors' Manual) (1610) and *Flores commentariorum Francisci Pegnae in Directorium Inquisitorum* (Flowers of the Commentaries of Francisco Peña in the Inquisitors' Manual) (1625), both by the Augustinian Luigi Bariola, reflect this move away from original production and toward brief summaries of prescient points, minus the complexity.

After its publication in the 1578, Eimeric's *Directorium* became the most influential inquisitional manual. It was printed eight more times in the late sixteenth and early seventeenth centuries.[41] The proliferation of editions suggests that Eimeric's *Directorium* was well read and widely distributed among the higher clergy and inquisitional authorities in the sixteenth and seventeenth centuries. And just as Eimeric streamlined the availability of inquisitional law and procedure in producing the original in 1376, Peña offered the same shift in the way inquisitors could do business by making the *Directorium* available in print. Peña's extensive commentaries not only showcased his knowledge, but also attempted to relate formerly medieval concerns to the contemporary Inquisitions. The result was that the average readers of the manual — local inquisitors — who were not usually academics like Peña, would not have spent considerable time distinguishing between Eimeric, Peña, conciliar legislation, and canon law. Instead, the inquisitor looked to Peña's *Directorium* as an authoritative source of inquisitional law. By contrast, academic theologians were more likely to look to Castro for discussions of the doctrine of the Inquisition as opposed to the lawyer-inquisitors who read Eimeric for concise explanations of procedure and citation of the law.

Works by Simancas, Villadiego, Castro, and Eimeric/Peña enjoyed widespread use and distribution in the early modern Spanish world. As the *Directorium* is composed of lengthy compilations of the edicts of popes and councils and of other theologians, it became a synecdoche of inquisitional and censorship theory. For the comprehension of sources in the *Directorium* and the theological sophistication of *De justa haereticorum punitione,* the works of Castro and Eimeric were dispersed far and wide in the early modern Hispanic world. In 1660 one of Mexico City's most influential book dealers, Paula de Benavides, was ordered by the Mexican Inquisition to produce a complete inventory of her stock.[42] Because Benavides's was the printing house for the Mexican Inquisition, having published the accounts of the autos de fe of 1649 and 1659, both of which were lavish events, one can safely assume that Benavides was one of the principal suppliers of European literature to the higher clergy and inquisitional authorities.[43] Among her inventory were numerous copies of the 1555 Louvain edition of Castro's *Aduersus omnes haereses.*[44] Other book dealers in Mexico City who also dealt mostly in religious and doctrinal books offered works by Castro and Eimeric's *Directorium* in the seventeenth century.[45]

In addition to the sales of inquisitional treatises, these books found their way into the Indies when Spanish inquisitors and prosecutors were assigned positions in the colonies. The inquisitor general of Peru, Serván de Cerezuela, assigned to the post in 1582, brought with him a variety of canon law treatises and inquisitional law books, and among his inventory one finds Simancas's *De catholicis institutionibus,* Castro's *Aduersus omnes haereses,* and Arnaldo Albertino's *De agnoscendis assertionibus catholicis et haereticis tractatus* (Treatise on the Necessity of Discerning Catholic from Heretical Assertions). The private collection of Tomás de Solarana, prosecutor of the Peruvian Inquisition from 1596 to 1606, included Castro's *De justa haereticorum punitione,* theological works by Cajetan and Silvestre, and legal theory by the "Spanish Bartolus," Diego de Covarrubias.[46] Even the remote town of Durango, the last Spanish town in the northern frontiers on the road to New Mexico, north of Zacatecas, had a Jesuit college which possessed a copy of Eimeric's manual in the 1610s.[47]

Definitions of Heresy

Inquisitional manuals and theoretical treatises began with the question of the definition of heresy. It was assumed that the eradication of heresy was the goal, and so, in a move to go to first principles, the manual writers looked to a variety of sources on which to draw their discussions of the meaning, origins, and dangers of heresy. In the case of Eimeric's *Directorium,* authoritative sources were copied at length, with Peña providing commentary. In works by Simancas, Páramo, and Castro, authorities were cited, but the discussion usually drew upon the manual writers' analysis of the origins of heresy, buttressed by scriptural, legal, or theological authority.

Jerome provided one of the earliest definitions of heresy, tracing the Greek words for choice to demonstrate that heresy was inherently a chosen error: "Heresy means choice in Greek, which in similar manner often means election."[48] The word *haeresis* is a Latinized form of αιρεσις, meaning choice or election; a system of philosophical thought or those who profess it; a proposal; a free will offering. The resulting participle, αἱρετικος (*haereticus;* heretical) thus meant able to choose, and the related word αἱρετίς (heretic), one who chooses.[49] Jerome's etymological proofs offered linguistic foundations for later canonists—for example, when the *Decretum* was compiled, Jerome's definitions were included in the section which dealt with heresy.[50] Aquinas also relied explicitly on Jerome's definition for his discussion of heresy in his *Summa.*[51]

Augustine offered another definition of heresy in his treatise *De utilitate credendi* (On the Usefulness of Belief), which would also be incorporated into the *Decretum.* With an approach more metaphysical than etymological, Augustine defined a heretic as someone who "offers new opinions as a result of his own pride." The idea that pride (or self-love) generated heresy became, as a result of Augustine's definition, a standard metaphysical explanation for the origins of doctrinal error. Furthermore, one could not properly be called a heretic solely on account of doctrinal error but had to be offered the opportunity to recant the error.[52]

If Augustine left any doubt about the relationship between refusal to be "corrected" and the crime of heresy in his commentary on the Letter to Titus, in his attacks on the Manicheans he made this intimacy palpable.[53] Augustine's exegesis was so succinct that it became one of the standard chapters of the *Decretum* to which inquisitors and theorists of heresy would turn for explanations about the need to offer canonical purgation before condemning an accused to the bonfire. In refuting the Manicheans, Augustine offered the general definition of heretics as "those who, among the Church of Christ, smack of something diseased or perverse, are corrected and thus understand the right and the healthy conclusion but contumaciously resist [correction], and refuse to emend their pestilent and fatal ideas, but persist in defending them."[54]

If the universal Catholic Church was to offer the only hope for salvation, it also needed to be kept as pure as possible and Augustine reasoned that "divine providence often provides for the expulsion of good men from the Church for committing too many turbulent seditions."[55] A succinct outline of his theory of the unity and cohesion of the Church can be found in one of his numerous attacks on the Manicheans, *De fide et symbolo* (Of Faith and Creed), in which he systematically outlined this ecclesial unity. The opening line set in motion the hierarchic metaphysics of both faith and Catholic unity: "For it is written and fortified by the most robust authority of the apostolic instruction *He who is just shall live by faith* (Habakkuk 2:4, Galatians 3:11). This same faith demands our duty by heart and by tongue, for the Apostle [Paul] asserts *For one believes with the heart and so is justified, and one confesses with the mouth and so is saved* (Romans 10:10)."[56] Thus faith and its opposite, heresy, required the two components outlined by Augustine: internal thought and external profession. Where salvation required faith (an internal act) and confession of faith (an external act), heresy would require the opposite: doubt and persistent rejection of the faith.

The foundational sections of the canon law dealing with the Inquisition and heresy began, just as Augustine did, with the fundamental principles of Catholic doctrine on which the entire apparatus of ecclesiological unity rests: monotheism, the Trinity, and the universal Church. Thus the first chapter of Eimeric's *Directorium* restated certain sections of the *Decretales* under the title *De summa trinitate*. Succinctly put by Innocent III in the Lateran Council of 1215, "There is truly only one universal Church of the faithful, outside of which absolutely no one can be saved."[57]

According to the metaphysics laid out by Jerome and Augustine on heresy as choice, the first decretal used in part 2 of Eimeric's *Directorium* was *Dubius in fide* (Doubt of the Faith), which began, "Whoever has doubt in the faith is an infidel."[58] *Dubius in fide* reflected a central component of the way in which inquisitors were supposed to act within the boundaries of inquisitional law and procedure. Heresy therefore required two stages. First, the accused had to understand that what they believed violated a specific truth or article of faith. According to Peña, "It is not enough that a Christian simply errs in the faith to be considered a heretic unless he knows that what he believes is contrary to Catholic truth."[59] Consequently, doubts arising from surreptitious or sudden temptations do not constitute heresy. Therefore, the inquisitor must first admonish the erring Christian to return to the fold. This leads to the second consideration: pertinacity. As Peña would comment, "The pertinacious man is said to be he who persists in error."[60]

The metaphysics of condemning heresy possessed terrible ramifications: to execute someone for heresy without allowing him or her the opportunity to recant would be to condemn someone not only to a horrible execution by immolation, but also to the considerably more distressful (and eternal) fire of hell. But Peña drew on Melchor Cano to argue that pertinacity could be as brief as a few minutes. This position significantly reduced the potential for reform, especially since many of the more liberal theorists of heresy argued that condemnation for heresy should be avoided unless the judge was absolutely certain of error and the complete absence of the possibility of reform.

At first glance one is struck by the continuity in Castro's *Aduersus omnes haereses* and *De justa haereticorum punitione* with various other discussions of heresy found chiefly among the canonists. But if one examines Castro's assessment of authority more closely, the extent to which his interpretations differed from those of other theorists becomes apparent. To this extent Castro's writings on heresy and the Inquisition were the most influential of the theologians' and conciliarists' that took up the theme.

Unlike the legal approach to explaining heresy, Castro focused on scriptural and theological proofs, commenting less on the law. The fundamental question concerned the definition of heresy. From the very beginning of both treatises, Castro made it clear that his conception of heresy as a doctrinal error had little to do with the law and everything to do with scripture. Thus, heresy was "an assertion deviating from the true faith" or "a false belief contrary to the orthodox faith." For Castro the origin of heresy was a rejection of divine knowledge and truth and an elevation of human knowledge in its place. Pride was thus the root of all heresy and the gravest mortal sin.

Yet like the canonists, Castro repeated the maxim that heresy must be twofold: internal doubt of the faith and external action asserting that doubt. Heresy must involve choice, not mere doubt. Therefore, Castro concluded that not all acts contrary to scripture — such as fornication and theft — were heretical unless accompanied by a belief that they do not reject scripture.[61] Using Matthew 7, by which the Council of Constance condemned Hus, Castro concluded that the fruits by which one is known are the external heresies making manifest one's internal doubt.[62]

But the question of doubt and conscience was among the principal concerns of Francisco Suárez in his treatise *De censuris* (On Censure) (1606). Suárez was born in 1548 in Granada and entered the Society of Jesus at the age of sixteen in Salamanca, where he studied theology. He taught theology at places as far-ranging as Rome before being appointed to the University of Coimbra in 1597, where he spent the rest of his career as holder of the prime chair of theology. An intimate of several popes, Suárez is best known for his defense of the Jesuit view of free will championed by Luis de Molina and his philosophy of law. An extremely prolific writer and sophisticated legal and metaphysical philosopher, Suárez took the theorization of law to its most extensive and erudite limits. Drawing on the Salamancan school of law as modern ethics and applying a good dose of Thomist metaphysics and rigorist neoscholasticism, Suárez, much to the chagrin of the Dominicans, would establish himself as the most influential theologian of his day.[63] Suárez remains arguably the single most important Jesuit philosopher. Most famous for his monumental work of legal philosophy, *De legibus* (On Laws), Suárez was equally skilled in metaphysics, ecclesiology, and systematic theology. *De censuris* was something of a combination of all these fields of study. Wide in scope, sophisticated in style, and complex in its logic, *De censuris* aptly demonstrated the Jesuit view of inner conscience and external action.

De censuris began with an examination of the concept of censure, addressing Roman Law — the *Digest* — which counted *censura* as the deprivation of the rights of citizenship. But according to Suárez, in keeping with the Thomist view of limited papal temporal power, the Church had no authority to deprive someone of material things. Rather, Suárez looked to the canon law in *Quaerenti* of Innocent III, which defined censura as excommunication, suspension, or interdict. The jurist Diego de Covarrubias — onetime professor of canon law at Salamanca, high court judge of Granada, and president of the Council of Castile — explained the punitive value of ecclesiastical censure and excommunication as corrective and medicinal. So did Suárez: "Censure is spiritual and medicinal punishment, depriving someone of the use of some spiritual goods. It is imposed by the ecclesiastical power and by it also can be absolved."[64] Nevertheless, Suárez noted that censura could not, by definition, deprive someone of internal spiritual things because they were inalienable. Rather, censura could only deprive someone of the external use of some spiritual thing — like the sacraments.[65] The goal was not merely to punish but to cure and convince the sinner to return to the fold of the Church; censura was thus "the act of binding one back to Christ."[66] In 1611 in the frontier town of Durango, the rector of the Jesuit school, Francisco de Contreras, understood this process in both customary and legal terms. The *alcalde* (chief local magistrate), Alonso López, seventy years old, revealed in confession that he had been living in excommunication for fifteen years — something that normally only the Inquisition could absolve. But Contreras argued in his letter to the inquisitors in Mexico City that the alcalde be absolved given his advanced age and repentance as well as Peña's arguments about customary relief of sin if pertinacity was not present. Therefore, according to Contreras, it was more important to "bind the sinner back to Christ" in this case than to risk his eternal damnation.[67]

If Suárez argued against the inherent ability of the Church to regulate truly internal conscience, he did so out of a specific conception of the Church as visible and militant, not invisible or diffuse. Therefore, where Matthew 16:18 was seen as proof of the apostolic succession, Suárez saw it as evidence that the Church had jurisdiction in the "exterior realm," or *in foro exteriori* in jurisprudential terms. Thus Christ's injunction that "whatever you bind on earth shall be bound in heaven" was proof for Suárez of the Church's jurisdiction in foro exteriori.[68] The Church was capable, in Augustine's words, of removing the "pernicious man" from its flock by excommunication, a proof derived from 1 Corinthians 5:13: "Drive out the wicked person from among you."[69] This, reasoned Suárez, was a far worse penalty than material punishment, since excommunication deprived a person of the rites of the Church, leaving one potentially unsaved at the hour of death.

This did not differ greatly from the ideas on excommunication offered by canonists like Peña, Covarrubias, and Innocent III and IV. But Suárez would prove to be an original thinker squarely within the emerging Jesuit view that internal conscience was inviolable even while one's actions necessarily fell under scrutiny. This view derives from Suárez's metaphysics of the Church. Arguing against various strands of condemned philosophy that suggested the Church was invisible and spiritual, Suárez put forth the Ignacian line that the "militating and visible Church should be governed by ministers who are in turn militant and visible in the Church."[70] The conclusion that Suárez drew from this conceptualization of the Church as visible, though, was at odds with the lengthy tradition that began in *Dubius in fide* and continued through Castro as well as the Catholic reformers who saw inner, not external, spiritual reform as paramount.

Covarrubias, for example, argued strictly against the view that excommunication removed only external privilege. His logic relied on an ancient ecclesiology that the Dominicans employed in arguing against the conquest of the Indies — namely, the Donatist controversy. The Donatists (in Augustine's time) believed that only those people living without mortal sin constituted the true Church. Their logic on mortal sin led them to conclude that any sacrament administered by a priest in a state of mortal sin was therefore invalid. Augustine, who argued repeatedly that both sinners and holy men constituted the worldly Church, attacked the Donatists for their position of ecclesiology and their rejection of the sacraments performed by priests in a state of sin. The ultimate result was that Donatism was condemned as a heresy. The controversy would rise again in the Council of Constance when John Wycliffe was condemned for arguing that only the chosen constituted the Church, which was, by his definition, invisible. Luther was excommunicated for similar views of an invisible spiritual Church. Covarrubias singled out Luther as a "heretical dog" for arguing that excommunication could deprive one only of external action but could never deprive believers of inner spiritual communion.[71] For Covarrubias, Luther and Wycliffe were of a piece: Wycliffe for saying that "censure of the Church is the censure of the Antichrist"; Luther for rejecting the inner quality of excommunication. Therefore, Covarrubias reasoned, "in order to extirpate the depraved opinion [of Luther] that excommunication is only external and not spiritual [or internal], it is necessary to show how excommunication is medicinal."[72] That nearly a century after Luther's excommunication and some five decades after Covarrubias' commentary on the *Sextus,* Suárez would essentially argue the same conclusion as that condemned by Covarrubias as Lutheran offers striking testimony to the inner disagreements among Catholic theorists of ecclesiastical censure.

In similar terms in disputation 4, section 2 of *De censuris* Suárez posited the following: "Whether censura can be brought because of a wholly internal sin?"[73] Anyone who doubted was an infidel, as stated in *Dubius in fide.* Likewise, Eimeric, in question 33 of part 2 of his *Directorium,* concluded that both manifest and secret heretics were subject to inquisitional authority, even if such secret heretics had not offered a word or external action reflecting an internal error.[74] Suárez's answer to this question, however, was no: "On account of only an internal act censure cannot be brought."[75] Suárez argued that while this was "an especially difficult question," Aquinas ostensibly provided the explanation in his *Summa,* in which he argued that "human law or judgment cannot be brought on account of interior motives."[76] Suárez employed the standard commentators on excommunication for his proof: Castro, Simancas, Hostiensis, Durand, and Antonius. While heresy required internal doubt and pertinacity, the commentators were unclear as to whether heresy required external pronouncement. Peña argued that mere internal doubt was good enough reason to question someone within the confines of inquisitional courts. Simancas, who could hardly be confused for a liberal, argued that the Inquisition had no authority over explicitly internal heresy if no physical manifestation of it had taken place. In fact, he argued that a "purely mental" heresy (one which has not been spoken) not only did not fall under the Inquisition's jurisdiction but could be absolved by one's confessor.[77] Moreover, "the Church has no power over purely interior acts."[78] Here Simancas made the distinction between thought and action and relied on the standard argument that heresy required external action in addition to internal doubt. If, on being admonished on the error of that doubt, the accused recanted, he was not a heretic. Simancas would go so far as to conclude that one's confessor could provide absolution for internal doubt — a conclusion at odds with some of the more radical Dominicans.[79]

All of this begs the question: if the act was purely internal and not accompanied by external pronouncement, how would such a doubt be known? One method was, of course, torture. It was to this problem that Suárez responded, less as a jurist concerned about the specifics of legal procedure, and more in line with his highly theoretical and metaphysical explanations of law. Ultimately, Suárez concluded that "the Church has no direct jurisdiction in internal acts" — an idea with profound consequences for inquisitors, confessors, and the laity alike. He replied that theologians in general "have taught that the Church has direct jurisdiction in purely internal acts, and consequently can prohibit them *sub censura.*"[80] But Suárez concluded in response that such internal thoughts were not mere thoughts. Suárez supported the view offered by the canonists that hidden acts fell beneath the jurisdiction of the Church, since these were acts and not mere thoughts. To this end Suárez discussed the difference between "truly" internal acts as opposed to "hidden actions," which were therefore still external. The result, reasoned Suárez, was that the Church could not claim to rule over the inner conscience of anyone but only over the external expression of conscience. Thus belief alone — for example, that Christ was not present in the Eucharist or that confession was not necessary — could not be reviewed by the Church if it was only unexpressed doubt. This rejected the arguments offered by the canonists who uniformly pronounced that simple "dubius in fide" was tantamount to infidelity and heresy.[81]

Suárez's (and Simancas's) view of the inability of the Church to judge purely internal acts was in keeping with Castro's limited view of ecclesiastical authority over the inner realm of thought. The Franciscans called for greater spiritual renewal by internal contemplation, as did the Jesuits with Loyola's *Exercises,* but both orders were loath to assign jurisdiction over those inner thoughts to the Church or to the Inquisition. Suárez was well aware of Castro's views on the matter and offered, among others, chapter 18 of book 2 of *De justa haereticorum punitione* as proof. Herein one sees the conflict between theological and legal visions of ecclesiastical censure. Castro concluded that "it is the common opinion of the theologians that the Church cannot compel internal acts."[82] He noted that the canonists argued precisely the opposite, with the gloss on the *Clementines'* chapter *De haereticis*, "deceived by poor intellect." Thus Castro argued that the gloss was faulty, and that Archidiaconus (the glossator) "did not understand the letter of that decree, nor consider its meaning. For that decree did not punish internal acts of the soul (as we have shown), in which the Church has no forensic jurisdiction, but punished external acts, which derive from those internal acts."[83]

Hierarchies of Knowledge

The question of heresy and error held various gradations based on levels of education, knowledge, and social position. Relying heavily on Aquinas's hierarchy of angels and men — in which theologians could be held to higher standards of knowledge than the laity — Peña offered pithy summaries and regulations for the distinctions of doubt, error, heresy, and inquisitional crime. The final section of part 1 of the *Directorium* — "twelve questions pertaining to the observation of the faith" — was an extended précis of Aquinas.

At first glance an exegesis on the theory of heresy might not appear to be closely connected to censorship. Yet in the jurisprudential and theological discussions of the dangers of heresy, censorship and control of doctrinal debate were the next logical considerations in such treatises. Indeed, Eimeric went directly from the definition of the faith and its rejection, heresy, to the problem of censorship. Fewer than four pages into the *Directorium,* Eimeric copied the bull *Damnamus ergo reprobamus* of Innocent III, which condemned Joachim of Fiore's analysis of the *Sentences* of Peter Lombard.[84] The title of Innocent's bull could hardly have been more succinct in linking doctrinal error with censorship: "We condemn and therefore we prohibit." In the concluding section of part 1 of the *Directorium*, Eimeric relied heavily on Aquinas's theory of the hierarchy of knowledge and its accompanying discussion of the issues of public doctrinal debate.

While Eimeric quoted from Augustine and Jerome on some select definitions of articles of the faith, his use of Aquinas was much more extensive and provocative. For example, his use of Augustine was simple quotation by manner of proof text. His use of Aquinas, however, was in scholastic *sic et non* formula in which he proposed his twelve questions pertaining to the faith and then offered quotations from Aquinas as the responses. Enriching this dialogue of the issue of the Church politic and its relationship with the exterior faith of its members were Peña's lengthy commentaries, updated for the late sixteenth century.

In the third of his twelve questions on the faith, Eimeric asked "whether someone is required to have explicit belief in the articles of the faith." Like the canonists and theologians, Eimeric distinguished between the requirement of inner faith in general, the doubt of which was condemned in *Dubius in fide,* and of the explicit vocalized faith—a faith that Augustine asserted "demands our duty by heart and by tongue." Aquinas argued that humans indeed "must explicitly believe in the articles of the faith, in as much as they are the first beliefs."[85] But both Peña and Eimeric concluded that the ordinary person could not be held responsible for all beliefs, but rather only for the most basic "articles of the faith," such as monotheism, the Trinity, and the resurrection of Christ.

Even while Aquinas, like Eimeric and Peña, asserted that all faithful were required to believe in the articles of the faith, he distinguished between the educated and the uneducated—a distinction that lay at the heart of the meta-physics of censorship. In Eimeric's fourth question on the faith, he asked "whether everyone is required to understand equally the explicit faith in the articles of the faith." The answer, unsurprisingly, was no. Eimeric again relied on Aquinas for the response in which he drew out his hierarchy of angels.[86] If angels have greater comprehension than men, prelates have a higher com-prehension and understanding than the laity. Accordingly, it was enough for the layperson to have a simple explicit knowledge of the faith but was excused from any further study or knowledge of it. For example, the average person needed only to accept the declared truth of transubstantiation of the Eucharist but was excused from understanding the subleties of that doctrine. Moreover, the layperson should not be questioned on the subtleties of the faith unless suspected of heresy, since "heretics regularly mislead the unlettered in regard to finer points of faith." Aquinas made a further, and central, contention by arguing that the ignorant are excused from doctrinal error when led to such error by their intellectual and theological superiors (i.e., priests).[87]

The exculpatory value of stupidity possessed numerous levels for Peña, who, in providing commentary on Aquinas, explained numerous rules for the definition of heresy as it related to pertinacity, error, and ignorance. First, "there can never be heresy without pertinacity." Second and third, "those who should know and must be presumed to understand the details of the articles must be considered heretics when erring in the faith." Fourth, the average person was not obliged to understand various subtleties of the faith, as in the metaphysics of the Trinity, but if one persisted in an error on this level one could be condemned as a heretic if one refused correction from the Church in the form of an inquisitor or ecclesiastical judge. Fifth, insuperable stupidity excused heresy absolutely. Sixth, whoever could not be expected to understand certain aspects of the faith and was led into error by a learned man was likewise excused of heresy.[88]

Much like Aquinas, though not relying on the *Summa theologiae* explicitly, Castro outlined a hierarchical view of doctrinal comprehension and responsibility. The ordinary laity was therefore, in his vision, required only to understand the articles of the faith but not more abstruse points of dogma or theology. At the same time, preachers must be held to a higher standard of understanding precisely because it was their responsibility to explain those finer points to the less educated. Like Peña, Castro viewed stupidity as exculpatory, especially if the ignorant person came to error as a result of a public sermon. Such a continuum of responsibility had direct consequences for the control of doctrinal debate and print, since Castro argued that absence of pastoral care of the flock resulting in heresy was not the fault of the laity but of the priesthood or bishop. Thus Castro concluded that if the laity committed doctrinal errors or mistakes from faulty teachings of a preacher they were guilty only of obedience to the Church. Moreover, Castro concluded that "idiots" or other ordinary laypersons could not be required to understand the most abstruse point of the doctrine.[89] In keeping with this view, Castro argued that "not everyone is held to the same level in belief."[90] If the illiterate laity needed to know only the articles of the faith, "the same cannot be said for preachers and prelates, who have no excuse for ignorance . . . and must not preach anything imperfectly."[91]

The theorists then asked, "Should one dispute publicly on the faith?" This question would apply both to spoken debate and to published material. The response to the query came partially from Aquinas's *Summa*, which played an important role in numerous theorists' discussions of censorship and the problems of open public disputation.[92] For example, Villadiego made extensive use of the *Summa* in his *Tractatus contra hereticam pravitatem*, asking, "If heretics persist in their error and wish to dispute publicly in order to confirm their errors, should we [in turn] dispute publicly with them?" His answer, like Eimeric's, was a direct quotation from the *Summa*.[93] Aquinas's conclusions gave a concise outline considering various possibilities: whether the disputation was held in the presence of the learned or ignorant men; whether heresy was present in the territory of the disputation; the lay-clerical divide.

In establishing the discussion of open doctrinal debate within the context of inquisitional theory, Eimeric quoted verbatim and at length from the *Summa*. Aquinas offered two considerations: on the part of the disputants (*ex parte disputantis*) and of the listeners (*ex parte audientium*).[94] Concerning the latter

Aquinas further divided the listeners into learned and unlearned, which meant learned in doctrine, theology, or canon law — all of which were by default in Latin. Therefore, "in the presence of learned men, firm in their faith, there is no danger in disputation of the faith."[95] This conclusion offered the theological basis of the censors' advisory power. By granting that censors were necessarily men learned and firm in the faith, they could be entrusted to hear arguments on the faith. Accordingly, it was proper that they review disputes and debates of the faith and printed material, even those that might be heretical.

The question of whether or not the unlearned laity might be allowed to hear disputation of the faith (and, by extension, read material related to the faith) "had to be distinguished."[96] When there was heresy to combat, Aquinas considered it licit to have public disputation of the faith in the presence of the uneducated in order to show the laity the error of heresies and false doctrines. This was the case with the newly established Order of Preachers — to expose the neo-Manichean ideas of the Cathars. Furthermore, Aquinas argued that "this public disputation of the faith should be undertaken only as long as there can be found those men, sufficient and capable for the task, who can refute errors."[97]

The explanations by Aquinas, Eimeric, and Peña outlined the argument for the provenance of the correction of heresy: to review suspect statements and books and determine whether or not they should be allowed, reproved, expurgated, or banned entirely. Moreover, the proofs offered by Aquinas reinforced the status of the censor, since he concluded that only those men capable of refuting the ideas of heretics were to be allowed to debate those ideas. The deliberations of the censors were not public but secret, but the results of their decisions were made public: the Indexes and declarations of censorship. All of this had very real public effects, since the censors were given the power to control this public arena of dispute.

There was a second consideration of public dispute *coram simplicibus* (in the presence of the unlearned): when there was no heresy to combat. The theologians suggested that such public disputation was gravely dangerous and should be prohibited because it would only suggest ideas that otherwise would remain unknown to the faithful, since heresy was seen as the result of contagion and infection. In addition to concerns about disputation ex parte audientium Aquinas (and thus Eimeric and Peña) had to consider disputation ex parte disputantis. Aquinas's and Eimeric's conclusions were hardly surprising: only the clergy were to be allowed to engage in the disputes — a conclusion codified in the canon law.[98] The logical extension of this conclusion, which would not have been lost on any censor, was that the laity was prohibited from writing and publishing books on doctrinal matters.

Book Censorship

In the 1370s Eimeric considered it sufficient to restate the various con-
demnations of heretical books issued by popes, such as of various apocryphal
books of scripture and Joachim of Fiore's works. In general, Eimeric did not
innovate on the question of censorship, and this is probably because wide
distribution of texts was rare, and manuscripts considered heretical were primarily found in the insular world of monasteries, mendicant houses, and
universities. But by the time Peña produced the critical printed edition of the
Directorium, censorship of print had become a crucial battleground of the
Spanish and Roman Inquisitions. Peña expanded the overall jurisdiction of
censorship, allowing for a variety of books to be censored without special
papal permission, as Eimeric had originally conceived.

By 1559 the first formal Index of the Spanish Inquisition was issued, and
this stemmed from the various privileges of Spain to have its own national
Inquisition separate from the papal Inquisitions. On the dispute over who
possessed the ultimate authority to issue edicts of censorship, Eimeric generally affirmed the right and responsibility of inquisitors by decree of the pope,
but Peña added commentary on this matter. Whereas Eimeric argued for censorship generally by special decree of the papacy, Peña reasoned that "this
seems to indicate that a bishop or inquisitor might not condemn those books
unless they have a special order from the Apostolic See."[99] Peña expanded the
bailiwick of censorship when he argued that "on the contrary, bishops and
inquisitors can indeed prohibit books suspected of heresy in their dioceses on
account of any suspicion of heresy, even if they were written by Catholic
authors."[100] The inquisitors of Mexico, Alfonso Fernández de Bonilla and
Francisco Santos García, asserted this very privilege in 1585 by fiat when they
banned the anonymously written *Oratorio y consuelo spiritual* (Prayerbook
and Spiritual Counsel).[101] The book was quite popular, as purges in Guadalajara, Tabasco, and the Yucatán from 1585 to 1588 turned up copies of the
book in the homes of several prominent citizens, including doña Catalina de
Bustamente, the wife of the governor of the Yucatán, who himself was discovered to have a banned edition of Luis de Granada's *Libro de oración y
meditación.*[102]

The diseased fruit from a diseased tree argument was an old one in theological and canonical reasoning. It was based on the Gospel according to Matthew
— "Are grapes gathered from thorns, or figs from thistles? . . . A good tree
cannot bear bad fruit, nor can a bad tree bear good fruit. Every tree that does
not bear good fruit is cut down and thrown into the fire."[103] Peña employed
similar logic in his justification for preventing the wide dissemination of books

deemed dangerous, arguing that "it is clear that a tree condemned for its pestilential fruit must also have its fruit forbidden, so that it does not instill venom, for the fruit of heretical doctrines is obviously contained in their books."[104] Extending this metaphysics of censorship further, Peña concluded that heretical books were more dangerous than heretics themselves because books could be widely dispersed and therefore read by more people than could ever be reached by mere men, as had been suggested by Simancas.[105]

Heretical books were not the only offending works for which Peña suggested censorship, and the mere suspicion of heresy was sufficient cause in Peña's estimation to warrant a work's prohibition. Furthermore, he argued that scandalous, dangerous, erroneous books, or those not conforming to Christian morals, must be banned for their ability to disturb the social order of the Church and the purity of the faith. Books containing double meanings also needed to be banned, reasoned Peña, because while one meaning might be construed as Catholic, the other could be heretical, as in the statement "faith justifies."[106] Peña's assessment was at odds with the rules of the Spanish Indexes, which allowed picaresque novels to circulate unless they attacked some doctrinal point, something for which the *Lazarillo de Tormes* was banned for some decades until it was allowed to circulate in expurgated form.[107] On this score Peña demonstrated his conservatism in comparison with his Spanish counterparts who tended to be less concerned with "light literature" than the Italians, who followed the negative injunctions of Plato and Augustine on the dangers of nonedifying literature.

According to his rigorist view, Peña expanded the boundaries of censorship on two points. First, Peña included "useless or unproductive books or [books] that deal with light or ridiculous subjects" among those to be banned.[108] Second, Peña argued in no uncertain terms that all books of heretics, regardless of content, must be prohibited. Besides his conclusions, Peña also showed novelty in his method of arriving at them. For example, he echoed the Tridentine rule against obscene books, but his justification reveals his eclecticism, for his authority for this conclusion was none other than Plato, who famously recommended the regulation of poetry in his *Republic*. To sixteenth-century theorists, Plato had long fallen out of fashion in favor of an Aristotelianism that was all-powerful in natural and moral philosophy as well as in Thomist metaphysics. But Plato as a ruling authority on censorship never went out of fashion even if his metaphysics did. Peña was familiar with Augustine's condemnation in *De catechizandis rudibus* of poetry and vain literature if it served no purpose other than esthetic pleasure: "If they [gentiles] try to represent the false stories of the poets, whose fodder is nonsense, and which are contrived for the pleasure of minds — even though they are the same vain and corpulent stuffing of the world — how fitting indeed that we should be guardians, so that these truths which we teach are believed without the redundant distribution of their causes or sweet inanity or pernicious lust."[109] While Peña did not specifically rely on this passage, Augustine's attacks on esthetics bereft of spiritual nourishment were well known. Though Augustine never had the kind of nightmares that Jerome did — like being accused by Christ of being a Ciceronian and not a Christian — Augustine shared Jerome's estimation of style as vacuous if not accompanied by Christian truth. This recalled Socrates' attack on Gorgias: sophists, making the stronger argument appear the weaker and vice versa, were nihilists because their only goal was to teach men to argue regardless of the inherent truth of the argument.[110]

Besides the discussion of the banning of books themselves, Peña considered the questions of punishment for printing banned books and the extent to which the ban should carry. In this regard, Peña viewed himself as a moderate, recounting the punishment envisioned by Justinian in his *Constitution* for transcribing banned text, which was to chop off one of the offender's hands. Peña suggested that excommunication would suffice since the "severity [of the Roman law] has long been absent from this tribunal of the Church, which was not founded on blood."[111]

Despite the grave dangers that Peña, like all censors, saw in books, he recognized the need for someone to read the books of the condemned. First, in order to refute errors, the preacher or censor needed to understand perverse ideas. Second, in order to obtain this information, exemptions would have to be made for those to read prohibited books. Initially, the privilege of reading prohibited books was granted to inquisitors, as Eimeric pointed out. But how this privilege was eventually extended to censors is not clear from a reading of the *Directorium*. Indeed, Peña suggested that the inquisitor could not extend the privilege of reading condemned books, as this was conferred by papal authority. The original privilege was extended to the inquisitor's vicars and substitutes, but neither Eimeric nor Peña specified the nature of vicarious power within the auspices of inquisitional law on this point.[112] Nor was this privilege absolute. For example, in 1618 the Augustinian censor of the Mexican Inquisition, Rodrigo Moriz, had his commission revoked for reading Martin Luther despite the fact that he had been appointed a corrector of books for the Inquisition.[113]

The question of licenses and privileges to read banned books revived the debate about the relationship between customary and codified, written law. True to his vision of inquisitional authority superior to diocesan power, Peña argued that bishops had no automatic authority to read prohibited books because in 1550 Julius IV and, on the termination of Trent and the publication of the Trent

Index in 1564, Pius IV revoked licenses to read prohibited books.[114] According to Peña's interpretation of these revocations, only inquisitors (because they were papally commissioned) could read prohibited books and only the pope could issue such licenses. This view conflicted with Castro's view that bishops were the first defenders of the doctrine and had an inherent role in regulating print and an explicit right to read prohibited books. Like Castro, a censor of the Roman Inquisition in the later seventeenth century, Thomas Delbene agreed that bishops could read prohibited books and even issue licenses to read them. He explained this both in terms of the ancient ordinary authority of bishops but also in terms of customary law and tradition. According to Delbene, even if a pope revoked such licenses, the point was moot in the Spanish Inquisitions because the Spanish Inquisition possessed specific privileges which exempted it from such papal fiat. In Delbene's view the collective value of tradition outweighed the attempts by any single pope to rewrite the legality of licenses to read prohibited books.[115]

Like Peña, Castro was relatively conservative in his assessment of what should be censored and for what reasons. Castro argued that censorship and heresy could not be separated; therefore, the various causes of heresy and the dangers of open doctrinal debate, translation of scripture, and the free distribution of banned books were all of a piece. Whereas the canonists, like Peña, would divide their discussions of the causes of heresy and censorship into more discrete categories, Castro intermingled them as fundamentally indissoluble. Consequently, Castro dedicated a significant portion of *Aduersus omnes haereses* to explaining the various causes of heresy, all of which were linked in some form or another with issues of censorship or the regulation of doctrinal debate. Likewise, in *De justa haereticorum punitione,* he addressed the concerns about public disputation as well as the validity of openly refuting heretics.

Castro began his explanation about public debate with Augustine's conclusion that pride was the mother of all heresy. Therefore, because heretics sought public approval for their doctrines, it was logical to ban public preaching of heretics, since "without the applause of the populace, the wind of pride ceases."[116] Moreover, the uneducated person might be duped by this public preaching, for, Castro continued, if one did not necessarily understand how to reject the arguments of the heretics one might conclude that the heretical doctrine was correct. For Castro, even true Catholic explanations of various topics ought to be banned publicly if the subject was especially complicated, as in the case of topics like grace and free will, predestination, and the mysteries of the Eucharist. The reasoning here shared much with Aquinas's view that coram simplicibus one must be careful not to dispute subjects unnecessary to the spiritual well-being of the laity. Accordingly, Castro concluded that only learned theologians should be allowed to dispute on the faith, since "any old cobbler or weeder could learn to argue on the subject of predestination or God's omniscience" even though he could hardly understand the true meaning of the words sallying forth from his lips.[117]

If Castro followed the standard canonist charge that laymen were forbidden from disputing the faith (as found in *Quicumque*), he did not consider all clergy inherently worthy of this privilege. He followed the Thomist conception of the need to refute heresy publicly when it had invaded a territory. The responsibility necessarily fell to theologians, since "among the learned men, constant in the faith" such disputation was acceptable.[118] But this did not mean Castro assumed that all priests and friars automatically fell under this rubric of *viri docti in fide constanti* (learned men constant in the faith). Just as the canon law empowered the Inquisition to prosecute priests suspected of heresy, Castro argued forcefully that the mere state of being a friar did not excuse doctrinal error. In harsh language, Castro condemned Dominicans who insisted that being a professed member of their order conferred immunity: "I cannot stomach those who, in order to praise their institute, have no shame in publicly declaring that he who has taken the habit of their same order cannot err in or desert the faith. . . . Is this not patent blasphemy when one attributes more to the habit one has taken than to the faith in or grace of God?"[119] Castro provided that there must be a distinction between oral, vernacular public disputation and written, Latin private debate among theologians. On this score Castro blended the Thomist conception of the distinction between coram simplicibus and coram sapientibus seamlessly with his own conception of the lay/clerical and vernacular/Latin divides. He pointed out that there was no logical inconsistency here, since he had warned against the dangers of public oral disputation before the populace. But since Latin written debate was available only to the learned, if an educated man should succumb to heresy on reading a treatise rejecting it, then the fault lay only with the reader. Therefore, in his estimation books disputing and attacking heresy in vernacular languages must be banned because the stupid cannot distinguish between right and wrong.[120] There seems to have been at least a rumor that fray Andrés de Olmos, an early Franciscan missionary to Mexico, translated the *De iusta haereticorum punitione* into Spanish, and one historian argues that it was translated into other vernacular languages, but there does not appear to be any contemporaneous evidence for this and such translations would have been illegal in any case. It may be the case that manuscript copies circulated but I have not seen any mention of them in the Inquisition's case law or correspondence.[121]

Castro linked various inherent causes of heresy to the need for censorship: pride, desire for glory, the lure of the flesh, avarice, and ambition. But besides these causes, other external causes of heresy were also linked to concerns about censorship. The first external cause of heresy resulted from the absence of the shepherd from his flock. The second external cause, also linked to pastoral concerns, was the "defective preaching of the word of God."[122] If preachers could not be trusted with this apostolic and pastoral responsibility, then the laity could not be held responsible for error. Castro drew on his personal experience of growing up in northern Spain in the early sixteenth century, asserting that he had seen many "mountain people" in Viscaya, Cantabria, and Galicia engaged in numerous superstitions, such as venerating the image of a goat. Prior to his appointment as inquisitor of Mexico, the Basque Franciscan Juan de Zumárraga had been an inquisitional investigator of witchcraft in nearby Navarre, sent to root out such superstitions in 1527—a campaign which had resulted in Castro's own discovery of this group. Such questionable practices, Castro concluded, were not the fault of the ordinary people who followed them but were the result of a lack of good preachers.[123]

Whereas Castro's first two external causes of heresy were directed at the conceptualization of pastoral care and the regulation of public, oral discourse, his third external cause of heresy was aimed squarely at printed books: the translation of scripture into the vernacular languages. As Castro argued in his own defense in *De justa haereticorum punitione,* heresies arising from perverted understanding of scripture or orthodox theology were not the fault of scripture itself but of the faulty understanding of it. Therefore, he concluded that it was "certainly doubtful that the uneducated masses [could] understand that which the most intelligent men [could] barely grasp with extensive study."[124]

Because heresy was a "pestilence . . . that could infect the entire Christian republic," Castro reasoned that heretical books posed an especially grave threat to ecclesial and social unity, employing specific scriptural allegories for his proofs.[125] His first was that of the Church as the shepherd, found in Luke 2:8: "In that region there were shepherds living in their fields, keeping watch over their flock by night." Castro, like most pastoral exegetes, associated this passage with that of Acts 20:28 to make the connection to the Church more apparent: "Keep watch over yourselves and over all the flock, of which the Holy Spirit has made you overseers, to shepherd the Church of God that he obtained with the blood of his own Son." The infiltrating wolf in sheep's clothing is an easily recognized metaphor for duplicitous evil, and Castro employed the image of such a wolf to represent the unseen heretic, as opposed to the well-recognized one. According to Castro, disingenuous heretics could corrupt and manipulate scripture or Catholic doctrine to trick the innocent or uneducated into error. Like Aquinas, Castro viewed the uneducated as the responsibility of the priests, who were to guide and protect them from their stupidity. Castro therefore blamed not the ignorant, if led into error by a preacher's error, but the preacher himself, since "not everyone must be held to the same standard" in the doctrine.[126] Therefore, it was the responsibility of the pastor or the bishop to offer an "antidote to the poisons" of the heretic.[127]

Because erroneous books passed more easily into the Church when they attempted to pass as orthodox, scrutiny of books—especially as they travel from diocese to diocese—was to be rigorous. The charge of such scrutiny fell, in Castro's vision, to the bishop, who acted as the shepherd of his flock. This view contrasted with others that viewed such scrutiny as primarily an inquisitor's responsibility. Furthermore, because most of the flock were ignorant and could not avoid error on their own, the bishop held the pastoral responsibility to keep out dangerous books—especially heretical books posing as orthodox. Once let in, according to the metaphor, the wolf could exterminate the flock.[128] In the context of heretical books, the bishop who allowed them to enter into Catholic lands failed in his pastoral duty and, Castro argued, should be removed from office and defrocked. Both Castro and Peña viewed the sealing of borders to prevent the influx of heretical or offensive books as of paramount importance in the overall hierarchy of episcopal responsibility. This was the case when, in 1563, the diocesan judge in Veracruz investigated Juan Díaz for having brought unapproved books with him on the ship *San Luis*. Díaz had been reported to be a Moor and was likely Portuguese, as he brought with him a copy of a book of hours in Portuguese—expressly banned in the 1559 Index.[129]

Because heresy was an infectious disease in Castro's metaphor, the cure was to stamp it out entirely. Heresy "vomits out poison," and in order to prevent its continual pollution of the faithful, the entire source, root and all, must be torn out and destroyed. Likewise, if a public well was poisoned, it must be walled up and closed. Castro employed both of these metaphors to explain his position on heretical books: confiscation and burning. Such a conclusion was more radical than much of what the Spanish and Mexican Inquisitions would institute. The Spanish Inquisition generally argued for the confiscation but not the utter destruction of heretical books. And in Mexico on numerous occasions inquisitors of the sixteenth century explicitly warned comisarios not to engage in public book burnings, lest the populace be scandalized by such action. But Castro suggested that if the books of heretics were left undestroyed the disease of heresy might rise again. Accordingly, he proposed destruction: "It is therefore necessary that all books of heretics be burned, so that no pestilent root remains out of which new heretics might arise."[130]

But ideas cannot necessarily be stamped out along with the books, which was why inquisitors and censors viewed them with such suspicion. The 1559 Index banned all prayer books of hours in Spanish and ordered most Latin books of hours to be reviewed. In addition to the question of outright prohibition, the question of memory flummoxed censors and inquisitors. For example, in 1575 the comisario of Yucatán noted that many "old devout women" might still remember the prayers contained in Spanish-language books of hours.[131] From a customary perspective, prohibited books were dangerous on numerous levels since memories of them could remain stuck in popular devotional conscience for decades. Nor could the prohibited books always be completely destroyed. Copies could be made; clandestine editions circulated. In 1574 fray Luis López wrote to the inquisitors in Mexico from Oaxaca that even though books of hours and Bibles in the vernacular had been banned and the edict of the faith was read publicly, he knew of bookshops outside the regional capital and in the hinterlands where one could purchase prohibited books; he attributed this state of affairs to the difficulties of hunting down and destroying the far-flung networks of trade in the geographic and climatologic complexity of the mountainous region of southern Mexico.[132]

But what of books that were not specifically heretical? Were there books that in Castro's view nevertheless ought to be forbidden? Like Augustine and Peña, Castro took a view at odds with the relative liberalism of the Spanish Indexes in relation to books not specifically heretical. Much as Augustine reproached the "sweet inanity" of the poets, Castro argued in *Aduersus omnes haereses* that one ought to be inherently skeptical of the potentially corrupting power of the books of the philosophers (meaning, pre-Christian authors). In them "one discovers irreconcilable discords of brothers, the bitterest reproaches of parents unto their children, the most pertinacious disobedience of sons, the most obscene loves, adulteries, rapes and Ganymedan abductions of the gods — all praised."[133] While he did not, as it were, name names, Castro had in mind works by authors like Homer, Ovid, Catullus, Petronius, Apuleius, and Terence. Yet the Spanish Index often allowed such works free circulation as long as they remained in Latin and were not translated into the vernacular. Concerning the case of works not deemed explicitly obscene or homoerotic (like Petronius's *Satyricon,* which circulated freely until it was banned in 1621 by edict of the Suprema), such as presumed moral classics like Vergil's *Aeneid* and Ovid's *Metamorphoses* (as opposed to the *Ars amandi*), the Spanish Inquisition had nothing to say.[134] Castro, however, would support no such lenience, recalling that "not for nothing did Plato cast out the poets from his Republic."[135]

Theorists and inquisitors also often saw dangers in the circulation or misuse of approved books. Sailors often reported that they viewed the *Flos Santorum* (a popular version of the lives of the saints) as entertainment and not as moral or spiritual guidance. In 1621 in Tepotzotlan (just to the north of the Valley of Mexico) rumors began to circulate about the sacrilegious use of the Gospels in the rural area where the Jesuits had established a school. Pedro Vidal had taken depositions from residents that a blind man was selling small (about two-inch-by-one-inch) copies of the Gospels to people who believed that possessing them would protect them from lightning. The blind book peddler had also convinced pregnant women that if they placed the booklets in their hair they would avoid painful or fatal childbirth. When witnesses were interviewed they said they knew nothing of anti-Catholic activities and when prodded about the case of the blind book peddler, they all responded that, oh yes, they knew about him but that they did not think he was doing anything wrong. The censors were thus pushed up squarely against the cultural mentalities of people who did not appreciate the rigorist view of censorship theory. The censor appointed in the case, the Jesuit Cristóbal Ángel, viewed these uses as superstitious, but the case was never brought to trial.[136]

The investigation in 1625 against Pedro Hernández in Mexico City brought together two strands of the theory of censorship — vernacular Bibles and the infection of territory by heresy. The Dominican Miguel Gaona wrote to the inquisitors that he had been aboard the lead ship of the Pacific galleon fleet, *Nuestra Señora de Alocha,* which Hernández had piloted from Manila and that Hernández had brought with him a vernacular Bible. The horror with which the Dominicans and the censors in general viewed the vernacularization of the Bible was considerable. In this case Gaona felt that the non-Latinized laity reading scripture was, as agreed Castro, a recipe for heretical incursions. Yet the matter went beyond the pilot's reading of a Spanish Bible: Gaona and other clergy had demanded that Hernández remove from his cabin the several female slaves with whom he had been sleeping. Sexual sins (especially sodomy) on board ships were often seen as bad omens for storms, and the Dominican insisted that such fornication would anger God.[137] The pilot had responded that he had sailed with priests only by chance and that moreover priests brought bad luck, since they scared the whores away — and that whores made for much better luck than priests on the high seas anyway. Gaona viewed this as proof that vernacular Bibles, the transport of books, sexual sin, and heresy were of a piece and that God would bring down his wrath on the blaspheming enemies of the faith for their disregard of the Church's guidelines.[138]

Infection and incursion were the metaphors on which censorship theory was based and the hierarchy of knowledge one of the principal pieces of the theoretical foundation for inquisitional censure. Eimeric, Castro, Simancas, and Peña were among the most widely esteemed theorists of inquisitional doctrine and practice in early modern Spain in colonial Mexico. Their works saw wide distribution and in the case of Aquinas mandatory memorization for advanced theological degrees. Their writings justified censorship in the Hispanic world. In particular their treatises offered what were considered infallible proof of the dangers of open debate, the prevention of wide dissemination of "dangerous" material, and the control of vernacular material. Both coram simplicibus and ex parte disputantis, the problem of print represented the ultimate challenge to all that was considered sacred for the soul and efficacious for the Church and body politic, which were often viewed as indistinguishable. Ultimately, the concern of the canonists and theorists of Inquisition and heresy was the unity and health of the Church politic as well as of the individual souls of believers.

As Covarrubias contended, the purpose of excommunication was to "heal the sinner from the fatiguing disease of sin," not to stain the hands of the inquisitors with blood.[139] The disease of heresy was thus seen as something that the Inquisition could excise in a kind of spiritual surgery or by doctrinal vaccination. Censorship lay at the heart of this enterprise precisely because canonists and theologians saw heresy as infectious. Therefore, if heresy was spread by books, as influenza is by a virus, then the best medicine was prevention. No censor would have failed to recognize this metaphysics or ignore the inextricable connection between books, censorship, and the prevention of the "spreading evil" of heresy.

3

Theories of Adjudication

"The Pope is not lord of the whole world," concluded the Dominican holder of the prime chair of theology at the University of Salamanca, Francisco de Vitoria.[1] On his return to Spain in 1523 after more than a decade in Paris (during which he earned a doctorate in theology) he was responsible for the introduction of the study of Aquinas into the theology faculty in Salamanca and the invigoration of neoscholastic discussions of contemporary ethical concerns associated with the School of Salamanca.[2] Vitoria argued in his discussion "On the Power of the Church," as he would do in his discussions "On the Indians," that the pope possessed spiritual but not absolute temporal power. This assessment flew in the face of Boniface VIII's claims of absolutism and generally against the views of influential canonists like Peña. And while Peña championed the Dominicans, one would be hard pressed to find a single reference to Vitoria in any of his thousands of commentaries. Specifically commenting on those who agreed with Boniface's assessment of temporal power in *Unam sanctam,* Vitoria replied unequivocally that "the supporters of the opposite view [i.e., that popes have temporal power] commonly assert that the pope instituted all temporal powers as his delegates and subordinates, and that he also instituted Constantine as emperor. All this is improbable make-believe, without a shred of logical proof or authority, either from scripture or from those true theologians, the Fathers. It is the glossators of (canon) law who, in their poverty of learning and substance, attributed this dominion to the pope.[3] Vitoria's view of canon lawyers differed little from his sometime colleague Alfonso de Castro, who remarked that glossators used proof texts for ostentation rather than for learning.

The differing visions of the relationship between the papacy, Church law, theology, and canonists were hashed out in various forms. The case of disputation on heresy and censorship was no exception. Rather than present a unified vision of censorship on all fronts, theologians and canonists provided fundamentally different understandings of these topics. Some tropes held consistently across this divide, such as the notion of heresy as a "creeping evil." But nowhere was the difference between the canonists and theologians manifested more greatly than in the assessment of authority in debate, as Vitoria's statement above so eloquently explained. The canonists, in his view, suffered from an impoverished understanding of the fundamental and highest authority: scripture.

The result was that as a specific outgrowth of the debate concerning which professional caste made the best inquisitor — jurist or theologian — a second question about the nature of expert advisor developed. Since jurists could not be expected to know theology as well as theologians, and theologians could not be expected to have studied the law with the same rigor as the canonists, the theorists of Inquisition recognized the need for specifically trained experts to advise the inquisitor on the discipline in which he was least qualified. By the sixteenth century this resulted in a professional segregation of knowledge between canonists and theologians.

In ecclesiological terms, authority that came out of one's office was called ordinary power or jurisdiction. Thus bishops were said to possess ordinary jurisdiction over the doctrine, the power of excommunication, and punishment for heresy. This was formally codified in *Ad abolendam*. When the papal legislation of the early thirteenth century began to empower Dominican friars to investigate heresy, however, this authority was transferred to delegated or vicarious jurisdiction. The logic was that since the pope was directly commissioning and delegating his authority, the Dominican friar–inquisitors possessed unique legal authority to investigate heresy that was separate from ordinary, diocesan authority.

Eimeric and Peña both recognized the primary responsibility of the bishop as pastor of the flock. This charge did not carry specific inquisitional duties even if, prior to the thirteenth century, it allowed bishops to punish parishioners for heresy. Therefore, Peña reasoned, a bishop who failed to impede heresy or the infiltration of heretical books ought to be removed from office. Consequently, it was the duty of the bishop to purge his diocese of heresy. If that was the case, did Peña or Eimeric conclude that bishops had specific inquisitional authority? Both Eimeric and Peña agreed that bishops held the authority, ex officio, to judge heretics but that their authority was automatically inferior to that of an inquisitor. Throughout the history of the Spanish Inquisitions, the question of whether delegated Inquisitions were usurpations of episcopal prerogatives would recur almost continuously.[4]

Part 3 of the *Directorium* discussed inquisitional procedure, and consequently the first subject Eimeric considered was the office of the inquisitor himself — the "delegate from the Apostolic See."[5] Eimeric had relatively little to say about the inherent professional qualities of the inquisitor. Rather, he limited himself to stating that an inquisitor had to be prudent, honest, circumspect, and "eminently skilled in the holy doctrine of the faith."[6] Because Eimeric wrote his *Directorium* when only friars acted as inquisitors, it would have been assumed that all inquisitors were theologians — this explains the absence of lengthy elaboration on this point. Peña, however, writing his commentaries from the 1570s through the 1590s, had no choice but to explain the professional background of the inquisitor.

Delegated judges — inquisitors — were those to whom "the faculty of judging heretics was given by the Apostolic See."[7] Peña understood this to mean theologians, not jurists, since the Inquisition judged the "sacred doctrine" — that is, theology, not jurisprudence.[8] This contrasted dramatically, as Peña subsequently noted, with Simancas's view that jurists were to be preferred to theologians as inquisitors. Indeed, Simancas said that "jurists are more elegant than theologians in their understanding of the law, as is seen when that foolish, mediocre theologian Occam rants and raves."[9] Splitting the two extreme views, Peña took a middle path, arguing instead that it was "certain that neither a sole theologian nor a sole jurist can easily dissect this issue."[10] Instead, Peña viewed the Inquisition as possessing such consequence that its court ought to be split between theologians and jurists; that an inquisitor should have studied theology or law; and that above all he must be versed in canon law and scripture, regardless of professional background. But Peña's balanced view manifested itself when he argued that "in those cities where there are two inquisitors, one must be a highly proven and extremely learned theologian, and the other should be a most expert canon law jurist, given the great magnitude and gravity of the subject of the faith."[11] In Mexico, where the Inquisition was run exclusively by jurists for nearly six decades (1573–1631), practice clashed with Peña's recommendation.

While Eimeric lived in a period of friar-inquisitors and Peña in a period during which friars ceased to operate as inquisitors in the Spanish tribunals, the debate on the supremacy of ordinary or delegated authority had changed little in theory. In drawing out the distinction between the two forms of religious authority in *foro exteriori*, Eimeric clearly delimited the jurisdiction of the inquisitor. Because an inquisitor was specifically delegated to investigate the doctrine, his authority *ipso iure* could not extend into cases that did not specifically deal with the faith or heresy. The real debate lay within a hierarchy of these two competing forms of authority. Writing in the fervor of the empowered Dominican order and its friar-inquisitors, Eimeric concluded that a judge ordinary could never prohibit or impede the procedure of the inquisitor.[12] This was the same conclusion that the inquisitors in Mexico made when they defended the jurisdictional attacks by the bishop of Guatemala against their inquisitional comisario in 1608 and 1609.[13]

In question 30 of part 3 of the *Directorium,* Eimeric considered whether or not a bishop or inquisitor could prosecute an inquisitor. Eimeric concluded that a bishop could not prosecute an inquisitor, since his ordinary power was inferior to the delegated power of the inquisitor and inquisitors held equal power and could therefore not prosecute another inquisitor. Peña, however, disagreed with Eimeric, concluding that a bishop might lawfully bring a case against an inquisitor given certain conditions: if (1) the inquisitor was a "manifest heretic"; or (2) preached against the faith or wrote or allowed to be written or preached anything against the faith; or (3) dismissed heretics without punishment; *and* (4) the pope could not be easily consulted; *and* (5) in the meantime the faith was endangered.[14] The fourth clause would be particularly important in the case of Mexico, where the Crown had endeavored, by its Council of Indies, to prohibit all direct communication between Mexican ecclesiastical authorities and Rome.

In rejecting the argument that an inquisitor was always, by definition, immune from diocesan prosecution for heresy, Peña rejected the immunity from inquisitional proceedings for inquisitors or Dominicans. In theory everyone, including bishops, was subject to inquisitional authority, though the Dominicans were granted exemptions in 1262. But Peña was not the only theorist to reject this immunity. Castro argued in *Aduersus omnes haereses* that only the Apostolic See or a general council had the authority to censure heresy. Drawing on a standard biblical proof for ecclesial unity in Ephesians 4:5 — "one Lord, one faith, one baptism" — Castro asserted the authority of the Church as complete over spiritual matters. For this reason, where there might be a multiplicity of opinions, the judgment of a "mere bishop" should not be binding in matters of the faith. Instead, there must be a judge who can pronounce sentence and whose conclusions "must be obeyed."[15] To this end Castro argued that only a general Church council, not a bishop or a theological faculty of a university, could define and judge heresy.

Moreover, if the opposite of Catholic truth was heresy, to whom fell the responsibility of defining heresy? In direct opposition to Simancas, Castro offered the following: "It is not the task of the canonists to judge heresy or faith but that of theologians, to whom such authority is committed by divine right."[16] If Castro elevated theologians to the highest jurisdictional level, Simancas offered the most representative defense of the jurists over the theologians, arguing that canonists, not theologians, were the correct professionals to run Inquisitions as courts. Simancas did, however, support the view that theologians were the proper experts on doctrine within inquisitional trials.[17] His praise of law over theology did not stop at discussions of inquisitional procedure. In his autobiography — in which he recounts his hatred for Carranza, in whose trial he was instrumental both in Spain and Rome — Simancas attacked numerous theologians for suggesting that theologians, not canonists, ought to be bishops. Simancas argued against the holder of a prime chair of theology in Salamanca, the Dominican Domingo de Soto, for suggesting that "better a cobbler than a jurist" does a bishop make. Though Simancas did not identify the source of the supposed statement by De Soto, the point was made clear when he continued by arguing that "other ambitious theologians and of lesser quality [than De Soto] followed this evil doctrine and therefore I added a defense of the jurists in the second edition of my *Catholic Institutions*."[18]

Whereas Peña, Eimeric, Simancas, and Castro had fairly specific ideas about who held the authority to define and judge heresy, Suárez's discussion was typically more diffuse, theoretical, and metaphysical. From the onset in *De censuris* Suárez distinguished between establishing and bringing censure, fundamental metaphysical differences. In his view only the papacy or the universal Church held the power to establish censure and heresy. But bringing the result of its punishment was, in his view, an explicitly human action that fell to specific human actors or judges. Drawing on a concept of human law vis-à-vis divine law, Suárez argued that the actual power of establishing censure was divine in origin, relying on the usual Petrine succession arguments. Yet at the same time Suárez saw Proverbs 8:15 — "kings rule through me" — as evidence that the actual application of divine law was not in itself divine but human. Therefore, the application of ecclesiastical censure, though it drew its origins from divine law, was itself a kind of human or natural law. The reason, he asserted, was that "the application of censure never occurs except when some particular form of penalty is prescribed" and "no censure exists except when it is concomitant with some human precept."[19] Diffuse concepts of the immutable and absolute power of the Church became concrete and human when specific penalties were appropriate. Christ instituted sacraments, but priests minister them; by way of simile, the same metaphysics applied to censure for Suárez: the Church instituted censure and human judges applied the penalties.

If the power to apply ecclesiastical censure was necessarily human, Suárez immediately considered who could hold this authority. As a Jesuit, Suárez argued that the pope was the first man to whom the power of applying censure fell. In asking whether "others can possess this power" Suárez provided a standard gloss on the distinction between ordinary and delegated authority.[20] Herein Suárez generally supported the jurisdiction of bishops, via ordinary authority, to bring censure and punish doctrinal error. For example, in disputation 3 of *De censuris,* Suárez tackled the question of the delegated authority of inquisitors, and, in his more philosophical rendering, ecclesiastical judges. In this context Suárez argued that if the Church was indeed "militant and visible," then its judges must be similarly militant and visible, not invisible.

Many of Suárez's negative conclusions about who could not legally bring censure were quite predictable: the excommunicated, women, and children. But he also insisted that judges must be above reproach and that any ulterior motives automatically nullified the legal authority as righteous champions of truth. For Suárez, causes brought by ulterior motives possessed no power of judgment. If one looks to similar arguments about the inherent moral qualities of judges, inquisitors, or bishops by jurists like Simancas or Peña or Dominicans like Eimeric, there was little discussion of this aspect of a judge's moral quality. These theorists were content, generally speaking, to argue that inquisitors needed to be firm in the faith and rigorous in their application of the law, but they said nothing about ulterior motives. One could see such ulterior motives in some of the more notorious inquisitional trials brought in sixteenth-century Spain — against Luis de León and Carranza, for example — and Suárez may very well have had such trials in mind. For Suárez, political motives had no place in religious tribunals because the only subject under review was religious orthodoxy. "Indeed," Suárez wrote of ulterior motives, "any such intent invalidates the moral act . . . sometimes such intent can make a judge so precipitant in bringing censure that he commits a substantial error."[21]

Even among theorists there did not appear to be much agreement about the essential nature of inquisitors and ecclesiastical judges. In some cases inquisitors were seen as inviolable guardians of the faith, as the Dominicans viewed themselves. But equally influential jurists, like Peña, and theologians with varying views of internal and external Church authority, like Castro and Suárez, saw the inquisitors as potentially flawed. For this reason the latter group of theorists tended to support preserving the jurisdictional sweep of bishops even in the context of an empirewide Inquisition.

The Experts: Theologians or Jurists?

Peña, among others, recognized that if an inquisitor were a theologian he would lack expertise in the law, just as a jurist lacked expertise in theology.

In order to rectify this imbalance, inquisitional law allowed the use of experts —whether in law or theology—to assist the inquisitor in rendering a fair verdict within a lawful trial. The origin of the office of an expert advisor to inquisitors lies in the *Sextus,* in the chapters *Statuta* and *Ut commissi. Ut commissi* offered the most explicit recommendation for such an arrangement, arguing that inquisitors were both commissioned and enjoined to call on experts in their proceedings.

Just as papal bulls conferred authority on the Crown and inquisitor general, the inquisitor general, in turn, bestowed the power of censorship on the theological advisors. In 1518 the Suprema ruled that "qualifier theologians must be called when some proposition needs to be reviewed, and those who seem to be the most learned and who have the necessary qualities, and for the determination, jurists [consultores] should be called."[22] In Mexico in the 1550s and 1560s, Zumárraga's successor, the Dominican Alonso de Montúfar, relied heavily on theologians as both his advisor-censors as well as delegated inquisitors ordinary, as when he delegated several dozen trials to Mexico's cathedral chapter *chantre* (director of the choir), the theologian don Rodrigo Barbosa.[23]

It was unclear what the respective roles of consultor and censor would be, but the instructions of 1518 suggested that both theological and legal experts were considered necessary in offering advice on difficult matters. The *Instructions* written by Torquemada in 1484, then recompiled by his successors to be used as a guide for procedure and law for future inquisitors, included no mention of the censor in keeping with the Dominican tradition of friar-theologian inquisitors. The *Instructions* of the Inquisitor General Fernando de Valdés of 1571 further elaborated the office of the censor as a specified role: "*Examination and qualification of propositions[:]* 1. When the Inquisitors gather together to look at the testimonies that result from some inspection . . . whose understanding pertains to the Holy Office of the Inquisition, being such that it requires review, theologians of letters and conscience should be consulted in whom concur the qualities required for this, who should give their opinion and sign with their names."[24]

The censor thus had no vote in inquisitional proceedings. He was an advisor and empowered to make recommendations that, in turn, were considered by the Suprema or, within the local Inquisitions, by its inquisitor general. Furthermore, the very definition of censorship—what should be censored; how it should be accomplished; what the penalties for heretical writing should be; why censorship should be such a pillar of social control—was bound up in mixed discussions of canon law and theology, overlapping in use and jurisdiction. The censors were theologians by definition; their purpose was to examine the details of doctrinal debate that were too abstruse for the canon lawyers who possessed votes—the members of the Suprema and the inquisitors. After the mid 1500s, the inquisitors were virtually never trained theologians and therefore, in the professional specialization of the later sixteenth century, were considered inadequate to split theological hairs.[25] The first inquisitor general of Mexico, don Pedro Moya de Contreras, was a canon lawyer, not a theologian or a friar.

Eimeric's discussion of experts was fairly brief, but Peña offered substantial commentary. Peña's academic style was eclectic, and he drew on scripture, theology, law (both civil and canon), and ancient classics to buttress his claims. For example, he drew from Proverbs (11:14), asserting that "where there is an abundance of counsel, there is strength." As was the case with other topics, the changing context of the Inquisition required Peña to modernize this section of the *Directorium*. Therefore, Peña understood this section to mean precisely the "abundance of counsel." If, in the medieval period of friar-inquisitors it was necessary to call jurists to assist the theologians on questions of law, Peña commented that "today, however, the inquisitors are jurists, as in Spain, and they should still call experts — in this case, theologians, whose duty it is to weigh the grade and quality of the propositions [of the accused]."[26]

In offering a lengthy commentary on Eimeric's more adumbrated consideration of "whether sentence should be brought by the Inquisitor and Bishop out of the advice of the experts," Peña considered the boundaries of jurisdiction between advisor and inquisitor.[27] His first conclusion was that "inquisitors are not compelled to follow the advice of the experts."[28] This view was supported by the Suprema's *Instructions* to inquisitors of 1561, which argued that the votes of the experts were not decisive.[29] This was reiterated in the trial of 1560 against the Mexico cathedral dignitary don Alonso Chico de Molina, when both the Augustinian and Franciscan censors called by inquisitor-archbishop Montúfar recommended absolving the cathedral archdeacon. Montúfar rejected their advice and condemned Chico de Molina as a heretic.[30] The discretionary power of the inquisitor notwithstanding, Peña ascribed an important role to the censors, concluding that inquisitors "may not, however, recklessly forsake the advice of experts."[31] Peña offered a balanced form of law — a central authority with the sole power to enact decrees and law, but restrained by the careful considerations of appointed experts in theology or canon or civil law.

Other jurists shared Peña's view of the utility of experts in the inquisitional procedure. Villadiego, for one, insisted that such experts were not only advisable but also necessary, arguing that "learned and wise men, fearful of God, must be called before sentencing." Moreover, he concluded that while experts should be consulted, their advice was more than consultative and should be binding, even if he stopped short of granting them a formal vote.[32] Such a view of inquisitional trial by committee held consistently with Villadiego's view that a general council, not the pope, was the correct representation of the Church.

Villadiego was not the only jurist to insist on the need for expert theologians in inquisitional procedure. Simancas recommended that censors be consulted in order to define the quality of suspect propositions, and while he recognized that such censors perforce were theologians, he did not accord them the power of a vote. Must the inquisitors follow their recommendation? Simancas concluded that only if that recommendation was unanimous must the inquisitors accept their advice but that if a split recommendation came from the theologians, the jurist-inquisitors should decide the doctrinal quality.[33] Martín del Río, the author of a treatise on witchcraft, and the Italian theorist Arnaldo Albertinus both recognized the role of theologians as being one of offering advice.[34] In all cases the jurists agreed that the advice of theologians was crucial, even if the theologians were deprived of a formal vote. Yet where Simancas would argue for the absolute power of jurists, Albertinus suggested that theologians were to be preferred over jurists for the papacy.

Juan de Rojas was another influential jurist to discuss the issue. Trained at Salamanca and made inquisitor of Valencia and Sicily as well as bishop of Girgenti, he composed the treatise *De succesionibus, de haereticis et singularia in fidei favorem*.[35] Rojas followed the line offered by Villadiego on theologian censors, arguing that whenever there was any doubt about heresy or when someone was suspected of heresy, "expert professors of Sacred Theology must be called, who commonly are called calificadores, and whose assertions inquisitors must always obey."[36] This was far from the purely consultative role that Peña and Simancas assigned to the censors; their view ultimately won in that the theologians had no vote in inquisitional proceedings in Mexico, though in the Suprema in Madrid the theologians played a more dominant role in fashioning decrees of censorship. In Rojas's view, and in Castro's also, if the censors did not have to be obeyed, then the entire apparatus might as well as be abandoned because if their "vote was solely consultative and not decisive, then in the same fashion the Inquisitors would not have to be obeyed."[37] And once that happened, Rojas concluded that the Inquisition might as well not exist, since the entire tribunal was based on the "Counsel of the Lord" and without it and its attendant hierarchy it would cease to function. Such was the case when, in 1574, after a lengthy trial, the Mexican inquisitor Moya de Contreras dismissed a heresy indictment against the mercurial don Diego Pérez Gordillo y Negrón, chantre of the cathedral chapter of Michoacán, who had been accused of Lutheran heresy and whose statements had been unanimously judged as heretical by the theologian-censors.[38] This was the inquisitor's legal prerogative, although theorists like Castro, Rojas, and Villadiego saw such vetoes as presumptive and rash.

Other theorists had little to say about experts as auxiliaries to inquisitors. Castro viewed theologians as the only worthy judges of heresy in the first place and for that reason accorded little authority to canonists, whom he considered intellectual buffoons. Likewise, Suárez, being engaged to a greater extent with philosophical matters, was more concerned with the authority of the ecclesiastical judges and less with specific discussions of procedure in specific courts. Because censorship relied so heavily on theological advisors and review, their formation in the inquisitional law and theory cannot be overlooked.

Typology of Crimes

In commentary 28 of part 3 of the *Directorium*, Peña offered a hierarchy of sin-crimes under the Inquisition's bailiwick, from the heretical proposition, to those contrary to good morals, to blasphemy, to sedition. Strictly speaking, then, Eimeric and Peña, following Aquinas, concluded that a heretical proposition was one that specifically repudiated an article of the faith or the definitions of the faith given by the Church or in scripture.

The question, however, was who or what would define heresy. In a lengthy commentary, Peña glossed Cano's definition of the eight rules of determining Catholic truth. Cano produced an influential text of systematic theology, *De locis theologicis*, on which Peña would rely for his definitions of Catholic truth and error. In that heresy was the rejection of Catholic truth, only by outlining the components of Catholic truth could one understand its opposite, heresy.[39] The first rule was that "those truths found in Scripture and whose meaning is all too clear, must be considered Catholic truths."[40] But what if the meaning was not clear? After all, the difficulties in biblical exegesis fell squarely in the center of the censorship enterprise. It was in this context that censure in general and censorship of books were inextricably bound within the inquisitional ideology of hierarchical knowledge and education. Peña concluded that it fell to the Church to define the more complicated meanings of scripture. But what was the Church in Peña's vision?

Peña answered this question by paraphrasing Cano's second rule of truth, contending that "whatever the doctors and pastors of the Church, in a legitimately convened council, teach is clearly true and must be accepted as such."[41] Both Cano and Peña were quick to point out that only those councils with papal approval carried the force of Catholic truth. This was a crucial distinction — one defended by Juan de Torquemada — because it meant that in the end the pope was the final arbiter even of conciliar decrees. The conclusion of the power of a general council, regardless of the interpretation of the See of Peter, was also supported by papal legislation. As early as 495 Gelasius asserted in what became the chapter *Maiores* in the *Decretum* that once an idea was decreed to be heretical in a general council or synod, the condemnation could not be revoked.[42] Likewise, Peña would agree with Cano's third and sixth rules that even while a general council could define heresy, the pope also held the power, as the Vicar of Christ, to define the faith. Drawing on papal absolutists like Juan de Torquemada, Peña concluded that the pope's definition of faith was itself *infallible*.[43] This derived from Cano's third rule of Catholic truth, which concluded that if the pope defined something, it must be accepted as true, since in his logic the pope could not err in the faith.[44] This logic conspired against the French barber Charles de Saligante in 1560 in Honduras when he said that the pope was merely a man and that only God, not the pope, could issue indulgences.[45] The Dominican censors called to review the case condemned Saligante as a heretic for denying the spiritual authority of the pope. The judge in the case sentenced Saligante to wear a sanbenito during three years of house arrest in Comayagua and to attend Mass every day for the same three-year period.[46] Such a triumphalist definition of papal infallibility was hardly uniformly accepted — both Castro and Villadiego concluded that the pope was not only fallible in judgment but could also fall into heresy, an eventuality for which only a general council could offer remedy. But many hardliners called the rejection of papal doctrinal infallibility heretical. In 1603 in Mexico a jurist was brought up on charges by the Holy Office for having said that the pope could err in the faith both as a person and as pope. The censors in the case, the Augustinian Diego de Contreras and the Dominican Luis Vallejo, argued that this was a manifest heresy condemned by Leo X in his excommunication of Luther.[47]

Cano's fourth rule asserted that the universal definition by the saints reflected Catholic truth, a conclusion with particular importance in the context of Lutheranism as well as in the practice of the Inquisition. His fifth rule was related but by culture: the common use of the apostles reflected Catholic truth. This meant that practices or rites not specifically ordained by Christ but adopted in early Christendom were to be accepted as truths on a par with the scriptures. Thus certain sacraments (like confession), the cult of the saints or apostolic traditions perforce were Catholic truths, and for this theologians would look for support to 2 Thessalonians 2:15: "So therefore brothers, stand firm and hold fast to the traditions that you were taught by us, either by word of mouth or by letter." The inclusion of "word of mouth" was crucial since it would offer a proof text that suggested that, even if not specifically contained in scripture, traditions carried the force of dogma. The tailor Blas Martín in 1571 in Mexico City discovered the force of this argument when he rejected images of the saints. In doing so, he rejected not scripture but the accumulated power of tradition; this formed a central component of inquisitional prosecution of iconoclasm.[48]

Rules 6 and 7 reiterated the authority of councils to establish truth, though in rule 7 Peña asserted that the common, unified voice of the theologians could establish Catholic truth. Thus rule 6 concluded that any dogma defined by the entire Church, a general council, or the pope must be accepted as truth. Seventh, anything pronounced in one voice by the consensus of theologians carried the force of truth. Finally, rule 8 argued that "if scholastic theologians state together with one voice a firm conclusion, and teach in order that a certain belief of theology must be perpetually and constantly embraced by the faithful, all faithful must embrace it as Catholic truth."[49] Overall, Peña and Cano pushed for a vision of Church doctrine heavily centered on theologians, one in which canonists were relatively uninvolved in the definitions of Catholic truth, even if they were to be counted on to hear the cases of law brought against those who rejected those truths.

It is not surprising that someone with as many opponents as Cano would wish to assert that the mere common opinion of scholastics could be used to define heresy without any inquisitional or diocesan oversight. But Cano's (and by extension Peña's) view that scholastics were empowered to define heresy was soundly rejected by Castro, who remarked that "the decrees of Paris do not cross mountains [i.e., the Pyrenees or the Alps]."[50] And so while Cano concluded that the common opinion of scholastics was sufficient authorization for doctrine, others were much less willing to allow certain academic faculties that authority.

Juan de Torquemada would be called specifically to defend the papacy against the claims of the conciliarists of the Basel Council; he had weighed in on the question of the definition of the faith.[51] In 1436 he wrote a treatise defending the supremacy of the papacy, arguing in favor of papal infallibility —even against the conclusions of Raymond of Peñafort and other Dominicans. In Torquemada's view a general council could indeed err, and it was the pope, not the council, who held the final decision in determining the doctrine of the Church. But in his "gradations" of Catholic truth enumerated in his defense of papal superiority, *Summa de ecclesia,* Torquemada outlined definitions that were even less certain than those of Cano.[52] For example, he offered some standard conclusions of what constituted Catholic truth: (1) that contained in scripture; (2) that which logically follows from scripture; (3) that approved by the apostles (even if not contained in scripture); (4) that approved by plenary universal councils; (5) that approved by the Apostolic See in matters of the faith; and (6) from traditions established by the doctors of the Church. But Torquemada innovated by arguing that anything that would logically follow from scripture or that would logically follow from councils, definitions of the papacy, or traditions offered by the Church doctors must be accepted as Catholic truth. The question immediately arose: who determined what could be logically inferred? For Torquemada, the answer was the pope or his trusted advisors. This vision was rejected by the conciliarists precisely because it left the definition of truth open to papal fiat instead of to rigorous debate by theologians or councils. Torquemada even went so far as to argue for an eighth method in which anything which was "propinquitous" to the faith and which could not reasonably be rejected must be accepted as doctrine. This view was frequently rejected by those theorists who argued that subjects not pertaining specifically to the faith did not fall under the purview of ecclesiastical law or censure.

Castro rejected a good deal of the papalist and conservative vision of the Church of Cano and Torquemada. For Castro, the Church had a duty to avoid the confusion of various authorities vying for the power to define religious error, "for not only many idiots and ignorant men, but even learned men, err in this by defaming many opinions in their writings even though they hardly merit such judgment."[53] That being the case, Castro outlined the various ways in which heretical propositions could be defined. The "first and most powerful" method of all was to rely on scripture. If there was not universal agreement among the theologians on the meaning of a scriptural passage, then an opinion ostensibly proven heretical by that same part of scripture could not be defined as heretical. The second method of defining heresy was by general council. Third, the general consensus of the Church could offer proofs against a statement, by way of tradition and oral memory. The papacy represented the fourth method of defining heresy, though here Castro was quick to point out that in his view the Apostolic See was not the person of the pope but the institution of the papacy. This was so because in his assessment the pope, in the form of a person, was capable of error, whereas the Church as a whole was not. Finally, the universal agreement of theologians could define a heresy, but as in his conception of biblical exegesis, Castro concluded that there could not be even a single dissenting theologian. Castro's view of the universal definition of the theologians was much stricter than Cano's common definition of them.[54] For Cano all that was necessary was the general consensus of theologians, whereas Castro viewed dissenting views of an opinion as invalidating the power of theologians to define the articles of the faith.

In Castro's reasoning the question arose when there was some doubt as to whether a proposition or idea was heretical and had or had not been previously condemned by a general council. In this case only the Church as a whole had the authority to proceed since regional authorities, lacking universal spiritual jurisdiction, could not define such cases. Castro found his whipping boy in Luther, who had argued that scripture was the only correct judge of spiritual matters. Not without irony Castro asked how scripture itself could physically manifest itself to bring judgment. While Castro did not place as much emphasis on the militant and visible Church as the Jesuits, he nevertheless argued that it was the Church as a whole that was the proper interpreter of scripture and that therefore the responsibility for defending the use of scripture against heresy fell to the Church.

If the Church held the authority of defining the faith and its opposite, heresy, Castro was quick to define the proper experts of the Church: "A particular Catholic truth must be defined not only by the Pope but by the Church."[55] In his view the judgment of the pope alone carried relatively little authority, and he went so far as to argue that the pronouncements of the pope without proper consultation with the College of Cardinals and other learned men carried no authority whatsoever.[56] This was the precise opposite of the view of Torquemada and others, who concluded that councils could have authority *only* with papal approval. Thus a papal fiat, in Castro's view, was empty and useless. While he would not go so far as to say so, this stance would have invalidated a good deal of canon law, including the more expansive, though traditional, papal claims of Boniface VIII: Boniface's *Unam sanctam,* for example, issued personally and without conciliar review, which claimed for the papacy and Boniface complete spiritual jurisdiction as well as the right to depose evil kings when the pope saw fit. According to Boniface's appraisal, the pope necessarily held spiritual as well as temporal power over all rulers.[57] In one stroke, Boniface solidified (at least for the canonists and champions of temporal papal power) the authority of the pope and, by extension, of the Inquisition to judge all men.[58] It would fall to Torquemada in the 1430s and 1440s to argue this line further in the context of the debate over conciliar authority after the schism of the Avignon papacy and the attempted reconciliation in the Councils of Constance and Basel.

Peña supported the authority of the papacy to establish and fix ecclesiastical law over and above that of the theologians in councils, and he associated the deprecation of the canon law with Wycliffe and Luther, both of whom argued that the *Decretales* was not inspired by Christ. Luther himself burned a copy of the bull of his excommunication, *Exurge Domine,* along with the canon law, during one of the public book burnings of his own work in Leipzig on December 10, 1520, arguing that "the canon law was included because it makes the pope a god on earth."[59] In contrast, for Peña and theorists of his mindset, the *Decretales* was by definition divinely inspired since the law it decreed derived from the pen of the pope, himself the direct representative of Christ. Moreover, according to Peña, the canon law could never be considered inferior to conciliar decrees ipso facto since only the pope could legitimize conciliar canons. Likewise, the attack on papal prerogatives was always a point of contention in both theory and practice. In Mexico, attacks on papal power and indulgences were common — and often punished severely. Such was the case in 1577, when the farmer from Michoacán Diego Muñoz (no relation to the inquisitional comisario of the same name) said that indulgences were useless and issued only to raise money — a clear echo of Luther's attack on Johann Tetzel; his words may also have been a reflection of a broader attitude in Mexico. Muñoz was convicted of heresy, sentenced to abjure *de levi* (a less severe sentence than *de vehementi*) in the church of Guanajuato, and exiled from Mexico for one year.[60]

Just as the Basel fathers promoted the supremacy of theologians in the fifteenth century (to the displeasure of Juan de Torquemada), so Castro was the most effective proponent of this conciliar view in the sixteenth century. But some notable jurists like Villadiego rejected papal supremacy and infallibility. Even Raymond of Peñafort, perhaps the most noted canonist to have lived, supported the view that a pope, as a person, could be a heretic and that if he were to fall into heresy must be despoiled of his office because the penalty for heresy must be "indistinct whether the [heretic] is a cleric, a Pope, or any other inferior person."[61] The reason? *Ad abolendam.* So the power to despoil a heretic pope came from the same argument that bishops were the first defense against heresy. The question arose immediately as to whether inquisitors could depose popes and bishops or whether bishops could depose heretic inquisitors — questions that would flummox the upper clergy both in Spain (notably in the Carranza case) and in Mexico.

Following Peñafort's and Villadiego's lead (though not explicitly), Castro argued that since it was possible for a pope to be a heretic, sometimes it was necessary for theologians to override the authority of the pope in order to correct and preserve the Church.[62] Given the elevation of papal law over pure theology (not Dominican jurisprudential theology) by the rigorist Dominicans and canonists, it is unsurprising that a significant portion of the first two parts of the *Directorium* were dedicated to redactions of the important decretals and concomitant glosses dealing with heresy and the Inquisition. If the first decretals quoted by Eimeric recapitulated the basic truths of the universal Church, part 2 of the *Directorium* redacted their counterparts: the condemnation of failure to adhere to the faith.

The Procedure of Censure

If there was a gradation of sin-crimes under the jurisdiction of the Inquisition, to whom did it fall to determine the nature of a specific crime of an accused? Peña concluded that theologians were the proper authorities to review the suspect statements of defendants. This fell within Peña's assessment that theologians were the best experts to discern questions of the doctrine, just as he assumed that jurists were the best authorities to run actual courts like the Inquisition. In part 1 of the *Directorium,* in which Peña considered the difficulties involved in removing banned books from circulation, he discussed who the proper authorities were to review books that contained "depraved doctrines" but had yet to be prohibited. As in his suggestion that theologians were best suited to review "suspect propositions," here too Peña believed that theologians were the best authorities to review suspect books. The reason was that only theologians could discern specifics of the doctrine, since, presumably, jurists were trained in the application of the doctrine but not in the doctrine itself.[63]

Peña often relied on Castro's vision of theological primacy, as can be seen in his frequent use of *De justa haereticorum punitione* as a proof text. In this treatise Castro explained his theory of religious error and its attendant typology. Thus the first distinction he made, drawing on Augustine, argued that while all heresy was erroneous, not every error was heresy. If it was true that not every error was heresy, then it was important to understand the levels of error and to whom their judgment fell, for "it is no small difficulty in understanding how they are to be distinguished."[64] Ironically, Castro's first authority for such distinction was Torquemada.[65] Castro pointed out that the necessary distinction was between beliefs that could be understood only by God and beliefs that could be understood without God. The second type, which depend on natural intelligence and not on God, could not fall under the rubric of faith/heresy. Therefore, "those propositions are not properly the object of the faith when they are understood by natural reason. [Rather] those propositions that can be proved false by natural reason are erroneous" but not heretical if they do not explicitly reject the faith. Consequently, "heresy properly speaking is against beliefs which are above and beyond human intellect."[66]

In a position that placed him squarely against the conception of scholastic authority of the Dominicans and their most curmudgeonly defenders, Torquemada and Cano, Castro argued that theological opinions did not carry obligation for the average person. For him, an opinion against the common opinion of theologians was theological error but not heresy. Such a conclusion had profound implications for the operation of the Inquisition, since inquisitors and more conservative censors routinely employed the argument that a proposition that went against the "common opinion of the theologians" was heretical. Not so for Castro, nor for numerous Jesuit censors. Therefore, Castro reasoned, to say that Mary was conceived in original sin was error but not heresy because the Church as a whole had not defined the Immaculate Conception as an article of faith; it was instead an opinion held by theologians.[67] Thus the commonplace view, expressed in 1600 by Felipa de Peñalosa, the wife of a goldsmith from Mexico City, that "the state of marriage was better than that of being a priest" was a frequent target of inquisitional investigation. In this particular case, the Franciscan censor Pedro de la Cruz concluded that although this opinion was erroneous it was not, strictly speaking, heresy.[68] Not so for the ironworker Rodrigo Cordero in Mexico City in 1574, who made similar statements about the state of marriage being superior to that of being a monk. The censors in the case — the Dominican Domingo Salazar, the Franciscan Antonio de Quixada, and the Jesuit Pedro Sánchez — unanimously considered the statement heresy, though luckily for Cordero the Thomist hierarchy of knowledge exculpated him from conviction.[69]

Despite the intense detail given to the point about defining the various gradations of sin-crimes under the inquisitional bailiwick, theorists like Peña had relatively little to say about the specific qualities of these heterodoxies. But in 1642 a "censors' manual" that addressed precisely those definitions appeared. The author of the manual, Giovanni Alberghini, was a Franciscan, a doctor of theology, and a censor of the Sicilian Inquisition (under the aegis of the General Spanish Inquisition) and his book strove to summarize in pithy fashion all the various crimes for which the advice of censors was sought.[70] In certain ways Alberghini's *Manuale qualificatorum* was for the calificación what Eimeric's *Directorium* was for inquisitional theory and procedure: it offered the standard views of the various problems under review along with the author's own interpretations. Simultaneously, the *Manuale qualificatorum* offered exegetical discussions of the most important questions of the various treatises on heresy, such as the definition of heresy, doubt, pertinacity, ignorance, and the inclusion or exclusion of heretics from the Church. Alberghini's glosses on the typology of offenses proposed the first comprehensive attempt by a censor of an Inquisition to define their hierarchy.

Chapter 12 of Alberghini's *Manuale* considered the "various propositions to be censured or qualified" — a centrally important point for inquisitional debate, given that "theologians dispute on this subject in treatises on the faith."[71] Alberghini mentioned Castro, Cano, Simancas, and Suárez — a motley group but a typical conglomeration of authorities used as proof text — as the most important of the writers to explain the gradations of calificación. Moreover, he saw in the Council of Constance the beginnings of this process of calificación and ordering of propositions, since therein Hus and Wycliffe had many of their ideas condemned as heretical, erroneous, scandalous, or offensive to pious ears.

The heretical proposition was the gravest — "that which is contrary to the faith in every way."[72] Moreover, drawing on Simancas, Albertinus, and Suárez's *De fide,* Alberghini added that the heretical proposition was "openly contrary to any truth of the faith of the Catholic definition."[73] Alberghini then took up the important question of internal and external error and contradiction of the faith. Thus Alberghini glossed the view from motive: "Some think that direct contradiction of the faith, or of the Catholic truth, was not enough for a proposition to be called heretical unless it approaches pertinacity in its utterance or is brought forth [uttered] from heresy, because if it is said from something else, it is said to be a proposition against the faith but is not heresy properly speaking."[74] Alberghini associated this supposedly liberal view of heretical statements with two of the sixteenth century's most notorious conservatives (both Dominicans): Tomasio de Vio (Cardinal Cajetan), the sparring partner of Luther, and Domingo de Báñez, successor to Cano and De Soto in the first chair in theology at the University of Salamanca and vitriolic enemy of the Jesuits.[75]

In the next section Alberghini asserted that "the better and more common opinion is that every proposition against the faith is heresy properly speaking."[76] This statement alone was open to interpretation. But Alberghini used Castro's *De justa haereticorum punitione* as proof for this position. Castro was absolutely against such a view and argued that the mental state and the intent of the person must be considered. Castro rejected the view that the physical statement of something against the faith was ipso jure heresy, concluding instead that it was always incumbent on the inquisitor to determine the inner state of mind of the person making the statement. If there was no inner doubt, then there could not, by definition, be heresy. In contrast, Suárez argued that the inner conscience of the person under suspicion was never rightfully within the jurisdiction of the Church and that the Church and Inquisition held authority only in foro exteriori, not in foro interiori.

Alberghini made this conclusion by a twofold definition of the heretical proposition. He argued the existence of both the "formal heretical proposition" and the "objective heretical proposition." The first required pertinacity, whereas the second, in his view, did not "because it consists only in the contradiction of the faith."[77] Here one might discern an affinity for the Jesuits' and Suárez's view that the Inquisition as a manifestation of the militant and visible Church was to be concerned only with external action, not inner conscience. But Alberghini seemed willing to include the traditional definition that heresy required both external action and inner doubt; yet he also expanded the overall range of the censors' authority by arguing that even objective heresy should be judged and punished.

After the heretical proposition a wide variety of propositions could be judged by the censors according to Alberghini. The proposition that "smacks of heresy" (*propositio haeresim sapiens* or *sapit haeresim*) was "that which contradicts the object of the faith not through evident consequences but which contradicts it morally by probable and certain consequences."[78] The proposition smacking of heresy led to the appearance of heresy only by indirect methods as opposed to being outright heresy by directly attacking an article of the faith. For example, a censor could have been empowered by this logic to conclude, unlike some more conservative jurists, that the suggestion that fornication was not a mortal sin was not heretical but smacked of heresy. In other words, it did not explicitly attack the sacrament of marriage—something that would be heretical—but by moral turpitude, as it were, it led to the appearance of the rejection of that sacrament. It was a common heterodoxy to say that "it is better to live together unmarried and be happy than to be badly married."[79] When, in 1605, the Tlaxcala hat maker Bartolomé López made this statement the Jesuit censors Pedro de Hortigosa and Pedro de Morales suggested that the statement was "bad sounding." López was convicted, condemned to abjure in an auto de fe, and was exiled from Puebla for six months, during which time he was to spend three months enclosed in a mendicant house.[80]

Thus the "bad-sounding proposition" (*propositio male sonans*) was that which by its double meaning had the potential of both Catholic and heretical value—for example, the statement "faith justifies." No Catholic theologian was about to reject the scriptural proofs that "the just shall live by faith," but by the same token Luther's attack on works and his soteriology of "by faith alone" (*sola fide*) brought this statement into constant suspicion, as was the opinion of Alberghini who drew on Luis de Páramo for such a view.[81] In similar fashion the scandalous proposition, or the proposition that offended pious ears, was one that denigrated the faith. Alberghini included within this definition propositions that others condemned as heretical. For example, Alberghini included here the following:

- Heretics should be tolerated, not destroyed.
- It is better to offer alms to the poor than for the Mass.
- It is useless to offer praise to the Virgin in prayer.[82]

In numerous other contexts—Erasmus not the least famous of them in his condemnation of saint propitiation, Mary veneration, and offering money for the Mass—these exact statements were condemned as outright heresy. One finds in Alberghini the enduring influence of Erasmus and a reformed Catholicism that was officially repudiated by Trent. But if such reform was officially condemned, it continued to survive in subtler forms—in this case, by demoting various condemned articles of the Erasmian and Franciscan reform project from heresy to scandal. This may seem disingenuous, but for the accused in inquisitional proceedings such distinctions were anything but insignificant. The charge of heresy could lead to torture and execution, whereas that of a scandalous or bad-sounding proposition did not carry the most severe penalties. It was relatively common for people to respond with scatological remarks about excommunication, which while considered scandalous were not always condemned as heretical. For example, in December 1569, in Guanajuato, when a representative of the diocesan officials went to inform Pedro Muñoz Maese de Roa that he would be excommunicated if he continued to refuse to pay his tithe, Muñoz responded, "I shit on the order of excommunication and its messenger."[83]

Other potential statements included the schismatic and the impious. Schism implied the rejection of the unity of the Church and as such was not exclusive of heresy. The impious proposition rejected external Catholic piety. And the injurious proposition attacked some statute or person of the Church. For example, in Alberghini's view this included the statement that mendicants living in private religious houses are not of the Christian religion. This was a common attack on the mendicant orders and often was viewed as heresy itself. The more rigorous censors, often Dominicans, viewed this as a rejection of the sacrament of orders and therefore as heresy strictly speaking. Alberghini, however, was unconvinced of this logic, as he was in the case of the statement that "the Roman Church is the synagogue of Satan" — an opinion condemned at Constance as heresy. Following Castro, Alberghini included this not among the heretical propositions but among the injurious.[84]

Like Alberghini, Castro weighed the various errors outlined by all inquisitional theorists in turn. His discussion of the scandalous proposition or of the proposition that was offensive to pious ears offers insights into Castro's relatively liberal conception of religious error. Under this rubric Castro included numerous opinions that were often condemned as outright heresies by Dominican inquisitors or censors in Mexico. For example, Erasmus was condemned in no small measure for his sarcastic rejection of the value of saint and Mary propitiation in his *Colloquies*. Castro, however, like many Franciscans, admired Erasmus, whom he described in *Aduersus omnes haereses* as "an eminently learned man."[85] Thus in his discussion of scandalous propositions, Castro concluded that the opinion that it was useless to offer prayer to the Virgin Mary was not heretical but simply scandalous. To say that fasting was unimportant to Christian perfection was likewise in his estimation not heresy but mere scandal. Another: better to bestow alms on the poor than to offer it for the sacrifice of the Mass. These statements were frequently condemned as heretical by authorities more conservative than Castro and often lay at the heart of the quashing of the so-called Spanish Erasmians who professed internal spiritualism over external devotion.

Castro also turned a relatively benign eye to seditious statements, which he likewise viewed as lying less within the jurisdiction of the Church. Any subject may depose a tyrant — heretical? No, merely offensive. Rejecting the election of a pope? Surely heretical. Again, Castro insisted that this was not heretical, since the Church did not enjoin the faithful to believe as an article of the faith the human election of a pope.[86] The result: rejecting a papal election was erroneous but not heretical. Castro also considered the statement that a bad priest does not need to be obeyed as merely seditious and not heretical.[87] Others would construe this as an outright rejection of the sacrament of ordination and therefore a heresy, or a rejection of the efficacy of the sacraments and therefore Donatist. Castro also viewed those who defended or aided heretics as schismatic but not heretical, since in his view the action of physical succor did not necessarily and automatically imply inner rejection of the faith.[88] This refuted the common view of the canonists and Dominicans, who viewed "aiders and abettors of heretics" (*fautores haereticorum*) as heretics themselves — something that Eimeric and Peña outlined in the *Directorium,* as did Villadiego and the canon law in numerous places. The distinction for Castro, however, was that of belief, not action, whereas the canonists argued the opposite, maintaining that the action of protecting a heretic was tantamount to rejection of the Church.

The temerarious proposition included a wide range of ideas that could not be strictly catalogued as heresy or that were qualified as such when in other contexts they might be condemned as heresy. A case from 1597 against the Franciscan Francisco Mexía of Tulancingo offered such a distinction. Mexía had said that it was better to hear a sermon than the Mass itself. The Augustinian censors Diego de Contreras and Pedro de Agurto concluded that while not specifically heretical the statement was "absolutely temerarious and false."[89] A stricter interpretation from a censor could have concluded that Mexía was harboring secret Lutheran tendencies of rejecting the mysteries of the Mass. In this case such a conclusion was crucial, as Mexía was never prosecuted. Castro explained that the temerarious proposition lacked absolutely any authority or reason and could not be proven by any reason or authority but simultaneously did not attack an article of the faith. Among the examples of the proposition defined as temerarious by Castro were the following:

- The Day of Judgment will arrive within a year.[90]
- All Romans are living in mortal sin.
- All bishops are damned.

One of the telling statements that Castro included under this rubric was, More married men will be saved than monks. In many cases similar statements about the relative soteriological value of the state of marriage vis-à-vis the state of being a monk, friar, or nun were qualified as heretical, as in the case against the ironworker Cordero. Many of Castro's examples could have been construed as heretical. Hus and Wycliffe were both condemned for suggesting that monasticism was useless, that Rome was a whore's den and the Roman Church an orgy of corruption.

The Question of Blasphemy

Among the various sins that might or might not fall under the jurisdiction of the Inquisition was blasphemy. Did the Inquisition have the authority to investigate and punish blasphemy in the same way it could heresy? A good amount of inquisitional ink was spilled over this very concern. Eimeric made the distinction between heretical and nonheretical blasphemy the linchpin of his argument. If a blasphemous statement contained no heresy, then the Inquisition did not need to proceed. Therefore, any blasphemous statement that did not specifically attack an article of the faith had no bearing on the Inquisition. At the same time a blasphemous statement that was also heretical fell within inquisitional jurisdiction. Eimeric argued that one's inner belief was unimportant for this crime, since any verbal expression of heretical blasphemy was cause for inquisitional investigation. This view contrasted with that of numerous later theologians, like Castro and Suárez, who argued that blasphemous statements that did not reflect one's true belief could not be investigated by inquisitors.

Eimeric rephrased the cliché that there are no atheists in foxholes — to wit, the fear of death or massacre cannot excuse heretical blasphemy.[91] For example, if, while fearing for one's life, a person were to say that Mary was a whore, he could properly be prosecuted by the Inquisition, since such a statement violated the article of faith of the virgin birth of Christ. Similar circumstances surrounded the case in 1629 against the carpenter Juan Zambrano, of Veracruz, who repeated the common belief that Joseph had "carnally known" Mary. The censors Juan de Ledesma, a Jesuit, and Francisco de Arévalo, a Dominican, concluded that the statement was heretical blasphemy since it attacked the doctrine of the virgin birth. They gave no consideration to the circumstances of the statement or to his inner thoughts, concluding that it was a prima facie case of heresy.[92] But others, like the Jesuit Hortigosa, considered exigent circumstances to insist that emotional turmoil clouding one's true beliefs must be considered in judging blasphemy, as was the case in Tlaxcala in

1602 when Juan Sánchez was accused of blasphemy for rejecting God and Mary when he was angered; for Hortigosa that meant that the accused, while guilty of blasphemy, had not committed any heresy.[93] Hortigosa did, however, find some attacks on the Virgin heretically blasphemous. In 1619 Mariana de los Reyes, an unmarried woman who had been the mistress of a married man for six years, was accused by her neighbor in Mexico City of being a slut who was "so easy that she gave her body to black, white and mulatto men alike." She responded by saying she was "as clean, chaste, and honorable as Saint Catherine" and that indeed she deserved treatment as a veritable Saint Catherine. Hortigosa concluded that this was in fact heretical blasphemy to demand the same reverence as a saint.[94]

But what exactly was heretical blasphemy? Rojas defined it as "that which has a meaning of infidelity or an abnegation of the faith." In commenting on Rojas and Eimeric, Peña concluded that the circumstances and location of the statement must be considered.[95] In his view the worst blasphemies were those attacking the Virgin Mary — a view also expressed by Simancas. For Simancas, blasphemy was to "speak wickedly against God or the saints . . . to attribute to someone else what exclusively belongs to God, to make false assertions about God or negate truth about God." Worse than this, argued Simancas, was to blaspheme the Virgin, or "to swear by the genitalia of the saints" — types of blasphemy over which inquisitors could claim jurisdiction in his view.[96] One suspects that the statement by Mateo Napolitano in Puebla in 1598 after breaking a vase of wine — that "Christ is a faggot" — would have fallen into that category, but Hortigosa argued that while gravely offensive, it was not heresy but simple blasphemy.[97]

Peña also concluded that imprecations of saints did not always constitute heretical blasphemy. The issue was inner belief, which immediately implied complex legal problems — Simancas viewed inner belief as unimportant in the case of particularly offensive attacks on the saints. After all, could not those accused of blasphemy say that their words did not reflect their inner belief and thus, in Peña's assessment, cover all their bases? The problem lay in discovering what the accused truly believed (a circumstance in which torture was employed). Nevertheless, Peña concluded that those who, by fear or other emotional disturbance, committed an external heresy or apostasy while retaining inner faith should not be tried by the Inquisition but rather should be reconciled by diocesan authorities.

Castro also did not view blasphemy as properly within the jurisdiction of the Inquisition because "theologians do not count blasphemy among the sins of infidelity."[98] Here he relied on a long tradition of spiritual theory that derived from Augustine's use of Romans 10:10 in *De fide et symbolo*: "This same faith demands our duty by heart and by tongue."[99] The mere external action of blasphemy, in Castro's view, could not be considered heretical if unaccompanied by inner doubt. As in the case of Suárez's understanding of ecclesiastical authority, it was precisely only the external action over which the Church held sway. But for Castro, blasphemy in the absence of "perverted will" should not be prosecuted by inquisitors. And even though, he asserted, all blasphemy was voluntary, it did not follow that all blasphemy derived from bad will or the actual desire to blaspheme. Therefore, blasphemy was not heresy if it did not involve belief but was simply the external expression of something against the faith.

For Castro both the "belief of the heart and the confession by the mouth" were necessary components for the perversion of the faith. If one was lacking, there could be no heresy. Thus blasphemy, while still a sin, was not "a vice opposed to the faith but a vice against the confession of the faith."[100] Therefore, since the Inquisition held jurisdiction only over heresy, simple blasphemy (as opposed to heretical blasphemy) did not fall under its authority. Moreover, Castro, like Peña, was willing to consider exigent circumstances and argued that the conditions of the person, place, and time must be taken into consideration when investigating blasphemy.

Castro enjoyed a considerable reputation beyond theology, despite his biting comments about canonists. His contemporary Covarrubias cited him as the ruling authority for the jurisdiction of blasphemy in his commentaries on pacts and oaths, *In constitvtionibis secvndae ex rvbrica de pactis*. Therein Covarrubias agreed entirely that the inquisitional authorities had no proper jurisdiction over nonheretical blasphemy. But it was to Aquinas that Covarrubias ascribed primacy over all other definitions of blasphemy, glossing Aquinas's definition of blasphemy as "that which diminishes the greatness of divinity or damns God himself, the virgin mother, or the saints with contumaciousness."[101] Yet like Castro, Covarrubias concluded that mere external attacks on the faith did not constitute heresy if not simultaneously accompanied by internal error. And like Peña, Covarrubias noted that the old (Mosaic) law made no distinction between thought and action when it condemned blasphemy and ordered its punishment in the form of execution by stoning.[102]

Overall, there was consensus on a limited range of subjects of inquisitional censure, even among the theologians. Most, if not all, agreed that external attacks on the faith were worthy of censure, but the real debate began when the question of motive, understanding, and inner conscience came into play. This was precisely the territory of debate that would unite those who, like Castro and, ironically enough, the canonists, whom he viewed as intellectual dullards, held the view that heresy and its punishment would depend on the two factors of inner doubt and external manifestation thereof to merit suitable censure. But the Jesuits, under the intellectual leadership of Suárez, argued for mitigating circumstances in assessing the all-important external actions. The ironies and strange bedfellows of politics overlapped for numerous intellectuals in conceiving practice of censorship.

PART **II**

Practice of Censure in Mexico

4

The Salamanca Connection

On August 13, 1521, Hernán Cortés entered a nearly destroyed Tenochtitlan as the undisputed victor in a horrific battle for dominance of the Valley of Mexico. His victory came about as a result of his combined use of technology, allying with the force of the enemies of the Mexicas, strategy, and the advantage of germs in a months-long siege in which some estimate that close to half the city of two hundred thousand died of epidemic disease. The military conquest of Mexico would not be matched necessarily by immediate "spiritual conquest," but the plan for conversion began immediately. Cortés called for Franciscans to be sent to Mexico, and in 1524 a group of Franciscan friars, numbering twelve as a symbolic imitation of the apostles, led by Martín de Valenica, arrived in Mexico.

The Franciscans, and by extension other mendicants like the Augustinians and Dominicans, were given privileges to engage in activities normally reserved to diocesan authorities, following the logic that friars were the most motivated clergy of Spain to bring about the conversion of the Indians. These privileges would set the tone for the Mexican Church, which would be quickly dominated by mendicants. The Crown also endeavored to isolate Mexico religiously by cutting off direct contact between the Mexican Church and Rome, forcing the Mexican Church to operate through the Council of the Indies instead. When the diocese of Mexico was founded in 1527, it was suffragen to the archdiocese of Seville. It was not until 1548 that Mexico would be elevated to the status of metropolitan see, and as late as 1571 the Inquisition in Mexico was composed of several local diocesan Inquisitions and one apostolic Inquisition of the (arch)diocese of Mexico.

When Alonso de Montúfar, the inquisitor-archbishop elect of Mexico, came to Salamanca to recruit Bartolomé de Ledesma around 1553, he would have found there the most intellectually illustrious Dominican house of Europe: San Esteban.[1] The theologian credited with reviving Spain as an important center of theological scholarship, Francisco Vitoria, had recently died and taking his place came the second generation of the so-called School of Salamanca. Vitoria's pupil Domingo de Soto, who succeeded him in the prime chair at the University of Salamanca, had professed his vows at San Esteban and was probably residing there when Montúfar arrived. Cano, the successor to De Soto in the prime chair, had professed at San Esteban in 1525.[2]

Salamanca was the principal university of Spain and could boast not only the most formidable systematic theologians of Spain, but also the most conservative and the strongest advocates of censorship among Spanish theologians. While today the School of Salamanca is often remembered for its theological rejection of papal temporal authority and its defense of the dominion of the Indians, there was an equally important line of thought encompassed by the Salamanca Dominicans represented by intractable hatred of the Jesuits, distrust of the laity, and an abiding belief in the Thomist hierarchy of doctrinal knowledge.

True to their medieval traditions, the Dominicans held firm to their sense that they were the special judges of the faith called to extirpate error, heresy, and sin. San Esteban had already sent one of its sons, Domingo de Betanzos, off to Mexico as its first inquisitor delegate in 1527. Besides being an enemy of Indian education, Betanzos was noted for his austerity and dedication to being in a state of poverty, supposedly walking barefoot from Spain to Rome. While his tenure as inquisitor delegate in Mexico was undistinguished, he came from a long line of friars who populated the first Inquisitions in Mexico.[3]

Ledesma had been raised intellectually and physically at San Esteban in the long shadow cast by Vitoria, having professed there when Vitoria was nearing the end of his life in 1543.[4] Domingo de Salazar, the future censor of the Mexican Holy Office and later bishop of Manila, professed there in 1546, and in 1547 so did Domingo Báñez, an enemy of the Jesuits second in vitriol only to Cano, who succeeded Cano in the prime chair at the university.[5] Juan Ramírez, a supposed descendant of Aragonese kings, also a future censor in Mexico and bishop of Guatemala, professed his allegiance to Santo Domingo at San Esteban in 1550.[6] In Salamanca Montúfar and Ledesma were in close contact with a good portion of the future censors of the Mexican Inquisition. Ledesma himself came from an economically impoverished but ostensibly noble family and was able to trade his considerable intellect for a distinguished career as censor, governor of the archdiocese of Mexico, and, ultimately, bishop of Oaxaca.[7]

The Dominicans who formed a hard core of conservative censors and diocesan inquisitors in Mexico in the sixteenth century were intellectually firmly placed in the context of Salamanca and its satellite theological schools. Many of them, like Ledesma, Ramírez, and Salazar, were themselves educated at San Esteban. Others, like the *criollos* (American-born Spaniards) who followed them in Mexico, like Bartolomé Gómez, were in turn educated in Mexico by Dominicans who had been trained in Salamanca and were the stalwarts of Tridentine counterreformation theology.[8] Pedro de Pravia, a Dominican censor appointed to the Mexican Inquisition in 1572, was a peninsular Spaniard who represented this group of influential friars.[9] He became the holder of the prime chair of theology at the University of Mexico from 1582 to 1590 while exercising his role as censor from that position. Having been nominated bishop of Panama in 1584, he abandoned his university chair in 1588 to begin his episcopal duties, only to die in 1590.[10] Along with Ledesma, who was also professor of theology, Pravia educated friars like Gómez who would then continue the Dominican line of theological conservatism. Pravia would solidify this connection as prior of Santo Domingo in Mexico City, which acted as the principal college for young Dominican friars.[11] And demonstrating the deep intellectual links between medieval thought and the milieu of the Mexican censors, Pravia wrote a commentary on Aquinas's *Summa theologiae*.[12]

The Dominicans of this early period in Mexico were firmly rooted in the medieval and early modern traditions of their order as well as in the ideological buttresses of inquisitional power: Aquinas, Eimeric, Torquemada, Cano, and Simancas. At the same time they were steeped in the conscious sense that they were the proprietary defenders of the faith, the de facto ideological owners of the Inquisition. After the establishment of the Holy Office in 1571 in Mexico, nine of the first sixteen censors appointed were Dominicans.[13]

The Dominican presence in the early years of the Mexican Inquisitions and the connection with old Spanish Dominican ideological traditions were cemented with the presence of Montúfar as inquisitor-archbishop and Ledesma as his principal advisor, vicar, and ordinary inquisitor. Born in 1489 of a noble family in Loja (in the diocese of Granada), Montúfar professed vows in the Dominican order at a young age in Santa Cruz of Granada. The archbishop of Seville, and later inquisitor general, Diego Deza, appointed Montúfar professor in the Dominican Colegio de Santo Tomás in Seville, where he taught arts and received his master's degree in arts. By 1524 he was lecturing on theology and received his master's degree in theology also from the Colegio in Seville. He served the Holy Office in Granada as censor before being nominated archbishop-inquisitor of Mexico in 1551. He arrived in Mexico in June 1554.[14]

Ledesma would become Montúfar's chargé d'affaires and long-term assistant and confidant.[15] Ledesma would come to play Richelieu to Montúfar's Louis XIII and eventually assumed most governing responsibilities of the archdiocese of Mexico as Montúfar's health steadily declined into the later 1560s and up to his death in March 1572.[16] Overall the presence of Dominicans in the corridors of inquisitional power beginning in the 1520s, furthered by their presence as censors and inquisitors ordinary, which solidified in the 1560s and 1570s, showed Mexico to be deeply connected to the ideological world of Spain and San Esteban in particular. This connection between early censorship activities in Mexico and Salamanca Dominicans was not figured only in terms of men who shared a common ideological background. For example, a letter of June 14, 1574, from the Suprema related that the general inquisitors had received two volumes of censorship decisions by the new Mexican Holy Office as well as the general censure of Bibles circulating in Mexico.[17] This investigation was then forwarded to Salamanca and to the Dominicans there who were in the process of fashioning the most extensive Index of Prohibited Books yet, which would be promulgated in 1583.[18] Thus the intimate nexus between Salamanca and Mexico was manifested here, showing that the Salamancan Dominicans were still closely allied with their confreres in Mexico and relying on their advice for decisions as to which books to place on the index.

The connections between Salamanca's Dominican force, Spanish thought on censorship, and the censorship efforts of Mexico were no more direct than in the case of Ledesma. He was raised intellectually during the most fertile period of Dominican intellectual brilliance at San Esteban and the university. He also deeply imbibed the central discussions on censure, excommunication, and the intimate connections between censorship and inquisitional control. He was well read both in the major Dominican theologians and in the influential canon law theorists of the day. In 1560 Montúfar asked him to write a treatise on sacramental theology, and in 1566 his *De septem nouae legis sacramentis summarium* (Summary on the Seven Sacraments of the New Law) was published in Mexico. Sophisticated and rigorous, it showed the deep, abiding connections to Ledesma's intellectual formation at Salamanca. His discussion of penance included a lengthy consideration of excommunication in which his first consideration was the very same portion of the *Decretum* which included Jerome's simile of heretics as putrid meat, offering his own metaphor of heresy as corrupted yeast which ruins entire batches of bread. He also included discussions of the standard deliberations on excommunication as being medicinal, drawing on notable glossators like Covarrubias.[19]

The connection between Salamanca and the Mexican Inquisition and its censorship apparatus was not, however, manifested solely among Dominicans. The diocesan priest don Rodrigo de Barbosa held a licenciate in theology from Salamanca and a doctorate from either Salamanca or Mexico.[20] Numerous Inquisition jurists who doubled as Audiencia judges held their doctorates in canon law from the University of Salamanca, including Mateo Arévalo Sedeño, a legal advisor to the Montúfar and Moya de Contreras Inquisitions who would eventually become professor of canon law and then rector at the University of Mexico.[21] Even at the local level the connections between Salamanca and Mexico's Inquisition ran deep. Born in Castellanos, don Juan de Zurnero was trained in canon law at Salamanca and in 1550 was made *maestrescuela (schoolmaster)* of the Michoacán cathedral chapter. In 1556 and 1557 he acted as the diocesan provisor and inquisitor ordinary. In 1560 he became archdeacon of the Mexico cathedral chapter and would also serve as Michoacán's diocesan ordinary to the Inquisition in the 1570s.[22]

Neither were Dominicans the only students of Vitoria to exercise influence in Mexico. Born in 1507 in Caspueñas, in the diocese of Toledo, Alonso de la Veracruz studied grammar at Alcalá de Henares and later arts and theology at Salamanca, where he was a pupil of Vitoria. In 1535, while the future friar was still a layman, Francisco de la Cruz, the *padre venerable* of the Augustinian mission in Mexico, came to Salamanca seeking recruits for Mexico. In deference to his recruiter, whose suggestion he accepted, the layman Alonso took the name De la Veracruz. The soon-to-be fray Alonso arrived in Mexico on July 2, 1536, and was the first Augustinian novice in the Indies, taking his vows in 1537.[23]

Fray Alonso had an illustrious academic career. Shortly after his profession of vows he was master of theology at the Augustinian Colegio del Nombre de Jesús in Mexico-Tenochtitlan. In 1540 he was commissioned by his order to found a provincial house of studies at Tiripetío in Michoacán. There De la Veracruz studied Purépecha under the tutelage of Antonio Huitziméngari Mendoza y Caltzontzin, son of the last Indian king of Michoacán, while De la Veracruz instructed the Indian noble in arts, the Spanish language, and theology. By 1548 he was vicar provincial of his order and in 1551 active in the establishment of the University of Mexico (which adopted as its constitution that of the University of Salamanca), becoming the university's first holder of the chair of scripture. From this position he trained many of Mexico's future ecclesiastical leaders, such as Pedro de Agurto, the Augustinian censor and

Figure 4. Title page of Bartolomé de Ledesma's treatise on sacramental theology (1566), compiled by order of his patron, archbishop-inquisitor Alonso de Montúfar. Courtesy of John Carter Brown Library

first bishop of Cebu in the Philippines, and the brothers and Augustinians Diego and Agustín de Carvajal, members of the criollo upper crust; fray Agustín became the bishop of Panama and Huamanga.[24]

De la Veracruz's career as philosopher and theologian also exemplifies the deep ideological connections between Mexico's theologians and Inquisition and Salamanca. For example, De la Veracruz was the only theologian who spent his career in the Americas whose works were published in Salamanca in the sixteenth century. In 1562 three of his most important works — *Physica speculatio* (on physics), a second edition of his work on sacramental theology and marriage among the Indians, *Speculum coniugorum (Mirror of the Betrothed)*, and his commentaries on Aristotle — were printed in Salamanca. In fact, of all authors printed in Salamanca in the sixteenth century, De la Veracruz ranked fifth in editions (fifteen), behind the eighty editions of works by Domingo de Soto and of Luis de Granada, thirty-six editions of Covarrubias, and sixteen editions of works by Luis de León.[25] The Salamanca connection was thus an ideological bond in the Iberian Atlantic world in which ideas, philosophies, and books traveled not only from metropole to colony but from the Americas to Europe.

Others would come from Salamanca to the Inquisition's court in Mexico. The Jesuit Pedro de Morales earned doctorates in both canon and civil law from the University of Salamanca. Having begun a promising career as a jurist in Granada and Madrid, he left the legal profession to become a Jesuit. Shortly thereafter he went with one of the earliest Jesuit cohorts to Mexico in 1575 and began teaching moral theology and canon law in the Jesuit College. He would later become rector of the Colegio del Espíritu Santo in Puebla, and in 1585 Moya de Contreras named him a canon law advisor during the Third Mexican Church Council. In 1592 Morales established the Casa Profesa (the Jesuit equivalent of a religious house).[26] In 1600 he was named censor of the Mexican Holy Office.[27]

In addition to San Esteban and the University of Salamanca, Alfonso de Castro himself trained some of the future censors of the Mexican Inquisition in the Franciscan house in Salamanca, where he was a famous and hugely popular preacher. Both of his known students who became censors in Mexico would spend considerable time in Guatemala. Antonio de Quixada was a rather conservative Franciscan who probably studied with Castro in Salamanca, had spent time in the Yucatán and was guardian of the Franciscan house in Guatemala before becoming censor of the Mexican Inquisition in 1572.[28] Another student of Castro's, Diego Ordóñez, was a corrector of Bibles in Guatemala (his uncle was cathedral canon, probably at Salamanca).[29] Ordóñez later composed treatises (today lost) on Duns Scotus.[30]

But if the Salamanca connection was strong there was a following trend in the Mexican Inquisition's censorship apparatus: the rise of the criollo elite and the increasing integration of the Inquisition's corporate membership with that elite. The extension of Salamancan pedigree could not have been more radically different from the experience of don Felipe Ruiz de Corral, dean of the Guatemala cathedral chapter and comisario of the Holy Office. In fact, his experience came up directly against that of the Salamanca Dominicans. For twenty years, from 1606 until 1626, Ruiz de Corral fought tooth and nail against the Dominicans—first, against Juan Ramírez and then against Antonio de Remesal, missionary, peninsular Spanish Dominican, chronicler of Guatemala, and biographer of Bartolomé de las Casas.[31]

Ruiz de Corral's biography demonstrates the extent to which the Inquisition in New Spain increasingly became less Spanish, more criollo, and less Dominican, more secular while retaining strong ties to its ideological roots in Salamanca. His story also demonstrates how the Inquisition and the censorship apparatus were increasingly linked to the criollo elite—straddling the Atlantic with one foot intellectually in Spain and one foot socially in the Americas. Don Felipe was born on a ship in the Atlantic in 1572 not far from Cuba. His father, licenciado Pedro Ruiz de Corral, was a lawyer whose family included several hidalgos from Huete, just west of Cuenca; his mother, doña María Orozco de Santa Cruz, was a daughter of hidalgos as well. The elder Ruiz de Corral had been elected *oidor* (judge) of the Audiencia of Guatemala, and in 1571 he and his pregnant wife, along with their two young daughters, Ana and Catarina, set sail for the Americas. After a long and insalubrious journey, during which Felipe was born and his father became ill and died in Cuba, the widow and her three children arrived in Guatemala. Doña María was received with open arms into the criollo aristocracy of Guatemala, which included the Alvarado and Díaz del Castillo clans, whose exploits as conquistadors and whose investments as encomenderos made them the wealthiest people in Guatemala.[32]

Doña María was quick to act. Within ten years her young daughters had married extremely well: fourteen-year-old doña Ana married Lorenzo del Valle Marroquín, a descendant of the former bishop; only a few years later doña Catarina married the grandson of the conquistador Bernal Díaz del Castillo, Pedro de Estrada Medinilla, whose mother was the oldest of Bernal Díaz's daughters. Young don Felipe was now an intimate member of the most powerful families of Guatemala.

By 1599, at twenty-seven years of age, don Felipe was made treasurer of the Guatemala cathedral chapter. In 1600 the Dominican and Salamanca-trained censor Ramírez, against his wishes, was nominated bishop of Guatemala. Two years later the dean of the cathedral chapter died, and within months, on October 28, 1602, the comisario, the Dominican Francisco de Cepeda, died. Don Felipe began to exercise authority as the comisario shortly thereafter, and in 1604 he was made dean of the cathedral chapter, converting him into the de facto inquisitor, given the distance from Mexico to Guatemala. Ironically enough, in the 1570s the Inquisition had given the comisario of Guatemala, the Dominican Alonso de Noreña (who was also censor) authority to act virtually unchecked in Guatemala and Chiapas, since it was impractical to remit all cases investigated in Guatemala back to Mexico.[33] The force of Dominican tradition, developed in the thirteenth and fourteenth centuries in Aragón and Languedoc, laid the ideological foundations on which a secular cleric and criollo, don Felipe, would rest his authority. Nothing could have been more infuriating to the new bishop, Ramírez.

A clash was inevitable. In 1604, shortly after his arrival in Guatemala, Ramírez stripped Ruiz de Corral of his authority as provisor (or chief diocesan prosecutor). Tensions began to build. Ramírez's predecessor, Fernández de Córdoba, had instituted a fiesta for the Assumption of the Virgin Mary on August 18, and Ramírez considered the date heretical. But the fiesta had become an important part of public culture in Guatemala by then. Nevertheless, Ramírez preached a sermon in the cathedral church on August 15 condemning the fiesta as being on the wrong date, attacking the encomenderos as oppressors of the Indians, and anathematizing his opponents as enemies of the faith. Ruiz de Corral and his sizeable cadre of supporters put on an even more elaborate spectacle three days later, with fireworks and elaborate pageantry, processions, and celebrations. The bishop condemned them from the pulpit again. Insults were exchanged, letters written to the inquisitors themselves in Mexico. Nothing was resolved, and hatreds simmered and festered.

By 1607 there were two clearly identified factions: one loyal to the bishop and the other to the dean-comisario. Two curas of the cathedral, Alonso Ibáñez and the new provisor, Diego de Vargas, defended the bishop. The Ruiz de Corral faction worked against them. Ibáñez had received a delivery of books from Spain, and Ruiz de Corral, who throughout his tenure as comisario proved perspicacious in regulating the flow of books, ordered the cura to show his books to the censor, fray García de Loaysa for review. Ibáñez seethed.

By November tensions boiled over. Ruiz de Corral and his partisans were determined to take the bishop down a peg through his surrogate. While attending choir and meetings of the cathedral chapter, Ibáñez had refused to remove his doctor's bonnet — a deliberate provocation. Ruiz de Corral demanded that he remove it in his presence as dean and comisario. The provisor refused. Since Ruiz de Corral was a priest he then enlisted the support of his relative, don Francisco de Corral, a layman, who on December 2 forcibly removed Ibáñez's bonnet in the choir loft while he verbally insulted him as an uncultured rogue (*bellaco malcriado*) — a grave insult both to his honor and status. Swords were drawn, blows exchanged. Ruiz de Corral was forced to flee the cathedral and hide in his familial house. Eventually he was arrested and imprisoned by Ramírez.[34]

In the aftermath and the same context bishop Ramírez began to assert his authority as inquisitor ordinary. He argued that bishops, from canon law and tradition, were the true guardians of the faith and excommunicated Ruiz de Corral. He published and pronounced the edicts of the faith. Imprisoned, Ruiz de Corral was eventually released when the inquisitors in Mexico City ordered Ramírez to relent. Ruiz de Corral and Ramírez then engaged in a vicious partisan legal war.[35] The dean-comisario and the inquisitors in Mexico City asserted the prerogatives of the Inquisition as superior to those of bishops. Ultimately, Ramírez was defeated and forced to relent, but he did not do so quietly. The Dominican died in 1609, seemingly leaving Ruiz de Corral to exercise inquisitional authority unchallenged. Ruiz de Corral continued, however, to feud with Dominicans into the 1620s.

If the experiences of peninsular Dominicans and the criollo new rich were fundamentally at odds with each other, the worlds of many other censors and inquisitors were far more integrated into a uniquely Mexican experience. The censors of the Mexican Inquisition were drawn from the major orders present in Mexico — Dominican, Franciscan, Augustinian, and Jesuit — and generally included few secular clerics. They were steeped in Thomist theology and well versed in inquisitional theory written by Spaniards and Italians. Ideologically, they were the heirs to the medieval Inquisitions. Prior to 1571 Mexico had several diocesan Inquisitions since the canon law provided for bishops to act as ordinary inquisitors when no specific delegated inquisitor was present. In many instances the bishops of nascent dioceses in Mexico appointed friars as their vicars and inquisitors.

Even if the majority of the inquisitors in the first several decades of the Mexican Holy Office had been born on the peninsula, they quickly integrated themselves into the socioeconomic world of the criollo elite and peninsular expatriate community in Mexico City. While the inquisitors can rightly be placed near the pinnacle of colonial ecclesiastical power, they did not, however, come from the middling or higher nobility, as did the viceroys.[36] Instead, the inquisitors of Mexico tended to be one step below the marquesses and dukes who ran the viceregal office. Many conquistadors and their children became fabulously wealthy from the hacienda system and the spoils of conquest. It is also well known that conquistadors in general had come from the middle and lower classes of Spain. Many, like Pizarro famously, were illiterate, but, as has always been the case of *homines novi,* the blueblood elites sneered at the low social pedigree of the Mexican conquistadors.

The shifting nature of the Inquisition in Mexico was both ideological and social. The seeds of the Inquisition may have come from Salamanca, medieval Spain, and the inheritance of Iberian legalism, but they were planted in American soil and they would sprout and grow into a particularly New World apparatus. Ideologically, the Mexican Inquisition was both metaphorically and literally the product of Salamanca and San Esteban. But socially, as the Inquisition in Mexico was forced to reckon with the power of the criollo elite, it was slowly moved away from its Salamancan rigor. Tamales, chocolate, pulque, and Indian mistresses were stiff competition for the austere vision of tracking down the heretical enemy. It is not accidental that the strongest local criollo comisario of the Mexican Inquisition, Ruiz de Corral, was heir to the socioeconomic success of the cacao plantations of Guatemala and Soconusco. And if theologians and court historians wrote lengthy treatises on whether or not chocolate could break the ecclesiastical fast, the inquisitional functionaries who had so completely integrated themselves into the criollo upper crust surely were asking other questions about the seductive cacao. The once mighty dominance of black-and-white-robed friars came up squarely against the exigencies of a colonial society and a mitigated ideology which had to account for more than the theories of Eimeric and Simancas and which considered the power of local religious custom.

The Early Inquisitions, 1525–71

Before the establishment of a formal, central tribunal of the Inquisition in Mexico in 1571, friars, bishops, diocesan councils, and delegated inquisitors vied for ecclesiastical authority in the Indies. In some cases, Inquisitions operated parallel to each other. In others jurisdictional conflicts boiled over into full-scale administrative wars. Overall, the period from 1492, the year of Columbus's arrival, to 1521, which saw the fall of Tenochtitlan, to 1571, when the Mexican Inquisition was established, was characterized, in the assessment of Miguel Ángel González, by "jurisdictional disintegration."[1] Others, like José Toribio Medina, refer to this period as the "primitive American Inquisition."[2] Irrespective of the name, the constant theme was that of tension between episcopal and missionary-mendicant authority.[3]

In 1493 a kind of virtual Inquisition in the Indies began. By royal decree, Jews and New Christians were prohibited from traveling to the Indies, and at the same time the Benedictine Bernardo Boil was appointed the apostolic vicar of all the Indies, a title that was largely ceremonial. The first American Inquisition was established in 1516 in Cuba when the Spanish inquisitor general, Ximénez de Cisneros, designated fray Juan de Quevedo, bishop of Cuba, as his inquisitor delegate. In 1517 Cisneros named the bishops of Santa María del Darién, Santo Domingo, and Concepción de la Vega (also on Hispaniola) as apostolic inquisitors. This Inquisition, however, was never actually put into practice. Cisneros died on November 8, 1517, and Cardinal Adrian became the new Spanish inquisitor general, naming in short order (in 1519) Alonso Manso, bishop of Puerto Rico, and fray Pedro de Córdoba, Dominican vice-provincial, as inquisitors of the Indies. Unlike the diocesan inquisitors ordinary, Manso and Córdoba were charged with specific delegated authority under the auspices of the Spanish General Inquisition.[4]

By 1527 Hernán Cortés, long hounded by his jealous enemies, was recalled to Spain to answer the various charges leveled against him. For those first six years after the fall of Tenochtitlan (1521–26) the prosecution of blasphemy and heresy was a haphazard affair, with Franciscans, Cortés, and civil officials vying for authority. There was no specific Inquisition set up, and there were no bishops to exercise their ordinary jurisdiction in prosecuting heresy. The Franciscans were the first mendicants to arrive in New Spain, at the behest of Cortés, and they asserted jurisdiction based on the privileges extended to them in the succession of bulls known as the *Omnímoda* in 1522, which granted to the mendicants the authority to carry out various duties and offices normally reserved to bishops and diocesan authorities.[5] The reasoning was that the Indies were so far-flung and geographically expansive and the missionaries so determined to make the Indies a new Catholic kingdom that it would be impossible to impart the entire evangelization process to diocesan authorities.[6] Thus *Omnímoda* granted the Franciscans the authority to baptize, hear confession, and catechize in ways that the friars and monks of the Old World never did. Various Franciscans and Dominicans would assert inquisitional authority as the result of the *Omnímoda* in lieu of an ordinary Inquisition carried out by a bishop.

Inquisitional authority from 1521 to 1526 is also obscured by the loss of documentation and the intermittent nature of its application. Richard Greenleaf shows that there was an inquisitional trial in 1522 against the Indian Marcos de Acolhuacan for bigamy, but the trial itself is not extant.[7] In May 1524 fray Martín de Valencia arrived as the head of the Franciscan mission of twelve in Mexico, and it appears that he and his coreligionists asserted some form of inquisitional authority for the next two years under the auspices of the *Omnímoda*. Valencia prosecuted some cases against Indians for idolatry and perhaps even relaxed some to the secular arm for punishment in 1524 and 1525 under the aegis of the *Omnímoda*. Ultimately in 1525 the Mexico City *cabildo* (city council) summoned the Franciscan missionary Toribio Motolinía before it to admonish the Franciscans for attempting to assert civil as well as ecclesiastical authority.[8]

In 1526 the Dominicans arrived in Mexico to establish a missionary project. In 1527 Betanzos was commissioned as the Holy Office's comisario and vicar general in New Spain by the inquisitors in Spain. In effect, since it would have been impossible for Betanzos to refer all inquiries across the Atlantic, he became the first inquisitor in Mexico.[9] In theory and in law a comisario did not possess full authority of prosecution, unless, as Peña noted, it was impractical to refer cases when the inquisitor was not available — as was clearly the case in Mexico. Still, there does not seem to be much evidence for a particularly vigorous Inquisition. Betanzos undertook twelve cases — mostly against conquistadors for blasphemy — in 1527. Even though he did not cast a wide net, he has the somewhat ignominious distinction of being the first inquisitor of Mexico to order inquisitionally sanctioned executions of Spaniards, those of Hernando Alonso and Gonzalo de Morales, for Judaizing, in an auto de fe in October 1528.[10] Two others were likewise commissioned to carry out inquisitional activities in Mexico — the Dominican Vicente de Santa María and the jurist Rodrigo de Torres. Like Betanzos, they were not especially active, together undertaking eight cases in 1527–28. Today there is one extant trial undertaken by Motolinía as a kind of protoinquisitional authority, though there surely were more.[11]

It is unlikely that Betanzos, himself a Dominican and trained in law at Salamanca before taking the habit of Santo Domingo, would have called on censors.[12] While by law he was enjoined by Eimeric and the canon law in general (in *Ut commissi*) to call on advisors schooled in that discipline in which the inquisitor was less expert, given Betanzos's background in Salamancan traditions, he ran his Inquisition along the lines of the medieval Dominican tribunals. While legal expert advice was recommended for theologians, it does not appear that such action was yet customary either in Spain or Mexico, and Betanzos's trials tended to be quickly dispatched and focused on a relatively specific group of conquistadors. This was partly a politically motivated Inquisition, as Betanzos went after partisans of Cortés — a faction whose members were supported by the Franciscans and who became enemies of the Dominicans.

There is some shadowy evidence for censors being used on occasion in the 1520s and for some kind of ideological specialization, though it would not have been important since most of the early inquisitors were friars in the medieval inquisitional tradition. In 1527 Motolinía appears to have continued to assert some kind of inquisitional authority, as there exists a trial in Texcoco against the aging conquistador Rodrigo Rengel for blasphemy in which the Franciscan acted as judge. Motolinía asserted his authority on the basis of his status as vicar and comisario of the Franciscans, though it is possible he was commissioned by Betanzos as a deputy. During the trial he relied on theological advice from fray Luis de Fuensalida in assessing guilt.[13] Santa María was equally commissioned by the General Council of the Inquisition as its vicar in New Spain and prosecuted a limited number (four) of cases.[14] In a trial over suspicious statements, Santa María employed the secular cleric Diego de Altamirano, the cousin of Cortés, in handing down a sentence.[15] Altamirano did not play an especially large role in the trial: he only signed his name to the sentence and other major procedural votes.

From 1528 to 1536 virtually no inquisitional authority in Mexico operated, with the exception of a single case tried by Alonso López as vicar and ecclesiastical judge in 1532.[16] In December 1528 Juan de Zumárraga arrived in Mexico as the bishop-elect of Mexico but had not been consecrated. Born in 1468 in Durango in the Basque Country, Zumárraga entered the Franciscan order and in 1527 was commissioned by the Spanish General Inquisition to investigate witchcraft in northern Spain. In 1528 he was elected bishop of Mexico and named the vaguely defined defender of the Indians. After his arrival in Mexico-Tenochtitlan he was involved in spectacular disputes with the Audiencia, whom he accused of raping and abusing Indians. At the high point of the dispute Zumárraga placed the entire Audiencia under interdict after one of its judges dragged a Franciscan, Antonio Ortiz, from the pulpit for denouncing the Audiencia judges in a public sermon.

In 1536 Zumárraga began activities as inquisitor of the diocese of Mexico, with wide authority granted him by the Crown and the inquisitor general. Zumárraga undertook a particularly vigorous Inquisition, one that was quantitatively as active as any Inquisition in sixteenth-century Mexico, which is impressive given his rudimentary apparatus — he did not employ censors, comisarios, familiars, or other auxiliaries. Instead, his zeal as a missionary seems to have powered his inquisitional activities. He was authorized to take up inquisitional investigations in the formative Mexican diocese, though by geographic necessity its purview was concentrated in central Mexico.[17] From 1536, when he began to adjudicate cases, until 1541, when he was rebuked for his zealotry and violence and stripped of his inquisitional commission, Zumárraga completed at least 120 cases — a rate of 20 per year, though all but 2 of the trials took place before 1541.

On examining the trials undertaken on Zumárraga's watch, one notices regular patterns. Blasphemy cases represented the single largest category and were prosecuted at rates far higher than in other Inquisitions (more than twice the overall rate for the first century of the Mexican tribunal), a fact which reflects the early missionaries' concerns that the social morality of conquistadors and early Spanish officials set bad examples for the Indians. The trials also tended to be speedy and expeditious. The accused were not afforded defense attorneys, as was required by inquisitional law, and Zumárraga only

Table 5.1. Inquisition Cases, 1536–41 (the Zumárraga Inquisition)

Charge	Number of cases	Number of cases with censors	Percentage of cases with censors	Percentage of caseload
Blasphemy	41	0	0.0	34.2
Bigamy	18	0	0.0	15.0
Propositions	13	1	7.7	10.8
Witchcraft	11	0	0.0	9.2
Heresy	10	0	0.0	8.3
Idolatry	8	0	0.0	6.7
Cohabitation	5	0	0.0	4.2
Flight	3	0	0.0	2.5
Processes of order	3	0	0.0	2.5
Desacato [disobedience to Church censure][a]	2	0	0.0	1.7
Judaizing	2	0	0.0	1.7
Querella [nondoctrinal complaints][b]	1	0	0.0	0.8
Sacrilege	1	0	0.0	0.8
Incest	1	0	0.0	0.8
Prohibited books	1	0	0.0	0.8
Doctrinal cases	87	1	1.1	72.5
Total cases	120	1	0.8	100.0

Source: AGN, Inquisición, volumes: 1, 2, 14, 22, 23, 30, 34, 36, 37, 38, 40, 42, 125, 212

a. Desacato was a charge of disrespect for the Inquisition and involved charges ranging from tearing down inquisitional edicts, refusing to attend the Lenten edict of the faith, attacking the authority of the Inquisition, and physically impeding the execution of inquisitional duties.

b. Querella, like processes of office, was a vaguely defined legal category. Usually these two types of charges involved nondoctrinal disputes involving one or more inquisitional officials who claimed some kind of immunity from civil or criminal proceedings, such as theft, assault, fraud, murder, rape, attacks on honor, and so forth. In some cases querella trials involved disputes over authority and jurisdiction between inquisitional and secular officials.

occasionally employed a prosecutor—Rafael de Cervantes, himself also a theologian. Instead, the Franciscan undertook the rapid succession of accusations and conviction himself. On limited occasions he deferred authority to vicars—to the Mexico Audiencia judge Francisco de Loaysa in 1537 and 1540, to Juan Gutiérrez de Olvera as comisario in 1538–40, and to the Mexico cathedral canon Diego Velásquez as diocesan provisor in 1539 and 1540.

Yet Zumárraga's rapid dispatch of convictions contravened at least the spirit, if not the letter, of inquisitional law. His handling of a trial against the Indian noble don Carlos Chichimecatecotl de Texcoco led to his downfall as inquisitor. Zumárraga prosecuted and convicted don Carlos for idolatry and bigamy and ordered him relaxed to the secular arm for execution in 1539. After don Carlos's execution on the bonfire Zumárraga was reprimanded by the Suprema for his overzealous activity and he was stripped of his inquisitional authority.[18] Nor did Zumárraga find it necessary to consult jurists even though he himself was a theologian not versed in the law. In a case in 1537 he employed fray Gregorio de Ávila for advice though Ávila did not provide a formal review.[19] Besides the question of severity, opinion was divided as to whether the Inquisition had authority over Indians — something that was settled in 1569 when the Suprema declared that the Mexican Inquisition could not proceed against Indians. The irony was that it was only in trials against Indians for idolatry that Zumárraga employed the advice of a jurist — the oidor Loaysa — in handing down sentence.[20]

Zumárraga's prosecution and relaxation to the secular authorities to execute don Carlos lend credence to the image of the Inquisition as ruthless, bloodthirsty, and emblematic of the Black Legend. But Zumárraga's handling of the don Carlos case was not representative of the Mexican Inquisition overall. The Mexican Inquisition, like the various local Spanish Inquisitions, did burn heretics at the stake, but in numbers well below those associated with the stereotypical image of the Inquisition. For example, in Mexico, about fifty miserables went to the bonfire in person in nearly three hundred years (from the first execution in 1528 until the Inquisition's abolition in 1820) — a slow week on Robespierre's watch. Others, who had escaped the jurisdiction, were burned in effigy. The two largest inquisitional autos de fe (public penances) in Mexico took place in 1596, when thirty-one Judaizers were condemned as heretics, of whom nine were relaxed to the secular authorities for execution, and in 1601 when fifty persons were condemned, four of whom were executed in person. For the period roughly covered in this book — 1527 to 1630 — some twenty-six individuals were executed in person (in 1,563 adjudicated trials), or 1.7 percent of those prosecuted, a rate almost identical to that in Spain.[21]

If the Zumárraga Inquisition was more zealous than other Inquisitions in the Mexican tribunal's history, it did present trends that in very broad strokes are typical of inquisitional activity in Mexico. There is a division between the charges for propositions, blasphemy and heresy (see table 5.1). But the charge of propositions included any heterodox or suspect statement that in later years would be reviewed by censors. The result is that many of the trials which were listed as propositions resulted in convictions for heresy, sapit haeresim, bad-sounding words, or other gradations of offenses. Whereas Zumárraga did not consult outside advisors in his trials, during the tenure of his successor, Montúfar, as well as under the administration of the Inquisition after 1571, trials for propositions would come to be an area in which censors were frequently consulted.

From 1541 to 1551 one finds only ten complete inquisitional trials for the entirety of Mexico — a low point in inquisitional activity never again equaled while the tribunal was in existence. There continued to be investigations undertaken by various diocesan Inquisitions, but very few cases were fully prosecuted and completed. For example, in the Yucatán and the dioceses of Oaxaca and Puebla there were sporadic investigations, and in Oaxaca some high-profile idolatry trials, but overall in the absence of a central Inquisition vested in the portfolio of the (arch)bishop of Mexico, inquisitional activities were low in this period. Having ousted Zumárraga as inquisitor, the Crown sent a royal inspector (*visitador general*), the civil lawyer Francisco Tello de Sandoval, to overhaul the colonial legal system, including the Inquisition. He undertook a severely limited inquisitional caseload in 1544. The primary purpose of Sandoval's *visita* (inspection) was the implementation of the New Laws, which were designed to curtail the power of the new conquistador-encomienda class and which had outlawed Indian slavery.[22]

In 1554 Montúfar physically took possession of the see of Mexico and simultaneously became apostolic inquisitor of Mexico. Unlike Zumárraga, Montúfar preferred to delegate his authority. For the majority of the cases investigated during his tenure — from 1554 to 1571 — Montúfar was conspicuously absent from the proceedings. In fact he participated as judge in less than 10 percent of the trials undertaken by his inquisitional authority. Instead, he relied on a highly educated group of canonists and theologians to handle the everyday business of the Inquisition. The theologians Ledesma and Barbosa, along with the canonists Luis Anguis, himself a spy for King Philip II, and the law professor Esteban de Portillo, formed the coterie that administered the inquisitional functions in Montúfar's stead.[23] For example, Barbosa was one of Montúfar's principal vicars and acted as inquisitor ordinary in at least forty-eight complete trials between 1563 and 1568 in Montúfar's stead.[24]

Like Zumárraga, Montúfar rarely employed censors per se. Instead, his Inquisition operated under the collective aegis of this group of canonists and theologians, who were delegated by Montúfar to prosecute inquisitional crimes. In this sense Montúfar followed traditional inquisitional procedure — and, indeed, law — much more closely than Zumárraga. But Montúfar did employ censors in some select high-profile cases of heresy and censorship. Even though he arrived in 1554 the first trial over which he presided did not

Table 5.2. Inquisitional Cases in Central Mexico, 1555–71 (the Montúfar Inquisition)

Charge	Number of cases	Number of cases with censors	Percentage of cases with censors	Percentage of caseload
Propositions	38	5	13.2	30.9
Bigamy	26	0	0.0	21.1
Blasphemy	23	0	0.0	18.7
Heresy	17	2	11.8	13.8
Cohabitation	4	0	0.0	3.2
Witchcraft	3	0	0.0	2.4
Processes of order	2	0	0.0	1.6
Flight	2	0	0.0	1.6
Querella	2	0	0.0	1.6
Prohibited books	2	0	0.0	1.6
Sacrilege	1	0	0.0	0.8
Imitating priest	1	0	0.0	0.8
Desacato	1	0	0.0	0.8
Solicitation in confession	1	0	0.0	0.8
Doctrinal cases	86	7	8.1	69.9
Total cases	123	7	5.7	100.0

Trials over which Montúfar presided as inquisitor: 10 (in 1558, 1560 (twice), 1561, 1563, 1564 (four times), 1565)

1555–59: 7 trials, 6 of which were overseen by Montúfar's delegates

Source: AGN, Inquisición, volumes 1A, 3, 4, 5, 6, 7, 8, 9, 10, 11, 15, 16, 17, 18, 19, 20, 21, 23, 25, 26, 27, 28, 29, 31, 32, 35, 36, 39, 41, 43, 45, 46, 49, 68, 72, 80, 91, 92, 95, 96, 97, 98, 110, 111, 112, 113, 114, 184, 251A

take place until 1558. Before 1560 only seven trials were themselves adjudicated in the archdiocese of Mexico, a rate of barely one a year.

While Montúfar's vicars did not act specifically as censors, their role demonstrates important traits of the Montúfar as well as of contemporaneous diocesan Inquisitions. Given his experiences as a censor in Granada before being elevated to the See of Mexico (and unlike Zumárraga, who seems to have had little patience for a multiplicity of legal and theological advice), Montúfar may have held in high estimation the notion of Peña that the more advisors, the better the result. Montúfar viewed his vicars and provisores as his trusted functionaries and generally allowed them not only to begin the investigations but also to finish them, passing judgment and sentence. The future of these advisors to Montúfar reflects the shift in authority from the pre- and post-

1571 Mexican Inquisitions. Ledesma and Barbosa would be among the first censors of the formal Mexican tribunal of the Inquisition.[25] Portillo became a legal consultor in the new tribunal, as did another canonist who exercised occasional authority as one of Montúfar's vicars, Arévalo Sedeño. During the Montúfar Inquisition, the same men who later would be divested of a vote and hold consultative positions possessed considerable actual authority.

The power of the friar-theologians and secular clergy as consultores and inquisitors themselves was not restricted to the Montúfar Inquisition. Throughout New Spain, numerous local, diocesan Inquisitions operated parallel to the Montúfar apostolic and archdiocesan Inquisition of Mexico. Where there was no special, delegated inquisitor present, canon law made clear that bishops still held the authority to act as ordinary inquisitors, even if that authority was steadily eroded in the late medieval period and effectively quashed in Spain after 1478. In Mexico, the difficulty of applying universal legal and ecclesiological concepts was the dilemma of derecho indiano. Since it was impractical for Montúfar to extend his authority to all of New Spain (and it was unclear whether he would have been legally allowed to do so in any case) diocesan authorities, either by order of the bishop himself or by the cathedral chapter *sede vacante* (without an appointed bishop), began to nominate inquisitors ordinary in the 1550s; they also began to rely heavily on a variety of advisors, diocesan provisors, and delegates.[26] In some dioceses the commissioned inquisitors ordinary were secular priests trained in canon law and associated with the local cathedral chapter. This was the case in Puebla, Michoacán, Nicaragua, and Honduras. In other dioceses the commissioned inquisitors varied between cathedral canon secular priests and mendicant friars, as was the case in Guadalajara and Guatemala. And in the Yucatán, the local Inquisition was run exclusively by the Franciscans, notoriously by Diego de Landa, who staged a massive auto de fe in Mani in 1562, executing several Mayans and destroying dozens of Mayan codices and thousands of idols. For De Landa as well as for Zumárraga and other practitioners of early Inquisitions, heresy, idolatry, and the written expression (of pre-Hispanic histories or heresies) were of a piece. Zumárraga, too, claimed to have destroyed hundreds of Nahua images. And like Zumárraga, De Landa was admonished for his procedural failings and was even required to stand trial before the Council of the Indies for staging an illegal Inquisition.[27]

These local inquisitors ordinary came from the same social background and status as men who, after 1571, would form the second tier of inquisitional authority. In fact, many of the inquisitors ordinary of the 1560s, including Melchor Gómez de Soria, Lorenzo López de Vergara, Pedro del Pozo, Cristóbal de Miranda, and Alonso Mexía, would become comisarios of the formal

General Inquisition of Mexico. While in some ways their power was only marginally diminished after 1571, in others this change represented a radical blow to their political power. Since comisarios were not allowed to pass sentence, the shift from inquisitor ordinary to comisario was dramatic. Yet at the local level, the average person probably did not split jurisprudential hairs over this issue, since the comisario held the authority to arrest and interrogate suspects.

The Early Reviews

The early theological advisors to local, diocesan Inquisitions were heavily steeped in Thomist scholasticism. The early theological reviews in Inquisition trials demonstrate that the internal debate within the Inquisition in Mexico began in the 1550s and remained a staple of that nonpublic intellectual forum until the dismantling of the Holy Office in the nineteenth century and the opening of its archives later. Despite their private nature, theological reviews reveal the beginnings of a scholastic debate on the nature of heresy, heterodoxy, and ecclesiastical authority in Mexico.

Outside of central Mexico the first statements by theological or canonical experts began to appear in 1558, in Guatemala, under the Dominican diocesan inquisitor Tomás de Cárdenas, who called theological advisors in three of the six cases he oversaw in Guatemala that year.[28] By 1560 opinions by theological advisors began to appear in other dioceses, like Mexico, as well as Oaxaca, Honduras, and Puebla. The use of theological advisors — not specifically called calificadores but serving the same purpose — was localized in the sense that it depended heavily on the inquisitor ordinary or the ecclesiastical judge in the particular diocese. In some dioceses, like the Yucatán, there was no use of such theological advisors, probably because the Franciscans guarded their jurisdiction carefully and because the Spanish population was so thin that there would scarcely have been enough men on which to call for such advice other than Franciscans.

The use of theological advisors was often ad hoc and varied from diocese to diocese in the pre-1571 period. Cárdenas, the prior of Santo Domingo in Santiago de Guatemala, was made inquisitor by the bishop of Guatemala, don Francisco Marroquín, as early as 1557, when he prosecuted doña María de Ocampo for witchcraft.[29] While in the cases overseen by the Dominican prior the theologians did not offer written opinions, they were included as integral members of the inquisitional team. The *audiencias* (or formal interrogations) of Cárdenas's Inquisition were held in the library of Santo Domingo in Guatemala, with Dominicans like Tomás de Vitoria and Diego Martínez as well as

the future censor the Franciscan Antonio Quixada (then guardian of San Francisco in Guatemala) attending.[30] In other cases Santo Domingo was turned
into a jail, and the accused were imprisoned there, as in the case of Juan
Rodríguez Herriero, who said that it was not a sin to eat meat during Lent
because the Church, not God, had instituted Lent. He both confessed and
performed his abjuration in the Dominican house in Guatemala.[31] In many
ways Guatemala closely followed the medieval model set by Dominicans in
the thirteenth and fourteenth centuries.

In many local Inquisitions, the theological advisors were consulted for points
of doctrine and empowered with votes in the proceedings, including sentencing. For example, Cárdenas allowed the friar-theologians to vote on sentencing
in the case against Ocampo. In 1560 Sebastián Bermúdez, the *cura* and vicar of
Trujillo (Honduras), was commissioned by Alonso Mexía, provisor of the
diocese, to proceed as judge. Mexía had himself operated as inquisitor ordinary
in 1559 but apparently was happy to defer to Bermúdez in the case in 1560
against Charles de Saligante, the French barber who was prosecuted for saying
that the pope was merely a man and that only God, not the pope, could issue
indulgences.[32] Bermúdez called two theologians for their advice, both Dominicans: fray Diego de Otáñez and fray Antonio Martínez. In addition to offering
their opinion — in both cases they condemned Saligante's statement for "denying the spiritual and temporal power of the Pope as head of the Church of
God" — the friars offered recommendations for punishment.[33] Otáñez recommended exile and sanbenito, and Martínez suggested six years of sanbenito and
imprisonment. Bermúdez took a seemingly less severe view of Saligante's view
of papal fallibility, sentencing him to wear a sanbenito for three years and house
arrest in Comayagua and to attend Mass every day for the same three-year
period.[34]

So too did the Dominicans Domingo de Salazar, prior of Oaxaca, Gerónimo
de Tixeda (who had been lector of theology in Oaxaca as early as 1561), and
Jordán de Santa Catarina (once subprior in Oaxaca) offer their recommendations for sentencing when they were called to give their opinion in 1569 by the
acting inquisitor ordinary, the cathedral dean don Juan Martínez Ruiz. The
accused, Pedro Sánchez de Reina, had said that it was "not a sin for a man to
sleep with a woman who was not his wife."[35] The friars countered that such a
statement was "formally heretical" and so obviously so that they did not need
to cite the "places where such a statement is condemned by Scripture." Nevertheless, they reasoned that when the accused "does not believe with contumacy or malice, mercy, rather than rigor, should always be used" in punishment. Therefore, in this particular case, the testimonies did not suggest such
contumacy and thus the accused should be sentenced according to neither the

"rigor of the law nor the ordinary penalty."[36] Thus even though he was suspect according to the logic of *Dubius in fide,* the lack of pertinacity exculpated him from heresy.

An earlier case of questioning the inner thought and faith of the accused involved the same friars — Santa Catarina and Tixeda — but with decidedly different results. In Oaxaca in 1561 the cathedral dean Martínez Ruiz, acting as inquisitor ordinary, prosecuted Mateo de Monjaraz for saying that for "a man to lie carnally with an Indian woman is not a sin."[37] When Sánchez said essentially the same thing in 1569, the friars Jordán and Gerónimo argued that such a statement was "manifestly heretical." But in the case in 1561 the same friars had concluded that while the statement about sex with Indian women was heretical, the man who said it was not himself a heretic. Why? The Dominican advisors concluded that because Monjaraz confessed and knew that such a statement was heretical and did not say it with the "intent of affirming it, but as a result of the anger of the moment in which he said it, he did not consider what he was saying."[38] Despite their seeming leniency, they reminded the inquisitor that such statements were all too frequent among the "common people" and that they should be eliminated given the "great danger" they presented to "ignorant people." The Thomist distinction of coram sapientibus and coram simplicibus manifested itself not as a simple theological abstraction, but as a real, practical concern of the theologian-friars who endeavored to Christianize an Indian and mestizo population.

While most of the theological advisory debates in the local Inquisitions were relatively brief, others offered fuller discussions on the nature of religious authority and heresy. An especially telling case occurred in Puebla in 1560–61 against Alonso Soltero for the following proposition: "Many saints that the Church has canonized are in hell because the Church canonized them for favors." The cathedral chapter, overseen by its dean don Bartolomé Romero, and acting as the supreme diocesan authority sede vacante, ordered the proposition sent to three different groups of friars for review: the Franciscans Gregorio Mexía (guardian of the Franciscan house in Puebla) and Juan Barrón; the Dominicans Hernando de Paz (prior in Puebla) and Juan Martínez; and the Augustinians Miguel de Alvarado (prior in Puebla) and Esteban de Salazar.[39]

On reading these three opinions, one is struck by their didactic nature. The Dominicans offered the most papalist assessment of the proposition. But in true scholastic form, Paz and Martínez began their opinion by arguing that "in order to understand the gravity of this proposition we must deal with it from first principles."[40] According to their assessment, the beginning and foundation of all things of the faith was Christ and, in his succession, Peter, "on which as a living stone our Holy Mother Church of Rome is built."[41] Here, the papal-conciliar debate found its way into the quotidian operation of ecclesiastical debate in the Indies. Paz and Martínez argued that the Apostolic See was the pope, who ruled as the head of the "body of this militant Church."[42] They drew on Innocent III, who had argued "that all the difficult matters which deal with the articles of the faith should be brought to the Apostolic See for definition."[43] By Innocent's definition, the Apostolic See could not err in matters of the faith. Even the most conciliar theologians accepted this, as did Castro. The distinction lay in the definition of the Apostolic See, and for this the Dominican censors in Puebla argued that it was the pope who represented that See. Hence they argued for papal infallibility on matters of the faith.

But was Soltero's statement heresy? According to Paz and Martínez, it was not in fact heresy because it did not reject a particular statement in scripture. This was a departure from the standards of heresy theory and inquisitional law, since statements that rejected decrees of general councils or apostolic tradition were considered heretical according to the definitions of theorists as distinct as Castro, Cano, and Torquemada. And even Paz and Martínez pointed out that Hus, Wycliffe, and Luther had all been condemned for rejecting saints and the authority of the Catholic Church to canonize them. But in the final analysis, these Dominicans argued for a limited view of conciliar authority and for the scope of heresy.[44]

The review offered by the Augustinians — Miguel de Alvarado, Esteban de Salazar, and Agustín de Salamanca — followed the line of papal superiority offered by the Dominicans.[45] But before offering this point, they explained one of the principal points for culpability in heresy: knowledge of the error and pertinacity in asserting the error, drawing on the standard explanations for these two points from Saints Anthony and Augustine as well as Castro. In their assessment, they instructed the cathedral chapter that not everyone who asserted a heretical statement was a heretic, since ignorance was exculpatory (again relying on Castro).[46] But when it came to the point of determining whether or not the statement under review was heretical, the Augustinians concluded that the determination of the pope was absolute and incontrovertible. For this they drew on Aquinas, who argued in *De potentia dei* that the pope was not required to convene a general council in order to determine matters of the faith. The Augustinian censors simultaneously offered Castro as proof of papal infallibility, which was either a deliberate corruption of Castro's view of papal fallibility or a misreading of Castro's definition of the Apostolic See. Thus they concluded that the pope "cannot err in defining something that deals either directly or indirectly with the faith."[47] Therefore, if the pope canonized a saint, it must be accepted as true and infallible. Consequently, the given statement was heretical on a level equal to that of Wycliffe and Luther.

The third opinion was given by the Franciscan Mexía, who argued for a heavily conciliar vision of ecclesiastical authority.[48] Like theorists of heresy and the Dominicans who offered their opinion in this case, Mexía first asserted a standard definition of heresy: "Only that proposition is heretical which truly and properly is contrary to some proposition revealed by God in the Holy Scripture, dealing with the Christian religion and against the determination of the Church."[49] Following this definition, Mexía embarked on an exegesis of the ways and rules by which one could discern a heretical proposition, revealing further his vision of ecclesiastical authority as conciliar and theologically — and nonlegally — based. Mexía then explained that he would leave alone the explanations of the canonists because "theologians explain with greater clarity and brevity" — a direct contradiction of Simancas.[50] Here he turned to Castro, whom he called the "light of our Spain and the universal Church," for the definition of the ways by which a heretical proposition — as opposite a Catholic, "true" one — could be known. Therein Mexía demonstrated a conciliar definition of religious authority.

In a précis of Castro's methodology, Mexía redacted five ways by which a heretical proposition could be known: (1) by scripture; (2) by conciliar decrees; (3) by religious custom and tradition; (4) by papal authority, but with the advice of theologians; (5) by unanimous consent of theologians. Following Castro's lead, Mexía argued that in understanding the opinion that "many saints canonized by the Church are in hell" the Church as the Apostolic See did not mean the person of the pope but the institution. Therefore, the pope, as a single man, could err, whereas the Apostolic See as an institution representing the Church was incapable of error. Consequently, the pope could err in canonization if he failed to consult learned men or a general council. For this reason, he concluded, as did Castro, that the definition of the faith should be entrusted not to a single man but instead to the universal agreement of councils and theologians. And although Mexía held this to be a basic tenet of conciliar theology, he warned that stating such a tenet among the "simple people" was dangerous because the uneducated might derive false ideas, like Lutheran anticlericalism, from it.[51] Ultimately, Mexía concluded that the statement under review was heretical since it violated the authority of the Church in the form of general councils, which, as in the case of the Council of Constance, had condemned Hus and Wycliffe for rejecting the authority of the Church to canonize saints.

The Puebla case offered the most complete instance of theological review among the local Inquisitions in this period. It also demonstrated the nature of theological debate within the confines of the Inquisition. Even in a case that might have seemed routine, considerable philosophical differences arose in determining the nature of religious authority and, by extension, the scope of inquisitional power. More telling perhaps was that all three opinions used similar proof texts and authorities: causa 24, question 1 of the *Decretum;* the chapter *Maiores* of Innocent III in the *Decretales;* Aquinas; Alfonso de Castro; and Juan de Torquemada. Yet, even in employing authorities as diverse as these — Torquemada and Castro could scarcely have been further apart in their conception of conciliar versus papal authority — the censors drew divergent conclusions.

Censorship Politics

While there was no shortage of politically motivated inquisitional proceedings in the various provincial dioceses from 1527 to 1571, perhaps nowhere was the level of political character assassination as great as in Mexico City itself. Here Montúfar and Ledesma engaged in the kind of inquisitional proceedings that made for fine reading within the rubric of the Black Legend. Indeed, so hyperorthodox were many of their cases and censures that the Suprema itself often reversed their judgments, as in the case of their censorship of Maturino Gilberti's *Diálogo.*[52] In fact, Montúfar proceeded against even the censor Gregorio Mexía for heresy and against numerous other hapless preachers caught in the wide net cast by the Dominican archbishop-inquisitor.[53]

The process of book censorship in Mexico prior to the establishment of the Holy Office in 1571 was uneven. Some authors were singled out for particular investigation, and on occasion inquisitional authorities investigated the reading habits of persons accused of heresy. For example, Zumárraga prosecuted Pedro Ruiz Calderón for superstitions, pacts with the devil, and black magic.[54] Ruiz Calderón was a priest from Guadalajara, Spain, educated at Alcalá de Henares, and a *racionero* (shareholder) of the Mexico City cathedral chapter, placing him in the lower religious elite. Among his many talents, he apparently knew a signature of Satan himself, undoubtedly a useful skill in conjuration. Arrested on January 31, 1540, he was processed quickly and sentenced on April 4, 1540, for preaching superstitions in Veracruz and invoking demons, for which he was to abjure his crimes while holding a candle during a mass in the cathedral church. He was also forbidden to say Mass for two years, though apparently he was not defrocked, and his books were to be sent to Spain. Zumárraga, true to the hierarchical notion of doctrinal responsibility, noted in the sentencing that he was "especially guilty given that he was an educated man."[55]

Other cases included information on reading habits. In 1568 Ledesma, as vicar for the ailing Montúfar, prosecuted the nun Elena de la Cruz of the Immaculate Conception in Mexico City for various opinions, such as believing that bishops could not issue pardons, that there were no venial sins, and that the pope's pronouncements were intended only to instill spiritual terror. Ledesma asked her what books she had read and discovered that she had read the *Libro de oración y meditación* of Luis de Granada.[56] This was not the only case in which reading habits and books were explicitly linked to resulting errors, and the archives reveal other cases in which the contagion fear is manifest.[57] While the theorists saw the infiltration into Catholic lands of prohibited books as threatening, the practice of questioning subjects on their reading habits was generally infrequent and depended on the specific inquisitorial judge.

But in general there is little to suggest that widespread and consistent purgation of prohibited books took place in this period. Indeed, when Zumárraga was inquisitor a formal Spanish Index did not even exist, so the process by which books were ferreted out was inherently ad hoc. Yet even after the publication of the Index of 1559, there was no systematic purge of libraries and bookstores in Mexico during the 1560s. Nor was a formal, effective apparatus for screening shipments of books and the circulation of personal books in Veracruz put into effect. There was some sporadic enforcement, as the port of Veracruz was in the diocese of Puebla and theoretically the diocesan provisor could prosecute cases originating there, as was the case when Lorenzo López de Vergara investigated heretical statements and possible smuggling of prohibited books into the port in 1563.[58] But this appears to have been an isolated instance.

That there was no centralized, widespread effort to enforce the Index and remove offending books from circulation in this period does not mean, however, that censorship was a dead letter. Instead, there were high-profile cases in which authors who had published books in Mexico saw their books censored, banned, or hunted down. In addition to Mexican published books, there was increasing concern about the influence of humanism and Erasmianism, strands of thought that were anathema to the conservatism of Montúfar and the Dominicans. We know a good deal about the rivalry between the Dominicans and Franciscans in the sixteenth century in Mexico as well as about Montúfar's efforts to rein in the privileges of the Franciscans. Generally speaking, the Franciscans, having arrived as the first missionaries in Mexico with the support of Cortés and the privileges of the *Omnímoda,* amassed considerable power and wealth, much to the displeasure of the more conservative Dominicans. Montúfar in particular viewed the Franciscans and Augustinians as a fifth column in Mexico, flouting diocesan rule and centralization, to say nothing of the many supporters of Erasmus and humanism within their ranks. Likewise, the regalist bishop of Michoacán, Vasco de Quiroga, the *jefe intelectual* (principal political-intellectual supporter) of Montúfar's antimendicant, prodiocesan reforms, has been well studied.[59] Montúfar and Quiroga would lead the attack on Franciscan and Augustinian projects of native-language publication, expansion of the non-Dominican mendicant missions, and mendicant privilege generally speaking, though Montúfar cast a blind eye to his own order in many illegal actions designed to benefit the Dominican presence.

Two notable cases have attracted attention: that of the *Doctrina* written by Zumárraga and of a *Diálogo* in Purépecha (the main native language of Michoacán) by his fellow Franciscan, Maturino Gilberti. In both cases Montúfar and Ledesma were the principal proponents of the bans on the Franciscan works. Zumárraga's *Doctrina* was printed first in Mexico in 1539 and had attracted the unfavorable attention of Montúfar by the 1550s. Montúfar convoked a meeting of theologians and jurists on November 3, 1559, to review the book, and on the advice of some of them and of Ledesma he ordered it banned pending further review by the Suprema, which would revoke Montúfar's decision two decades later.[60]

Two principal areas of dispute overlapped in these high-profile censorship cases. The first reflected a broad debate occurring throughout the Hispanic world concerning humanism and Erasmianism. Erasmus had exerted influence in the court of Charles V, but by the 1530s his work had come under fire principally from conservative Dominicans who viewed both humanism and Erasmian leanings as heretical or at least highly suspicious. Simultaneously, the conservative faction from Spain that was influential and ultimately victorious at Trent began to formulate the first indexes, particularly the editions of 1554 and 1559, formalizing the attack on various works of Erasmus, on vernacular translations of scripture, and on other humanist projects. Montúfar was aligned with this general antihumanist ideology, and his overall prosecutorial activity as inquisitor in Mexico reflects a staunchly conservative vision of Catholic counterreform. To this can be contrasted the admiration for Erasmus shown by Zumárraga as well as by other influential members of the Franciscan mission in Mexico.[61] In the case against Zumárraga's *Doctrina* and Gilberti's works, a principal argument made by Montúfar and Ledesma in banning the works was their distrust of humanism and their view that doctrinal discussions in Indian languages were suspect, especially if the authors evidenced Erasmian tendencies.

The second major point of confrontation was jurisdictional. Montúfar, along with Quiroga, promoted a Tridentine reform of the Mexican Church parallel to efforts in Spain. Despite the fact that Montúfar was a Dominican, he and Quiroga championed and promoted a systematic attack on mendicant privileges in New Spain. The Franciscans in general bore much of the brunt of this centralizing reform in Mexico. The content of Zumárraga's and Gilberti's work was, in many ways, less important than the fact that they were Franciscans. Similar missionary works by Dominicans did not receive nearly the same level of scrutiny from Montúfar's vicars.

In the censorship trial of Zumárraga's work, the principal ostensible point of contention was an obscure opinion of Zumárraga that the blood Christ shed at the Crucifixion and absorbed in the cross was subsequently reincorporated into Christ's divinity — a point so abstruse that the Suprema did not even take Montúfar's ban seriously.[62] There were clearly other, ulterior motives for banning Zumárraga's *Doctrina*. Among them were Zumárraga's unabashed enthusiasm for Erasmus and his call to translate the Bible into all languages of the world. Zumárraga had also published a work by Seville's cathedral canon, Constantino de la Puente, who was later convicted, after his death in the Seville inquisitional jail awaiting trial, for heresy in 1559.[63]

The attack on the Franciscan missionary Gilberti reflects two important facets of a Tridentine thrust. The inquisitional trials against Gilberti and his books were part of a broader assault on the Franciscans and their humanist activities; likewise, Gilberti was caught in the cross fire of the battle for control of Michoacán in particular and the Catholic Church overall. These censorship trials and surrounding feuds highlight a broader debate about the influence and nature of a counterreform manifested at Trent. The forces that ultimately triumphed at Trent — symbolized in their broad agenda but also in the relentless effort to rid Spain of humanism, witnessed, for example, in the arrest and trial of the Augustinian professor at Salamanca, Luis de León, and in the prosecution of Carranza — were reflected organically in Mexico in Montúfar's broad agenda.[64] This ideology in incipient form in Mexico was expressed through Montúfar's attempts to control the friars, rein in humanism, and crush his opponents whenever he saw fit.

Gilberti was a Franciscan from Toulouse who went to Mexico in 1542 as part of the already impressive conversion efforts of the Minor Brothers. He was quickly dispatched to the west in Michoacán, where he would spend several decades as a priest and student of Purépecha language and culture. He found himself caught squarely in the crosshairs of a vicious and at times violent partisan battle for jurisdiction in Michoacán between the mendicants and Quiroga. The two factions had been battling each other within the confines of the law over episcopal power as it related to mendicant privilege with the result that partisans of Quiroga went so far as to burn down the Augustinian church and conventual house in Tlazazalca in 1560.[65]

Much of Gilberti's production has been lost, though from contemporary discussion we know he was extremely active on many fronts as a preacher, writer, and translator. In addition to his famous *Vocabulario* and *Diálogo* in

Purépecha he translated several popular spiritual works into Purépecha, including the *Flos Santorum* and works by the Dominican Felipe de Meneses that he entitled *Luz del alma cristiana en lengua tarasca*.[66] Meneses was allied with the Dominican faction of reform and humanism associated with Luis de Granada, Saint John of the Cross, and Carranza — targets all of the conservative faction led by Cano (and spiritual teachers of Ledesma) that censored, prosecuted, and placed on the Index works by these confreres.

Gilberti was a member of this group as well, promoting Purépecha study and use among Franciscan missionaries and producing a Purépecha grammar in addition to major works he translated into Purépecha. This productivity, like that of the Franciscan Nahuatl scholars Bernardino de Sahagún and Alfonso de Molina, came under fire from the Dominicans in Mexico, much in the way Erasmus's work was subjected to scrutiny and censorship efforts (often by Dominicans) in Spain.[67] Many will recognize the broad contours of Dominican hostility to humanism and of the rivalry with the Franciscans; of inquisitional censure of Franciscan efforts to produce a native-language corpus of exegetical and grammatical material for their enterprise; and of deep concerns about the millennial character of the Franciscan mission in Mexico. In particular, readers will find a familiar echo in the final confiscation of Sahagún's ethnographic projects and in the failure of the idealistic school at Tlatelolco.[68] The Franciscans had established a theological school, the Colegio de la Santa Cruz, which was intended to train Indian elites in Spanish and Latin and in Catholic theology with the goal of producing an indigenous clergy. Castro himself had weighed in on the controversy, writing a defense of Indian education and intellect.[69]

Quiroga had denounced Gilberti to Montúfar's Inquisition on December 3, 1559, for having printed his Purépecha works without diocesan license and for suspicion of heresy. According to the review offered by secular cleric censors, including the mastermind of the Tlazazalca fire, the Michoacán cathedral chapter chantre don Diego Pérez Gordillo y Negrón, Gilberti had professed a variety of heresies to the Indians. Among them — what became the linchpin of the censorship trial — was that Gilberti had argued in his works that the Indians should be discouraged from worshipping images of Christ and the saints. Montúfar ordered the works' recall from circulation in April 1560. In 1563 the Crown issued a formal ban on the *Diálogo,* which was ultimately overturned by the Suprema by 1588.[70]

To Gilberti and many Franciscans, the discouragement of promoting the images of saints among the Indians made perfect sense given their concerns about veneration of pre-Hispanic deities. When, in January 1561, Gilberti was called before the inquisitor ordinary acting on Montúfar's behalf — the provisor Portillo — he admitted that he had written about discouraging the worship of images. Gilberti had written a dialogue in which a master and pupil discuss matters of the faith. The master in the dialogue said that one should not worship images because the image itself was not God, Jesus, Mary, or a saint but only a reminder of the mercy of the divine. This was recognized as a potential iconoclastic heresy, but Gilberti argued that the problem was linguistic and that he had a difficult time translating the fundamental concept of divine symbolism into Purépecha. Linguistics aside, he maintained that it would be best to discourage the Indians from venerating images so as to avoid idolatry. Portillo did not recommend a judgment against Gilberti, though the *Diálogo* had been banned.[71]

As the censorship trial against Gilberti's works transpired, Pérez Gordillo was determined not only to see Gilberti's works banned, but also to have the missionary arrested and tried himself. The chantre denounced Gilberti for a variety of public opinions.[72] Among these, according to Pérez Gordillo, was that Gilberti had supposedly taught the Indians that the end of the world was near and that when it came only the friars would remain faithful to the Church. Such a view was hardly unique among the Franciscans. The difference was that there was evidence that a missionary openly preached this eschatology to the Indians in a likely attack on the diocesan clergy. The outcome of this charge remains a bit nebulous since Gilberti was never formally convicted of heresy.

Another high-profile censorship case involved one of the cofounders of the University of Mexico, the Augustinian Alonso de la Veracruz. Yet while De la Veracruz was a student of Vitoria, a scholastic theologian, and a formidable intellectual in his own right (writing treatises on law, the sacraments, and missionary activities), he riled Montúfar's efforts to cleanse Mexico (like Spain) of humanism.[73] De la Veracruz waged intellectual battles with the archbishop-inquisitor. As early as 1554 he acted as a censor, reviewing books before publication. He received the humanist Cervantes de Salazar's commentaries on Luis Vives, *Commentaria in Ludovici Vives exercitationes linguae latinae*, giving it his approval. De la Veracruz also defended Gilberti against charges of heresy, approving Gilberti's *Diálogo*.

But it was De la Veracruz's opposition to tithing the Indians that landed him in trouble with the inquisitor. In his treatise *De decimis* he argued that the Indians could not be obliged to pay tithes because they would only support the diocesan clergy and that the Indians were too poor to pay the tithe in any case. He also had argued that there was no need for a diocesan Church in the Americas and that friar-missionaries were sufficient for the administration of the new Church.[74] The Dominican considered De la Veracruz's ideas so contumacious that he denounced him to the Spanish General Inquisition for heresy. In his letter to the Suprema, dated January 31, 1558, Montúfar singled out no fewer than eighty-four propositions of De la Veracruz for condemnation, many of which he called heretical. Close behind Montúfar followed Ledesma, who signed a brief (*parecer*) along with Montúfar condemning the Augustinian scholastic.[75] Montúfar then wrote to Philip II on June 20, claiming that De la Veracruz was attempting to "found a new Church" in the Indies by asserting that only the mendicants had authority to catechize.

De la Veracruz appealed his case, which Montúfar had submitted to the General Council directly, and he was absolved by Philip II and the Suprema but not before he crossed the Atlantic to insist that Montúfar was an obdurate tyrant. De la Veracruz was also able to successfully defend the mendicant privileges which Montúfar and Quiroga had been attacking before the Council of the Indies and have most of them restored by Pius V in 1568. De la Veracruz was instrumental in having the proclamation *Bvlla confirmationis et novae concessionis priuilegiorum Mendicantium* (Bull of the Confirmation and New Concession of the Mendicant Privileges) published in Mexico in 1568. But much of the damage had been done. Despite Montúfar's enforcement of a centralized Tridentine Church in Mexico he did not enforce the Index with nearly the same level of verve.[76] This was probably the result of his tendency to delegate authority to vicarious representatives of diocesan power and of his physical debility, which left him ill and virtually bedridden for most of the final years of his tenure as archbishop-inquisitor.

Gilberti and De la Veracruz were not the only influential clerics to have faced the wrath of the Dominican archbishop-inquisitor. Montúfar and his cadre of advisors also proceeded against numerous other clerics for moral and intellectual infractions. The most notorious of these trials were the lengthy imbroglios between two principal factions in the viceregal capital. One was led by the cathedral archdeacon and later dean, don Alonso Chico de Molina, who also represented the Cortés faction and the Franciscans who sympathized with him and who had grown leery of Montúfar and Quiroga's repeated attacks on mendicant privilege and conquistador-family power. The other faction was led by Montúfar, who represented the Dominicans and a substantial portion of the diocesan clergy, including Barbosa. There was first an informal caucus trial in 1560 against Chico de Molina, followed by bitter and rancorous feuds in the cathedral chapter, a second trial against Chico de Molina, and finally the treasonous conspiracy of Martín Cortés to overthrow the viceroy and install himself as emperor of Mexico. Chico de Molina had enlisted in the conspiracy. All the while ecclesial and academic politics swirled about. Chico de Molina was no straw man, but whereas De la Veracruz and Gilberti were either shrewd enough or lucky enough to have been spared the ignominy of an inquisitional conviction, the same cannot be said for Chico de Molina, who spent a good portion of the 1560s battling Montúfar and Ledesma and losing every time.

Chico de Molina, like Gilberti, was caught in forces much larger than himself. On his arrival in Mexico in 1554 Montúfar began his counterreform not only ideologically but also politically. He stacked the archdiocesan cathedral chapter with cronies and relatives, giving his nephew Bravo de Lagunas a seat on the council within weeks of his arrival. He treated the cathedral dignitaries with haughty disdain, often refusing to attend their meetings despite his role as archbishop. On one occasion Lagunas, along with another nephew and crony of Montúfar, Juan Cabello, left the meeting in a huff, after the chapter's secretary contradicted Lagunas on a procedural point. In turn, Montúfar's servant, Lázaro de Álamo, called the secretary a bastard and slapped him. Viceroy Luis de Velasco insisted that Montúfar punish his servant, but Montúfar never did. This was the climate fostered by the former censor of Granada as he ran the archdiocesan court.[77]

Much has been made of the controversies of Montúfar and Chico de Molina. Recent scholarship suggests that rather than a full-press attempt at revolution the investigations and executions of Cortés's partisans contained considerable procedural illegalities and were intended to punish a specific faction rather than dispense justice.[78] Likewise it is now clear that Chico de Molina's encounters with Montúfar were not isolated events. For example, shortly after arriving in Mexico Montúfar jailed both the archdeacon Juan de Zurnero and the maestrescuela Sánchez de Muñón for disobedience. By 1561 the cathedral chapter itself was complaining to the king that the new archbishop-inquisitor was a tyrant. The charges seem to have stuck, as eventually the crown dispatched an inspector, Jerónimo de Valderrama, to investigate the claims.[79]

The new cathedral archdeacon, Chico de Molina, had been in Mexico for only six months when, on September 5, 1560, he attended a dinner party at the archbishop's quarters along with Ledesma and the prior of Santo Domingo, Diego de Osorio. According to statements made by witnesses an argument about the sacraments had broken out, and Chico de Molina claimed that those already in a state of grace did not receive grace from the sacraments.[80] The Dominicans Ledesma and Osorio had attacked Chico de Molina for this, and it was reported not only that Chico de Molina refused to relent or recant, but also that at one point he grabbed Osorio by the coat, telling him that "not even he and his entire black order" could force him to recant. On informing the archdeacon that Trent had differed with him, Chico de Molina noted, in a supreme twist of theological irony for the Dominicans, that since Trent had yet to receive papal approval, its decrees were not binding. The next day Ledesma came before his colleague Montúfar to denounce the archdeacon.[81]

At the ensuing trial Chico de Molina's potentially Lutheran rejection of the sacraments as well as his anti-Trent sentiment was put on display before an illustrious group of theological and juridical advisors brought in to offer expert testimony. No fewer than eleven formal opinions were written before the case was closed. Priors of the major mendicant houses of Mexico-Tenochtitlan were called in, as were the judges of the Audiencia. All told it was an impressive team of some of the leading intellectual figures of Mexico. That the leaders of the Mexican political-intellectual elite would be called should not be surprising: Chico de Molina was a symbol of everything the enemies of Montúfar stood for, and the archbishop-inquisitor as well as Ledesma was determined to make an example of him. By the same token, Montúfar realized that Chico de Molina had powerful allies and that he could not afford to alienate them with the appearance of hubris. The Dominicans were also worried that the case would spiral beyond their control. Anguis, Montúfar's provisor, suggested that the entire case be sent to the Suprema for adjudication.[82] Meanwhile, Chico de Molina had met with Augustinians and Franciscans at San Francisco for advice. They had written the equivalent of amicus briefs in his favor stating that while the archdeacon's behavior may have been rash, it was certainly not heretical. The briefs were then entrusted to De la Veracruz for safekeeping. The trial record eventually would include them, and they provide telling clues about the nature of theological debate in the viceregal capital imbued with high-stakes politics.

Montúfar accorded two of the witnesses against the accused, Ledesma and Osorio, the right to give expert theological advice (calificación). Inquisitional law stated that witnesses in inquisitional trials could not make statements with ulterior motives, as Suárez explained in various places.[83] Chico de Molina was well aware of the legal errors of the case. Anguis had tried to convince Chico de Molina to accept correction from the archbishop, which he refused. Finally, after testimonies from Osorio and Ledesma were heard, Chico de Molina was called before Montúfar on September 9. The archdeacon impugned the inquisitor's authority and demanded that Montúfar recuse himself.[84] His argument was that Osorio and especially Ledesma were Montúfar's close companions. Moreover, he claimed that Montúfar was well known to harbor ill will toward him and was therefore disqualified from judging the case. Inquisitional law provided for the disqualification of testimonies from "known enemies" of the accused.

Montúfar was not pleased. He ordered the Augustinians Antonio de San Isidro, prior of San Agustín in Mexico City, and Joseph de Herrera, lector in theology, to appear on September 13 and provide written opinions on the matter. Much to the archbishop-inquisitor's displeasure, in their view Chico de Molina's statements about the sacraments did not even merit inquisitional censure. They concluded that his statement that Trent had no authority was bad sounding and scandalous because it was uttered publicly.[85] Their assessment stood in sharp contrast to the theology of the other advisors. The Augustinians were in close alliance with De la Veracruz, and it would be the Augustinians who dominated the theological faculty two years later when Chico de Molina was named to the prime chair of theology at the University of Mexico. It was all but certain that in refusing to return a recommendation of heresy the Augustinian censors were giving their enemy Montúfar the back of their hand politically. They surely had not forgotten the fire at Tlazazalca only three months earlier, known to have been the direct result of Quiroga's policies, and his ally Montúfar was painted with the same broad brush by the mendicants.

Montúfar continued his illegal actions by calling Ledesma and Osorio as censors in the case. From September 13 to 22, the Dominicans offered their opinions. Osorio concluded that Chico de Molina's statements about the sacraments at the very least "smacked of heresy."[86] Juan de Ozpina called the same statements heresy outright — for suggesting both that the sacraments did not confer grace by their inherent nature and that a person in a state of grace did not need the sacraments. Ozpina defined the rejection of the legitimacy of Trent as "temerious" but not manifestly heretical.[87]

Whereas Osorio and Ozpina limited themselves to brief statements, Ledesma employed lengthy metaphysical arguments for the efficacy of the sacraments. Ledesma was himself Montúfar's designated sacramental theologian, and he asked whether someone's rejection of the instrumental salvation of the sacraments had to be understood in the context of the Crucifixion and Resurrection of Christ. For Ledesma, Chico de Molina had effectively rejected the soteriological value of the blood of Christ given that the Eucharist presumes to represent that blood. Therefore, such a view rejected the instrumentality of the Law of the New Testament as given in Galatians 3, in which Paul explained that the Old Law was abolished to free the Christian from its burden by the efficacy of the New Law, meaning the grace of Christ — specifically, through the sacrament of baptism: "For all of you who were baptized into Christ have clothed yourself with Christ."[88] The former prior of Santo Domingo in Mexico-Tenochtitlan and censor of Zumárraga's *Doctrina*, Domingo de la Cruz, applied the exact same scriptural proof of Galatians 3 for his conclusion that Chico de Molina's rejection of the innate power of the sacraments was heretical.[89] Along with Galatians, Ledesma relied on the canons of Trent and Florence, which stated that "the sacraments of the New Law contain and confer grace."[90]

When it came to the sacrament of the Eucharist, Ledesma unequivocally condemned Chico de Molina's view as heretical. His authority was the Council of Trent, which had anathematized anyone who rejected the sacraments.

Ledesma's explanations, in consonance with those of Trent, relied on the ecclesiological notion that only within the Church was one saved and that those who, like Luther, suggested that salvation could be obtained by faith alone without the Church and its sacraments were heretics. Ledesma saw scriptural proof for this in John 6:53-54 when Christ spoke of the Eucharist: "Amen, amen, I say to you, unless you eat the flesh of the Son of Man and drink his blood, you do not have life within you. Whoever eats my flesh and drinks my blood has eternal life." For Ledesma this was proof of the soteriological efficacy — indeed, the exclusivity — of the Eucharist.[91] Concerning Chico de Molina's rejection of Trent's authority, Ledesma stopped short of calling it heresy. This was likely a nod to the Torquemada line that councils had force of law only after papal approval, in opposition to the conciliar line, which saw councils as binding legal custom.

Rafael de Cervantes, the onetime prosecutor for Zumárraga, secular cleric, and doctor of theology, offered his calificación on September 22. He suggested that Chico de Molina's statements about the sacraments could have been the result of ignorance, but that by all appearances they were dangerous and similar to Luther's views on the inefficacy of the sacraments for salvation. Cervantes did not call them heretical but made the point about the dangers of ordinary people hearing such ideas when they otherwise would be uninfected with such heresies — a near perfect rendition of Aquinas's (and Innocent III's) discussion of the dangers of debating the faith coram simplicibus.[92] Cervantes was not alone in stating this concern. Domingo de la Cruz employed the same argument about the "dangers of these times" in arguing that it was "scandalous especially in this time when it leads to the contempt of the sacraments and drives men away from devotion and from the participation in them."[93]

But it was the Franciscan Juan Focher who put up the strongest theological opposition to Montúfar's case. Understanding the case in terms of the metaphor of infection and heresy, he argued that the suggestion that the sacraments did not contain or confer grace by their nature was condemned by numerous authorities, most recently Trent. Focher thus saw the various statements about the sacraments as dangerous and scandalous, but he stopped short of calling them heretical. His combined use of theologians like Saint Bonaventure, the *Decretales* and the *Decretum,* and conciliar authority made the lengthy review appear to be a condemnation of Chico de Molina. In two separate written opinions Focher argued that such propositions could "scandalize and perturb the faithful" and that their propinquity to heresy "in these days allows heretics to defend their errors" with the same statements.[94]

Just as Castro argued that heretics slay the faithful with "unseen javelins" and as Innocent III argued that "heretics creep more stealthily in the open," so

Focher understood the potential of heretical-seeming ideas to allow heretics to "trick" the faithful. Thus Focher reprimanded the propositions of Chico de Molina, concluding that they were "propinquitous to errors of heretics."[95] Focher was also the only censor to make the connection between Chico de Molina's statements and Donatism by pointing out that the efficacy of the sacraments and their ability to confer and contain grace bore no relationship to the ministers of the sacraments—borrowing a refrain from Augustine's attacks on the Donatists.[96]

But Focher's conclusion took a different direction. He repeatedly argued that Chico de Molina's statements were condemned by theologians and by Trent but refrained from judging them outright heresy. His conclusion would surely not have been what Montúfar, Ledesma, or Osorio had anticipated. Focher concluded that Chico de Molina was in fact innocent of any error and should be exonerated: "I assert that in nothing in the aforementioned did he err . . . and that concerning these propositions there is nothing worth being punished. And this matter having been brought and decided, it must be declared that he is innocent and must be absolved of the crime of which he was accused."[97] Focher's rationale was that those not explicitly guilty of heresy ought not to be judged harshly, lest they be lost entirely from the Church. Thus he relied on Romans 13: 3 in conclusion: "For rulers are not a terror to good conduct, but to bad. Do you wish to have no fear of the authority? Then do what is good, and you will receive its approval, for it is God's servant for your good." Focher did not clarify how this tied in to exonerating the statements of Chico de Molina, but one can suppose that the words only drove the wedge that much further between the Dominicans (via Montúfar and Ledesma) and the Franciscans. Focher's conclusion was also likely a carefully orchestrated attack on Montúfar. Focher, along with De la Veracruz, was one of the principal mendicants who strove to preserve the privileges of the papal bulls of 1521 and 1522 and was a bitter enemy of Montúfar.

In any case Chico de Molina saw the political balance tipping in Montúfar's favor and opted to confess on September 25 despite his attempt to have Montúfar recused from the trial. In the chambers of Montúfar and realizing that if he did not confess he could easily be harshly punished, his pride gave way to expedience. Montúfar fined him two hundred pesos (a substantial sum in an era when a parish priest could expect to earn a little less than that in a year) and ordered him never to repeat similar statements in the future. He was also ordered not to mention the trial in any form.[98]

Further developments complicated this uneasy détente. On November 5 reports came to Montúfar that Chico de Molina had preached a public sermon despite the ban placed on him. Montúfar conferred with his legal advisors.

The jurists—the provisor Anguis and the Audiencia judges Villalobos and Vasco de Puga and the Audiencia prosecutor Maldonado—as well as the cathedral canon Cervantes de Salazar argued for the transferal of the trial to the General Council in Spain.[99] In what must have been an infuriating rebuke to Montúfar, the archdeacon was vindicated when the Suprema overturned the ruling against him sometime in 1561, though the exculpatory sentence was lost at sea.[100]

The various calificaciones of Chico de Molina's statements turn a microscope on Mexican ecclesiastical and theological politics of the 1550s and 1560s. The university had been recently established in 1553, and the Dominicans did not dominate it in the way they had that of Salamanca. The Augustinians, who chafed at Montúfar's Tridentine centralism, rebuked the archbishop-inquisitor by refusing to hand down a calificación supporting a claim of heresy. The Franciscan Focher rejected Montúfar's designs outright, claiming that Chico de Molina was not only not guilty of heresy but of nothing in particular. On the other hand, Montúfar's allies, the Dominicans, despite the illegality of their presence, supported Montúfar's trial against Chico de Molina wholeheartedly.

By 1562 Chico de Molina was elected to the prime chair in theology at the university by order of the viceroy and the Audiencia, both enemies of Montúfar.[101] The cathedral chapter at this time was rent by the deep factionalism of the anti-Montúfar bloc, led by Chico de Molina, and the pro-Montúfar, anti–Chico de Molina group, led by Barbosa. It was no accident that the principal enemy of the archbishop-inquisitor was given the prime chair of theology. Many saw Montúfar and Ledesma as imperious and much too active in the application of their view of ecclesiastical order. One cannot discount either the influence of De la Veracruz, who had populated the university with his pupils and still held a prime chair of theology in 1562, when Chico de Molina was given the other prime chair. The chair in arts was held in 1562 by another Augustinian, Herrera, who, along with fray Isidro, had opted to qualify Chico de Molina's statement about Trent as merely bad sounding, a significantly lesser charge than heresy. Holding the chair of grammar was the humanist Cervantes de Salazar, who may have been a neutral party but whose humanism would have made him suspect to the Dominican conservatives. De la Veracruz's approval of Cervantes's commentaries on Luis Vives as well as his approval of Gilberti's works prior to publication had placed the Augustinian in Montúfar's sights. While it would be impossible to gauge the psychological motives for the election of Chico de Molina to the chair of theology, it is clear that the faculty of 1562 was anything but friendly to Montúfar. The election of the archdeacon would have been an infuriating rebuke to the Dominican inquisitor, and De la Veracruz and his pupils understood its symbolism as well as its practical fallout.

Chico de Molina was apparently emboldened by events following his first trial. He appears to have pushed his position forcefully, so much so that Montúfar filed a lawsuit against him after Chico de Molina began to say that he was not required to obey the archbishop as his superior. It was rumored that he may even have asked Montúfar's forgiveness, but the archbishop-inquisitor viewed the apology as false, and in a letter to the king in 1563 he called Chico de Molina a Judas.[102] By 1564 Chico de Molina was dean of the Mexico City cathedral chapter, and in the spring he made the first of a series of career-ending mistakes: he initiated a proceeding in the Inquisition against both Ledesma and Barbosa. It is difficult to fathom the political myopia of such a move, given that Montúfar was inquisitor and Ledesma his right-hand man and that Barbosa was Montúfar's provisor of the archdiocese. The cathedral dean probably thought he could force the hand of the inquisitor and possibly have Barbosa removed from office by the power of the cathedral chapter over which he ostensibly ruled. Instead, Chico de Molina's effort was repaid in a spectacular volte-face: he was himself accused of heresy, though the final outcome of the reverse trial is apparently lost.[103]

The charge that Chico de Molina leveled against Ledesma was not entirely clear. The cathedral dean claimed that Ledesma had preached certain heretical propositions, though these were not specified.[104] Testimonies indicate that Ledesma may have preached something about rich and poor alike being able to enter heaven, though the witnesses insisted that they were rather unclear on the nature of the intellectual scuffle. Ledesma was anything but vague, saying that the cathedral dean was "known in all this territory as his mortal enemy."[105] Ledesma was quickly informed of the charge against him by his crony Montúfar. Someone merely accused within the confines of an inquisitional court was not supposed to be informed of a potential trial against him and certainly was not supposed to have the luxury of knowing the identity of the accuser at the outset. This had been standard procedure for centuries, and inquisitors were admonished that, in general, to break the secrecy of the deposition would lead to the anarchic dissolution of the integrity of the system as well as to concatenations of backbiting. It appears that Montúfar informed Ledesma of the charge based on the "mortal enemy" exception. Thus Ledesma stated, "Don Alonso Chico de Molina has said and published before many people, affirming that I have said certain heretical and bad-sounding propositions in the pulpit or outside of it against our holy catholic faith . . . therefore I ask and supplicate your reverence [Montúfar] that the said dean appear before you and swear what the propositions are that I have said and that if he has them written that he show them."[106] The effort of Chico de Molina was flummoxed, and Montúfar, along with Anguis and Sedeño, acting as judges, found no cause to continue with the trial beyond taking depositions, reiterating Ledesma's right to preach publicly.[107]

On the same day that the cathedral dean came forward to denounce Ledesma — April 20, 1564 — he simultaneously leveled a charge against Barbosa, who had apparently made a sarcastic remark in a sermon that if men committed adultery, it would only be fair if their wives repaid them in kind.[108] Attacking Ledesma would have sufficed to seal his career but planning a stealth attack in what appears to have been an attempt to oust Barbosa from the cathedral chapter only made Chico de Molina's strategy fail more grandly. Perhaps he had counted on the support of the other canons and dignitaries of the cathedral chapter to back up his version of Barbosa's "scandalous, heretical and bad-sounding propositions." Instead, Barbosa enlisted various members of the chapter as witnesses for his defense, including the maestrescuela, don Sancho de Sánchez Muñón. The result of the two cases was that Montúfar and Barbosa leveled a proceeding and accusation of heresy against Chico de Molina. It is contained in the same case files as the information and accusation against Barbosa but does not include an arrest order, formal audiencia with Chico de Molina, or sentence from Montúfar, who acted as judge in the two proceedings begun by Chico de Molina. Consequently, one is left to speculate as to the exact outcome.

In the summer of 1566 Montúfar sentenced Chico de Molina to permanent exile from New Spain for his presumed role in the Martín Cortés conspiracy. He was ordered to return to Spain to answer charges that he was involved in the seditious plans of Martín Cortés to overthrow the viceroy and install himself as the sovereign of an independent Mexican kingdom.[109] He was accused of treason, stripped of his ecclesiastical *fueros* (exemptions from civil court prosecution and torture), and judicially tortured, leaving him a literally broken and defeated man. Because the conclusion of the second trial against the dean for heresy, begun in 1564, is no longer extant, it is difficult to determine whether this recall was strictly a royal decision or whether Montúfar engineered it as inquisitor. Even after Montúfar had rid himself of Chico de Molina his venomous hatred for the dean continued, noting in a letter to the king of January 31, 1568 that Chico de Molina had said that he considered the archbishop the most evil man in the world.[110] Regardless of the machinations, it is clear from the trials against high-profile clerics like De la Veracruz, Gilberti, Chico de Molina, and Zumárraga (via his literary memory) that Montúfar intended to reform the Mexican Church more through the stick than the carrot and that he was willing to stake both his political fate and his historical legacy on his vision of a tightly controlled Tridentine Church—an approach the mendicants opposed every step of the way. The tool of inquisitional censure was for Montúfar the rod he employed in attempting to bring what he viewed as the much too independent Franciscans and Augustinians into line. Yet in 1561 the first holder of the prime chair of theology, the Dominican Pedro de la Peña, had been accused of heresy by none other than Chico de Molina. Instead of calling in censors and initiating a vigorous investigation, as he did in the case against Chico de Molina, Montúfar allowed De la Peña to write his own defense and never investigated the charge—a clear illegality.[111] For Montúfar, De la Peña's word was good enough for exculpation. That the original accusation had come from Montúfar's archenemy also seemed to clarify the archbishop-inquisitor's view of the law in favor of ignoring it. The maxim that politicians believe not in principles but in expedience was never so clear.

As Montúfar's health steadily declined in the late 1560s the archdiocese and the Inquisition, which operated as part of the archbishop's portfolio of power, was controlled increasingly by his trusted surrogates: Portillo as provisor and Ledesma as governor of the archdiocese. The last Inquisition trial in which Montúfar acted as a judge was in 1565.[112] By 1568 it was rumored that the archbishop was virtually bedridden, and by 1569 he began to disappear from correspondence, suggesting that he may have been suffering from dementia.[113] By 1570 the archdiocesan Inquisition under Montúfar's authority was run almost exclusively by Portillo, who had adjudicated eight cases in 1569, ten in 1570 (one of which Barbosa also adjudicated), and ten in 1571. Ledesma also prosecuted three cases in 1571.[114] In any case the stage was set for the shift in power from the Dominican- and friar-run Inquisitions to the modern, jurist-run Inquisition that would replace them.

Censorship and censure formed an integral part of the early Mexican Inquisition. Debates over the education of the Indians, humanism, and the relationship between diocesan and mendicant control of the Church all sparked notable efforts of control of print and speech. In many cases there were no formal trials, as happened when Ledesma and Montúfar denounced De la Veracruz to the Suprema, which, it seems, did not take up the case. In other instances, Montúfar asserted his authority as inquisitor to ban works printed in Mexico, such as those by Gilberti and Zumárraga. And in the case of Chico de Molina, Ledesma and Montúfar crushed a powerful opponent within the diocesan administration and university and replaced him with their own man: Ledesma. The overall image one derives from the Montúfar Inquisition and censure is one of the implementation of an organized cudgel of control.

6

The Holy Office Established, 1571–90

In 1569 an assembly was convened in the Council of the Indies to discuss the restructuring of the administration of the overseas holdings of the Spanish empire. As part of this change the Council of the Indies recommended the establishment of independent tribunals of the Holy Office for Lima and Mexico. The result was that the Suprema commissioned the jurist Moya de Contreras as inquisitor general and Juan de Cervantes and Alfonso Fernández Bonilla as prosecutors (*fiscales*).[1] In November 1571 the formal tribunal of the Holy Office of the Inquisition was physically established in Mexico. Unlike the previous diocesan Inquisitions that held only local authority or even the apostolic Inquisition of Zumárraga and Montúfar, the new tribunal held universal jurisdiction over all of New Spain, from Costa Rica to Durango (and, eventually, New Mexico). The next two decades witnessed the solidification of the Holy Office in Mexico and its rapid ideological specialization. Beginning in 1571 the first censors (calificadores) were appointed, formally marking the professional division within the Inquisition between jurists and theologians as well as establishing censors as a central component of inquisitional procedure. Having served as inquisitor general, Moya de Contreras became archbishop of Mexico in 1573 and in 1585 convened the Third Mexican Provincial Church Council, which established the basic rules of ecclesiastical governance of the Mexican Church for centuries.

Moya de Contreras was born around 1530 in Pedroche, in northwestern Córdoba, to a family of the lower nobility. He attended the University of Salamanca, where he studied canon and civil law; he subsequently earned his doctorate in canon law either from Salamanca or the University of Seville. His career flourished under the patronage of Juan de Ovando. By the mid-1560s Moya de Contreras was appointed maestrescuela of the cathedral chapter of the Canaries, while his patron, Ovando, was promoted from provisor of the archdiocese of Seville to a seat on the General Council of the Spanish Inquisition. Eventually, Ovando, through the influence of Cardinal Espinosa, was appointed visitador of the Council of the Indies in 1567. Ovando found the administration of the Indies in a sorry state of disarray and would recommend the meeting of 1569. While Ovando was still conducting his inspection of the council in 1569, Moya de Contreras was appointed inquisitor of Murcia. Shortly beforehand Philip II had signed the royal order commissioning a formal tribunal of the Holy Office in Mexico on January 25, 1569. Moya de Contreras served little time in Murcia; in August 1570 he was named inquisitor of the newly established tribunal of the Holy Office in Mexico. Moya de Contreras left Seville with his prosecutors Cervantes and Bonilla and secretary Pedro de los Ríos, but the entourage was stranded in the Canaries from November 1570 to June 1571, having missed their connecting ship headed for Hispaniola. On June 2 they managed to find passage to the Indies, and, on their arrival in Cuba, Cervantes died of fever. Setting out for Mexico, on August 1, Moya de Contreras and De los Ríos ran aground, fled in a small boat, and found passage on yet another boat. On August 18, 1571, in what surely would have been sweltering heat, they arrived in Veracruz.

Martín Enríquez de Almansa, lord of Valderrábano, was viceroy of New Spain from 1568 to 1580. He was born into the higher nobility of Spain, a descendant of Castilian royalty. When Moya de Contreras made his journey from Veracruz to Mexico City he was greeted by three cathedral canons outside of Mexico City. When he entered the city on September 12, 1571, the usual dignitaries arrived to greet him, but the Audiencia members and the viceroy were notably absent. Enríquez's absence was not accidental but rather a carefully planned political and social snub which was repeated by other viceroys over the years. During Moya de Contreras's short term as inquisitor he would spar often with the viceroy. Concerning their first meeting, before which a large crowd had gathered to observe, Moya de Contreras complained in a letter to Ovando that the viceroy kept him standing and did not ask him to cover his head, thus offending his hidalgo honor. Numerous other symbolic acts of political war broke out: Enríquez balked at taking an oath to the Inquisition, though eventually he did so; the viceroy also originally refused to give Inquisition officials a place to sit in the cathedral sanctuary; Moya de Contreras insisted that the viceroy bow to the inquisitional authority in issuing travel licenses to leave New Spain.

Finally, on Sunday, November 4, 1571, the formal oath taking and installation of the Inquisition in Mexico took place, with all manner of pomp. Moya de Contreras processed with the reluctant viceroy, the senior Audiencia oidor, government officials, and the faculty of the university. At the cathedral church the canons and representatives of the Dominican, Franciscan, and Augustinian orders greeted him. The archbishop Montúfar, who had been bedridden for years, was too ill to attend the ceremony. Ledesma, acting as governor of the archdiocese, read the sermon for the official swearing-in ceremony. But if Moya de Contreras seemed to have triumphed over Enríquez with the ceremony, in which the viceroy was forced to swear fealty to the Inquisition, Enríquez in turn refused to allow the inquisitor to read the Index of Prohibited Books in the cathedral. As was often the case, the Inquisition, despite its authority, could not always convince the civil officials of their legal fealty to the Holy Office.

Within this climate of distrust for the inquisitional office and authority Moya de Contreras entered his tenure. Despite this atmosphere, the new inquisitor proved equal to the task. He oversaw the vigorous prosecution of English and French pirates; enforced the Index of 1559 and commissioned a wide-ranging and ambitious purge; prosecuted and convicted important printers and later laid the foundations of the administrative structure of the Mexican Church as archbishop in the Third Mexican Council of the Church in 1585. He was also commissioned to conduct a visita of the notoriously corrupt Audiencia in the early 1580s.

After Moya de Contreras left his position as inquisitor general of Mexico, other jurists followed.[2] Bonilla, licenciado in Spain and later doctor in canon law at the University of Mexico, was the fiscal of the Mexican tribunal from 1571 until 1573, when he was elevated to inquisitor in Moya de Contreras's place, a position he would hold until at least 1592. That year he was nominated to replace the deceased Moya de Contreras as archbishop of Mexico, although he did not live to take physical possession. Another jurist, Alfonso Granero Dávalos, accompanied Bonilla as inquisitor from 1574 to 1577 (after being prosecutor in 1574 briefly), and by 1579 he had been appointed bishop of La Plata in Bolivia. Replacing Dávalos and Bonilla as fiscal in 1575 was Francisco Santos García, a canon in the Mexico City cathedral chapter and founder of the prestigious Colegio de Santa María de Todos Santos, corporate home of numerous powerful criollos of the sixteenth and seventeenth centuries, including Cortés's grandson.[3] Like so many of the new generation of jurists who came to dominate the various Spanish Inquisitions, Santos García was promoted from fiscal to inquisitor in 1580. He eventually received the miter of New Galicia (Guadalajara). The overall picture of the men who came to run the newly founded Mexican Holy Office was that of career-oriented ecclesiastical administrators of the highest level, trained in law and viewing the Inquisition as a formal court of law in ways that theologians would never have conceptualized.[4]

In the context of the new jurist inquisitors, the office of the censor was formalized within the Mexican Inquisition. While during the various diocesan Inquisitions and even under Montúfar's apostolic Inquisition there were theologians called on to act as temporary censors, after 1571 the inquisitor general of the Holy Office in Mexico was empowered to appoint permanent censors as his auxiliaries, as well as consultores, comisarios, civil deputies (familiares), bailiffs (*alguaciles*), and notaries.

With this professional specialization came increased reliance on censors for their advice on doctrinal points. Whereas in the local Inquisitions as well as during Montúfar's Inquisition theologians often acted as inquisitors themselves, with the dominance of jurists in the inquisitional office also came the need to consult with theologian-censors for clarification of doctrinal points. This could be seen both in terms of the prevalence of censors in the proceedings as well as in the shifting landscape of inquisitional personnel.

Quantitatively this shift was profound. During Zumárraga's Inquisition, advisors were used in very few cases — fewer than 10 percent in fact. The same can be said of Montúfar's as well as of various local diocesan Inquisitions. After 1571, however, theologian censors were called with rapidly increasing frequency. In cases involving doctrinal disputes — suspect oral statements, heresy, blasphemy, and superstitious activities — in this period censors were called at a rate of about 30 percent of the time (tables 6.1, 6.2). Moreover, the newly established Holy Office proved to be extremely active and vigorous, terminating on average more than thirty-two trials per year from its inception in November 1571 until the end of 1579, making it quantifiably the most vigorous period between 1527 and 1640. While doctrinal cases came under the increasing scrutiny of censors, issues involving either clear violations of inquisitional law — like Judaizing — or in which there was no specific doctrinal issue involved — like bigamy, attacks on inquisitional jurisdiction (desacato), escape from prison, or prosecution of inquisitional officials for civil crimes for which they had immunity — censors were rarely, if ever, consulted. The result was that the censors came to represent a highly specialized kind of expert on whom jurists relied to elucidate the finer points of doctrine and ideology.

The data show that censors were quickly incorporated into inquisitional

Table 6.1. *Inquisitional Cases, 1571–79*

Charge	Number of cases	Number of cases with censors	Percentage of cases with censors	Percentage of caseload
Bigamy	90	0	0.0	31.4
Heresy	63	21	33.3	21.9
Propositions	44	17	38.6	15.3
Blasphemy	16	6	37.5	5.6
Desacato	13	1	7.7	4.5
Querella	10	0	0.0	3.5
Flight	8	0	0.0	2.8
False testimony	7	0	0.0	2.4
Solicitation in confession	7	0	0.0	2.4
Processes of office	6	0	0.0	2.1
Apostasy[a]	6	0	0.0	2.1
Witchcraft	6	2	33.3	2.1
Judaizing	4	0	0.0	1.4
Imitating priest	3	1	33.3	1.0
Cohabitation	1	0	0.0	0.3
Idolatry	1	0	0.0	0.3
Inhábil[b]	1	0	0.0	0.3
Prohibited books	1	1	100.0	0.3
Doctrinal cases	152	48	31.6	53.0
Total cases	287	49	17.1	100.0

Source: AGN, Inquisición, volumes:
1A, 29, 46, 47, 48, 49, 50, 51, 52, 53, 54, 54bis, 55, 56, 57, 58, 59, 68, 69, 70, 71, 72, 74, 75, 76, 77, 78, 79, 80, 81, 82, 83, 84, 85, 88, 91, 92, 93, 94, 95, 96, 97, 98, 99, 100, 101, 102, 103, 104, 105, 106, 107, 108, 110, 111, 112, 113, 114, 115, 116, 117, 118, 128, 131, 134, 149, 175, 181, 184, 187, 212, 213, 224, 226, 1494

[a] The charge of apostasy ("renegarse") included priests who married while being priests and in doing so were considered apostates for violating their vows of chastity.
[b] Violating sumptuary punishments (like being stripped of the right to bear arms or ride a horse) for conviction of heresy.

procedures after the establishment of a central Holy Office in 1571. But numbers tell only part of the story. They reveal the extent to which certain inquisitors relied on theologian censors for their understanding of their position as defenders of the faith. By all appearances, the inquisitors in the 1570s and 1580s appear to have placed a good deal of confidence in their censors for the definition of heresy, blasphemy, and various offending statements.

Table 6.2. Inquisitional Cases, 1580–89

Charge	Number of cases	Number of cases with censors	Percentage of cases with censors	Percentage of caseload
Bigamy	29	0	0.0	22.5
Propositions	24	7	29.2	18.6
Solicitation in confession	16	0	0.0	12.4
Judaizing	12	0	0.0	9.3
Desacato	11	1	9.1	8.5
Blasphemy	7	0	0.0	5.4
Processes of office	7	0	0.0	5.4
Heresy	5	0	0.0	3.9
Sanbenitos	5	0	0.0	3.9
Witchcraft	4	0	0.0	3.1
Imitating priest	4	0	0.0	3.1
Inhábil	2	0	0.0	1.5
Querella	2	0	0.0	1.5
Flight	1	0	0.0	0.8
Doctrinal cases	77	7	9.1	59.7
Total cases	129	8	6.2	100.0

Source: AGN, Inquisición, volumes: 1A, 89, 90, 119, 120, 121, 122, 123, 124, 125, 126, 127, 129, 130, 131, 132, 133, 134, 135, 136, 137, 138, 139, 140, 143, 174, 175, 184, 232, 558, 1487, 1488, 1494, 1553

In addition to the quantitative preponderance of censors in trials involving censure of heterodoxy, the censors reflect their generally high social prestige. Even if these first censors were a diverse lot in terms of their corporate identities, they shared similar educational, social, and class backgrounds. While there is no internal documentary evidence to suggest that Moya de Contreras, Bonilla, or Dávalos had a specific agenda, the diversity of the censors seems to speak for itself. Fifteen censors were formally appointed from 1571 to 1590: seven Dominicans, four Franciscans, one Jesuit, one Augustinian, one secular priest, and one whose corporate identity is unknown.[5] The numbers suggest dominance by the Dominicans, which should not be surprising. The jurists who came to run the Inquisition were trained in canon law and hence would have understood the deep traditional associations between the Inquisition and the Order of Preachers. And it was no accident that the Inquisition was physically erected across the street from Santo Domingo.

The Mexican Holy Office was now under the reins of highly educated canon lawyers who would have been familiar both with the letter and spirit of *Ut commissi* as well as the various disputations on heresy and Inquisition of theorists like Eimeric, Peña, Villadiego, Rojas, Simancas, and Castro. Theological review as a process had been operative in the major tribunals of the Spanish Inquisition in the peninsula for some decades by 1571. The new inquisitors would have been well aware of the new trends in inquisitional procedure, which involved the deferral of complex doctrinal points to the theologians from the legally trained jurists. Cano, for one, had been called to review Carranza's catechism, as had other notable theologians.[6]

The new censors were accorded respect according to their uniformly high intellectual pedigree. The first generation of censors came from the upper ranks of ecclesiastical government and mendicant administration. Five of them would become bishops: Tomás Cárdenas of Verapaz, Bartolomé de Ledesma of Oaxaca, Domingo de Salazar of the Philippines, Juan Ramírez of Guatemala, and Pedro de Pravia, bishop elect of Panama.[7] A sixth, Alonso Noreña, ruled the bishopric of Chiapas sede vacante for several years as its governor, just as Ledesma had ruled the archdiocese of Mexico as Montúfar's governor.[8] In addition to their ascent into important diocesan administrative positions, the first generation of censors represented the upper echelons of the mendicant power structure. For example, the Augustinian Martín de Perea, a pupil of De la Veracruz, saw his role as defender of the prerogatives of mendicant privilege as well as of Thomist orthodoxy. While he completed his duties as censor he was also prior of San Agustín in Mexico City, one of the three most important mendicant houses.[9] The Dominican Pravia led Santo Domingo as its prior.[10] Both Perea and Pravia would hold the prime chair of theology at the University of Mexico, as would Ledesma. Perea, Pravia, and Ledesma were nearly always present for the censors' meetings (*juntas de calificación*) — the oral debates on heterodoxy — demonstrating the close links between the mendicant houses, the university theological faculty, and the inquisitional review process. The Franciscan employed in these meetings, Antonio de Quixada, was the exception to major administrative power, as he does not seem to have risen much higher than the guardianship of San Francisco in Guatemala, when he also served as an ad hoc censor for the diocesan Inquisition there.[11]

By contrast, the two nonmendicant censors employed in the juntas of the 1570s were hardly untrained or incompetent. Rodrigo de Barbosa had been inquisitor ordinary during Montúfar's tenure.[12] Pedro Sánchez was no less prestigious. Having been trained in Alcalá and professed in the Society of Jesus, Sánchez rose to the rectorship of the University of Alcalá — an academic position second only to the theology and law faculty of Salamanca.[13] He left behind one of the most prestigious academic careers to come to Mexico to establish the Jesuit province. He was the first provincial of the Jesuits in New Spain and was quickly appointed censor. These men, while not necessarily members of the highest socioeconomic elite of sixteenth-century Mexico, represented a highly ambitious group interested in the projects of conversion, catechesis, and development of the new Mexican Church.

In the daily operation of the Inquisition in this period, the review of suspect opinions tended to be carried out by committee, which meant that the Dominicans, in practice, did not dominate the tribunal to the extent that the numbers suggest. Rather, many of the censors were appointed to oversee such projects as the expurgation of books, the review of unexpurgated books, and the functioning of the tribunal at the local level. For example, the Dominicans Tomás de Cárdenas and Juan de Castro do not appear in archival documentation as censors per se and spent their careers in Guatemala for the most part. Alonso de Noreña spent his career as a comisario in Chiapas as well as a censor, active in rooting out suspect books and manuscripts and writing erudite opinions that he forwarded to the main office in Mexico City.

But when the time came for the inquisitors in Mexico City to call on censors, this period saw an almost uniformly consistent team drawn from among the following: Ledesma, Salazar, Pravia (as holder of the prime chair of theology at the university), Quixada, Sánchez, Perea (as professor of theology), and Barbosa. This review by a diverse group was intended to blunt the control of theological review by any one faction or ideological viewpoint.

In general, censors in this period lived in the orbit of the Mexican archdiocesan polity, residing in Mexico City in their orders' houses, and were called by the Inquisition for their advice in the physical chambers of the Inquisition. After the 1580s, a sizable number of censors remained in Mexico City, but increasingly the inquisitors also appointed censors in provincial cities or areas to act primarily as book correctors in libraries of religious houses or among the populace in general after the comisarios had recalled books. On other occasions, the inquisitors appointed noncensors as specific book correctors. One exception to this trend in the 1570s and 1580s occurred far to the south of Mexico City.

Moya de Contreras delegated wide authority to a group of Dominicans in Chiapas and Guatemala. The result was that the Dominicans increased their already significant power in that area and came to view it as largely their religious fiefdom. On February 15, 1573, Moya de Contreras wrote to Diego Carvajal, comisario of Guatemala, with lengthy instructions on his duties. Along with this missive Moya de Contreras commissioned the Dominicans Cárdenas (the former inquisitor ordinary), Castro (provincial of his order),

and Noreña to correct Bibles and other books needing expurgation.[14] Sometimes comisarios acted to delegate their authority — which usually included
the right to confiscate prohibited books — to friars to undertake the expurgation; for example, Cristóbal Miranda in the Yucatan in 1573 appointed fray
Thome de Arenas and fray Diego de Cañizares to correct Latin Bibles.[15] The
Oaxaca cathedral chapter dean and comisario, Sancho Alzorriz, did the same
when he informed the inquisitors in a letter of March 16, 1588, that he was
too ill to carry out the inspections of libraries and had delegated this authority
to various friars.[16] Moya de Contreras also delegated authority of doctrinal
review within the physical confines of the Guatemala comisario's bailiwick.[17]
The effect was to turn Guatemala and Chiapas into a satellite Inquisition with
much wider powers than those held by other provincial commissions.

Besides the establishment of censors, the tribunal and its inquisitors commissioned two other new offices central to the project of censorship, control,
and orthodoxy: the consultor and the comisario. The consultor was by definition a jurist who acted as an advisor on matters of law to the inquisitor. The
comisarios, on the other hand, were established as the vicars of the inquisitor
in the major cities and ports of New Spain — from Durango in the north to
Honduras in the south and all major cities in between, such as Zacatecas,
Guadalajara, Valladolid, Puebla, Oaxaca, Mérida, and Santiago de Guatemala. The comisario had various functions, the most important being the daily
operation of the Holy Office outside of Mexico City and its immediate en-
virons. This meant reading the annual edict of the faith and overseeing the
continual machinery of hearing testimonies and, if necessary, making arrests
of the accused when ordered to do so by the Inquisition.

In establishing censors, comisarios, and consultores — as well as the other
vital offices needed for the tribunal's operation — the Mexican Inquisition embarked on an ambitious project of jurisdictional centralization. For example,
Moya de Contreras insisted that the viceroy — his personal bête noire — did
not hold royal jurisdiction over pirates from John Hawkins's crew, but that the
Inquisition was commissioned to prosecute such men, since they were suspect
of Lutheran or Calvinist heresies.[18] The new inquisitors also began much more
vigorous enforcement of the Index, enjoining the comisarios to recall all prohibited books and issuing numerous redactions of the most common prohibited books. And, for the first time in fifty years of Spanish control of Mexico, official inquisitorial port controls in Veracruz were set up with the aim of
stemming the constant entry of prohibited books. The comisarios chosen by
the new inquisitors were men of relatively high learning and were expected to
uphold the new program of inquisitorial control. Ultimately, there occurred
within the Mexican Inquisition a radical shift of professional specialization
and separation of spheres of knowledge during the 1570s and 1580s.

Calificaciones

During the formative decades of the 1570s and 1580s, the Mexican Inquisition prosecuted the supposed major heresies, like Lutheranism and Erasmianism, with particular vigor, and on numerous occasions propositions sounding like such heresies were sent for review. The concern over European heresies was linked inexorably with the theorization of heresy as viral and infectious, and one would be hard-pressed to find in the case law of the day opinions that did not reproduce the rhetoric of jurisprudential theory — like that expressed by Innocent III or Páramo. Simultaneously, the tribunal prosecuted bigamy on a wide scale. This fell in line with several trends stemming from Trent and a move toward reining in the relatively liberal sexual mores of Spanish culture, which were at odds with the increasing conservatism of the Church. In the context of Mexico, many Spanish men had left wives behind in Spain, only to marry again in the Americas or take up with an Indian mistress. Moya de Contreras and Bonilla were determined to root out these men and punish them. Yet such a crime was viewed as not needing review by the censors but rather, Moya de Contreras once wrote, should be resolved to the extent that the accused understood their crimes without any need for lengthy theological peregrination.[19]

One of the common characteristics of the censors' reviews of this period was their brevity. While there were occasional cases in which censors wrote multipage opinions, in general they issued brief statements on the relative scale of the proposition under question. For example, Cristóbal de Gurrola Vizcaíno, a citizen of Seville, was accused of heresy in 1572 in Mexico City. Under review was his statement that if a man slept with an unmarried woman and paid for the sex it was not a mortal sin and that furthermore "he had read this in a book."[20] The censors Pravia, Ordóñez, and Perea did not share Gurrola's enthusiasm for premarital coitus and responded tersely that "this proposition is heretical." Inquisitor Moya de Contreras agreed with the assessment of the friars and convicted Gurrola of heresy, sentencing him to two hundred lashes and a fine.[21]

Opinions about sex formed their own subset of propositions for review both by the Inquisition and the censors. The most common idea to be prosecuted by the Inquisition was that fornication was not a sin, or that it was only a venial sin. As Castro had pointed out — and as the inquisitors and censors would have known — the difference between sin and heresy was thought. Therefore committing fornication, while considered a sin, was not heretical. But expressing the opinion that fornication was not a sin transformed the accused into a potential heretic. Usually, this kind of idea was not sent to censors and was considered manifest evidence of guilt. But more subtle variations on the theme of sexual mores were considered complex enough to warrant review by the censors. Sexual crimes of cohabitation and bigamy became high-profile targets of the Mexican Inquisition. These crimes were seen as especially problematic since the ratio of Spanish men to women was extremely high (sometimes as high as five to one), which led to all manner of informal sexual relationships between Spanish men and Indian and mixed-race women.[22] For example, the common idea that "it is better to be happy in concubinage than badly married" found its way into the friars' review on various occasions, as in the case in which Bonilla prosecuted the mulata Ana Caballero in 1574.[23] The key to such statements was the use of the term *concubinage* for informal marriages. But in the case of Caballero the censors Sánchez and Quixada concluded that her statement "smacked of heresy" (sapit haeresim), whereas Perea argued that it was bad sounding and offensive to pious ears (*suena mal piarium aurium offensiva*). Caballero was convicted and sentenced to hear Mass in the Holy Office's chapel with a candle in hand, abjure her crimes, and pay a fine of fifty gold pesos.[24]

Just as picaresque literature did not raise the hackles of the Spanish inquisitors, obscene propositions were reviewed for their doctrinal rather than their sexual content. In 1573 a man (his name does not appear in the incomplete case file) said that having ejaculated into his wife's hand, he had not committed a sin. Presumably, he had made the common assumption that so-called unnatural sexual acts with one's wife were acceptable — a view not shared by inquisitors or theologians, who considered all acts incapable of procreation inherently against nature. (The legal phrase reflected the exclusivity of heterosexual, missionary-position intercourse: *recto vaso, recta positione,* or "in the correct vessel [the vagina] and in the correct position [man on top].") In this case the censors viewed his statement as heretical, and while they gave no explanation for this they likely viewed his opinion as a violation of the socially acceptable expressions of sexual behavior.[25] But when the Franciscan Juan de Amezquesa refused to obey an excommunication order against him by his bishop in Guadalajara and stated further that he "wiped his ass with the excommunications placed on him" the censors were more interested in the doctrinal than the scatological question. On September 20, 1574, the Dominican Salazar and the Franciscan Quixada reviewed Amezquesa's statement and argued that the statements "degrading the censures imposed by the bishop or his judge are scandalous, bad sounding and offensive to pious ears."[26] Ultimately, though it is unclear why, Bonilla suspended the case, even though he could have sentenced the Franciscan for bad-sounding words rather than for heresy.

Another major object of inquisitional prosecution in Mexico in the 1570s and 1580s was doubts about the sacraments. If the caseload of the Mexican

Inquisition can be believed, laypersons as well as friars had imbibed Erasmus's reforming ideas about the superiority of inner spirituality over external actions. This widespread familiarity reflected the high level of ideological fluidity between Europe, Spain, and Mexico, in an Atlantic system in which books traveled widely and freely, exposing people in Mexico to the prominent religious debates of the days. There appears to have been a good deal of lay skepticism about the usefulness of the Eucharist, confession, and attendance at Mass. For example, in 1572 Moya de Contreras prosecuted Sancho de Aldana for blasphemy for having said, according to the initial accusation, that "only Jesus Christ was present in the consecrated host and neither the Father nor the Holy Spirit was present therein."[27] The committee of censors — Barbosa, Salazar, and Ordóñez — viewed this as worse than blasphemy and said that it was formal heresy. Aldana was not let off nearly as easily as one might think, given the complexity of the Trinity even for theologians. He was sentenced to appear publicly in an auto de fe, be stripped to the waist, and, with a candle in hand and a gag about his tongue, abjure his crimes — how he was supposed to pronounce his abjuration while gagged is a mystery. This was to follow his public humiliation of being paraded through the streets of Mexico City on a mule while his crimes were publicly announced. Following the festivities, he was administered one hundred lashes and then exiled from Mexico for four years.[28]

In theological metaphysics, Christ, God the Father, and the Holy Spirit were considered coeternal as well as concurrent and therefore all present in the Eucharist. Trinitarian dogmatics represented an important component not only of orthodox theology but also of the theory of heresy. Eimeric, for one, began his *Directorium* with an exegesis of the orthodox view of the Trinity. True to the general form of doctrinal reviews of the 1570s, there was no discussion given in Aldana's case, the censors assuming that the inquisitors would have deferred to their superior theological understanding as well as recognizing the orthodoxy of Trinitarian metaphysics that said that Christ was neither generated nor generating.

Aldana's case reflected the strictness to which the censors of the 1570s and 1580s held the laity to some of the most complex theological subjects as well as the severity of the punishment meted out by the tribunal for his infraction. Aquinas argued that the laity and the common man were not compelled to understand the more difficult aspects of the doctrine — a conclusion supported by Peña, Castro, and other inquisitional theorists and jurists. The censors of the 1570s, however, tended toward a strict enforcement of even the more rarefied points of the Catholic doctrine not shared by later censors — a trend in keeping with the generally vigorous nature of the newly founded tribunal.

Questions of the Eucharist were not restricted to Trinitarian metaphysics within the inquisitional purview. The explanation of the metaphysics of the Eucharist relied on two components to explain the transformation from wine to blood: the accidents (physical wine and bread) remained constant while the true substance changed miraculously, wine to blood and bread to flesh. The accidents — that is, the physical appearances — of the wine remained the same in this transformation. Many Protestant reformers in varying degrees rejected the Aristotelian explanation of the Eucharist, which insisted that the accidents of the wine and bread could remain the same while mystically turning to blood and flesh. Some, like Zwingli, rejected entirely the transformation of wine into blood and argued that the Eucharist was nothing more than a memorial of Christ and his Crucifixion. This view was, of course, condemned as heretical, and even Luther saw it as going too far. While one does not find the books of Calvin or Zwingli in Mexico, one does find the austere simplicity of their vision of Christian ritual. Juan de Torres, a miner in Santiago in New Galicia, was prosecuted in 1574 precisely for holding such views. His statements — (1) the host is a remembrance; (2) the sacrament is only a demonstration or memorial — were given to the censors for review. Salazar, Quixada, Perea, and Sánchez stopped short of condemning the statements as heretical but argued that in the first case it resembled "the language of the heretics." The second "smacked of Lutheran heresy," they said, and normally, if "taken rigorously," such a statement would be heretical, but because the miner had said them in a state of confusion they only "smacked of heresy."[29] If the miner had gone so far as to suggest that the Eucharist was *only* a remembrance he likely would have been condemned as a heretic. Torres died before formal sentencing, so one is left to speculate on the extent of his potential punishment.[30]

The doctrinal distinction hinged on the sacramental nature of the Eucharist. In 1572 Joan de Valderrama said that "the sacrament of confession and of the Eucharist were ceremonies and not sacraments." The censors Barbosa, Pravia, Ordóñez, and Perea agreed unanimously that this statement was heretical.[31] The fiscal, Bonilla, had asked that Valderrama be relaxed to the secular arm for execution, but Moya de Contreras, in consultation with the episcopal ordinary, Portillo, rejected this charge. Nevertheless, Moya de Contreras found him guilty of being suspect in the faith, and for this Valderrama was sentenced to appear in person in the next auto de fe, candle in hand, and abjure his crimes publicly, after which he was exiled from the archdiocese of Mexico for one year.[32]

This sentence contrasted starkly with that given to Aldana because Valderrama had explicitly rejected the sacramental nature of the Eucharist whereas Aldana had committed a metaphysical indiscretion. Why was this the case then? The distinction between implicit and explicit rejection of a sacrament was no small one and had concrete effects in prosecution, but the practice of sentencing revealed that even when overseen by an ostensibly scrupulous canonist like Moya de Contreras sentencing varied from case to case. Francisco Gómez de Triguillos was similarly accused, saying, among other scurrilous things, that "mere toasts do not console me," referring to the Eucharist.[33] The censors found this perverse but not heretical. But Gómez made the further mistake of insisting that attending Mass was not required, which two censors, Barbosa and Salazar, called formal heresy and two others, Ordóñez and Perea, viewed as erroneous. Gómez dug his hole even further when he said he had read in "some books of hours" that Saint Augustine had said that having attended Mass one would not lose one's soul. In response Gómez had said publicly that Augustine had lied because the "alcalde Mercado" had attended Mass and this did not prevent him from going to hell and that Judas had communed and still was condemned. The censors did not seem to appreciate Gómez's humor in attacking his apparent enemy, the alcalde, and said that such a statement was "injurious to saint Augustine." But it was his view that no poor man could be saved that was considered formal heresy. Gómez had even said that he wanted to live under Moorish kings because they would feed their subjects. Ironically, Gómez's materialism was vanquished when he was ordered imprisoned and his goods impounded. Ultimately, he perished unvindicated, as he died before sentencing.[34]

The Eucharist was not the only sacrament impugned that witnessed the review of the censors; confession also was debated by the laity. For example, Hernando Dávila had scolded his wife for her proclivity to go to confession and said that "one confession made to God was worth more than ten made to a priest."[35] This alone would have placed the accused in danger, but he apparently added that Erasmus's *Colloquies* was his proof for this view; this probably did not amuse the censors or the inquisitors, though secretly many Franciscans may have agreed with Dávila. The case occurred in 1573, long after the *Colloquies* had been banned by the 1559 Index, and one wonders whether Dávila had known of the prohibition. In any case, the Index obviously was not effective in preventing Erasmus's *Colloquies* from reaching Mexico. Quixada and Sánchez said the statement was heresy, Barbosa and Perea said it was erroneous, and Salazar that it "smacked of heresy." The absence of unanimity concerning the heretical nature of the statement likely stemmed from the absence of an explicit rejection of confession as a sacrament and instead argued for the higher valuation of internal confession over the physical confession before a priest. But Dávila was said to have heretical ideas by all the censors in the same trial for saying that one needed to confess only once in a lifetime and that devotion to saints was useless. This rejected the rule of IV Lateran of 1215 and was thus an explicit heresy. The censors' review occurred in 1573, but the full trial is lost, though Barbosa and Montúfar had already prosecuted Dávila in 1565 in a similarly incomplete case file.

Iconoclasm was not taken lightly in the context of Calvinist views of adornment and was viewed, along with Luther's rejection of the priesthood and papacy, as one of the more dangerous heresies of the day.[36] This view was seen as especially perilous in Mexico given the long tradition of Indian religious symbolism and the concerns of missionaries about the best way to convert them to Catholicism without allowing them to retain worship of the old gods. Missionaries treaded a fine line between promoting a cult of Catholic saints while rejecting the old gods, and on many occasions missionaries were themselves accused of iconoclasm in their promotion of a stripped-down, Erasmian devotion, as happened with Gilberti.

Rejections of papal authority, too, were considered serious attacks on Catholic ecclesial unity, given the apostolic and Petrine claims of the Church to continuity. And rejection of papal absolutism was not rare in late sixteenth-century Mexico, even among Spaniards. In 1574, the Franciscan Alonso de Ordoz preached in Tlaxcala that only God or Christ, not the pope, could absolve sin. This rejected the authority of the pope to issue indulgences and jubilees—a central component of Luther's initial rejection of papal authority. The censors Salazar, Quixada, Perea, and Sánchez agreed that such a statement was outright heresy.[37] There is, however, no extant trial, though it would be nearly impossible, given the explicitly Lutheran nature of his propositions, that no trial was held. One needs no speculation to determine the fate of Diego Muñoz, an agricultural worker of Michoacán, who said in 1577 that indulgences were worthless and were concocted only to make money.[38] Predictably, the censors Ledesma and Rodrigo de Seguera, comisario general of the Mexican Franciscans, replied that such a statement was heretical and scandalous. Muñoz was subsequently sentenced to abjure in the main church in Guanajuato during Mass and was exiled from Mexico for one year.

Unlike heresies and the specific rejection of the sacraments, idolatry, folk magic, and witchcraft were viewed by both the inquisitors and censors in Mexico as being relatively benign. Unlike the so-called witch-hunting crazes of Italy and Germany in the early modern period, inquisitors in Spain and Mexico tended to avoid prosecuting such crimes and to leave them instead to the diocesan authorities.[39] This seems to reflect concerns on the part of censors and inquisitors alike that heresies like Lutheranism and Calvinism were more dangerous than allowing the "simple folk" to continue to practice folk medicine and rituals. Such leniency did not, however, mean that the crime of *hechi-*

cería was never pursued in Mexico, but that hierarchically it represented a lesser offense. Even Simancas supported this view. For him the issue was one of doctrine and belief — if divination or superstitions involved no heretical belief or explicit pact with the devil, the Inquisition did not possess jurisdiction. Thus in his view "the mixing of wax images, fortune-telling, or vain observations to provoke love, which do not mix the sacred with the profane, are mere superstition and do not properly belong to inquisitional investigation."[40]

Inquisitional cases in Mexico followed this basic approach (though it appears to have changed according to the censors and inquisitors involved). For example, in 1577 the inquisitor Bonilla prosecuted doña Felipa de Atayde for a variety of superstitious activities, including using various powders and waters to determine whether or not a marriage was good. According to the censors Ledesma and Perea, such activity, while idolatrous, was not heretical or erroneous.[41] Doña Felipa was sentenced to appear with a candle, abjure her crimes, and pay the hefty fine of four hundred pesos, which would have been debilitating even for an upper-class woman, after which she was exiled from the diocese of Mexico for three years.[42] Likewise, in prosecuting doña Margarita Pacheco in the same year for using various potions made from donkey brains, corn, and water, Ledesma and Perea again concluded that she was not guilty of heresy though her actions revealed a "tacit pact with the devil."[43] Like doña Felipa, doña Margarita was sentenced to abjure, pay a four-hundred-peso fine, and serve a five-year exile from Mexico.[44]

Another sin-crime that found its way to review by the censors was a kind of early modern cultural relativism. Its most common manifestation was the suggestion that every person could be saved according to his own law — the Moor in Islam and the Jew in the Hebraic law.[45] Such a belief was not an approved theological truth. The Franciscan Pedro de Azuaga of Extremadura was charged with this crime in 1572, having stated it in Guadalajara. The censors Barbosa, Ordóñez, and Perea agreed that his statement was heretical.[46] For this he was sentenced to abjure publicly in Guadalajara and forever stripped of his license to preach. Another Franciscan, the Italian Miguel de Bolonia, was charged with making the same statement in 1572.[47] Again, Barbosa, Ordóñez, and Perea concluded that his behavior was heretical, but strangely enough Moya de Contreras suspended the trial.

Others made their opinions about the potentially good characteristics of non-Spanish cultures made known with more subtlety, like Francisco Gómez when he said he wanted to live under a Moorish king because Moors fed their subjects (see above). In 1571 Josepe Lomelín made a similar argument by saying that the Venetians were correct to make a pact with the Turks to avoid war because "it is better to eat than die of hunger."[48] The censors Ordóñez and Perea thought that this was "bad-sounding, temerious, and scandalous," whereas Salazar argued that it had no relation to the Catholic faith.[49] Some years later, in 1580, Gerónimo Monte, of Milan, a merchant in Soconusco, was accused of having said, "Lutherans are not as evil as they are made out to be and some do good things."[50] The Dominican censors Juan de Castro and Lope de Montoya concluded that the first part — that Lutherans were not as bad as supposed — was "bad sounding, scandalous and offensive to pious ears," though it contained nothing explicitly heretical. The second part, they reasoned in classic natural law fashion, could have a Catholic meaning, since "not all works of the infidels are wicked," but, given the first part of the statement, the friars concluded that it "appeared to favor heretics." *Fautor haereticorum* (aider and abettor of heretics) was a lesser criminal indictment than outright heresy but severely punishable nevertheless. The opinions were given within the context of a civil trial begun by the governor and justicia mayor of Guatemala, León Páez Chumacero de Sotomayor, who remitted the trial to the Inquisition, demonstrating the independence accorded the censors — Dominicans all — in Guatemala. Having reviewed the information sent to Mexico City (the censors' report included), Bonilla concluded that the fiscal, Santos García, had failed to make his case, acquitted Monte, and ordered the return of his previously confiscated property.[51]

Overall, the use of calificación in the 1570s and 1580s was a kind of procedural formality. Granted, the censors wielded considerable power and authority both within and without the tribunal. But the theologians had once and for all been stripped of their voting power and had to content themselves with advisory gravitas. Moreover, even if Moya de Contreras and Bonilla did call on the censors for frequent hearings to help the jurist-inquisitors decide the fate of the miserables accused before the court, the inquisitors did not ask them to write lengthy displays of theological subtlety. In nearly all the cases in which the censors were called for advice, their review was limited to an oral discussion which the notary recorded and to which the censors affixed their assenting signatures.

While in general the new tribunal operated with little written feedback from the censors, there were cases in which formal theological debate was asked and given. These cases, however, are the exception. Of fifty cases in the 1570s and 1580s in which the inquisitors used censors, fewer than ten involved the censors writing their own opinions.[52] For example, Pravia, the Dominican, wrote a brief opinion on rejecting the sacramental nature of the Eucharist and confession. His review relied on standard theological and heresy theory proofs. In assessing the nature of the Eucharist and penance he first relied on the argument that acts accepted as traditions within the cult of worship could be accepted as orthodox. Just as theorists like Torquemada, Peña, and Cano suggested that nonscriptural traditions carried the same weight of Catholic truth, the contravention of which was equated with heresy, so too Pravia made a historical-cultural argument for the sacramental quality of confession and Eucharist—relying explicitly on Cano's theology. Buttressing his argument with theological authorities, he added that Trent, in session 7, canon 2, had condemned the view that sacraments of the New Testament did not differ from rites of the Old Testament and were therefore not sacraments but mere actions, and in session 7, canon 1, Trent condemned those who said that the sacraments were only ceremonies.[53]

In other cases numerous censors were called, for example, in the trials against Alonso Cabello, a young Franciscan who found himself at odds with both the Inquisition and some of his more conservative confreres for his fondness for Erasmus and various Erasmian beliefs. Cabello had been raised the son of a middling bureaucrat, the former alcalde of Oaxaca, and professed his vows to the Franciscan order in Mexico-Tenochtitlan in 1569 when he was thirteen. He became embroiled in a controversy over Erasmus's influence in the Mexican Franciscan order and was prosecuted twice for heresy for having professed opinions such as "monks are no species of men and are alien to God" and for arguing that men should be allowed to leave the Franciscan in order to marry. He was convicted in 1573 and 1577 for heresy and was eventually shipped back to Spain for further adjudication after he had endured the ignominy not only of conviction but of numerous censors' reviews that saw him not only as an Erasmian heretic but also as a dangerous renegade.[54]

The Question of Print

If the debates about the nature of heresy and heterodoxy were often settled in the confines of internal debate of the Holy Office, the same held true for the fate of printed books circulating in Mexico. In particular, there was a debate at the heart of the humanist endeavor and particular to the New World: the question of the translation of scripture into the vernacular. The concern over Indian-language translations of scripture came as a specific outgrowth of the prohibition of 1599 on all vernacular translations of scripture.

When Montúfar was inquisitor and archbishop and Ledesma his vicar governing the archdiocese, it appears that there was no widespread application of the 1559 Index in the 1560s. Such a purge may in fact have occurred and the documentary results thereof been lost, but there is no anecdotal discussion of any such application in the voluminous inquisitional documentation that remains. The absence suggests that Montúfar never ordered a full-press enforcement of the 1559 Index. This is difficult to understand given that Montúfar, in addition to hunting down his enemies, was a champion of central political control, having published the canons of Trent in 1565, with Ledesma preaching the sermon on the day of their publication in Mexico City.[55] Whatever the reasons, Mexico did not witness large-scale enforcement of the 1559 Index until after the establishment of the tribunal in 1571.

In the wake of the establishment of the Holy Office in Mexico, the inquisitors Moya de Contreras, Bonilla, Dávalos, and Santos García embarked on numerous programs intended to enforce the Index. From late 1571 to 1574, Moya de Contreras ordered a massive purge of books prohibited in the 1559 Index; this was largely undertaken by Ledesma. Simultaneously, there was a flood of correspondence between the Holy Office in Mexico City and the various comisarios throughout New Spain in an effort to centralize and coordinate the rigorous application of the 1559 Index, then more than a decade old. The correspondence and initiative dwindled in the late 1570s, as it appears that the inquisitors — by then Bonilla and Dávalos — viewed the process of taking prohibited books out of circulation as more or less complete. Then in 1583 a new Index was issued. From late 1583 to the end of the 1580s, the inquisitors in Mexico sought to apply the rules and laws of the new Index in Mexico. Correspondence was voluminous: reminders to comisarios about their duties in publishing the edict of prohibited books; of ordering all citizens under their jurisdiction to relinquish all prohibited books in their possession under penalty of excommunication; and the forwarding of books for expurgation to proper authorities. Such correspondence became nearly as common as the everyday discussions of pending trials and arrests sent along with depositions by the comisarios.

The 1559 Valdés Index was somewhat spare and brief; the 1583 Index, formally issued by the inquisitor general Quiroga, was lengthy and comprehensive. Therein appears the first index of expurgations — books that would be allowed to circulate once offending portions were purged. But perhaps more important was the impetus of centralization of the control over censorship. Whereas in the past, censorship decisions had often been relegated to the censors, the 1583 Index had as one of its goals the scaling away of that local autonomy through the creation of an encyclopedic, wide-ranging Index.

While technically the Index of 1583 was promulgated by Quiroga, its real authors and drafters were the Dominicans of Salamanca.[56] They had tried on several occasions in the 1560s and 1570s to eliminate the works of their enemies, such as those by Luis de León, Loyola, and John Wild, only to find that such works continued to be popular. They realized that the only way to codify their agenda was to have it promulgated in the form of an Index.

Designing the 1583 Index in the wake of Trent, the Salamanca Dominicans harnessed their considerable intellectual power to the General Council of the Spanish Inquisition. For at least a decade prior to 1583 the Salamanca Dominicans controlled the internal meetings convened for the purpose of drafting a new, much more comprehensive and ambitious Index. As could be expected, the 1583 Index covered every questionable Catholic author known to Christendom. It was no accident that whereas the 1559 Index attacked primarily vernacular translations of the Bible and major Protestant heretics like Luther and Calvin, the 1583 version turned its focus inwardly to the enemies within the gates.

If the goals and purposes of the 1583 Index differed from those of the 1559 edition, in the 1580s the Mexican inquisitors rallied the comisarios to do the work of enforcing it in the provinces.[57] Likewise, the comisarios flooded the offices of the Inquisition with correspondence informing their superiors of their completion of the required duties — publishing the Index and the edict of the faith and recalling prohibited books.[58] Besides attempting to enforce the books banned or ordered expurgated by the indexes of 1559 and 1583, the inquisitors in Mexico occasionally made their own prohibitions. Such ad hoc censorship compounded the already difficult task of enforcing the Index in a territory as far-flung as New Spain, over which a single Inquisition held sway.

The concern over vernacular translations of scripture and prayers was one of the central issues of the 1559 Index and its subsequent enforcement. Such a ban extended, specifically in the case of Mexico, to Indian languages. The Suprema intervened on this issue when the Mexican inquisitors informed it in 1577 that a manuscript version of Ecclesiastes translated into "an Indian language" was circulating widely in Mexico. The Suprema supported what the Mexican tribunal had already done by banning not only the manuscript of Ecclesiastes, but also all Indian language translations of scripture.[59] The inquisitors Dávalos and Bonilla had also banned a Nahuatl translation of the Parables of Solomon written by the Franciscan Luis Rodríguez in 1577.[60]

The question of translating scripture into Indian vernacular languages was part of a much broader debate about the nature of catechesis and the missionary project and about the relative value of Hispanicization compared with Christianization. Many missionaries viewed the Hispanicization of the Indians as less important than their immediate Christianization. For this reason, despite royal efforts to the contrary, Franciscans began studying Indian languages and promoting evangelization in Indian languages while relegating Hispanicization to secondary concern. Antonio de Nebrija may have famously said that "language is the handmaid of empire" and the Crown may have promoted a policy of bringing about the slow death of Indian languages in

INDEX
ET CATALOGVS
Librorum prohibitorum, mandato Illuſtriſſ. ac
Reuerédiſſ. D. D. GASPARIS A QVIROGA,
Cardinalis Archiepiſcopi Toletani, ac in regnis
Hiſpaniarum Generalis Inquiſitoris,
denuò editus.

CVM CONSILIO SVPREMI
Senatus Sanctæ Generalis Inquiſitionis.

MADRITI
Apud Alphonſum Gomezium Regium Typographum,
Anno, M.D.LXXXIII.
Taſſado a cinco marauedis el pliego.

Figure 5. Title page of the most comprehensive Index to date, the 1583 Index. It had more Catholic authors than Protestant authors on it and was also the first Index of the Spanish Inquisition to include an index of expurgation. Courtesy of Beinecke Rare Book and Manuscript Library, Yale University

favor of a cultural and linguistic Hispanicization, but missionaries saw the conversion to Christianity as more immediately important. Such primacy was especially recognized by Franciscans, many of whom developed an eschatology derived from Joachim of Fiore, in which in the final mendicant age of history only friars and their followers would remain faithful to the Church and thus achieve salvation. This eschatology lent a sense of urgency to the Franciscan missionaries' project, leading to mass baptisms and conversion projects.[61]

The most noted expression of this fervor and linguistic project of studying Indian languages and using them to promote the Franciscan missionary project was the school at Tlatelolco.[62] The Franciscans had a house in Tlatelolco, but they also established a school for Indian aristocrats for the study of Latin and formal theology with the goal of producing an Indian clergy caste. Castro had argued that Indians were just like Europeans — some were inherently stupid and others had the facility and drive to become learned theologians and priests.[63] He supported Tlatelolco as a school of linguistics in which Spanish Franciscans studied Nahuatl and Indian nobles studied Latin and Spanish and Catholic thought. In the end, the combined forces of epidemic disease, languishing royal support, and the opposition of the Dominicans doomed the idealistic project of Tlatelolco, but not before its most famous resident, Bernardino de Sahagún, produced a massive multilingual history of Mexica culture, society, and religion based on his decades of work with Indian informants and students who provided thousands of interviews about Mexica society.

Sahagún had produced a wide range of materials, including Nahuatl devotional works, but it was his *Historia general de las cosas de Nueva España* that drew the greatest attention. Produced over several decades in the 1550s, 1560s, and 1570s it is today known as the Florentine Codex and represents one of the crowning achievements of the Franciscan project of studying and using Indian languages to promote their missionary endeavor. By the late 1560s, however, the Franciscans were divided over the use and potential dangers of the project. Ultimately Philip II would issue a royal ban on the *Historia general* in 1577, demanding that all copies of the lengthy manuscript be forbidden and sent to the royal court in Spain.[64] The manuscript remained unprinted until its rediscovery in the late eighteenth century. But even though Phillip II had banned Sahagún's masterwork, it appears that illegal copies of at least portions of the work survived and continued to circulate. As late as the 1630s and 1640s the Florentine Jesuit Horacio Carochi, living in Tepotzotlan, seems to have relied on portions of books 6 and 12 of the *Historia general* when he composed his Nahuatl grammar, published in 1645.[65]

This was the context for the clandestine circulation of the Ecclesiastes manuscript. Dominicans like Montúfar and Ledesma had succeeded in casting a wide shadow of suspicion on Indian language intellectual production. But the question of scripture remained. Many lobbied for an exception to the 1559 Index's rule banning vernacular scripture. They reasoned that Mexico was a unique case and that conversion efforts would be fatally hampered without accurate Indian language translations of scripture. At the very least a reliable translation should be made, went this line of reasoning, for priests and missionaries, a translation that presumably would not have been available to the laity.

Thus the ban on Indian language translations of scripture did not come without a debate. When the inquisitors in Mexico sent out a letter affirming the prohibition, they asked "whether the execution of this prohibition would result in some diminution in the doctrine of the Indians, and in case such books are absent whether they are necessary for the administration of the doctrine."[66] Diego de Landa, as bishop of Yucatán, argued against this ban in a letter to the inquisitors on January 19, 1578, stating that "until now there has been no chapter of the Sacred Scripture translated into Indian language in this land" and that it would be vitally important for such translation in the missionary project.[67] He added that he would be happy to recall prohibited books; this offer must have been a desperate attempt to reassert the inquisitional authority that was ignominiously stripped from him after the debacle of his questionable Inquisition of the late 1550s.[68]

Besides De Landa's complaint, the inquisitors formally solicited the advice of various well-known friars. The questionnaire is not dated, though it is in the inquisitional notary's hand of the 1570s, and the ban on Ecclesiastes came in 1577, so it was likely sent out either shortly before or after that same ban.[69] It asked the following:

> Presupposing that the Holy Office has prohibited a manuscript that appears to be Ecclesiastes translated into an Indian language or any other of the Holy Scripture into the same language or any other vulgar tongue, we ask the following:
>
> what books of Holy Scripture have been translated into Indian languages?
> also, will this prohibition result in some diminution in the doctrine of the Indians?
> also, in case it would cause diminution, what books would be specifically necessary for the ministers for the administration of said doctrine?
> also, would it be wise to prohibit the same Indians entirely from having such books so that they have nothing translated into their language, given their capacity and lowness of their intelligence?[70]

Among those for whom there exist replies to this questionnaire were the Franciscan Nahuatlists Alonso de Molina and Sahagún; the Dominican provincial and vicar Juan de la Cruz; and Domingo de la Anunciación, also a Dominican, who had been in Oaxaca in 1560 and whose specific location for the Ecclesiastes debate was not noted.[71] The friars were chosen specifically for their expertise in Indian languages — Sahagún and Molina in Nahuatl; De la Anunciación had written a doctrina in Zapotec in 1565.[72]

The responses to the poll highlighted the extent to which such internal documentation was a form of intellectual debate, underscoring the fissures between Dominican and Franciscan conceptions about how best to catechize Indians. Both Sahagún and Molina began by asserting that they were unaware of any Indian language translations of scripture, including that of Ecclesiastes. One cannot be certain whether this was true or whether it was intended to avoid confrontation for such knowledge. It seems unlikely that two of the premier Nahuatlists of the day would have been ignorant of what appears to have been a well-known manuscript of Ecclesiastes. Molina, for one, claimed that while unaware of the Ecclesiastes manuscript, he did know of Rodríguez's Nahuatl translation of the Parables of Solomon, describing him as "a good theologian," and the translation as being in "excellent Mexican [and] . . . very useful and advantageous for the ministers who preach to the Indians."[73]

Sahagún and Molina viewed the prohibition of Indian-language scripture as detrimental both to the Indians and to the Christianization project. They considered the questionnaire in the context of the difficulty of indigenous languages and the need for non-Indian language specialists to have access to accurate translations for sermons and preaching. Moreover, both men — especially Molina — saw the denial of such works to the Indians themselves as manifestly uncharitable and un-Christian. For example, in his review, Molina said that the Indians had a right to possess the same kinds of books that other Christians did and that "it is not just to deprive them of such a great favor to have the spiritual consolation of devotional books for their souls and salvation."[74] Molina, however, did not point out that Spaniards possessed no right to have Spanish-language Bibles.

The Dominicans De la Anunciación and De la Cruz did not share the Franciscans' view of Indian intellectual rights or their customary interpretations of inquisitional censorship. De la Cruz thought that the prohibition on the Pauline Letters and Gospels in Indian languages would indeed be detrimental to the missionary project. De la Anunciación, however, felt that such a ban was wholly justified, given that such a prohibition would result in "very little or no" detriment to the Indians or to Christianization. Furthermore, he argued that such Indian language translations were not necessary for preachers, unless they had been rigorously reviewed and corrected beforehand. In his view, the dangers of incorrect and heretical translation outweighed the pastoral

Presupuesto que por el S.to officio se prohibe un libro de mano que parece ser el, Ecclesiastes traduzido en lengua yndia, y otro qualq. de la Sagrada scriptura en la dicha lengua, o en otra vulgar se pregunta. Lo prim.

- Que libros ai de la Sagrada Scriptura traduzidos en lengua de los yndios

- Item si de la execucion desta prohibicion Resultara alg. diminucion y falta a la doctrina de los yndios

- Item en caso que vuiese la dicha falta, que libros de los dichos son precisamente necessarios a los ministros para administracion de la dicha doctrina

- Item si es bueno prohibir a los mesmos yndios Intotum q. no tengan cosa alguna de molde ni de mano traduzido en su vulgar vista su capacidad, y baseza de su yngenio

1. X A lo primero es mi parecer que ningun libro de los de la sagrada escriptura ni parte del ni capitulo ni parte del traduzido en la lengua vulgar lo tenga otro ninguno que los predicadores desta lengua.

2. A lo segundo lo que se es que estan traduzidos los Euangelios, y Epistolas que se cantan en la yglesia por todo el año. Tambien sep que ay traduzidos ciertos capitulos de los prouerbios modo paraphrastico: tambien e sydo que el Eclesiastes esta traduzido por el mismo modo paraphrastico: todo esto me parece que lo pueden tener los predicadores desta lengua tan solamente.

3. A lo tercero me parece que aun ay mucha falta de ayuda para los predicadores por tanto me parece que una Postila con sus sermones que se a hecho de pocos años aca la puedan tener los predicadores, porque les dara gran de ayuda es sobre todos los Euangelios y Epistolas de los Domjngos y principales fiestas del año.

4. A lo quarto digo, que me parece que lo que esta empreso y si quisiero imprimjr basta por agora para la predicacion de los yndios.

5. A lo vltimo me parece que la gente vulgar pueda tener todo lo que esta empreso tocante a la Doctrina Xptiana. y de mano pueda tambien tener algunas doctrinas y orat.

Figure 6. This document was the redaction of the questionnaire given to Indian-language experts in the debate on the Ecclesiastes manuscript. One notes how the Inquisition's notary summarized the issues to be considered by the censors. The signature, less fluid than earlier ones, by Bernardino de Sahagún reflects his advanced age. Courtesy of Archivo General de la Nación, Mexico

gunas doctrinas y oraciones con tal que esten firmadas del author: pero n[i]

sermones ni de mano, ni impresos.

needs of preachers in Indian *doctrinas* (or proto parishes). He pointed out that Latin and Spanish did not always translate into Indian languages and for this reason offered numerous potential doctrinal problems. Therefore, he concluded that because so many manuscript translations of scripture into Indian languages were "full of errors" the Indians were rightly prohibited from possessing or reading any such translations.[75] De la Cruz shared this evaluation, suggesting that if any book should be allowed, it ought to be De la Anunciación's *Doctrina*.[76] De la Anunciación recommended his *Doctrina* along with Molina's *Confesionario* as justifiably allowed to the Indians.

Shortly after the prohibitions on the Ecclesiastes manuscript in 1577, the inquisitor Bonilla responded in a letter of January 18, 1580, to Noreña in Chiapas, repeating the ban on translation of scripture into all vernacular languages, including Indian languages. Bonilla added that in sermons where scripture was read in translation, even though the Spanish and Mexican Inquisitions did not expressly prohibit this, such homiletic translations ought to be forbidden as well.[77] This differed from the Mexican Inquisition's stance in 1587 that Spanish translations of scripture within sermons were acceptable.[78] Despite the ban on Indian-language translations of scripture, in 1577 Bonilla and Dávalos allowed "the ministers of Indians" to keep their Indian-language Gospels and Pauline Letters for their instruction and catechesis of Indians.[79] This position was reiterated in 1587 by Bonilla and Santos García.[80] Thus to a small degree the inquisitors relented in the face of the need to adapt the rigid censure of vernacular scripture given the circumstances of Mexico and the need for conversion efforts.

The Indian-language Ecclesiastes — the language of which was never specified — was not the only recipient of ad hoc prohibitions of books by the Mexican inquisitors. For example, the popular comedy *Celestina* was widely censored by the Mexican tribunal, even though it did not appear on the Index. While any original order prohibiting the *Celestina* is not extant, frequent correspondence refers to its being banned in Mexico. The comisario of Yucatán, Miranda, reported diligently to the inquisitors Bonilla and Dávalos in letters of April 28 and December 28, 1574, that in addition to having published the edict of prohibited books he had recalled and confiscated all copies of *Celestina* he had found.[81] This appears to be in response to Bonilla's letter to Miranda of April 28, 1574, concerning the recall of *Celestina*.[82]

Moya de Contreras also signed the literary death warrants on several popular works during his tenure. The 1565 edition of the papal history *Historia pontifical,* a book appearing frequently in book inventories and inspections, was banned by inquisitional edict by Moya de Contreras. So too were numerous works of the German Franciscan Wild, including his exegesis on Romans as well as any of Wild's exegeses on John printed "outside the kingdoms of Spain." His works were suspect in part because of his emphasis on a soteriology based on faith, which many Dominicans viewed as thinly veiled Lutheranism. Yet Moya de Contreras's prohibition went further than that of the 1559 Index, which had not yet prohibited the numerous editions of Wild's works that it did in 1583.[83]

After the 1583 Index was published and began circulating in Mexico, a devotional work titled *Consuelo espiritual* was banned.[84] The Mexican inquisitors apparently viewed this book as especially dangerous, if the volume of correspondence on the book indicates anything. The tribunal sent out missive after missive to its comisarios, warning them to seek out this book and purge it from their midst. It was, at least in the Yucatán, a very popular work among the laity, who possessed it more frequently than any other prohibited book by 1586, when the comisario of Yucatán, the Franciscan Hernando Sopuerta, carried out a general inspection of the diocese for prohibited books.

In addition to the prohibition of specific works and works produced in Mexico, printers themselves were viewed with suspicion as potential enemies of Catholic orthodoxy. Two high-profile cases against the typographer Pedro Ocharte and his blockcutter Juan Ortiz in 1572 underscored the new emphasis Moya de Contreras would place on the regulation not only of books but also of the people who physically created them.[85] Ocharte was a Frenchman from Normandy and had come to Mexico to ply his trade as a printer; Ortiz was also French, from Gen, but had been raised in Valladolid, Spain. Their careers were typical in the printing trade in the Spanish world, which was dominated by non-Spaniards.[86] And as in the case of centers of printing like Seville, foreigners were viewed with suspicion as potential Lutheran heretics. The trials against Ocharte and Ortiz were little different.

Printers were seen as worthy of greater scrutiny given their trade and their generally high levels of literacy — they had to be able to read in order to function as printers. In his trial Ocharte, for example, was not accused of printing heretical books or even of possessing them. The charge against him was that he had praised a book in which it was said that simple prayer was sufficient for salvation. The book itself was never identified in the trial. According to Ocharte, the book in question had come up in discussion, and he had asked to see a copy of it. But he denied, even under extensive torture, that he had ever seen the book or that he had rejected the sacraments. But Bonilla viewed the mere mention of the possibility of a French Protestant book as sufficient to have Ocharte imprisoned. Ultimately, under torture Ocharte denied the numerous charges of Lutheranism against him, and he was absolved of all charges in 1574.

Ortiz was not so fortunate. He was accused of a litany of heresies. According to numerous witness statements he had committed various Lutheran offenses. He had supposedly rejected the presence of the Devil, saying he was only present in hell and did not tempt people on earth. Ortiz had also rejected the miracles of Our Lady of Monserrat and in addition had said that God did not perform miracles in battles. He had also apparently rejected the need to observe saints' days and obligatory Church holidays by abstaining from work. The censors Pravia, Barbosa, Perea, and Ordóñez viewed his various statements and actions as ranging from sapit haeresim to outright heresy, in the case of rejecting the existence of the Devil. Ortiz was also accused of praising the same book that Ocharte had. And like Ocharte, Ortiz was accused of pronouncing a variety of heresies during the discussion of that book. Both Ocharte and Ortiz were accused of rejecting purgatory and of saying it was useless to pay for masses for one's soul.

Ortiz, however, was also accused specifically of having physically produced a heretical imprint. Ocharte's shop had frequently printed images of Our Lady of the Rosary, and Ortiz had convinced him to add the inscription, "These beads are innumerable and the sinner who prays them will never lack grace."[87] The censors viewed this statement as suggesting that simply praying the rosary would provide eternal grace and therefore a potentially heretical view of the role of sin. Whereas Ocharte was absolved, Ortiz was found guilty. The difference in outcomes seems to be the overwhelming evidence against Ortiz. In Ocharte's case there was little corroborating evidence whereas Ortiz had a lengthy list of witnesses who made sworn statements against him for his various Lutheran heresies. He was condemned as a heretic and made to abjure de vehementi, fined two hundred pesos, and exiled permanently from all Spanish territories.

Ocharte and especially Ortiz were used to make an example of the dangers of Lutheranism in Mexico, as were the various English and French sailors associated with John Hawkins who were condemned as heretics. Overall Moya de Contreras and then Bonilla oversaw a reinvigorated centralized Mexican Inquisition, and they saw the rooting out and punishment of heretics related to print and books as being of central concern. The enforcement of the Index, the ban on Indian language scripture, and the *motu propio* ban on various other works were part of a strategy to clamp down on humanism, Erasmianism, and cultural production that went afoul of the conservative forces that came to dominate the Mexican Church after the brief period of humanist projects of prior decades. It is difficult to gauge, in quantitative terms, the effects on cultural production this trend had, but one can safely assume it had an impressive chilling effect. Certainly the Franciscans bore the brunt of this assault as their libraries and schools came under increasing scrutiny. But the laity surely also understood the terrible consequences of flouting the inquisitional apparatus. At the same time prohibited books continued to circulate in wide numbers in Mexico despite the best efforts of inquisitors and censors.

The beginnings of censorship under the auspices of the Mexican Holy Office were characterized by personally diverging visions of censorship. This stands in relative contrast to the overall centralization of the Holy Office as a formal tribunal. But much of this centralization was marked by the exigencies of a geographically vast and culturally diverse territory. The Mexican Inquisition held jurisdiction over an area slightly more than four times greater than all of Spain, which had more than ten individual Inquisitions in contrast to Mexico's one. While the efficacy of the Inquisition in central Mexico may indeed have been impressive, its far-flung areas were often neglected and left to the idiosyncratic application of inquisitional law and procedure by its comisarios. Likewise, the establishment of formal censors allowed for a new form of official debate on the very nature of heresy and its punishment. Gone were the days of local, diocesan control of orthodoxy, and in its place an imperfect and contentious tribunal was forged.

7

The Ebb of the Holy Office, 1591–1640

In 1607 a farmer from Lisbon living in Mexico, Francisco Gómez, was accused of making suspect statements which were reviewed by the inquisitors in Mexico City. According to various testimonies, Gómez was in the countryside and on his way home when he engaged in a conversation with several men. In the course of the conversation he said, "Whoever does not fornicate in this lifetime will be fornicated by the devil in hell."[1] Heresy? Blasphemy? Earlier censors like Ledesma would likely have seen this as worthy of punishment and possibly as heretical, since in the statement Gómez implied that fornication was both laudable and necessary for avoiding hell. The inquisitors don Alonso de Peralta and Gutierre Bernardo de Quiroz sent the statement to the Jesuit censors Pedro de Hortigosa and Pedro de Morales, who concluded that Gómez's statements "conform to the quality of his person and the occasion in which they were said and appear depraved and disconcerting like the obscenities that farmers tend to say, but they do not bring any suspicion of thinking badly of the faith."[2] After reviewing the testimonies and the censors' recommendation, the inquisitors decided to absolve Gómez without punishment, given his "minimal [mental] capacity."[3]

The consideration of the social and educational status of the accused as well as the circumstances under which a suspect statement was made became common factors in the calificaciones of the late sixteenth and early seventeenth centuries in Mexico, largely under the tutelage of Hortigosa. Unlike the more stringent standards applied by censors of a previous generation, the Jesuit rarely saw heresy in statements that only decades earlier were singled out as attacks on the sacraments and the Catholic Church. From the 1590s to the 1630s, a shift in personnel and, with it, a fundamental change in the view of the Inquisition and its reach redirected the sweep of the Mexican Inquisition's purview of sin-crimes.

Hortigosa often considered the exigent circumstances of a statement. Castro had argued for the same contextual approach to inquisitional proceedings, unlike more hard-line censors, theorists, and inquisitors, who viewed such circumstances as immaterial. In the early seventeenth century, the inquisitors relied on Hortigosa's advice to dismiss charges on occasions when the circumstances of the accused provided evidence that the person did not actually mean to say the offending statements. For example, on numerous occasions black slaves who renounced God or committed blasphemies while being whipped were absolved of heresy or blasphemy because censors concluded that they did not truly believe what they were saying, given the circumstances of extreme pain. Such was the case of Sebastián, the black slave of Cristóbal Ossorio, the notary of the Audiencia of Mexico, in 1602, when, on being whipped by Ossorio, he yelled, "I renounce God and the saints."[4] Hortigosa and Morales argued that "this proposition said on such an occasion and being reported *in continenti,* does not merit much consideration."[5] Case closed. That Sebastián was both a slave — Thomist hierarchy of intelligence — as well as being under painful duress — exigent circumstances — combined to produce his exculpation.

The coming of the Jesuits to Mexico and their increasing influence highlight the limitations of interpreting censorship as purely functional. The debate surrounding grace and free will — known among ecclesiologists as the *de auxiliis* controversies — illustrates the limitations of such functionalism. Taking the lead of Luis de Molina, the Jesuits rallied to a view of free will that was fairly radical for Catholic baroque theologians: the *scientia media*. According to Molina and, to an extent, Suárez, the efficacy of grace was at issue. In his view free will was such that one could choose to sin but not violate the efficacy of grace. Thus grace that was efficacious did not prevent someone from committing a sin.[6] On the other side of this debate were, generally speaking, the Dominicans, whose rigorist view of soteriology saw in Molina the Pelagian heresy. Báñez was the leader of the Dominican attack on Molina's work; along with his Dominican confreres, he launched a censorship campaign against Molina, arguing that to suggest that efficacy of grace did not prevent sin was heretical and smacked of Pelagianism. The Jesuits, in response, called the Dominicans pseudo-Calvinists, linking their implication of predetermination with Calvin's providential absolutism.

The result was that beginning in 1597 special *congregationes de auxiliis* (tribunals on grace) were formed, with formal sessions held before numerous popes. Ultimately, a definitive decree was given in 1612, and each side was left to simmer in its animosity with the warning that neither would be allowed to attack the other's view of grace and free will as heretical. But why so much discussion of obscure theological subtleties? If the functionalists are correct, then all of this would have only been cover for social control. Yet, the de auxiliis debate was about both the relationship of behavior to theology and about the metaphysics of God's provenance and relative free will of humanity. At the risk of grossly simplifying the debate, the Jesuit view of free will meant that they were more interested in the actual social action of people as it related to the spiritual and mental impetus for such actions. The Dominicans, on the other hand, viewed heterodox action or thought as independent or at least as equally important pieces of the construction of heresy and religious error. Thus the notion that baroque culture was expressly directed in the sense of social maintenance, as Maravall suggests, implies that Spaniards thought the same. But theologians, as directors of moral culture, did not see things in such simplified terms.

We have, then, on the one hand the relatively concrete universalism of the Dominican tradition, which saw heresy and the Inquisition squarely in redemptive and soteriological terms. Heresy was eternal and noxious; there was no mitigation. This assumed that a heresy expressed an ancient and eternal error, as Gelasius explained: "Achatius is not the inventor of a new error, but the imitator of an ancient one."[7] This would form the section of the *Decretum* on the definition of heresy — a section which included Jerome's vision of heresy as akin to putrid meat. On the other hand, we have a vision of understanding heresy and heterodoxy which relied on customary law, local culture, and the circumstances surrounding a particular offense to the Church.

These distinctions between a consuetudinary Jesuit view of human action and moral failings and Dominican providentialism and rigorism were especially crucial in Mexico. By the late 1590s Hortigosa was the unrivaled intellectual of the Mexican Inquisition. Scarcely a single calificación passed through the inquisitional proceedings without his signature from 1594, when he began to operate as a censor, to 1626, when he died. For Hortigosa the circumstances and personal characteristics of the individual accused of a religious crime were as important as the absolute value of the statement under review. The emphasis on and championing of free will by the Jesuits had direct and significant consequences for the Mexican Inquisition and its censorship efforts. Both in the theoretical world, as in the erudite and sophisticated *De censuris* by Suárez, and in the practical world, reflected in the daily calificaciones by Hortigosa in Mexico, the rising influence of a Jesuit metaphysics of human action and moral theology changed the way the Mexican Inquisition censored.

The final consolidation of the juridical control of the inquisitor's office came in this period. Along with this consolidation came the identification of the inquisitor's office in Mexico with the emerging criollo elite in Mexico. Over the next five decades some of the most influential Spanish families with size-able criollo membership saw either their sons or sons-in-law placed as inquisitors or legal advisors to the Inquisition in Mexico, among them the Quiroz, Bazán, Albornoz, Peralta, Guerrero, and González Soltero, families linked to conquistadors, hacendados, viceroys, rectors of the university, and the lower Spanish nobility.

While the criollo elite formed important connections with the inquisitorial office, they also appear to have made a concerted effort to have their sons installed as censors. While the censors drew no salary, the prestige in having a family member as an inquisitional official was important enough that many of the criollo elites sought to place their second and third sons in the censors' office. All told, the period from 1591 to 1640 saw a proliferation of censors. In this period 136 censors were given the office; from 1571 to 1590, only 15.[8] The rate at which censors were given office from 1591 to 1640 was thus nearly four times that of the period from 1571 to 1590. The overall effect was to dilute the actual activities of the censors; most of the censors do not appear in any trial or proceeding whatsoever, while a few, like Hortigosa, became the principal advisors to the inquisitors.

Inquisitorial Activity

For two decades — from 1590 to 1610 — the Mexican Inquisition continued its heavy case load, adjudicating on average more than thirty cases per year in the 1590s. This number was lower in the first decade of the 1600s — some thirteen per year — but was still higher than in decades to come. As with the period immediately following the establishment of the Holy Office in Mexico in 1571, these two decades continued the move toward a highly specialized professional group of censors on whom jurist inquisitors increasingly relied. In fact, these two decades were the same years in which inquisitors were the most likely to rely on censors — and Hortigosa in particular — of any period of the first century of inquisitorial activity in Mexico. Charges like blasphemy, oral statements, heresy, and superstitions saw censors consulted on well above 30 percent of all trials. For the more loosely defined charge of propositions during this period, well over half of all such cases involved the consultation of theologian censors. The numbers may actually be higher as the

Table 7.1. Inquisitional Cases, 1590–99

Charge	Number of cases	Number of cases with censors	Percentage of cases with censors	Percentage of caseload
Judaizing	66	1	1.5	21.2
Heresy	56	16	28.6	18.0
Propositions	33	18	54.5	10.6
Blasphemy	31	10	32.3	10.0
Witchcraft	25	7	28.0	8.0
Apostasy	18	1	5.6	5.8
Bigamy	17	1	5.9	5.5
Desacato	15	1	6.7	4.8
Processes of office	14	0	0.0	4.5
Sacrilege	8	0	0.0	2.6
Solicitation in confession	7	0	0.0	2.2
Imitating priest	5	1	20.0	1.6
Querella	4	0	0.0	1.3
Flight	4	0	0.0	1.3
Sanbenitos	2	0	0.0	0.6
Islam	2	1	50.0	0.6
Revelations	2	2	100.0	0.6
Inhábil	1	0	0.0	0.3
Fautor	1	0	0.0	0.3
Doctrinal cases	255	57	22.3	82.0
Total cases	311	59	19.0	100.0

Source: AGN, Inquisición, volumes: 127, 143, 144, 145, 146, 147, 148, 149, 150, 151, 152, 153, 154, 155, 156, 157, 158, 159, 160, 161, 163, 164, 165, 166, 167, 168, 174, 175, 176, 177, 180, 182, 183, 184, 185, 186, 187, 188, 206, 207, 208, 209, 210, 211, 213, 214, 215, 216, 217, 218, 234, 238, 239, 240, 242, 244, 246, 247, 248, 249, 251A, 977, 1489, 1490, 1491, 1492, 1493, 1529

extant archival material includes dozens of freestanding reviews by censors with no record of the trial attached. It is safe to assume that from 1590 to 1610 the intellectual prestige and ideological influence of the theologian censor began to reach their highest points, and this enhancement corresponded with Hortigosa's first decade and a half as censor.

If the influence of the censor reached an apex in these decades, it coincided with the ascendance of hidalgo jurists as inquisitors. The intense period of investigation and prosecution by the Mexican Inquisition of the 1590s was almost single-handedly engineered by the inquisitor don Bartolomé Lobo Guerrero, a man made famous by his intense and violent extirpation cam-

Table 7.2. Inquisitional Cases, 1600–1609

Charge	Number of cases	Number of cases with censors	Percentage of cases with censors	Percentage of caseload
Blasphemy	33	8	24.2	25.2
Propositions	20	16	80.0	15.3
Bigamy	17	0	0.0	13.0
Heresy	13	4	30.8	9.9
Querella	11	1	9.1	8.4
Desacato	11	0	0.0	8.4
Apostasy	5	1	20.0	3.8
Sacrilege	4	3	75.0	3.0
Imitating priest	4	0	0.0	3.0
Witchcraft	3	1	33.3	2.3
Flight	3	0	0.0	2.3
Solicitation in confession	2	0	0.0	1.5
Processes of office	2	0	0.0	1.5
Inhábil	2	0	0.0	1.5
Judaizing	1	0	0.0	0.8
Doctrinal cases	85	33	38.8	64.9
Total cases	131	34	26.0	100.0

Source: AGN, Inquisición, volumes 165, 166, 167, 174, 183, 210, 249, 253, 254A, 255, 256, 257, 258, 259, 260, 261, 262, 263, 264, 266, 267, 269, 270, 271, 272, 273, 274, 275, 276, 278, 279, 282, 377, 386, 452, 454, 463, 464, 466, 469, 470, 471, 472, 478, 481, 483, 508, 823, 916, 1493, 1495, caja 161

paigns in Peru.[9] From 1581 to 1593 Lobo Guerrero was chief prosecutor for the Holy Office in Mexico, and his intensity can be seen in his vigorous calls for guilty verdicts.[10] He was made inquisitor in 1593 — an office he held until 1598. Studies of his activity in Peru — where he was archbishop from 1607 to 1623 (after having been bishop of Santa Fé de Bogotá from 1598 to 1607) — reveal a zealous man who directed a massive extirpation campaign in the Andes. He had cut his teeth in Mexico and oversaw as prosecutor and judge the most fertile period of inquisitional censure that Mexico had seen.

Lobo Guerrero appears to have taken quite seriously the charge to ask theologians for expert advice. This practice was followed by his successors, but whereas Lobo Guerrero was extremely proactive in prosecuting heterodoxy, his successors were much less active. In the inquisitional office followed jurists who came from well-connected families and who, in many cases, were

not even ordained priests. Don Alonso de Peralta was inquisitor from 1594 to
1609 and was ordained only after being appointed inquisitor—a situation
repeated with the appointment of Gonzalo Martos de Bohórquez as inquisitor
in 1609.[11] There was no specific law against a layman jurist being inquisitor,
but it goes a long way toward demonstrating just how different the Inquisition
of Mexico in the early 1600s was from the medieval Dominican Inquisitions.
The Bohórquez was a powerful criollo clan in the Indies, as were the Bazán
and Albornoz, one of whose members, don Francisco, was made inquisitor in
1617. Rodrigo de Albornoz, for example, was the first contador of Mexico
and a wealthy encomendero. The Dominican Juan de Bohórquez was bishop
of Venezuela.[12]

There may have been a purely ideological reason for the decline in inquisitorial activity in the early decades of the seventeenth century, although
physical circumstances seem to offer equally compelling reasons. It may have
been owing to malaise. Some, like Solange Alberro, suggest that once the
major heresies were stamped out, the Inquisition tended to withdraw or focus
on lesser heterodoxies and blasphemies.[13] The inquisitors, however, were no
longer highly motivated ideologues but social climbers whose appointment
represented important sociopolitical strategies for influential colonial families.
By the 1610s the Mexican Inquisition was adjudicating about eight cases a
year. This number remained fairly constant, and, in the aftermath of numerous floods in the 1620s, by the 1630s the Mexican Inquisition completed
only some fifty-seven trials in a decade.

There were also profound financial and political reasons for the steady,
sharp decline in activity of the Mexican Inquisition in the first decades of the
seventeenth century.[14] The floods of the 1620s, especially the massive one
of 1629, alone would have produced significant declines in inquisitional activities, since the tribunal was located in the capital and in the lowest-lying
region in the valley. The Mexican Inquisition was also facing dire economic
problems. The salaries of the Mexican Inquisition alone totaled, in theory,
close to 10,000 pesos annually.[15] But it was never entirely clear who would
pay this or where the money would be found. There is considerable controversy over the subject, since it has long been assumed that one of the ulterior
motives of the Inquisition was financial and that the real reason for prosecuting conversos and Judaizers was to impound their property to pay for the
expensive operation of the Inquisition.[16] Philip IV issued decrees in 1621,
1624, and 1629 stipulating that viceroys withhold inquisitional salaries until
the Inquisition provided the viceroy with detailed accounting. The Mexican
Holy Office refused. But it appears that the Inquisition was taking in incredi-
bly small amounts of income—merely 15,000 pesos from 1614 to 1637, or

Table 7.3. Inquisitional Cases, 1610–19

Charge	Number of cases	Number of cases with censors	Percentage of cases with censors	Percentage of caseload
Bigamy	22	0	0.0	26.5
Propositions	14	9	64.3	16.9
Blasphemy	9	2	22.2	10.8
Solicitation in confession	6	2	33.3	7.2
Querella	6	1	16.7	7.2
Imitating priest	5	0	0.0	6.0
Witchcraft	5	3	60.0	6.0
Desacato	4	1	25.0	4.8
Apostasy	3	0	0.0	3.6
Heresy	2	1	50.0	2.4
Sacrilege	2	2	100.0	2.4
Prohibited books	2	1	50.0	2.4
Inhábil	1	0	0.0	1.2
Revelations	1	0	0.0	1.2
Processes of office	1	0	0.0	1.2
Doctrinal cases	49	20	40.8	59.0
Total cases	83	22	26.5	100.0

Source: AGN, Inquisición, volumes: 178, 254, 287, 288, 291, 292, 294, 298, 299, 300, 304, 306, 307, 309, 310, 311, 313, 314, 315, 317, 319, 320, 321, 322, 325, 327, 455, 464, 474, 477, 478, 479, 480, 482, 486, 491, 659, 683, 1530

only 625 pesos per year, which was less than 7 percent of the costs even of the salaries of the Inquisition (the inquisitors in theory received close to 3,000 pesos a year each).[17] The fiscal from 1634 to 1641, don Francisco Estrada y Escobedo, prosecuted only a handful of cases before becoming inquisitor of Mexico in 1642. Seventeen years later he would be the focal point of a royal investigation into widespread corruption and abuse of power in the Mexican Inquisition. The result, as became clear in the visitas conducted by Pedro Medina Rico in the 1650s, was that inquisitional officials were taking bribes and illegally confiscating property on a wide scale to make up for the lack of consistent pay.[18]

While the caseload and activity declined sharply in these decades, the prominence and preponderance of the censor did not. Censors were consulted in 30–50 percent of cases involving various doctrinal charges like heterodox statements, blasphemy, and heresy in the period before 1620. But into the

Table 7.4. Inquisitional Cases, 1620–29

Charge	Number of cases	Number of cases with censors	Percentage of cases with censors	Percentage of caseload
Judaizing	15	0	0.0	16.8
Propositions	13	6	46.1	14.6
Witchcraft	12	4	33.3	13.5
Solicitation during confession	10	0	0.0	11.2
Blasphemy	6	5	83.3	6.7
Querella	6	0	0.0	6.7
Imitating priest	5	1	20.0	5.6
Heresy	4	2	50.0	4.5
Bigamy	4	0	0.0	4.5
Apostasy	3	1	33.3	3.4
Processes of office	3	0	0.0	3.4
Desacato	2	0	0.0	2.2
Cohabitation	2	2	100.0	2.2
Prohibited books	2	0	0.0	2.2
Islam	1	0	0.0	1.1
Revelations	1	1	100.0	1.1
Doctrinal cases	74	22	29.7	83.1
Total cases	89	22	26.2	100.0

Source: AGN, Inquisición, volumes: 178, 219, 221, 303, 319, 326, 327, 328, 329, 330, 331, 332, 333, 337, 338, 341, 342, 344, 345, 346, 347, 348, 349, 350, 352, 353, 355, 357, 358, 362, 363, 364, 366, 371, 488, 489, 509, 510, 659, 683, 823, 1495, 1552

1620s and 1630s this number declined along with the overall activity of the tribunal. Overall, the picture of inquisitional and censorship activity in the period from 1591 to 1640 is one of decline and mitigation. On the one hand there was a clear and consistent decline in both the quantity and legal quality of the inquisitional prosecutions. On the other hand the increasingly liberal, casuistic approach to censorship led to an inquisitional apparatus that had considerably less bite. (This would change dramatically after 1640, when the Mexican Inquisition experienced a kind of brief revival with the vigorous investigation of mostly Portuguese crypto-Jews, but that is a subject for a different book.)

Table 7.5. Inquisitional Cases, 1630–39

Charge	Number of cases	Number of cases with censors	Percentage of cases with censors	Percentage of caseload
Bigamy	11	0	0.0	19.3
Judaizing	8	0	0.0	14.0
Propositions	7	5	71.4	12.3
Desacato	6	0	0.0	10.5
Querella	4	0	0.0	7.0
Imitating priest	4	0	0.0	7.0
Witchcraft	4	1	25.0	7.0
Processes of office	3	0	0.0	5.3
Solicitation during confession	3	1	33.3	5.3
Apostasy	3	0	0.0	5.3
False testimony	2	0	0.0	3.5
Blasphemy	1	0	0.0	1.7
Flight	1	0	0.0	1.7
Doctrinal cases	30	7	23.3	52.6
Total cases	57	7	12.3	100.0

Source: AGN, Inquisición, volumes: 268, 340, 359, 361, 366, 367, 370, 372, 373, 374, 375, 377, 378, 379, 380, 382, 384, 386, 387, 389, 464, 479, 493, 495, 495, 636, 640, 659, 695

Hortigosa

Father Hortigosa would be dreaming soon. Having put away his edition of Aquinas, to which he turned nightly for intellectual rigor, he closed his eyes and listened to the sounds of the city around him. The *zócalo* (main plaza) was only two blocks away, and he was accustomed to the often noisome activity and fecund smells. He did not mind so much and slept easily. The public criers had gone home for the night, and in their place the streetwalkers had come out to ply their fleshly wares along Mesones Avenue and even sometimes scandalously beneath the seal of the Inquisition across the street from Santo Domingo. Hortigosa, however, did not have such enticements on his mind. He drifted off and saw a luminous white cloud hovering over a spare landscape that he only imagined in his sleep, having never been to Durango before. He saw it as rocky and mountainous, somehow arid, filled with exotic cacti that he supposed the Indians ate or turned into some kind of alcoholic drink. But he could not be sure. His only image of Durango and the land of the Tepehuanes came from his disciple and student Hernando de Tovar, a precocious young man whom Hortigosa looked after like a son. The cloud hung in a sharp November sky, for it was in that temperate month that his student had been run through with a spear. Suddenly, seven white doves flew out of the left side of the cloud, trailing behind them a banner on which was written "Praecipites atra ora tempestate columbae" — a reference to lines from the *Aeneid:* "Here Hecuba and all the princesses took refuge vain within the place of prayer/Like panic-stricken doves in some dark storm."[19]

The doves flew above father Hortigosa's head and alighted on his shoulders, sitting there serenely and feeling somehow soft and light and producing a tingling down his spine, as if he had felt the Holy Spirit itself. The doves began to sing, "Let us praise the Lord of all." Staying with him for some time, one dove led the others away into the sky again and showed him a face made red by the sun that he recognized as that of Tovar, who raised his hand in the sign of benediction. When Hortigosa awoke he took the dream as a sign of the peace of salvation and quickly wrote down on a piece of paper "coram Deo et Christo Jesu non mentior" (before the Lord and Jesus Christ, I do not lie).[20]

Hortigosa was born in 1546 or 1547 in Ocaña, just to the south of Madrid. By all appearances he was a precocious student, having begun liberal arts and theology at the University of Alcalá at a very young age. Some suggest he had begun his university studies as early as age ten or twelve. When he entered the Society of Jesus in 1564 at the age of seventeen or eighteen he ostensibly had completed a significant portion of his training at Alcalá. By 1570, doctorate in hand, he was sent by his order to the Jesuit College of Plasencia to teach theology, and in 1571 he was ordained a priest. His activities over the next few years remain unclear, but he was ultimately nominated to take part in the third Jesuit expedition to New Spain and in September 1576 arrived in Mexico.

In Mexico Hortigosa began an illustrious career that placed him in the highest levels of theological authority. His erudition and advice were so highly esteemed that he was often referred to as the "guiding light of this kingdom" (*Sol de este reino*) — an honorific designation repeated in the funeral orations that followed his death in 1626. Soon after his arrival in Mexico he was appointed to the prime chair in theology at the recently formed Jesuit Colegio Máximo de San Pedro y San Pablo, a position he held almost continuously for more than forty years. Archbishop Moya de Contreras quickly made Hortigosa his personal master in theology after his arrival in Mexico, inviting him to give the former inquisitor individual lessons. These lessons continued over a period of nearly a decade, from 1576 to 1585, when Moya de Contreras convoked the Third Mexican Provincial Church Council, sometimes known as the Mexican Trent. Hortigosa was Moya de Contreras's personal advisor at the council and was also the author of the council's Latin decrees (the council's secretary, Juan de Salcedo, redacted the decrees in Spanish).[21] After the completion of the council, Hortigosa was called to Rome in 1586 by his order as *procurador* (a kind of solicitor general) for the Mexican province. He returned to Mexico in 1588 and never returned to Spain.

While the original nomination of Hortigosa as censor to the Mexican Inquisition appears to be lost, he began to act as a censor in inquisitional proceedings by 1592.[22] At this time Hortigosa undertook a commentary on the second part of Aquinas' *Summa* (*segunda segundae*), known also as commentaries on faith, hope, and charity. Never published, it was nevertheless an ambitious project for a man who was simultaneously involved in pedagogy, studying Nahuatl, advising ecclesiastical officials, and offering calificaciones for the Holy Office.

After the 1590s the use and form of the calificación underwent substantial changes. Beginning in the mid-1590s, the inquisitors tended to summarize the offending or suspect statement in a brief. This summary, usually beginning with the phrase "The following is to be reviewed," was then given physically to the censor. In nearly all cases, the written redaction was then reviewed by the censor in his residence. Thus the censors signed the date of their review along with the location, whether Santo Domingo, San Francisco, San Agustín, or San Pedro y San Pablo in Mexico City. This is another indication that the inquisitors were increasingly less involved in the day-to-day operations of the Mexican tribunal and willing — or relieved — to let the censors stand in for them. The process of censors' reviews now did not even take place in the Inquisition's chambers — they were in a sorry state — but were instead delivered by courier to the various regular orders' houses and returned from those houses to the tribunal's offices.

The written arguments by the censors expanded the internal debate on heresy and censorship. Instead of brief statements by censors, the calificaciones of the 1590s and early decades of the seventeenth century were rich in moral theological speculation. Ostensibly having quashed various impulses of reform in the sixteenth century, the Hispanic Inquisitions turned their attention to lesser offenses like blasphemy and obscene statements. Trials for heresy became increasingly less frequent in the first four decades of the seventeenth century in Mexico. But that decline did not mean that the inquisitors in Mexico turned a blind eye to such offenses.

Hortigosa's calificaciones were not isolated instances of a single man changing the face of the Mexican Inquisition, though his efforts certainly had a profound impact on the tribunal's choice in convictions and sentencing. Rather, Hortigosa's liberal views of heresy, blasphemy, and apostasy were part of the more general trend of the Jesuit impact on Mexican religious culture. Whereas the Dominicans were rigorous and unflinching in their defense of orthodox methods and conclusions about moral theology, the Jesuits were fluid and adaptable. Suárez's argument about the scope of the Church's power over the interior realm would have been familiar to Hortigosa. It was this attitude toward what the Jesuits viewed as the inviolability of the confessional and personal conscience that made them such popular confessors.[23] Since they arrived relatively late to Mexico compared to the mendicant orders and secular clergy, the Jesuits in general focused their energy on the Spanish population. Their educational efforts were likewise aimed at the criollo and peninsular elite.

The debate on behavior was intimately linked to the Ignacian understanding of the inner conscience and its perfectibility. Explained most notably in Loyola's *Exercises,* the Jesuits held that one could strive toward spiritual and moral perfection by close and personal examination of one's conscience and faith. Cano was livid with rage at the idea and fulminated consistently against the Jesuits for what he viewed as religious vanity. In a manuscript opinion he wrote as a kind of ad hominem attack on Loyola and the Jesuits, Cano charged the founder of the order with superciliousness and alumbradismo and even referred to the teachings of Loyola as "shit."[24] By 1600 the poisonous intellectual rivalry between the Jesuits and Dominicans came to its vicious political denouement in the de auxiliis controversy.

But the de auxiliis controversies represented more than an arid metaphysical debate on the distinctions between efficacious and prevenient grace. It was a fundamental clash between two opposing visions of personal conscience, behavior, and, ultimately, the power of the Church to determine the propriety of either. The Dominicans had not been used to the kinds of defeats they experienced at the hand of the de auxiliis stalemate. Neither were they accustomed to seeing their beloved handmaiden, the Holy Office, hijacked by the Jesuits. Yet that was precisely what happened in Mexico in the seventeenth century. True, the inquisitors themselves continued to be secular clergy trained in canon law, and they deferred to the traditional role of the Dominicans as forebears of the Inquisition. In the seventeenth century the inquisitors who died while in Mexico were generally buried in the church of Santo Domingo. But this was a symbolic gesture, much like the physical proximity of the Mexican Holy Office's headquarters across the street from the same Santo Domingo. In practice, it was Hortigosa, not his contemporary, the Dominican Luis Vallejo, who held the greatest influence over the inquisitors as theologian and censor. Wealthy criollos did not send their sons to the Dominicans for education; they sent them to the Jesuits. One can only imagine the fury that such a demise in intellectual status caused the Dominicans, though one may see it reflected in the streets of Guatemala in 1608, red with the blood of partisan riots.

Jurisdictional Disputes

The Jesuits were not the only interlopers standing in the way of the Dominicans' vision of an orthodox New World kingdom. One of the most scurrilous and ruthless jurisdictional battles — in addition to the very real physical battles — ever waged within the context of the Mexican Holy Office occurred in Guatemala between the comisario Ruiz de Corral and Bishop Ramírez.

Intellectual debates and currents are often swept under the tide of archival material and the secrecy of the Holy Office. Ruiz de Corral was an extremely active comisario. Most comisarios tended to send terse, pithy correspondence to the inquisitors in Mexico, summarizing important events, like the reading of the edict of faith. Ruiz de Corral, however, tended to write lengthy letters detailing the contents of his investigations into religious error. When Ramírez began to insist that as bishop he possessed ordinary jurisdiction, the debate flared into a war. Ramírez excommunicated Ruiz de Corral, who had previously, as cathedral dean, prohibited various devotional processions Ramírez had attempted to institute. Ruiz de Corral in turn began writing lengthy disquisitions on canon law and the superior authority of the Inquisition as a delegated tribunal.

At issue in Guatemala in 1608 were two related questions. First, Ramírez had insisted that as bishop he retained inquisitional authority as the principal defender of the faith in the diocese. According to this logic it was the bishop, not the comisario, who should publish and announce the edicts of the faith that enjoined the faithful to denounce heresy. Ruiz de Corral countered that as the direct deputy of the inquisitor, who was himself the direct delegated vicar of the pope, his authority was superior to that of the bishop and hence only the comisario, not the bishop, should publish and announce the edicts of the faith. Ramírez argued the opposite, concluding that episcopal prerogatives trumped inquisitional privileges — a perverse irony since it was his own order, the Dominican, which had benefited from precisely the opposite argument.[25] Ramírez had repeatedly published and announced inquisitional edicts in the cathedral church of Guatemala, leading Ruiz de Corral to denounce him to the inquisitors in Mexico in a series of letters explaining that his edicts were torn down from the cathedral door in April and May 1608.[26]

The second issue also involved jurisdiction but in a much more spectacular fashion. The cathedral cura Ibáñez had defended the bishop's position vigorously. By late 1608 tensions were high, and a vicious feud engulfed Guatemala's high criollo society. Partisans lined up on both sides. Ruiz de Corral had strong support among the criollo-encomendero elite of Guatemala, who were not going to go down without a fight—especially against some moralistic friar. But Ibáñez asserted the rights to prosecute anyone within the diocese for crimes against the Church—even the dean and comisario.[27]

But Ruiz de Corral was unbowed. He wrote vigorous defenses of his prerogatives as comisario and argued that it was Ramírez who had incurred penalty by infringing on inquisitional authority by publishing the edicts. He said it was Ibáñez's contumacy that was the true affront. Ramírez excommunicated the comisario for this defense. The inquisitors in Mexico were forced to intervene to demand the release of their comisario and to chastise the bishop. All this took place as the capital of Guatemala was engulfed by partisan street fights, the escape of Ruiz de Corral on one occasion to avoid arrest by diocesan officers, and high-stakes deals brokered between the two factions as they appeared to face full-fledged armed battle over the jurisdictional disagreements.

As tensions boiled over the inquisitors called in censors to attempt to settle the dispute. At issue was the very nature of inquisitional authority itself. The question of the relationship between bishop and inquisitor was never entirely settled. Some, like Simancas, argued that bishops never completely gave up the jurisdiction over heresy and related matters. Others, like Peña, tended to view the authority of bishops as inherently inferior to that of inquisitors. It was always understood that inquisitors were expected not to directly contravene the bishop's will, but simultaneously it was generally agreed that authority delegated by the papacy to inquisitors tended to trump the authority of bishops to act as inquisitors ordinary. Nevertheless, many bishops, like Ramírez, continued to assert this privilege as laid out by *Ad abolendam* and Simancas.

In October 1608 the inquisitors commissioned two sets of censors to review the competing charges: Hortigosa and Morales and the secular cleric (and future inquisitor) Diego de León Plaza.[28] León Plaza offered a fairly standard defense of the privileges of the Inquisition, arguing that while the bishop was empowered by law to investigate heresy as judge ordinary, this authority was trumped by the superior power of papally delegated inquisitors and comisarios.[29] According to his assessment, the Inquisition derived its authority from the papacy, so inquisitors enjoyed vicarious authority from the papacy; their comisarios therefore possessed the same authority. Consequently, bishops, having inferior authority, could not under any circumstances prosecute or excommunicate comisarios.

Moreover, the actions of the bishop by extension violated the power of the inquisitors because inquisitors were empowered to appoint their comisarios in all areas falling under their jurisdiction. For authority on this point, León Plaza cited *Ut commissi* and *Per hoc,* the various plenary privileges and immunities given by Urban IV to Dominican inquisitors, Villadiego's *Tractatus contra hereticam prauitatem,* and Rojas's *De haereticis.* The irony was cruel — the exact same decrees Urban IV had issued more than three centuries earlier to immunize the Dominicans and give them special status as inquisitors were now turned against one of their own. Ramírez's moral indignation is palpable in his vicious commentaries written in the margins of the inquisitors' eventual rebuke. And one can only imagine the sadistic glee it must have given Ruiz de Corral and the criollo descendents of Bernal Díaz and Pedro de Alvarado. At long last they would see the arrogant Dominicans and peninsular Spaniards humbled in a land which the encomenderos had long seen as their private moneymaker and quasi-feudal possession.

León Plaza argued that because comisarios were the delegates of the inquisitors in every district, they enjoyed the same privileges as inquisitors, as Alexander IV, Páramo (himself a staunch fan of the Dominicans), and John XXII all demonstrated. Thus "there cannot be anyone who can deny that the comisario is the official of the Apostolic See, which, according to the chapter *Inquisitores* of the *Sextus,* says that 'a bishop cannot prosecute the inquisitor during the exercise of his office.' "[30] Moreover, "the manner in which the bishop ordered the excommunication against the comisario was temerity as it is prohibited by the law . . . and being obliged to favor the causes and ministers of the Holy Office he can be considered suspected of blocking it, which is a grave crime — that is, to impede the free exercise of the Holy Office."[31] Thus, in violating the privileges as spelled out in the *Directorium Inquisitorum,* León Plaza concluded that Ramírez's excommunication of the dean-comisario was null and void; he hinted even that Ramírez had committed a chargeable offense by impeding the exercise of inquisitorial authority.

The Jesuits Hortigosa and Morales came to essentially the same conclusion, but they did so for different reasons, and the process by which they did so highlighted the divide between law as immutable and universal — a position from which León Plaza essentially argued — and as customary and fluid. Hortigosa and Morales began their review by asking whether a bishop in New Spain could rightfully publish the edict of the faith. They responded that yes, he might, because he derived his power to extirpate heresy from his office as bishop.[32] Moreover, they continued, this privilege was reinforced by positive law, as spelled out in *Ut inquisitionis* and *Ut officium.* Again, these dilemmas were never completely and indubitably resolved, since even the most highly trained canonists like Peña, Covarrubias, and Simancas disagreed on whether the establishment of inquisitors eliminated ex officio episcopal rights to in-quisitional power.

In addition to positive law (i.e., the canon law) and the inherent authority vested in bishops, the Jesuits argued that many influential theorists supported the view that bishops retained inquisitional prosecutorial powers — among them, Simancas, Albertinus, Villadiego, and Sylvestro.[33] The irony was surely not lost on the inquisitors who had just finished reading a brief by León Plaza that used Villadiego to argue the opposite position. According to the Jesuits, these theorists all agreed that bishops and inquisitors compete with the same privileges and powers to investigate and punish heresy.

But the Jesuits here turned to the issue of custom as trumping positive law. In New Spain, they concluded, the coequal status of bishop and inquisitor was no longer in effect because in Spain the privilege of publishing the edict of the faith had long been stripped of bishops and delegated exclusively to inquisi-tors. Therefore only apostolic inquisitors, not bishops, could proceed against crimes of heresy because this had been established by custom for decades in Spain and New Spain. The refusal by bishops to defer to inquisitors could cause divisions. Drawing on Rojas, the Jesuits concluded that by custom bish-ops must cede this authority in New Spain.[34]

The Jesuits added a second proof to support this view.[35] Again, this derived from customary expectations and the force of tradition — a powerful form of proof not only for theologians but also for censors and inquisitional theorists. The papacy delegated authority to inquisitors to investigate heresy beginning in the thirteenth century. Therefore they, not bishops, were the express repre-sentatives of the papacy and apostolic authority, since the inquisitors were specifically delegated as a necessary auxiliary in these causes. Consequently, only inquisitors could maintain prisons for heretics. If bishops and inquisitors simultaneously investigated heresy, it would lead to confusion, though Sim-ancas supported such simultaneous investigations. But the predominant view was that the bishop could appoint an ordinary to take part in the process, but only as an advisor.[36]

Ultimately, the Jesuits, along with León Plaza, dealt a crippling blow to the claims of Ramírez. It must have been humiliating for the Dominicans to realize that four hundred years after their zealous founders had hunted down Cathars and established a series of privileges for their order, their enemies, the Jesuits, were now using those same privileges to assert the supremacy of the Holy Office, operated by lawyers and Jesuits, to run roughshod over a Dominican in Guatemala. It was a tough pill to swallow and probably explains their con-tinued embitteredness, especially when dealing with Ruiz de Corral.

The inquisitors demanded that Ramírez cease and desist, and they ordered the diocesan authorities to respect the inquisitional comisario. But they also admonished Ruiz de Corral not to arrest the bishop and to try to work with him. Having been reviewed by the censors, the inquisitors concluded that Ruiz de Corral did not incur any penalty or heresy.[37] In a series of heated letters in late 1608 and early 1609 the inquisitors Quiroz and Peralta explained their rejection of Ramírez's claims and their support of the conclusions by the censors. Ramírez had asserted that various sections of the canon law supported his claims to jurisdiction over inquisitors or comisarios who violated Church doctrine and to claims of diocesan authority over heresy — *Ad abolendam* and *Inquisitionis* as well as the *Clementines'* chapter *Multorum querella.* The inquisitors rejected this assertion completely.[38]

At the heart of the inquisitors' support of Ruiz de Corral was an argument, like that of the Jesuits, based less in the law than in custom. As Peña explained it, inquisitors could be understood to be allowed, if delegated by the papacy to do so, to prosecute renegade bishops, whereas the reverse was not true. Quiroz and Peralta repeated this logic by telling Ramírez that he based his argument on authority that predated the Inquisition and that subsequent legislation had trumped. Moreover, they instructed Ramírez that he was "ill-informed" of the law and that he must relent unless he would prefer to be prosecuted himself by the Holy Office. Ramírez did not relent easily. He called the censors who reviewed the case "blind, tricked, duped" and said his supporters were as holy as Saint Michael the Archangel — a statement in itself potentially blasphemous.[39]

Ramírez died in 1609, but the hatred Ruiz de Corral harbored toward the Dominicans did not evaporate. Little more than a decade later, in 1620, the Dominican Antonio de Remesal, the biographer of Las Casas, returned from Spain to Guatemala (where he had lived in the 1610s). He brought with him his substantial personal library and, it seems, several hundred copies of his *Historia de la prouincia de S. Vicente de Chyapa y Guatemala* (History of the Province of Saint Vincent of Chiapas and Guatemala), which had been printed in Madrid in 1619.[40] Ruiz de Corral demanded that Remesal show him the license from the Seville Inquisition that was, by law, required for transatlantic shipment of books.[41] The comisario-dean argued to the inquisitors that Remesal could have been smuggling prohibited books along with the Dominican history, which was rumored to have attacked the Guatemalan encomenderos and criollos as murderous oppressors of the Indians. Remesal refused, arguing that as a Dominican he was exempt from such impositions. Ruiz de Corral, however, had the friar clapped in irons and imprisoned in the diocesan jail, payback for the treatment he himself had experienced, in the same jail, a decade earlier. In the end Ruiz de Corral was ordered to relent, but the point was made: he was going to repay the Dominicans in spades for their attacks on his privileges and on his criollo lineage.

The debate on jurisdiction between Ruiz de Corral and the Dominicans fills volumes. It was never intended for public view and has to this day remained unpublished. Yet there is no doubt it reflects important intellectual trends of the seventeenth century over religious authority and jurisdiction. In many ways the skirmishes played out in Guatemala would be repeated all over the Spanish territories throughout the seventeenth century. The problem of ordinary versus delegated authority became a central leitmotif of seventeenth-century Mexican church history. When Juan de Palafox y Mendoza came to Mexico as visitador general and archbishop elect of Mexico in 1640 it was precisely this issue that consumed his career and led to violent demonstrations in the streets of Puebla in 1642.[42] Palafox chose the see of Puebla and there attempted his vigorous application of the diocesan control of the Mexican Church that the Tridentine decrees had envisioned nearly a century earlier. Palafox would run into the substantial power and popularity of the Jesuits in Puebla, and ultimately, when he attempted to enforce his authority as bishop, riots — both pro and contra Palafox — erupted in Puebla. The battles between Ruiz de Corral and the Dominicans in Guatemala were of a similar piece in the seventeenth century, which saw nearly constant battles between diocesan and regular clergy as well as between the Inquisition and diocesan authorities for control of the Mexican Church.

The Question of Custom

Jurisdiction was not the only issue to divide Catholics in the first decades of the seventeenth century, even if it would be one of the more pressing. A host of issues confronted Mexico in the period, and at the heart of many debates was the question of circumstance, context, and immutable law. The debate about eternal and unchanging law and inquisitional rigor in the face of the new Jesuit vision of ethics would lie at the center of many of these issues of popular religion and its regulation. Blasphemy, sexual innuendo, satire, the debate over the conception of Mary, and the activities of priests were all fodder for debates within the Mexican Inquisition.

Witchcraft and superstitious activities continued to be regulated by the Mexican Inquisition and the censors throughout this period, even if the cases were often left to founder. This can be seen in a rare surviving series of lists of inquisitional caseloads (or *memorias de testimonios*) drawn up by the notary in 1626 and 1627. In 1626 at least 180 separate testimonial denunciations were drawn up by comisarios from New Mexico to the Yucatán. In 1627 the number is 183. (There were many more — these were only those formally detailed in one specific inventory.) Yet from 1626 to 1629 only 33 cases were adjudicated by the Mexican Inquisition. In 1626 a scant 6 cases were tried in

Table 7.6. Summary of themes of depositions from comisarios in New Spain, c. 1621–26 (mostly 1626)

Propositions	32
Powders	25
Spells (*hechizos*)	23
Herbs	22
Apostasy	7
Divinations	7
Superstition	6
Judaizing	6
Bigamy	5
Solicitation in the confessional	4
Desacato	4
Possessing an image of the devil	3
Powders and menstrual blood spells	3
Menstrual blood spells	1
Echar las habas [probably a reference to a type of divination involving tossing beans]	3
Eating meat on prohibited days	2
Not going to Mass	2
Islam	2
Donkey brain spells	2
Enchanting men	2
Trickery [magical]	2
Suspicious Flemish person	1
Circumcision	1
Revelations	1
Astrology	1
Revealing inquisitional testimony	1
Revealing confession	1
Drinks	1
Worms in spells	1
Sacar la landrecilla [removing the sciatic nerve from a leg of lamb to make it kosher]	1
Cave in Guadiana where the devil resides	1
Blasphemy	1
Being a convicted heretic from Llerena	1
Being married while being a friar	1
Not being baptized	1
Kissing a dog	1
Not confessing	1
Not valuing images of saints	1

Source: AGN, Inq., vol. 356, exp. 6

Table 7.7. Summary of themes of depositions from comisarios of New Spain, 1627

Herbs	33
Peyote	1
Propositions	27
Superstitions	18
Spells	18
Powders	15
Bigamy	15
Blasphemy	8
Rebaptism	6
Apostasy	5
Desacato	4
Orations	3
Possessing a familiar	3
Sacar la landrecilla	2
Prohibited books	2
Solicitation in the confessional	2
Pact with the devil	2
Menstrual blood spells	2
Abusing a crucifix	2
Being suspicious in the faith	1
Touching the Host	1
Suspicious book	1
Absolving a case reserved to the Inquisition	1
Imitating an inquisitional official	1
Absolving a deceased person	1
Spell using a frog	1
Possessing an image of the devil	1
Speaking with the devil	1
Divinations	1
Consulting astrologists	1
Disrespect for an image of a saint	1
Stones (in spells)	1
Cave where the devil lives	1
Pool of water where the devil lives	1
Burying a piece of wood	1
Incest	1

Source: AGN, Inq., vol. 360, exp. 1

Mexico. The numbers speak for themselves: the vast majority of investigations in this period were left to die on the vine. And the cases most likely to be investigated, and then ignored, were cases involving some form of folk medicine, ritual, magic, or potion: the use of herbs, peyote, menstrual blood used as a sexual love spell, powders. As was the case with Hortigosa's casuist approach to heresy and inquisitional crime, the same basic relaxed attitude to so-called lesser crimes continued to be applied, for both ideological and structural reasons, after his death in 1626.

Diego Muñoz, the Franciscan comisario of rural Michoacán from the 1580s until his presumed death in 1626, gathered voluminous testimonies about folk medicine, superstitious rites, and suspicious pacts. But in general the inquisitors in Mexico did not respond or prosecute those he denounced. Such was the case when Muñoz conducted a lengthy investigation in 1614 in Celaya against Isabel de Aguiar and other Spanish women. Several witnesses claimed she was a witch, yet the Inquisition never responded.[43] However, the inquisitors did respond to another case brought during Muñoz's investigations in Celaya at the time. The physician of Querétaro (still very much a rural pueblo at the time), Sebastián de Cepeda, had remarked on seeing a wooden statuette of the baby Jesus that he "had a very good backside for 200 lashes." The inquisitors did not appreciate the humor and ordered Muñoz to give Cepeda "grave punishment."[44] In numerous other instances prosecutions against Catholics for refusing to abstain from meat on Fridays were left untouched by the inquisitors in Mexico City or virtually ignored by rural comisarios. Yet this customary approach violated previous, more conservative case law and the doctrine laid out by theorists like Peña, who stated that eating meat on prohibited days was grounds for inquisitional conviction.[45]

Unlike previous or even contemporaneous cases against women for applying folk remedies or amorous love spells, cases that the Inquisition often dismissed as mere superstition (and that even conservative jurists like Simancas viewed as not falling under inquisitional jurisdiction), the Inquisition did prosecute non-Spanish women for such activities. One suspects there was a racial component, as opposed to an eternal theological one, to the selective prosecution of witchcraft. In 1622 the Inquisition prosecuted Leonor de Isla, a mulata who was born in Cádiz and was a citizen of the port of Veracruz. As was relatively common, she had been mixing menstrual blood into drinks in order to ensorcell men for the sake of romantic fealty. Often this was overlooked as mere superstition, but at issue in this case was the charge that she had mixed the sacred and the profane, using holy water and small pieces of a church altar along with love letters and the menstrual blood in drinks. The result of such combining, argued Hortigosa, was that she was guilty of express pacts with the devil and of grave damage to the Church. She was found guilty and sentenced heavily to abjure de levi in an auto de fe, receive one hundred lashes, and be exiled from New Spain for six years.[46] But this was not the case when the Portuguese Mariana Gomes, also of Veracruz, was prosecuted in 1623. Hortigosa reviewed her case as well and concluded that, like Isla, Gomes was guilty of making explicit pacts with the devil. Gomes was subjected to torture, but unlike the mulata she was absolved of the charges by the inquisitors.[47]

The question was different, however, when the case involved more than love potions. The Inquisition cast a great deal more scrutiny on cases that involved the mixing of the sacred and the profane — which, as Simancas argued, was an inquisitional crime — and in cases of suspected false mysticism. These offenses were seen as grave threats to the unity of the Church in Mexico and tended to be dealt with severely. In 1597 Juana de Espinosa, a widow, was accused of witchcraft in Mexico City. She had apparently promised a woman she would offer prayers to Saints Augustine and Mary Magdalene to determine whether the woman's husband was angry. The Augustinian censors Pedro de Agurto and Diego de Contreras concluded that in addition to being superstitious, her "evil disregard" for holy things proved she had an explicit pact with the devil. The inquisitors Lobo Guerrero and Peralta may have agreed, but they were willing to let her off with a warning because she confessed her errors freely and was seen as too ignorant to understand the gravity of her crimes.[48]

The trials against the suspected alumbrados Juan Núñez and Marina de San Miguel took up similar themes, but the crimes were viewed with considerably more gravity. Núñez was an official of the royal mint and San Miguel a Dominican *beata*. They were involved in a small circle of alumbrados in Mexico City — like a group that had been uncovered in Llerena in Extremadura and persecuted with vigor by the peninsular Inquisitions for their attacks on external forms of worship, their emphasis on internal spirituality, and their disregard for various sacraments and traditions.[49] In particular, the alumbrados were seen as potential Lutherans or Erasmian Catholics who refused to accept external spiritual display.

Núñez was accused of having seduced the beata Marina. This alone would have placed him in danger, since he facilitated the breaking of her vows of chastity. But what was worse, he had mixed discussions of God, scripture, and the ineffable love of the spirit with his sexual advances, pondering the love of God while his hands were up her skirt.[50] He had also told her that standard forms of the mortification of the flesh like fasting, cilices, and self-flagellation were useless. When called to review the case, Hortigosa and Morales concluded that his statements and actions were scandalous and injurious but not heretical. The Franciscan censors Sancho de Meras and Juan de Salas, however, saw the clear heresies of the alumbrados.[51] Moreover, Núñez was accused of being a crypto-Jew for, among other things, having always worn a clean shirt on Saturdays, attacking external worship, and having said that the Jews observe the Law and the Old Testament better than Christians. He was arrested, tortured, and convicted of the alumbrado heresy in 1603, sentenced to abjure de vehementi, six years' reclusion to work in a hospital, after which time (if he survived) he was to be perpetually exiled from Mexico. He was also fined five thousand ducats, a spectacular sum for a conviction.

Marina, for her part, did not resist the advances of her spiritual advisor and lover. While her sexual sin — as a beata she had taken a vow of chastity — would have been frowned on, her spiritual crimes were seen as graver. She claimed to have "seen Christ crucified with her interior eyes" — a clear sign of her alumbrada tendencies. She also claimed she was able to transport herself spiritually. She was convicted of heresy and condemned to abjure de vehementi, to be paraded publicly as a heretic nude from the waist up with a gag in her mouth and to be given one hundred lashes. She was stripped of her beata habit in perpetuity and was ordered to serve in reclusion in a hospital for ten years, to pay one hundred pesos, and to hear a mass in Santo Domingo every Sunday and every feast day for two years.[52]

There was a clear distinction made by censors like Hortigosa and others like Meras, Salas, Agurto, and Contreras. Whereas Hortigosa was more likely to take into consideration the mental condition of the accused and to provide a relatively mitigated interpretation of the perceived offense to doctrine, other censors of this period were much more likely to construe those same acts within a context of immutable truths ratified not only by scripture and conciliar decrees, but also by the force of Catholic custom and tradition. For example, when the alumbrado Núñez attacked the use of cilices and the adoration of images, Hortigosa said it was "bad sounding," whereas the Franciscans called it condemnable. Likewise, when Núñez was accused of saying that "the perfect man does not need vocal prayer, only mental prayer," Hortigosa said there was nothing to worry about. The Augustinian Contreras concluded the opposite and called the statement heretical. One sees in this relatively brief, albeit notorious case of 1600–1603 that there were wide divergences in the ways heresy could be construed, though in the end, Núñez and his circle were effectively quashed by the Mexican tribunal.

Such divergence was laid in bold relief in the case of the denunciations against an unnamed Portuguese man in 1603. According to the redaction of the case given by the inquisitors to the censors, the man had, after having been robbed and struck with a piece of metal, sworn by the life of Christ. Having been admonished not to repeat such offenses, the Portuguese man repeated his curses, stating "by God and by the wounds of the devil, I swear that if I find out who stole from me, I will kill him even if it was Christ himself." Hortigosa concluded that "these blasphemies said under such circumstances are not heretical." But the Dominican Vallejo was not interested in the circumstances and said that such a statement was heretical. According to Vallejo, by saying he would kill Christ if he were the one who threw the metal the accused had rejected the immortality of Jesus.[53] The literalism of the Dominican thus came up squarely against the situational ethics of the Jesuit.

Other cases reveal the same culturally specific interpretations of Hortigosa in which he tended to distinguish between moral corruption or physical sin and the considerably graver crime of heresy. For example, the cura of Ocaba in the Yucatán, Cristóbal de Valencia, was accused in 1609 not only of soliciting young women in the confessional but also of having fellated several men. When challenged for his sodomitical activities, the priest remarked that it was a very Christian act, that Saint Peter himself had engaged in the same, that it led to the path toward sainthood, that the apostles had taught it, and that in any case he had permission from the bishop to engage in it. Hortigosa and Morales remarked that such acts and statements were indeed manifest error and perniciously blasphemous, but in the end they also concluded that they reflected more "the carnal blindness of vice than disbelief in the faith."[54] The Augustinian Contreras agreed with this assessment but called the statements outright heresy. Valencia was convicted of solicitation, but not of heresy, and was sentenced to abjure de levi in the private chambers of the Inquisition, was exiled from the Yucatán for six years, stripped of his license to hear confession for two years, and fined one hundred pesos. Overall, this was a relatively light sentence, especially in light of the much heavier sentence for similar offenses in the Montúfar, Moya de Contreras, and Bonilla Inquisitions.

One also finds distinctions between condemnation of sexual innuendo and heresy. In January 1619, the comisario of Puebla heard testimony against Rodrigo del Carpio and forwarded the depositions to the inquisitors in Mexico City. According to those who testified against Del Carpio, he had made obscene statements about the Virgin. The inquisitors then forwarded a redaction of Del Carpio's opinion to Hortigosa and the Dominican censor Bartolomé Gómez. The censors read that "a certain crude layman who swore frequently was talking with certain persons on the morning of the expectation of Our Lady. Hearing the church bells ringing he asked what festival it was, to which one of the persons present replied that it was of Our Lady of the O. The other man [the accused] replied [in an untranslatable pun] Our Lady of the Fucked One."[55] Numerous jurists, like Peña and Simancas, considered statements against the Virgin to be the worst kind of blasphemy and deserving of

Figure 7. Written in the inquisitional notary's flowing hand, this document lists the accusations to be reviewed by the censors and is typical of the procedure of redacting statements for censors' reviews. Courtesy of Archivo General de la Nación, Mexico

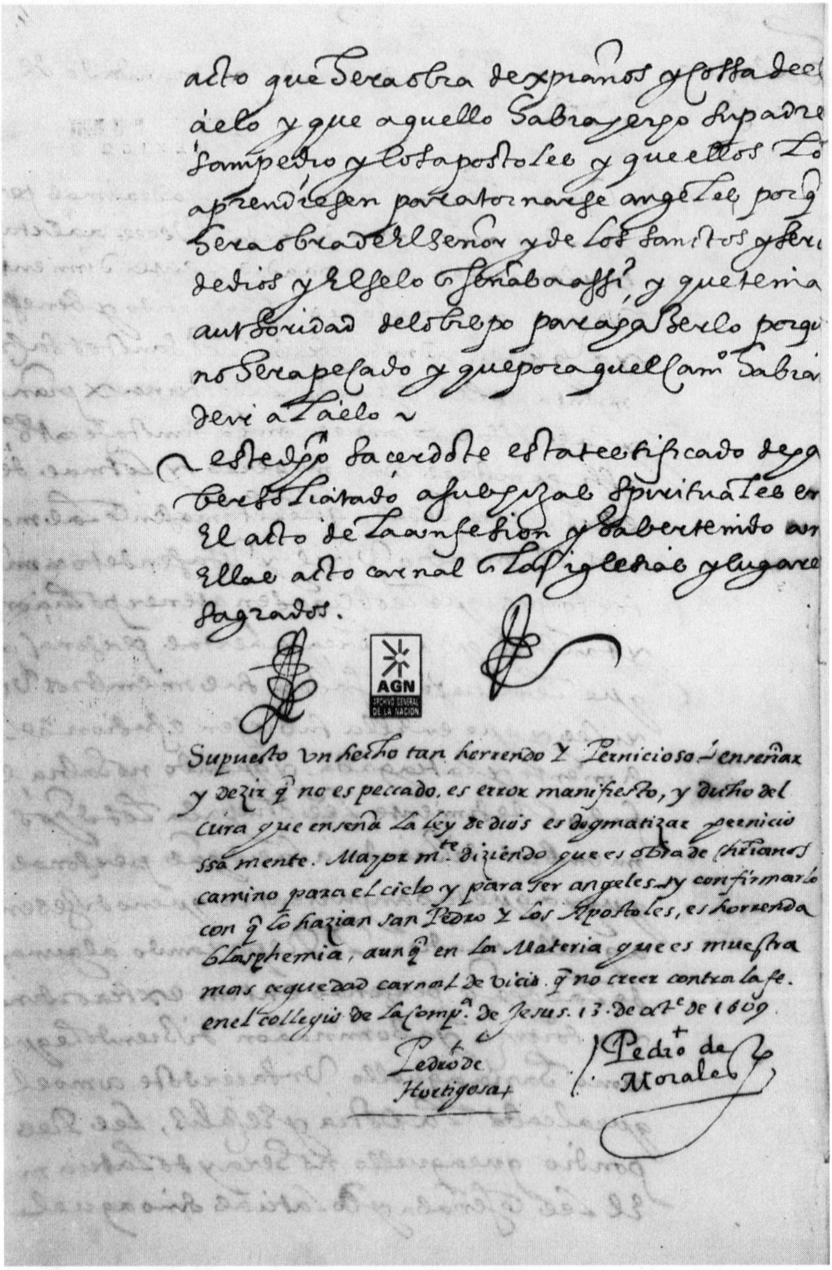

Figure 8. The conclusion of the statement sent for review along with Pedro de Hortigosa's and Pedro Morales's review of and conclusions about the offensive statements sent to them for censure. Signed in the Jesuit College in Mexico City, October 13, 1609. Courtesy of Archivo General de la Nación, Mexico

severe punishment. Gómez agreed with this line of reasoning and concluded in his calificación that Del Carpio's statement was a "great blasphemy and sacrilege . . . as the bishop Simancas warned in his book *De catholicis institutionibus*."[56] Hortigosa, however, did not share Gómez's or Simancas's view of blasphemy in this particular case, concluding that Del Carpio's words were "bad sounding . . . but contain no blasphemy or indication of thinking evilly about Our Lady."[57]

More important than any statistical assessments of the rise and decline of the activity of the Mexican Holy Office was the qualitative shift in the review of suspect statements. Internal debates on the nature of heresy and religious error took on more sophisticated nuances in the seventeenth century. While the debates were less likely to concern the so-called major heresies of the sixteenth century, the censors and inquisitors were no less interested in the definition of heresy. What did change was the view of the Inquisition.

In the first decades of the seventeenth century, the Mexican Inquisition continued to assert its primary role as censor, but even the Holy Office would be brought into the circle of jurisdictional battles time and again as the Mexican Church underwent these power struggles. While autos de fe continued as popular activities of a sadistic, carnivalesque quality, censorship and censure continued to be unpopular. This manifested itself in various forms. Members of the cathedral chapters or Audiencias across New Spain frequently snubbed or boycotted the annual Lenten readings of the edicts of the faith. On numerous occasions even the viceroy boycotted the autos de fe.[58] People refused to relinquish prohibited books after they were instructed to do so in the same edict of the faith. Others regularly ridiculed the Holy Office and the inquisitors. For example, Ana de Aranda said in Mexico City in 1615 that "the inquisitors are nothing but a bunch of drunks and fools who do not know what they are doing or consider their own vices."[59] She was not even accused of heresy, since she attacked no specific article of the faith, though some inquisitional authorities, like Eimeric, had argued that attacks on inquisitors could be construed as heresy. The review by Hortigosa, the Augustinian Juan Morillo, and the secular cleric (and future inquisitor) Bartolomé González Soltero stated that "these words are scandalous and offensive to pious ears and disrespectful of the Holy Office of the Inquisition and its mandates"[60] This was not enough to sustain prosecution, and the inquisitors dismissed the case.[61]

Besides these popular manifestations of discontent with the apparatus of control of the Inquisition, there were institutional barriers to the enforcement of the censorship project. In 1591 the comisario of Veracruz, López de Rebolledo, died. This began a period of almost complete dominance by the Franciscans of the port's controls for censorship. With the shifting of control from secular to mendicant, Franciscan authority in Veracruz over the institutionalization of the *visita de navío* (inspection of ships) appears to have reached fruition. The Franciscans routinely allowed books on the 1583 and 1612 Indexes to circulate through Veracruz. The Franciscans had lost a lengthy series of censorship battles over some of their most lauded sixteenth-century writers, like Zumárraga and Wild. The result was that the enforcement of the Index at Veracruz, where theorists like Peña and Castro saw it as most critical, failed or was so lax that it became nearly useless. In any case the popular discontent with the Inquisition's projects of literary, religious, and cultural control does not appear to be an isolated phenomenon in the early seventeenth century. If men as powerful as Chico de Molina, the Mexico City cathedral chapter dean, were crushed under the rigorous authority of a Montúfar in the sixteenth century, in the seventeenth men openly flouted that same inquisitional authority.

The Question of Print

The general trends of this period between 1590 and 1640 — the decline in vigor of the Mexican Inquisition, the fascination with prestige, the backbiting — were reflected in much of the inquisitional censorship of written material. Likewise, the presence of Hortigosa was felt in this area of inquisitional activity. While the Mexican Inquisition made occasional prohibitions of books known to circulate in Mexico — the *Celestina,* for example — the bulk of its energy focused on unapproved manuscript material and on lesser heterodoxies.

The censures of manuscripts and books issued from the Mexican Inquisition in this period tended to be limited and specific. A spiritual guide titled *Repartimiento del tiempo y de las horas en que Jesu Cristo padeció* (Assessment of the Time and Hours in Which Jesus Christ Suffered) by Agustín de Orosco, printed in Madrid in 1612, was reviewed for a variety of minor errors. For example, Orosco had written that the "divine inspirations that Christ communicated to Judas were strong and efficacious."[62] Vallejo weighed in on the subject, arguing that according to "good theology" this could not properly be called "efficacious" since the words Christ said to Judas did not prevent him from committing a mortal sin. The de auxiliis debates and the recent unsatisfactory denouement could not have been far from Vallejo's mind; he would have understood perfectly the implication of his conclusion and interpretation, supporting the Dominican line on grace.

In other cases books were reviewed and ordered expurgated or banned less for theological heresy than for scandalous statements. For example, in his *Catalogus gloriae mundi* (Catalogue of the Glory of the World) (published first in 1529 in Lyon) the French jurist Barthélemy de Chasseneuz had written that while giving birth to Jesus, Mary was watched to see if she was, in fact, a virgin. As a noted theorist of customary law of his day, Chasseneuz was probably attempting to bring a cultural understanding to the old question of the virgin birth of Christ. But this would tread dangerously close to rejecting the virgin birth, and in his review of the book on February 16, 1604, the Augustinian Juan de Contreras concluded that such a statement was erroneous and temerarious, though he did not call it heretical or blasphemous.[63]

Other books were also banned by inquisitional fiat in this period. As had always been the case, the Mexican inquisitors could ban any book they deemed worthy of censure, as they did the Yepes biography (although the reasoning behind the ban was not entirely clear). But the inquisitors were having a difficult time of compelling legal compliance with these bans. As can be seen in the order to ban the Yepes biography, the inquisitors reiterated the legal position held by the Inquisition that no one, regardless of legal or clerical status, was exempt from inquisitional censorship or from inquisitional inspections of libraries and personal collections. As so often happened, deliberate foot-dragging or opposition to censorship — especially among the clergy and higher royal officials — made for an uphill battle in enforcing the strict theoretical models of censorship outlined by Castro, Peña, and others.

The Mexican Inquisition also strove to regulate manuscript satires that were popular forms of social and political expression. Individual Jesuits and the Jesuit order were repeated targets of satirical verse circulating in manuscript form in the 1610s and 1620s. In numerous instances, Jesuits, themselves sometimes censors, such as Luis de Molina, brought libelous or satirical manuscript verse before the inquisitors. There was very little seriously heretical or even blasphemous quality to these various satires. Compared with the many common scatological and pornographic blasphemies of the day, the satires of the Jesuits were quite mild. For example, in a satire that Cristóbal Ángel, the *prepósito* (guardian or provost) of the Jesuit house in Mexico City and himself a censor, brought before the Inquisition in 1621 one struggles to find the punch line. The basic attack was that the Jesuits were falsely pious and sanctimonious. The Jesuits were described as being a little fat and perhaps enjoying life too much. But the satire does not deliver the kind of trenchant anticlericalism that characterized Erasmus and Luther and those influenced by them. Nevertheless, the censors, Hortigosa among them, ordered the manuscript banned for attacking an "approved religion" and its prerogatives.[64]

In addition to controversies over the satirizing of Jesuits or of Catholicism or the Church in general various manuscripts that were frauds of indulgences or other privileges circulated in early seventeenth-century Mexico. Such manuscripts and printed lists of indulgences circulated widely, if the large

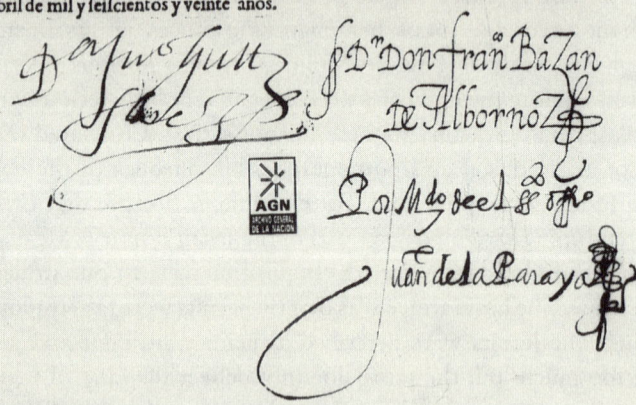

239

OS LOS INQVISIDORES CONTRA
LA HERETICA PRAVEDAD, Y APOSTASSIA. EN
la Ciudad de Mexico, Estados, y Prouincias de la Nueua España, Yslas Phi-
lippinas, y todo nuestro distrito, por Authoridad Appostolica &c. Por que al seruicio
nuestro Señor conuiene recoger dos Libros, el vno intitulado vida virtudes
y muerte del Benerable Varon Francisco de Yepes, vezino de Medina de el Campo, com-
puesto por el Padre Fray Ioseph de Velasco, de la Orden de Nuestra Señora del Carmē,
de Regular obseruācia, de la Prouecia de Castilla, impresso en Valladolid, Año de 1616.
Y otros qualesquiera quadernos impressos, o escritos de mano, tocātes en qualquier
manera a la vida de el dicho Francisco de Yepes. ¶ El segūdo que tiene por titulo el
Solitario cōtéplatiuo, y Guia Espiritual, sacada de diuersos Santos, y padres espirituales, cōpuesto y recopilado por el Padre Fray Iorge de San Ioseph, religioso descalço, de
la ordē de nuestra Señora de la Merced, Redempcion de Captiuos, de la Prouincia de
el Andalucia, impresso en Lisboa, Año de 1617.

¶ Por tāto por el tenor de la presente mādamos, à todos los vezinos, y moradores, es-
tantes y residētes, en todo nuestro distrito de qualquier grado, calidad, preheminēcia,
ô dignidad, que sean, que luego que este nuestro Edito venga à vuestra noticia, ò del
supieredes en qualquier manera, traygais, y exiuais, ante Nos, ò ante nuestros Co-
missarios, en las partes y lugares, donde os hallaredes fuera desta Ciudad, qualesquiera de los dichos Libros, de las dichas impresiones, ò de otras qualesquiera que sean
ó quadernos impressos, ò escritos de mano, dētro de seis dias primeros siguientes de la
promulgacion deste nuestro Edito, lo qual ansi haced, y cumplid, en virtud de Santa
obediencia, y sopena de Excomunion mayor latæ sertentiæ trina Canonica monitione
præmissa, y de quinientos ducados para gastos extra ordinarios deste Santo Officio,
y solas dichas penas mandamos, que ninguna persona los pueda tener, leer, imprimir,
ni vender, y porque nadie pueda pretender ignorancia lo mandamos, publicar, Dada
en la Ciudad de Mexico, en la Sala de nuestra Audiencia, en treinta dias del mes de
Abril de mil y seiscientos y veinte años.

Figure 9. Order banning the *Vida, virtudes y muerte del Benerable Varón Francisco de Yepes*
(1616), issued and signed by the inquisitors don Francisco Bazán de Albornoz and Juan
Gutiérrez Flores in Mexico City, April 30, 1620. The order states that no one of any position or
benefice was allowed to read the book. Courtesy of Archivo General de la Nación, Mexico

number of confiscated materials is any indication. For example, a list of the alleged utilities of hearing the Mass was drawn up as a redaction of a work of the fifteenth-century Carthusian Joan de la Peña, a Parisian theologian. Brief broadsides and summaries of theologians' conclusions were composed as short discussions of important points. For example, in the case of De la Peña, twenty-four of his principal conclusions about the utility of the Mass were redacted in a one-page broadsheet, drawn from his original treatise *Resolución de las dudas que a cerca de la celebración de la Missa* (Resolution on the Doubts surrounding the Celebration of the Mass), printed in Rome in 1498. The broadsheet was printed in Mexico City in 1605 under the license of the archdiocesan provisor of Mexico, Francisco de Loya, and was directed to the Franciscan censor Juan de la Cieza.

Like many indulgence summaries or summaries of theological points, their brief character notwithstanding, De la Peña's summaries were sent for review to the Augustinian censor Diego de Contreras, who concluded that in general most of the propositions were "temerarious" and false. For example, the broadsheet claimed that Jerome had argued that while attending Mass one's soul was temporarily freed from the agonies of purgatory, which Contreras viewed as false.[65]

Some lists of indulgences were drawn up and circulated in broadsheet form without specific papal or diocesan approval. One such catalogue, which circulated in both manuscript and printed broadsheet form around 1605, listed indulgences supposedly granted by the holy actions of the abbess of Our Lady of the Cross, Juana de la Cruz, whom the broadsheet called a saint. It claimed the indulgences were granted by Gregory XIII and Adrian VI. The broadsheet may very well have been an outright fraud. Hortigosa was among those called to review the claims, and he viewed the broadsheet and its claims as superstitious and false since there was no clear author or proof of its authenticity. For example, the broadsheet claimed that anyone who prayed on a feast day was given plenary indulgence, a position Hortigosa rejected as false since there was no mention of contrition. Likewise, the broadsheet claimed that anyone who kept a copy of it with them would be freed from temptations of the devil. Hortigosa did not view this as heretical but found it problematic because, in his assessment, it would lead to false confidence and an avoidance of the proper method to overcome one's temptations. The list also claimed that praying nine Hail Mary's was as good as attending nine masses, an assertion Hortigosa also considered false.[66]

Overall the debates on print and censure in the seventeenth century began to focus on these specifically defined questions of doctrinal points, on the question of grace, and of the issue of authenticity. Whereas the sixteenth-century

Inquisitions in Mexico had focused on broad issues of humanism, Indian language production and catechesis, and Spanish Catholicism in an American context, by the seventeenth century the focus shifted. Censors were called in more often to review specific issues and to resolve questions about the fitness of the Spanish laity to be exposed to potentially fraudulent claims about theology or the appropriateness of Catholic participation in traditional activities, as dozens of indulgence lists and suggestions about how to avoid purgatory circulated.[67]

In many ways these changes forced the censors to take a narrower focus. Not that they ceased reviewing other cases, but that they saw the intricacies of questions about grace, free will, indulgences, and salvation become increasingly more complex. In the context of battling factions in the de auxiliis controversies and their practical fallout in Mexico, an eager lay audience read discussions, in broadsheet form, about grace and salvation.

Don Francisco Estrada y Escobedo was variously bishop of Guatemala and Havana and bishop-elect of Puebla. In 1634, on becoming the inquisitional prosecutor in Mexico, he took office at the very nadir of inquisitional activity and zeal. He became Mexico's inquisitor in 1642. In many ways his career and familial profile resemble those of his predecessors. But circumstances had changed dramatically from the heyday of the 1570s or even from the zealous decade of the 1550s, when friar-theologian missionaries acted as inquisitors. In 1634 the Mexican Inquisition, was, for lack of a better word, broke—financially, morally, and intellectually. The Inquisition's most talented censor, Hortigosa, had died. The new censors were underachieving, venal social climbers like Martín de Peralta, scion of an old conquistador family that had married into the Castilian *hidalguía*. The Inquisition itself was prosecuting only a handful of cases a year. Mexico-Tenochtitlan was only barely scraping away the muck from years of floods. And Estrada was taking bribes from the accused and dismissing cases of heresy in exchange for payment of his salary, which the Crown and the confiscation of goods could not provide. In 1642 he began arresting people on trumped-up charges and dismissing others in exchange for cash; he was about as far from the ideal inquisitor that Eimeric and Castro had in mind as possible. Ultimately, when Medina Rico finished his visita nearly two decades later, he had issued no fewer than 175 indictments, 111 of them against Estrada.[68]

The censorship apparatus had reached the end of a lengthy cycle by 1640. Long gone were the days when theologians squared off in serious, solemn fashion within the secret confines of the Holy Office. And long gone were the ideological zeal and rigor of the Dominican extirpators of heresy, of the grim-faced jurists who redacted complex discussions of the faith and heresy. What had been an imposing, fearful edifice was now a farcical caricature of that image. The air had gone out of the enterprise, and in its place remained a system intended to benefit local gentry and in many ways the ultimate expression of customary law, derived from local ideas about the role of regal power. One can imagine Domingo de Guzmán calling for an Inquisition into the Inquisition and the Cathars remarking smugly that in the end the material world really was the product of the devil.

PART III

Censors and Their Worlds

8

Lucre and Connections

The Sociopolitical World of the Censors

From the Mexican Inquisition's inception in the 1520s until its (temporary) decline in the 1620s and 1630s the nature of theologians and censors as a group shifted considerably. During the diocesan Inquisitions prior to 1571 and in the early years of the Holy Office in the 1570s, friar-inquisitors and censors came from the ecclesiastical elite. They were often hidalgos, frequently became bishops, and were highly educated theologians near the apex of intellectual power of New Spain. They may have suffered a political setback in 1571 and in the decades that followed, when the inquisitors were drawn from the legal profession and the theologian censors were stripped of their votes in the Inquisition, but given their politically high status and intellectual prestige, they were not a force to be ignored. By the 1630s, however, the censors were more likely to be drawn from a middling criollo gentry, ne'er-do-well second and third sons, often of little intellectual or political accomplishment.

The shift away from theologian-inquisitor mirrored a shift in power broadly conceived in Spain and Mexico. Contreras and Henningsen remarked that there were really two "different 'Inquisitions': one aggressive, expanding, militant, and dogmatic; the other, decadent and bureaucratic."[1] The first occurred in the second half of the sixteenth century, mostly in the wake of Trent and the triumph of a Counter-Reformation. The second took place after the mid-seventeenth century, when ostensibly the tribunals came to be dominated by gentry more interested in the social prestige attached to their offices than in extirpating heterodoxy. To what extent did the Mexican tribunal follow this general trend from zealous believers to corpulent holders of sinecures? In terms of caseload certainly the Mexican tribunal followed the global trend, and in sociopolitical terms it generally did so, although signs of the shift were visible well before the mid-seventeenth century.

Using the collective data of *limpieza de sangre* statements (purity of blood genealogies required for nomination to prove Old Christian and non-Jewish ancestry), nomination rolls, Inquisition case law, and diocesan registries, I offer here a collective biography of various inquisitional officials. Various components of social status and political power are considered. Some information gleaned was self-explanatory: criollo or peninsular background; affiliation with a religious order. The same can be said of the inquisitors, comisarios, and consultores: status as a bishop, canon of a cathedral chapter, or oidor of an Audiencia. One aspect that involves interpretive analysis, however, is that of class. Class was one factor among others, including ethnicity, geographic origin, family ties, prestige, and social order in a complicated social calculus for colonial Mexico. Thus in assessing what I have chosen to label rather generically as class I considered a number of variables. Since most of the censors were friars, they held no private, personal property. To unravel their status in the social order requires other types of information. For this I relied both on the administrative positions they exercised and on their family connections.

At the top of the sociopolitical ladder in viceregal Mexico ruled an administrative elite. Jurisdictions and authority overlapped, and this is generally seen as a deliberate strategy of the Spanish Crown to curtail the centralization of power in the hands of a criollo and conquistador-encomendero elite. At the apex of colonial power was the viceroy as the representative of the king. But since ecclesiastical and civil power overlapped and because the Church always strove to assert its role as judge of the divine, the viceroy's rule did not go unchallenged. The archbishop of Mexico and the inquisitor general of Mexico vied for the position as supreme arbiter of the Church in New Spain. In the case of Spain in the 1560s, for example, the Inquisitor General Valdés was able to assert himself as the most powerful cleric in the land by imprisoning the official primate of the Spanish Church, archbishop of Toledo Carranza. Such a dramatic move never came in Mexico in the period under review here, but Montúfar would defeat the cathedral chapter dean Chico de Molina, and the seventeenth century is filled with lurid stories of political rivalry between bishops, inquisitors, and comisarios, as was the case in Guatemala between Bishop Ramírez and Dean-Comisario Ruiz de Corral. Likewise, the judges of the Mexican Audiencia often acted as a body to flummox viceroys, and visitadores of New Spain wielded power second only to the king and were able to depose viceroys. Censors, generally speaking, did not ascend to this political power elite, although in some cases they were able to rise higher, as was the case of the censor and diocesan cleric Bartolomé González Soltero, once rector of the university, who became inquisitor of Mexico.

I have defined the administrative elite as those men who ascended to these highest positions of power in New Spain (archbishop, viceroy, inquisitor, university rector, Mexico's cathedral chapter dean) or those whose direct relatives (i.e., brothers, fathers, or uncles) occupied those same positions. Close behind this political elite was a high administrative caste of jurists, theologians, cathedral canons, and university professors whose power was considerable. Because theologians and friars did not count their social status in pesos but in power and intellectual prestige, I have classed them accordingly. I have placed in the upper administrative class (generally they were members of the economic upper classes) those who occupied positions one tier below the archbishops and inquisitors. These upper administrative men held important positions within their orders, such as being priors or guardians of the main mendicant or Jesuit houses in Mexico City. Some became bishops of suffragen sees like Oaxaca or Guatemala. The upper administrative class also counts those whose direct relatives held important royal or ecclesiastical posts, like *regidores* in major cities, Audiencia judges, or metropolitan cathedral canons. Below this administrative elite fell a large group of middling administrators who held lesser positions within their orders, such as being in charge of smaller, provincial houses, and whose relatives did not hold major administrative positions. Finally, a small portion of the censors appears to have come from the rural middling or lower classes in Spain. They were sons of peasants who had fallen perhaps on hard times and whose Spanish pedigree would have instantly placed them on a higher ethnic-social plane in Mexico than they occupied in Spain. Overall, this structure for defining the class status of the inquisitors, consultores, censors, and comisarios of the Mexican Holy Office avoids the problem of placing them in a strict socioeconomic model on which their careers were not based. In addition to this administrative scale of class I have also considered hidalgo status, which was not always directly tied to administrative accomplishment. I include as hidalgos those whose direct relatives or who themselves employed the honorific don or doña.

The Inquisitors Ordinary before 1571

With the exception of the Zumárraga and Montúfar Inquisitions from 1535 to 1541 and from 1554 to 1571, respectively, the other various Inquisitions operating in Mexico before 1571 were run by authority of individual bishops. The various local Mexican Inquisitions between the 1530s and 1560s followed a diocesan model but also retained many features of specially designated ecclesiastical judges. On the one hand, in most dioceses inquisitors were deputized by the bishop himself or by the diocese sede vacante, as when the Oaxaca cathedral chapter dean Martínez Ruiz acted as inquisitor ordinary for nearly two decades, from 1554 to 1572, overseeing a vigorous diocesan Inquisition, adjudicating thirty-one cases, and acting as investigator in several others.[2] In other instances the bishops themselves undertook inquisitional investigations under the aegis of their own ordinary power, as was the case with don Francisco Marroquín in Guatemala in 1557.[3]

For the purposes of this book, the most important facet of these local Inquisitions was the dominance of theologians, friars, and cathedral canons. Some dioceses tended to have ordinary Inquisitions run almost entirely by cathedral canons, as was the case in Oaxaca, Michoacán, and Guadalajara. For example, the cathedral canon Gerónimo Rodríguez and then the cathedral chapter treasurer don Pedro de Yepes ran the ordinary Inquisition in Michoacán from 1561 to 1575.[4] In the diocese of Guadalajara the cathedral dean, don Bartolomé de Ribera, acted as visitador and inquisitor ordinary in Zacatecas from 1557 to 1562, overseeing an itinerant Inquisition in the mining city.[5] In 1569 and 1570 the Guadalajara archdeacon, don Pedro Bernardo de Quiroz (relative of the future inquisitor Gutierre Bernardo de Quiroz), exercised similar authority as diocesan visitador and ecclesiastical judge ordinary.[6] Puebla's bishop also deputized cathedral canons, like the chantre don Alonso Pérez de Andrada from 1569 to 1571, to act as inquisitor.[7] Using cathedral chapter dignitaries as diocesan inquisitors was an outgrowth of the system of colonial administration by *letrados* (legally trained functionaries), who formed the vast bulk of royal officials in New Spain. In later times men like Yepes, Ribera, and Martínez Ruiz would become comisarios of the Mexican tribunal. While they engaged in many of the same activities — taking depositions, hearing denunciations — once the shift was made from inquisitor ordinary to comisario there was a plunge in power and status. As inquisitors ordinary Martínez Ruiz and Yepes were both investigator and judge. As comisarios, the later generation of provincial cathedral canons had no power to pass sentence or reach a definitive conclusion to a trial. They were reduced from being judges to being vicarious representatives of the same system.

Other diocesan Inquisitions of the period before 1571 followed the lengthy medieval tradition of employing friars as inquisitors. This was a locally determined phenomenon. In areas where Indian populations were dense and friar involvement equally dense, such as in the valley of Mexico, Guatemala, and the Yucatán, the diocesan Inquisitions tended to be run by friars. For example, in the Yucatán, in addition to the infamous Inquisition run by De Landa, the

Franciscan bishop Francisco de Toral acted as inquisitor ordinary from 1563 to 1569.[8] In Guatemala the Dominican Tomás de Cárdenas was inquisitor ordinary from 1557 to 1559, including in the noted trial for witchcraft against doña María de Ocampo, tried by both Cárdenas and Bishop Marroquín in 1558.[9] Later the Augustinian Bishop Bernardino de Villalpando was inquisitor ordinary of Guatemala from 1566 to 1570.[10] Like their cathedral canon counterparts, the friar-inquisitors of the pre-1571 period saw their influence and power as inquisitors adumbrated after 1571. In some local Inquisitions, there were examples of friar theologians being employed as *consultores teológicos* (theological advisors). Cárdenas, for one, brought in his coreligionists Juan de Castro and Tomás de Vitoria for advice, empowering them with a vote in the sentencing proceedings.[11]

The shift from theologian-inquisitors to censors was not merely a thematic one. Rather, literally some of the same men who acted as theologian-inquisitors before 1571 were among the first generation of censors of the Mexican tribunal. Antonio Quixada appeared as a theological advisor to Cárdenas in the Ocampo trial in Guatemala.[12] He would later be censor of the Mexican Holy Office. Quixada was not the only theologian to undergo this transformation. The same had happened with don Rodrigo Barbosa, who was among the most active and powerful of Montúfar's deputies in the 1560s.[13]

The inquisitors ordinary and theological advisors of the 1550s and 1560s tended to come from a highly motivated group of missionaries and early arriving Spanish bureaucrats. These were men who came to Mexico with a genuine sense of vocation and even of messianic fervor. De Landa is a perfect example of this group.[14] While one may debate his character, there can be no doubt he saw his mission to the Yucatán in terms of salvation of the Indians and of the global aspirations of Spanish Catholicism. Likewise, men like the Dominicans Juan de Castro and Tomás de Vitoria were both theological advisors and missionaries in Guatemala, viewing their charge in both catechetical and inquisitional terms.[15]

Inquisitors

When the formal tribunal of the Mexican Inquisition was commissioned in 1569 and began functioning in late 1571, there were diocesan, local Inquisitions operating in Veracruz, Puebla, Michoacán, Guadalajara, Zacatecas, Oaxaca, Yucatán, Guatemala, Nicaragua, and Honduras. The establishment of one central Mexican Inquisition was intended to supersede the multiple claims to jurisdiction in matters concerning the faith that the proliferation of bishops and ordinary Inquisitions had asserted up to 1571.

There was really only one *Mexican* Inquisition prior to 1571 — that which

Zumárraga and Montúfar had exercised through the powers vested in their (arch)bishop portfolio. One cannot accurately speak of them as the only inquisitors of Mexico prior to 1571, but one might speak of the Michoacán Inquisition run by Yepes or the Guatemala Inquisition run by Villalpando.[16] Given the general chaos of having ten simultaneous, independent ordinary Inquisitions in New Spain by 1571, it should come as no surprise that the Suprema appointed Moya de Contreras, a canon lawyer, as the first inquisitor general of all Mexico.[17] While Moya de Contreras's election as a canonist to the position in Mexico mirrored the shift in the other Inquisitions, it also had practical reasons. The Crown, Council of Indies, and the General Council of the Spanish Inquisition were looking for ways to centralize the American Inquisitions under the jurisdictional sweep of two centralized tribunals, and lawyers seemed the best candidates to resolve the various legal questions surrounding these multiple claims.

Moya de Contreras's reception as the new inquisitor general was not especially well received by the power elite of Mexico City, who had grown accustomed to having relative autonomy from Madrid.[18] Nevertheless, the election of a canonist to the position of inquisitor general in 1571 signaled the end of the friar-inquisitors or theologian-inquisitors as the ruling judges of Inquisitions in Mexico. Following Moya de Contreras from 1573 until 1642 came a steady stream of canonist-inquisitors. The only exception was González Soltero, who held a doctorate in theology.[19] But the other inquisitors to follow Moya de Contreras — from Alfonso Fernández de Bonilla to don Francisco de Estrada y Escobedo — were lawyers. If the shift in practice toward jurists was not enough as a fait accompli, in 1608 Philip III ordered that no one could be appointed inquisitor without legal training and education, thus putting a formal end to theologian-inquisitors.[20]

Besides the shift from theologian and friar-inquisitors of the earlier periods before the 1560s, the inquisitors general of Mexico can be characterized by their particular social status. Being an inquisitor carried a great deal of social prestige, to say nothing of political power. As was the case in Spain, the appointment as inquisitor in Mexico was often a stepping-stone to an important bishopric.[21] The annual salary (on paper, at any rate) of the inquisitor general was also quite impressive — 800,000 maravedíes (2,941 pesos).[22] There were problems, though, when the salary was not paid, but it is safe to assume that the inquisitors were quite wealthy men. This placed the inquisitor near the apex of the Spanish administrative elite — Audiencia judges could expect to earn about half this figure, and even the best-paid royal officials, like the royal treasurer, were earning about half a million maravedíes in the sixteenth century.[23] But the question of salary was not absolute. Often the Inquisition had to rely on confiscated property for income, and inquisitors were barred from accepting other forms of income. Moreover, the inquisitional salaries — to say nothing of their payment — were stagnant for seven decades while other officials saw consistent pay raises.[24]

The appointment as inquisitor was a central part of the ecclesiastical elite's career pattern. Obtaining a bishop's miter offered much greater opportunities for social prestige, peculation, and power, though suffragen sees like Michoacán and Oaxaca offered salaries below that of inquisitor.[25] Nevertheless, of the sixteen inquisitors general appointed from 1571 to 1642 in Mexico, eight went on to hold bishoprics in prestigious dioceses, such as Guatemala and Puebla. Moya de Contreras became archbishop of Mexico and don Bartolomé Lobo Guerrero that of Lima. For many, obtaining a bishop's miter came after they had enjoyed benefices in cathedral chapters, illegal appointments that were quite common. Instructions to inquisitors explained that they were forbidden from holding paying positions in the Church while acting as inquisitor. Yet this did not seem to affect their appointments. Bonilla was dean of Mexico's cathedral chapter before being nominated archbishop. Don Alonso de Peralta was archdeacon of Mexico, and don Francisco Bazán de Albornoz was dean.[26]

An appointment as inquisitor general of Mexico capped the careers of some, while others continued within the empirewide Inquisition. These men generally had served some Inquisition previously, either as inquisitor or fiscal. For example, Bernardo de Quiroz terminated his tenure as Mexico's inquisitor when he was appointed inquisitor of Toledo in 1618.[27] Juan Gutiérrez Flores had been prosecutor of the Spanish Inquisition in Sicily and inquisitor of Mallorca. Bazán de Albornoz had served as inquisitional prosecutor in Cartagena de Indias. In any case the elevation to the inquisitor's office, whether as the final step in one's career or as the penultimate one before a bishop's miter, followed similar career lines in Mexico and Spain, the inquisitors generally coming from the lower but untitled nobility and being closely connected to the ecclesiastical power structure.[28]

The inquisitors in Mexico were also the beneficiaries of social climbing by the criollo new rich, who married off their daughters to peninsular Spanish men to raise their racial pedigree. For example, the inquisitor Bazán de Albornoz, a criollo who came from the highest political circles of Mexico, gained his position as a result of strategic marriage. Francisco Verdugo, from Cogeces de Iscar near Cuéllar, accompanied Cortés as a crossbowman in the conquest of Mexico. There is no evidence to suggest he came from anything other than a middling or lower-class background. After the conquest he received several encomiendas at Teotihuacan, Yauhtepec, Tepotzlan, and Cuestlaguaca with a combined income of 500 pesos — a spectacular sum in 1520s money. Eventually he married Isabel Velásquez, the sister of Diego, the failed pursuer of Cortés and governor of Cuba — a definite step up the social ladder for Verdugo.[29] The result was that Verdugo's and Velásquez's daughter, Francisca Verdugo, carried the honorific doña and married Alonso de Bazán. Their children included illustrious gentry of Mexico, including a Knight of the Order of Santiago — don Antonio Velásquez de Bazán — who was also a familiar of the Holy Office, and Francisco Verdugo de Bazán, the first bailiff of the Mexican Inquisition. Francisco married doña Magdalena de Albornoz, the daughter of doña Isabel Vázquez de Tapia and niece of the conquistador and later regidor of Mexico City, Bernardino Vázquez de Tapia, and relative of Mexico City's first contador, Rodrigo de Albornoz.[30] The ultimate result is that Francisco Verdugo de Bazán and doña Magdalena de Albornoz bore the inquisitor general Francisco Bazán de Albornoz as well as Gerónimo Bazán, a censor. A relative of the Bazán de Albornoz, from the Verdugo side of the family, Francisco Verdugo, a doctor and professor of canon law at the University of Seville and inquisitor of Peru from 1622 to 1636, was made archbishop of Mexico in 1636 but died without being consecrated.[31]

The same doña Isabel Vázquez de Tapia had a sister, doña Catalina de Tapia, who married Antonio de Carvajal, who had come to Mexico with Julián de Aldrete and who was the son of a fishwife and a priest. He became alcalde ordinario of Mexico City and received an encomienda at Zacatalan worth 1,840 pesos.[32] If there ever was a case of successful social climbing it was that of Carvajal, whose grandchildren, having mixed with the progeny of the first comendador of Mexico, Leonel de Cervantes, included the Augustinian don fray Agustín de Carvajal, bishop of Huamanga; don Antonio Cervantes Carvajal, comisario of Puebla; don Leonel Cervantes Carvajal, bishop, variously, of Santiago de Cuba, Guadalajara, and Oaxaca. Antonio de Carvajal also had two daughters, both named doña Luisa and both of whom married familiares of the Mexican Inquisition.[33]

The inquisitors in Mexico were characterized by their upper-crust status but moved closer into the realm of the criollo, instead of peninsular, elite. Before 1571 it is not clear how many of the inquisitors ordinary were hidalgos. But of the inquisitors from 1571 to 1642, nearly half (seven) were hidalgos. Half (eight) held doctorates and seven licenciaturas, and one presumably held at least a licenciatura. Later, two — González Soltero and Bazán de Albornoz — were confirmed criollos. It is likely that Gonzalo Martos de Bohórquez was a criollo also for a possible total 19 percent of inquisitors appointed between 1571 and 1642. Overall, their group identity was that of the highest ranks of ecclesiastical power and society. This compares dramatically with those clerics who would remain in secondary positions as cathedral canons but whose career path — studying canon law and ordination in the secular clergy — mirrored that of the inquisitors. Family status and connections and geographic origins, not intellectual prestige, represented the point on which this distinction turned. The inquisitors of Mexico were characterized by their professional training in canon law and their considerable social standing. While there was some variation — from nouveaux riches descendants of conquistadors to blueblood defenders of the ethnic and social hierarchy of old Spain — in general they stood near the pinnacle of the Mexican sociopolitical world.

Consultores

Along with the shift from theologian-friar inquisitors to jurist-inquisitors there was a second blow to the power and prestige of the theologians as brokers within the Inquisition. After 1571 the inquisitors also began to appoint legal advisors to trials. These were jurists called in to advise the inquisitors on points of law and were also accorded votes in important procedural points as well as in sentencing. Their power within inquisitional trials contrasts with that of the censors, who had no vote.

What is known about the new group of *jurisconsulti?* The majority were judges of the Audiencia of Mexico. There is information on at least forty-three of the consultores of the Mexican Holy Office for this period (1571–1640). Sixty percent of these were judges, and all but one of these served in the all-important Audiencia of Mexico.[34] As individuals the Audiencia judges exercised regal power on a level second only to the viceroy and as a group possessed power on a level nearly equal to that of the viceroy. Other consultores (16 percent) were cathedral canons in the Mexico City cathedral chapter. Usually, cathedral canons and oidores pursued similar educational careers in canon law, but oidores in general were laymen and jurists whereas canons were members of the diocesan clergy. The Mexican Inquisition thus increasingly saw itself not as an arm of the diocesan power but sui generis, even if many inquisitors would become bishops.

Socially, the consultores were on a level nearly equal with that of the inquisitors. Nearly half (42 percent) were hidalgos, and many, like the Mexico Audiencia judge Pedro Suárez de Longoria, consultor from 1606 to 1617, married into the lower nobility with women who bore the honorific title doña.[35] Whereas the inquisitors tended to be or become bishops, the consultores were never bishops because they were usually not ordained priests and were married men. Their social position tended to be that of the first sons of the important Spanish families in Mexico, and their function was to ascend as high as possible in the legal hierarchy and simultaneously marry as well as possible.

More than 60 percent of them possessed doctorates, always in law, and the rest were licenciados. These were men who measured success not only in prestige and privilege, but also in royal power and lucre.

The average salary of Audiencia judges in Mexico in 1589 was about half that of an inquisitor, at 1,500 pesos. This placed the judge-consultores economically well within the upper classes but considerably below inquisitors, archbishops, and viceroys, though they were more likely to receive their salary than inquisitors, given the royal patronage of the Audiencia.[36] They were often closely related to various other members of the ecclesiastical elite in Mexico and came from the leading families of New Spain: the Quiroz, Hurtado de Mendoza, Barrientos Lomelín, and Carvajal. Family networking was an important part of horizontal growth of clan power, and placing a son within the Audiencia was an important step for the criollo elite. Being incorporated as a consultor—a prestigious appointment—solidified that power as well as extended numerous privileges to the family and consultor.

The cathedral canon consultores in Mexico City also exercised broad ecclesiastical power and earned considerable salaries. In economic terms, they lived alongside the second-tier officials of the Inquisition. Whereas the inquisitors' salary was constant from 1572 up to the 1640s at 2,941 pesos per year, the holders of the honorary positions within the metropolitan chapter—the treasurers, chantres, deans, and maestrescuelas—were earning around 2,000 pesos as late as the 1670s.[37] Cathedral canons in provincial cities earned less—sometimes less than 1,000 pesos annually. Nevertheless, the cathedral canon consultores of the Inquisition were clearly within the upper socioeconomic ranks of society.

Another shift in the composition of the consultores reflected a trend opposite to that of the censors. Whereas after 1571 censors were more likely to be the intellectual elite of Mexico's theologians, the consultores after that date were now less likely to represent the academic ruling caste. For example, during Montúfar's tenure as inquisitor general of Mexico, he relied heavily on a cadre of highly trained canonists both to run and advise the Inquisition in the diocese of Mexico. Luis Anguis was a trusted canonist and held the chair of *Decretum;* Esteban Portillo as inquisitor ordinary thereafter held the prime chair of canon law (of the *Decretales*) in the university.[38] Mateo Arévalo Sedeño, who had received his licenciate in canon law at the University of Salamanca in 1551, acted as a consultor during the Montúfar Inquisition and held prime chair of canon law before Portillo in the 1550s and 1560s.[39] These were the men who, as respected jurists, were acting inquisitors in Montúfar's stead.

After 1571, however, the consultores were more likely to be called upon as familial favors and nods to royal authority than for their intellectual prestige. The Audiencia was notoriously corrupt in the early years of the formal Mexican tribunal of the Inquisition.[40] While archbishop of Mexico Moya de Contreras was empowered to conduct a general visita in the 1580s and a major object of his reform was the Audiencia of Mexico. At the time the connections between the Audiencia and the Inquisition had reached a zenith. Nearly all the consultores were also Audiencia judges under the leadership of Pedro Farfán, a bitter enemy of Moya de Contreras. The result was that Moya de Contreras pursued, prosecuted, and obtained convictions of several Audiencia judges, including the Inquisition's consultores Farfán, Hernando de Robles, Diego García de Palacio, Pedro Sánchez de Paredes, and Sanctiago del Riego. These were hardly straw men: Farfán had been rector of the University of Mexico, and as a group they exercised near complete civil power in Mexico in the early 1580s. Robles was made consultor in 1575 after presenting what appears to have been a falsified limpieza de sangre. In 1580 rumors began to fly that Robles — from Alcazar, married into the low aristocracy, and alcalde and then oidor of the Audiencia — was the grandson of a condemned Judaizer, Hernando Atracho. The inquisitor Bonilla ordered an investigation in Toledo and on March 24, 1581, stripped Robles of his commission as consultor.[41] It was left to the vigor of a man like Moya de Contreras to prosecute the oidores, but well into the seventeenth century there continued to be a strong connection between the Audiencia of Mexico and the corps of consultores for the Holy Office.

Comisarios

A sketch of the general makeup of the comisarios places the censors in their broader sociopolitical context. Once the Mexican tribunal was formally established, so too was the office of comisario. Like that of censor, this was an auxiliary position, though it sometimes carried a small salary — comisarios in provincial areas might earn 150 to 200 pesos annually for their efforts, though they usually had other professions from which they drew salaries — to say nothing of the potential money to be made in kickbacks.[42] These officials fell much further down the overall socioeconomic ladder than inquisitors and bishops and can be placed among the middle bureaucratic class of New Spain. But, like the office of censor and familiar, the comisario enjoyed social prestige, political-religious power, and immunity from civil court litigation.

The composition of the comisarios was highly localized. In the more important locations, like Puebla, Oaxaca, Valladolid, and Veracruz, there tended to be relative continuity of officeholders. In other areas, more remote or considered less important, there were lengthy periods in which no comisario held office, and the area in question would have fallen under the jurisdiction of the bishop, resident cura, or ecclesiastical judge ordinary. In other instances diocesan vicars exercised authority on religious orthodoxy in lieu of comisarios. This meant, however, that a formal visita would have been required to investigate religious heterodoxy — an activity that did not happen with much regularity after the end of the sixteenth century. The corporate character of the commisariate of any given city or location also tended to be locally determined. Veracruz and New Mexico, for example, had a long line of Franciscan comisarios.[43]

Generally speaking, the comisarios of the Mexican Inquisition from 1571 to 1640 came from various groups: the regular orders (mostly Franciscan), the cathedral canonry, and, in more remote regions, the lower diocesan clergy or lower-ranking missionary-clergy. These provincial cathedral canons represented a kind of second tier of the Mexican criollo elite. Unlike the canons of the Mexican cathedral chapter, who came from the higher ranks of criollo society, the local cathedral canons represented the provincial elite, earning considerably less than inquisitors and Audiencia judges. For example, by the mid-seventeenth century, Isidrio de Sariñana earned 779 pesos per year as canon in Toluca and 1,066 pesos in Querétaro.[44]

But if the salaries of the inquisitional officials stagnated, those of cathedral dignitaries did not. For example, in Michoacán in the 1570s a cathedral canon could expect to earn about 400 pesos a year from his position, a meager amount compared to the dignitaries in the Mexico City cathedral, the inquisitors, and Audiencia judges. But with increased tithe collections came better salaries. By the 1640s cathedral canons in Michoacán were earning about 1,400 pesos, the dignitary posts (like maestrescuela, the cathedral teacher, and chantre) 1,700, and the dean 2,000, placing them economically well within the upper classes.[45] But salaries were not the only methods of financial gain in provincial cities. Like alcaldes, members of provincial cathedral chapters used their positions to engage in lucrative business scams. Don Pedro de Yepes, the cathedral treasurer and comisario of Michoacán, willed thousands of pesos in specie, property, slaves, and religious donations in his will in 1577, despite the fact that his official position paid less than 300 pesos a year.[46]

Many provincial comisario cathedral canons were hidalgos, but few can be traced to the most influential families of Mexico. Instead, they were tied to provincial wealth, and their appointment to an inquisitional commission, often in their hometown, represented an important step for their families in either moving up the social ladder or solidifying their position within the provincial order — as was the case in Guatemala with Ruiz de Corral. But these comisarios did not, like many censors and inquisitors, move on to more lucrative positions. They neither became bishops of their respective dioceses nor were they advanced to positions of greater prestige within the Inquisition as inquisitors. Instead, their appointment as comisario represented the high point of their political careers.

Don Antonio Cervantes Carvajal was comisario of Puebla for twenty years, from 1620 to 1640. As a younger son in a large, wealthy family, his appointment in Puebla represented an important connection for his family, which counted among its ranks bishops, hidalgos, and censors. But the Cervantes Carvajal, and its progeny don Antonio, represented the highest end of the social spectrum of the comisarios of Mexico, and even don Antonio never enjoyed the privilege, wealth, and power of a bishop's miter — something that went to his brother don Leonel instead. Rather, don Antonio's appointment was likely intended to provide further familial connections within the Holy Office and thereby solidify its social power. Likewise, from 1609 to 1636 the archdeacon of the cathedral in Oaxaca, Cristóbal Barrosso de Palacios, served the same diocese as comisario without seeing a promotion. His predecessor, the dean of the Oaxaca cathedral, Sancho Alzorriz, a peninsular Spaniard, served more than three decades (1572–1606) without a promotion. But this begs the point. Being dean or canon of a middling city like Oaxaca or Valladolid was no minor position and carried a good deal of prestige, and the salary attached to a position within those cathedral chapters was hardly a meager one even if less than that of the high upper classes.

Men like Ruiz de Corral and Cervantes Carvajal were, however, a far cry from the considerably more humble comisarios of less important cities and locales. One finds among them few high-ranking members of the ecclesiastical power elite. Unlike the censors, who were often guardians or priors of their orders' houses or provincials of territories, the comisarios of smaller cities and regional towns were more likely to be historically unknown men who boasted few other achievements. Few remember men like Esteban Prieto, the Franciscan comisario of Campeche in 1633, or don Diego Jurado Prieto, comisario of Tabasco (1627–32). There is probably some regional historian or local genealogist who remembers them, but the point is that their influence in the larger picture of Mexican society was negligible. This does not mean it would be worthless to study such men: they represent, after all, an important facet of what came to form a kind of criollo identity in the eighteenth century — men who began to resent the imperious bearing of the peninsular Spaniards, who lorded their supposed racial and geographic superiority over people who increasingly saw themselves as Mexican, not Spanish. But that is another story.

If one considers the overall composition of the comisarios compared with that of the censors, consultores, and inquisitors, their position, while within the upper-middle sociopolitical ranks of New Spain, placed them closer to the bottom in the hierarchy of the Inquisition. When a man like don Ambrosio Díaz del Castillo Valdés, the grandson of Bernal Díaz and relative of Ruiz de Corral, found himself comisario of Guatemala in the 1640s, he would have understood that for all the hopes and dreams of two generations earlier — of easy women, fabulous wealth, and sprawling haciendas — his position as a member of a provincial elite was spurned by the powerbrokers of Mexico City. They would see in don Ambrosio his grandfather's low social status, and in his commission, a distant, and Indian, diocese. Nevertheless, like don Felipe, Bernal Díaz's descendents accompanied their wealth with the prestige of commissions of the Holy Office. With this prestige powerful criollo clans were able to diversify their power between civil and ecclesiastical spheres, adding to their encomienda and hacienda wealth.

Censors

In Mexico theological advisors began to be appointed on a largely ad hoc basis in the 1550s both by Montúfar and by the various diocesan inquisitors ordinary operating throughout New Spain. These men were not nominated as censors on a permanent basis, and it does not appear that any formal procedure, except fiat, was involved. After 1571, however, censors were appointed as permanent functionaries.

Like the families associated with the inquisitor's office, those who placed their progeny as censors were tightly linked and connected members of the criollo elite. The Augustinian Martín de Peralta and the Dominican Luis de Castilla were grandsons of the conquistador and regidor Vázquez de Tapia and connected to many hidalgos, inquisitors, and royal officials. The Franciscan censor Gastón de Peralta was their distant uncle (Peralta's maternal aunt was married to Vázquez de Tapia). Vázquez de Tapia's uncle, don Francisco Alariz, was himself the inquisitor of Toledo. The brothers Agustín and Diego de Carvajal, both Augustinians, were the great-grandsons of Vázquez de Tapia, through his daughter doña Catalina's marriage with Antonio de Carvajal. The Cervantes Carvajal were also connected to this line — Vázquez de Tapia's daughter doña Catalina and Antonio de Carvajal were the grandparents of don Leonel Cervantes Carvajal, the bishop of Guadalajara, and don Antonio, the comisario of Puebla. Doña Catalina and Antonio de Carvajal were also the great-grandparents of the Augustinian censor Alonso de Valdés, who was the son of doña Luisa Cervantes Carvajal, who was married to an inquisitional familiar, Alonso de Valdés. Overall the clan connections among censors, inquisitors, bishops, and royal officials ran both wide and deep in colonial Mexico, and placing a family member in the censor's chair was only one piece in an overall political calculus of the criollo elite.[47]

There is information on 151 censors appointed between 1571 and 1640.[48] From 1558 to 1579 there were 45 additional theological advisors who were never specifically mentioned as censors or who were not admitted permanently.[49] In the first group, the majority had some kind of evidence concerning their background, religious order affiliation, class, and occupation. Those who, prior to 1571, were never formally appointed as censors do not have as much information, though in some cases their backgrounds are known, as they were mentioned in the trial transcripts. In other cases the early censors were known for other activities, like the Dominican Pedro de la Peña, who, in addition to acting as a censor for the Oaxaca Inquisition in 1560, became prior of Santo Domingo in Mexico City and had held the prime chair of theology at the University of Mexico from 1553 to 1560.[50]

As was true of the missionary effort in Mexico in general, the friar-theologians who became censors and theological advisors to inquisitors were virtually all peninsular Spaniards in the sixteenth century. The first criollo censor (nominated in 1591) was Agustín Dávila Padilla, the Dominican known for his history of his order in Mexico.[51] There is confirmed geographical birth data on 84 of the official censors from 1571 to 1640 and on 11 others for whom geographic origins are likely.[52] The majority of the censors were peninsular Spaniards. Of the 151 censors, between 54 and 62 were peninsulars (36–41 percent of total; 57–65 percent of those with background data).[53]

A significant percentage of the censors, however, were criollos. This contrasts with the inquisitors, who were overwhelmingly peninsular. Of those censors for whom there is data, between and 30 and 33 were criollos, or 32–35 percent for which there is data (20–22 percent of the total). The frequency of criollo censors was also a function of time. Before 1591, all censors were peninsulars as far as is known, but from 1591 to 1640, 36–39 percent of those with confirmed data were criollos. This was considerably higher than for other positions of authority in Mexico in the period under review, such as inquisitors (19 percent). In the sixteenth century as a whole, 96 percent of bishops in the New World were peninsulars. Sixty-seven percent of all seventeenth-century bishops in the Indies were peninsulars. Peninsular archbishops of Mexico represented 85 percent of all appointments up to 1850, and similarly high numbers can be found for other prominent sees of the Indies, like Lima (77 percent).[54] The criollos were better able to insert themselves into the hierarchy of the Inquisition in Mexico than they were in the more lucrative bishoprics. This suggests, as do the various appointments and familiar connections among other officials, that the Inquisition operated as a patronage network for the criollo elite. Although these positions were of honorific value and carried social and intellectual prestige, men who were better able to ascend the Church hierarchy often did so in more lucrative positions as bishops, inquisitors, and canons of cathedral chapters.

While the criollo prominence among censors outpaced that of bishops and inquisitors, the shift from a mendicant Church to a diocesan-run Church was not matched in the ranks of the censors. Until 1640, 92 percent of all censors came from the regular clergy. In either case there was no flattening of the influence of the regulars going into the seventeenth century, as was the case in the overall structure of the Spanish American Church. For example, in the sixteenth century 75 percent of all bishops in the Indies came from the regular orders. By the seventeenth century this fell to 58 percent, and by the eighteenth century a minority 35 percent of bishops were regulars while 65 percent were diocesan clergy.[55]

The Mexican Inquisition honored the long tradition of mendicant inquisitional activity by placing almost exclusively mendicants (and some Jesuits) in the corps of the censors. But in terms of absolute numbers, the Franciscans formed the plurality among Mexican censors. Franciscans represented 36 percent, Dominicans 24 percent, Augustinians 17 percent, Jesuits 11 percent, Mercedarians 4 percent, and only 6 percent came from the diocesan clergy. But these numbers also tend to reflect the dominance in numbers by the Franciscans in the mendicant Church in Mexico. In terms of activity in the Holy Office, Dominicans and Augustinians and, later, Jesuits dominated the censure process.

The domination of the censors by the mendicants complicates one's ability to conduct a thorough survey of their educational background. After the reform in the 1850s and 1860s and the nationalization of Church property, significant portions of the mendicants' archives were lost or destroyed. Consequently, there is incomplete documentation on individual education within the houses of the regular orders. At first glance this might not appear to be an especially important point. After all, were not many censors university professors trained in important universities? True, but in Mexico friars were barred by their orders from receiving their theological education at the university even though they were allowed to serve the university as professors.[56]

After the first wave of censors, of whom several were trained at Salamanca, information on the educational background of the censors fades significantly.[57] The Franciscans established their own schools within their major houses. San Francisco of Mexico City was a major school in its own right. Many mendicants received master's degrees from within their own order. While the Dominicans had a lengthy tradition at Salamanca, even there many of their major scholars were trained not at the university but at San Esteban, as was the case with Ledesma.[58] The Jesuits followed the same general pattern in Mexico and established their own Jesuit-run colleges throughout Mexico.[59] The Augustinian censors Martín de Perea, Pedro de Agurto, Juan Morillo, and Cristóbal de la Cruz were all listed in the University of Mexico rolls as having been trained and given their master's degrees in theology within the Augustinian order. They appear within the university's archival documentation thanks to their roles as chair holders of the university and had their degrees incorporated within the university. Where the mendicant and Jesuit censors were educated in their own corporate colleges, the diocesan-clergy censors continued their higher education within the universities. For example, Diego León Plaza, a member of a well-placed wealthy family who would become rector of the University of Mexico, received his doctorate in theology from the University of Mexico in 1597. Juan de Cervantes, who became an episcopal ordinary sitting in on inquisitional proceedings, received his master's degree in theology from the University of Mexico in 1586.[60]

Overall, however, the censors as a group had a lower educational profile than inquisitors and consultores. For the period considered here, 33 censors held master's degrees, 13 held doctorates, and 1 held a licenciate in theology or canon law, representing about 30 percent of the total. There is a problem, however, with determining educational level. Not all genealogical statements are available, and in many cases the censors did not sign with their titles (some friars eschewed titles as a form of humility). For example, the Dominican Luis Vallejo was appointed censor in 1603, and nowhere in inquisitional records does one find information on his educational level. Yet he was holder of the Aquinas chair of theology at the University of Mexico in 1617, and it is difficult to believe he did not hold at least some degree in theology; this was a proprietary chair of the Dominicans, however, so he may have been appointed in spite of not having an advanced degree.[61] There were probably other cases like this, and it is unclear, in light of the lack of archival evidence for them, how many of the censors held higher degrees.

Overall, unlike the inquisitors, who came from the social and political elite, the censors tended to come from a kind of middling gentry, or what one might call high middle class. There were exceptions, but as a group the censors were lower in status, educational levels, and class than the inquisitors, oidores of the Mexican Audiencia, and the canons of the metropolitan cathedral chapter. By the same token, the censors as a whole ranked higher than the comisarios of the Mexican Inquisition and well above the minor administrative officials of New Spain, such as the alcaldes of lesser cities and small towns. While close to a majority of the inquisitors and consultores were hidalgos, the percentage for censors was decidedly lower (21–25 percent). One-fourth is certainly not negligible, given the overall makeup of colonial Mexican society, but it is roughly half the rate of the inquisitors and consultores. In determining hidalgo status, I have relied on a crude methodology: those whose direct relatives bore the honorific don/doña or who held titles of lower nobility (Knights of Santiago, for example). Friars in general avoided using the honorific *don*, though some censors who came from the diocesan clergy, like Juan de Cervantes and Antonio de Peralta, used the title. In any case, the censors did not, as did many viceroys, come from the upper nobility. The Dominican Juan Ramírez was supposedly the descendent of Aragonese kings, and the Augustinian Martín de Peralta and the Dominican Luis de Castilla drew their genealogies to the kings of Castile, though such lineages were often faked. Francisco Velasco, a Franciscan and a criollo appointed in 1623, seems to be an exception to this general rule: his father and grandfather were both Knights of the Order of Santiago, and his grandmother was the sister of Viceroy Velasco.[62]

Further description of the class status of censors comes from a variety of factors. In comparison to the inquisitors and the consultores, slightly less than 10 percent of the censors belonged to that upper echelon of the political elite. The censors were more often members of an ecclesiastical high caste — nearly half (60) for whom there is reliable data (48 percent) were members of the administrative upper class — as priors and guardians of major mendicant houses in Mexico City or as bishops of lesser sees. Numerous censors held these important positions within their orders or as governors of the main mendicant provinces or as comisario general of their order. While garnering for their holders significant levels of social prestige, these positions would not place the censors who held them in the true administrative elite.

But if the censors as a whole can be classified as coming from a middling to higher administrative ecclesiastical caste, this profile is also temporally determined. In the early decades (1571–1605) of the Mexican tribunal, the censors tended to come from the higher levels of colonial society and politics. Of the first 42 censors, the density of administrative power and social status is impressive. Among them one counts the following:

- 11 bishops
- 8 provincials of their respective orders
- 8 priors or guardians of important mendicant houses
- 6 holders of the prime chair of theology at the University of Mexico
- 4 inquisitors or ecclesiastical judges ordinary
- the former rector of the University of Alcalá
- 3 cathedral chapter canons of Mexico
- 3 diocesan governors
- 3 consultores to the Third Mexican Church Council

This collective profile was never again matched in the corps of the censors, as it increasingly became a group of well-connected social elites placed by nepotism. From 1571 to 1605, 79 percent were among the administrative elite or the upper administrative class. By contrast, after 1605, about 40 percent came from those same administrative upper classes.[63] Thus the major shift was downward from the upper to the middle administrative class. From 1571 to 1605 only two censors, Diego Ordóñez and Antonio de Quixada, came from the administrative middle class, and Ordóñez was an hidalgo. From 1605 to 1640, about a quarter (22 percent of the total and 27 percent of those for whom there is data) were from that middle class, and nearly a tenth (7 percent of those for whom there is data) in this period can be called lower or working class. The overall shift was dramatic: from highly placed administrators and political players to underachieving distant cousins of the administrative upper classes.

This sketch, however, tends to flatten the distinctions between censors. On the one hand there were men who rose to the very zenith of ecclesiastical power in the Indies. The see of Santo Domingo was held nearly continuously for three decades, from 1590 to 1621, by former Mexican censors — from 1597 to 1605 by the Dominican Dávila Padilla, from 1612 to 1619 by the former holder of the prime chair of theology at the University of Mexico, Augustinian Diego de Contreras, and from 1619 to 1621 by the Augustinian Pedro Solier (formerly bishop of Puerto Rico).[64] Ramírez was elevated to the see of Guatemala in 1600 and held that position through rancorous times until his death in 1609.[65] Ledesma obtained the miter in Oaxaca, as did Juan de Cervantes later.[66] Cervantes, like González Soltero, became an inquisitional ordinary, and both ended their careers as bishops — Cervantes in Oaxaca and González Soltero in Guatemala.[67]

But these cases were the exception — of the 151 censors in the period of study, 15 were elevated to bishop; 11 of those appointments occurred before 1605, and some to minor sees like Panama and Manila. The censors were much more likely to reach their career apogee within their order or in their appointment as censor itself. Numerous friars exercised positions of importance in their orders as priors and guardians. In fact, a substantial proportion of the priors and guardians of the three important mendicant houses in Mexico City were censors. Perea and Juan de Contreras served as priors of San Agustín; Pedro de Pravia, Francisco de Arévalo, Lázaro de Prado, and Juan Díaz Arce as priors of Santo Domingo; and Sancho de Meras, Juan de Lormendi, Pedro de la Cruz, Francisco de Velasco, and Francisco Rodríguez as guardians of San Francisco.[68]

Nevertheless, by the seventeenth century, far more censors found themselves in relatively unimportant, small, or impoverished houses. And not a few of these middling administrators came from the ostensibly upper classes. Joseph Morán de Cerda, despite being an hidalgo, managed only to become guardian of the Franciscan house at Tocolotlan. It was rumored that his maternal grandfather, an hacendado, had married an Indian noblewoman, an act that theoretically would have disbarred him from both the priesthood and inquisitional office.[69] Juan de Cornejo was guardian of Tlatelolco in 1622, decades after its demise as a humanist educational project.[70] And while these positions would be considered less than prestigious, after the end of the sixteenth century it became increasingly more common for censors to have no administrative responsibilities whatsoever. Luis de Castilla, while coming from one of Mexico's most prestigious and wealthiest family (his cousin was the governor of the Philippines and count of Santiago) appears to have achieved virtually nothing in terms of career.[71]

There were some exceptions to the general decline in status and prestige of the censors into the seventeenth century. Many were nominated as censors in the seventeenth century and maintained a relatively high profile. The Franciscan Bartolomé de Burguillos was the confessor to the viceroy in the 1620s.[72] The Dominican Agustín Aldrete became censor of the Toledo Inquisition.[73] And the Dominican Antonio Hinojosa — whose uncle was the disgraced censor and professor at the University of Mexico Hernando Ortiz de Hinojosa — became censor of the General Council of the Spanish Inquisition — all the more impressive since he was a criollo.[74]

As academics the censors excelled at about the same rate as they did in higher ecclesiastical positions — that is to say, a relatively small portion of the censors as a whole occupied the highest academic positions. From 1554 to 1640 12 censors were also chair holders (*catedráticos*) of theology at the University of Mexico. Over the same time period there were 24 catedráticos of theology at the university, which means that half of all the university's theological chair holders of the period were censors.[75] If one includes De la Peña, who acted as a theological advisor in 1560 in the Oaxacan ordinary Inquisition and who held the prime chair of theology at the University of Mexico from 1553 to at least 1560, then 13 of the 24 catedráticos in theology were censors over a period of nine decades (1553–1640).[76] But if the theology faculty was dominated by the regular clergy and counted a high proportion of censors, theologians rarely ascended to the rectorship of the university. This position was reserved almost exclusively for canonists. González Soltero and León Plaza, both censors and theologians, were exceptions to this general rule.[77]

The canonists and their domination of the rectorship of the university followed similar lines of social prestige and status as observed above. In strictly economic terms, the theologians could never compete with the canonists and nonordained jurists. Even the provincial cathedral canons could expect salaries from 400 to 1,000 pesos per year in this time period. In contrast, the junior professor of theology at the University of Mexico earned 200 pesos per year in 1587.[78] At Salamanca the salaries were not significantly more impressive for theologians. By 1634 the prime chair of theology earned an annual salary of 500 pesos. The prime chairs in canon and civil law, by contrast, collected approximately 915 pesos per year.[79] At the same time a provincial cathedral canon in Michoacán could earn a 1,400-peso salary.[80] But university professors also tended to have other forms of income — often as cathedral dignitaries — so they were wealthier than these salaries suggest.

Social prestige and class, however, cannot be measured in purely economic and political terms. The clergy, both diocesan and regular, asserted over and over their proper role as guardians of the soul and therefore the idea that they were of the highest importance in the overall social order. There can be no mistaking the high prestige associated with the upper-level clergy in colonial Mexico, given the heavily Catholic public and intellectual cultures. But while the clergy continued to assert the primacy of theology over law as of divine, instead of human, origin, the realities of colonial society were such that the clergy represented an important component in familial clans' social status diversification. León Plaza came from a well-heeled family; his father was familiar in Cuernavaca.[81] Others, while less well placed, nevertheless were part of extended networks of family ties with the Inquisition. The father of the Dominican Tomás de Sant Juan was a familiar of the Seville Inquisition.[82]

Except for the presence of the censors on the theology faculty at the University of Mexico, as a whole the censors were not high-powered intellectuals and academics in the way that censors of the major inquisitional tribunals in Spain were. In the peninsula, some of the early modern period's most formidable minds were simultaneously censors. De Soto and Cano both served extensively as censors for the Suprema. In the Mexican tribunal, by contrast, most censors served within their orders as priors and provincials. Nevertheless, some notable men were academics themselves. Hortigosa was variously professor of theology at the Colegio de San Pedro y San Pablo, as was his fellow Jesuit Juan de Ledesma, who ultimately held the prime chair of theology at the royal university as well.[83] Pedro Sánchez had been rector of the University of Alcalá de Henares before coming to Mexico in the first Jesuit mission to New Spain.[84] Others served as lectors in theology within their orders' colleges. Ten censors held such positions in their orders, which still is a very low figure overall — less than 10 percent of all the censors for the period of study.

Even if there was a general decline in the intellectual prominence of the censors, some were active as writers, theologians, and preachers. Ledesma's *De septem nouae legis sacramentis summarium* was influential among Mexican theologians in discussing questions of administering sacraments to the Indians. One of the major debates was whether or not Indians should receive the Eucharist. In line with their view that Indians were dull witted and should be treated as children, the Dominicans in general argued against administering this sacrament to Indians. While not perhaps as extreme as some of his coreligionists, like Diego Durán, Ledesma reasoned that daily communion was acceptable in absolute terms but that if someone was in a state of mortal sin daily communion was not recommended.[85]

Others supported Indian communion, and another censor, Agurto, argued like his mentor, Alonso de la Veracruz, that it was precisely the weak who needed the Eucharist the most and therefore Indians should receive communion. He wrote a treatise to that effect titled *Tratado de que deven administrar los Sacramentos de la Sancta Eucharistia y Extrema unctión a los indios de Nueva España* (Treatise on Whether the Sacraments of the Holy Eucharist and Extremunction Should Be Administered to the Indians of New Spain) in 1573.[86] After the completion of the Third Mexican Church Council of 1585 it appeared that the faction in favor of Indian communion had prevailed, as the council supported Indian communion. Hernando Ortiz de Hinojosa, the one-time holder of the prime chair of theology and canon of the metropolitan cathedral chapter, wrote a memorial to the council in his capacity as advisor noting that many priests, arguing that it violated Church law, continued to refuse this sacrament to Indians.[87] Nevertheless, it appears that Ortiz de Hinojosa had a generally low opinion of Indians in general, arguing, for example, that priests should not demean themselves by accepting invitations for dinner at Indians' homes and that Indians should be forbidden to depict demons (as in Saint James paintings) for fear they might backslide into paganism.[88]

Other censors engaged in more traditionally European theological endeavors, the most typical of the period being commentaries on Aquinas. Hortigosa wrote several manuscripts, including commentaries on Aquinas "In 2.am 2.ae quaestionae divi Thomae commentarii de Fide: spe et charitate" (Commentaries on the Second Part of Saint Thomas: On Faith, Hope and Charity) from 1590 to 1592. Later, in 1603, he completed a discussion on confession and confirmation, "De sacramentis poenitentiae et confirmationis" (On the Sacraments of Penance and Confirmation).[89] In 1606 he completed further commentaries on Aquinas's discussion of angels, "Ex prima parte Angelici Doctoris Divi Thomae quaestio 50a de substantia Angelorum absolute in quinque articulos divisa" (From Question Fifty of the First Part of the Angelic Doctor Saint Thomas Aquinas on the Absolute Substance of Angels, Divided into

Fifty Articles).[90] Other works he completed included a discussion on indulgences, "Disputatio de indulgentis ecclesiae," and treatises on the nature of theology, "De natura theologiae," and on the Trinity, "De Mysterio SS. Trinitatis," though it appears that the two latter manuscripts have been lost.[91] There is some evidence that Hortigosa's commentary works may have been printed contemporaneously. A lengthy, untitled manuscript from 1610 dealing with general theology and doctrine exists today, and in the margins of the prologue is written "a work authored by father don Pedro de [H]ortigosa which was sent to the printer," though it is not clear if it was ever published.[92]

Hortigosa's collaborators and fellow censors wrote extensively as well on a variety of subjects, and as a whole the Jesuits were the most active theologians of the censors. For example, Diego de Santisteban wrote several treatises, including one, *De divina gratia* (On Divine Grace), which defended the Jesuit position against the Dominicans on free will and grace and which contained discussions of human action and laws.[93] Santisteban also wrote a commentary on Aquinas, "De sacramentis materia in genere incipiens a quaestione 68a 3ae partis theologiae D. Thomae" (On the Subject of the Sacraments Beginning with Question 68 of Part 3 of Saint Thomas [Aquinas] c. 1603), a discussion of the Trinity via an analysis of Aquinas's "De Sanctissimo et Ineffabili Trinitatis Mysterio in 17 quaestiones Angelici Doctoris D. Thomae a quaestione 27 usque ad 43 1ae partis" (On the Most Holy and Ineffable Mystery of the Trinity in 17 Questions of the Angelic Doctor Saint Thomas Aquinas from Questions 27 to 43 of Part One) sometime between 1605 and 1611, commentaries on the sacrament of the Eucharist "Comentaria circa materiam de sacrosancto eucharisticae sacramento," and an analysis of the sacrament of baptism, "Comentaria circa materiam de Baptismo" (Commentary on the Subject of Baptism).[94] Likewise, Hortigosa's frequent colleague on the inquisitional court, Pedro de Morales, offered various defenses of the Jesuit enterprise in Mexico and of Jesuit views of Church authority. He defended the early efforts by the Jesuits in Mexico in which they brought substantial numbers of relics and conducted large, ostentatious public ceremonies to impress upon the public their recent arrival and dedication to the criollo elite. Morales related the particularly notable ceremony of 1578 to that end in his summary of the event for the order's master general, Everardo Mercuriano.[95] Morales also weighed in on formal theology with a treatise on excommunication, "Materia de excommunicatione" (c. 1585). In Lyon in the same year of his death, 1614, he published a biblical exegesis, on chapter 1 of the Gospel of Matthew, *In capvt primvm Matthaei. De Christo domino, sanctissima virgine deipara Maria, veroque eius dulcissimo, et virginali sponso Iosepho* (On the First Chapter of Matthew, of the Dominion of Christ, and of the Most Holy Virgin Mother of

God Mary and of Her Most Sweet and True Virgin Betrothal to Joseph) as well as other biblical commentaries.[96] Andrés de Valencia wrote a *Tractatus de Incarnatione Dominica* (Treatise on the Incarnation). Juan de Ledesma completed part of his planned *De Deo ut uno* (On God and Unity).[97] Ledesma also completed a discussion of the Jesuit line on providence, "De ideis divinis, veritate et falsitate, justitia, providentia et praedestinatione tractatus" (Treatise on Divine Ideas, Truth and Falsehood, Justice, Providence and Predestination) in 1619.[98]

Other censors besides the Jesuits wrote treatises of formal theology. Juan Focher, a man who held a doctorate in law from Paris but who simultaneously was a respected theologian, wrote numerous treatises (lost today) on subjects such as ecclesiastical law in general, penal law, ecclesial immunity, and pastoral care. In addition to being confessor to the viceroy Luis de Velasco, the elder, and the first holder of the prime chair in theology, Pedro de la Peña left a manuscript commentary on Aquinas, "Commentarium in primam partem Sancti Thomae" (Commentary on the First Part of Saint Thomas).[99] The Dominican Hinojosa wrote a treatise on Thomist metaphysics, "Clypeum thomistarum ex quaestionibus metaphysicis et theologicis affabre compactum" (The Sturdy Shield of the Thomists Skillfully Designed from Metaphysical and Theological Questions).[100] In 1596 Pravia, the onetime prior of Santo Domingo in Mexico City, completed an analysis of the sacrament of the Eucharist as part of a commentary on Aquinas, "De sacrosancto Sacramento Eucharistiae quaestio 73–83 tertiae pars Divi Thomae" (On the Most Holy Sacrament of the Eucharist from Question 73 to 83 of the Third Part of Saint Thomas).[101] Antonio del Pozo, a Dominican who had taught theology in Oaxaca for some thirty years, wrote a treatise on monastic theology in 1618.[102] Besides the numerous and notable achievements of De la Veracruz and his students, Juan de Contreras, the peripatetic prior of various Augustinian houses, also wrote a commentary on Aquinas, "Tractatus de sacratissimo mysterio Incarnationis" (Treatise on the Most Holy Mystery of the Incarnation) in 1596.[103] Another student of De la Veracruz, Diego de Contreras, the archbishop of Santo Domingo, was a biblical scholar who left behind a now-lost "Exposición de los lugares más difíciles de la Sagrada Escritura" (Discussion of the Most Difficult Sections of the Holy Scripture).[104]

Other censors discoursed on practical and historical questions. One of the most famous, in twenty-first-century terms, of the censors' works was also one of the least influential contemporaneously: Dávila Padilla's *Crónica,* which Dominican historians used extensively but which had little to say about theology. Others offered works remembered today. The Franciscan Juan Baptista, who was a censor in the Chico de Molina trial of 1560, wrote a confessional, a sermon book in Nahuatl and worked on translating the *Contemptus mundi,* while also serving as guardian in Texcoco. Other works were less notable. For example, the Franciscan Miguel Agia apparently wrote several books on theology that are not extant, but his discussion of Indians, *Tratado o consulta sobre el servicio personal de los indios* (Treatise or Consultation on the Personal Service of the Indians), published in Lima in 1604, survives.[105]

In any case, by the mid-seventeenth century the censors appear to have ceased being influential theologians. While many held important administrative positions within their orders and in the universities and colleges, they produced little intellectual work. Instead, they tended to oversee funeral ceremonies and write eulogies. The Dominican Antonio de Gutiérrez offered a dedicatory sermon to the Templo de Jesús María in Mexico City in 1621.[106] Another Dominican censor, Francisco de Arévalo, noted as a famous orator, gave the feast day sermon for Aquinas in 1632 in Mexico, shortly before being elected provincial of the main Dominican province of New Spain.[107]

All told the personnel of the Mexican Holy Office represented the socioeconomic upper classes and the ecclesiastical ruling elite. There were important hierarchical distinctions within this tribunal and deep cleavages in status, power, and prestige between theologians and jurists. It was long a commonplace in early modern society to suggest that theology was the queen of the sciences and ruled the intellectual universe of Catholic politics and society. But if the Inquisition is any guide, the battle for primacy was far from settled in the minds of the jurists and theologians. If theologians and jurists held fundamentally different visions of authority and religious power, those same divisions played out also in the sociopolitical spheres in the Mexican Church. And while the theologians may have lost their status and position as the sole judges of the Inquisition, they retained important power, status, and class in Mexican colonial society.

Cordon Sanitaire:
Efforts and Failures of Book Censorship

On the afternoon of June 24, 1610, the feast of the birth of Saint John the Baptist, after rumors of an impromptu auto de fe, the cathedral bell rang ostentatiously to indicate that something important was about to happen in Mexico-Tenochtitlan. Shopkeepers grumbled at the interruption to business but also perked up their ears, knowing there would be a spectacle. The Franciscans wondered whether the Dominicans had again found cause to invade their libraries or chastise one of their liberal confreres. The inquisitor himself, accompanied by his bailiff and his Jesuit chargé d'affaires, solemnly exited the cathedral into the Zócalo. The Jesuit, in particular, had urged the inquisitor to avoid this spectacle, given that people would only be encouraged to read yet more banned books, which everyone in Mexico knew could be found in taverns and bathhouses for the right price. What would be next? Spanish editions of Petronius?

A great display was made, even if the viceroy himself was conspicuously absent. Standing on a raised platform before the crowd, the Dominican censor preached a rousing sermon on the dangers of the heretical plague, looked out at the Jesuit, and choked on his bile. He was one of the beloved dogs of the pope called to exterminate the heretics, but the casuist had outflanked him on so many occasions, convincing the inquisitor to exculpate men when they had cursed God in a card game or blasphemed the Virgin, tricking the lawyer into believing that efficacious grace had no bearing on the sinful actions of men. The Pelagian!

The Jesuit, for his part, had other concerns on his mind — Horace. He wondered if one might make an interesting translation of the Roman poet's work into Nahuatl. The Dominican was so crude, so inelegant. He tried to ignore him. Too late; the match was struck. The books gathered in the square — the unapproved Bibles, the Spanish prayer books, the coveted and rare copies of Erasmus — were engulfed. The crowd, always eager to enjoy the suffering of others, cheered. Ashes fell on the great plaza where Aztecs had seen an eagle devouring a serpent and where priests tossed war captives down pyramids with their chests gaping wide, raising pulsating hearts in their hands, devouring symbolic pieces of them. *Pulque* sloshed out of cups; dogs scavenged.[1] Young men cast furtive glances at the town lovelies and risked an indiscretion or two with their lovers, accompanied by their Indian governesses. Snow-covered Popocatepetl and Iztaccihuatl were visible on the horizon, reminding the Spaniards that they were, indubitably, not in Spain.

This bonfire never took place, but the image of such book burnings remains popular in the collective construction of the Black Legend of Spanish rapacity for which the Inquisition served as a central pillar of propaganda. But in Mexico the Inquisition did not burn books in public, and the populace did not cheer bonfires. So unpopular were the Index of Prohibited Books and its remarkably conservative theology that the inquisitors warned their deputies to avoid public book burnings for fear the public would turn against the Inquisition. Even if the bonfire is an illusion, the cast of characters is not. We have met most of them already. The Dominican, Luis Vallejo, was a rigorous defender of the hard-line Counter-Reformation programs of censorship. His sermons (like the ones he may have preached in front of autos de fe) were well known; in 1614 he was called to deliver the sermon on the beatification of Teresa of Ávila.[2] The Jesuit, Hortigosa, was confidant to inquisitors, personal theologian to the archbishop, master of theology in the Jesuit college, Nahuatl expert, and, indeed, reader of Roman poets. The inquisitor, Gonzalo Martos de Bohórquez, came from an old Spanish aristocratic clan and, unlike the censors, had not been an ordained priest.[3] Perhaps it was he who once referred to Hortigosa's role in the Inquisition: "Where is my old man, without whom I am lost? This court cannot function without his advice."[4] The differences between these three were emblematic of the many contradictory strands of the everyday efforts to rid Mexico of banned books and remove others from circulation.

In the 1570s the newly formed Mexican Holy Office, under Moya de Contreras and then Bonilla, prosecuted high-profile heresy and piracy cases against the English slaver John Hawkins and other English corsairs as well as some

French.[5] These trials prompted an alert for Lutheran and Calvinist books as well as vernacular scripture reaching Mexico. The foreign national and linguistic identities of the corsairs thrust them into the larger debate about the transatlantic diffusion and regulation of books and religious ideology. The issue of trade violations by Hawkins and others paled in comparison in the collective Catholic apprehension over the possibility that the newly conquered Mexico could become infected by Lutheranism. Among the central concerns was the possibility that vernacular translations of the Bible or books by Calvin, Philipp Melanchthon, or John Knox would reach Mexico, infiltrate Catholic homes and minds, and result in an ecclesiological disaster in which the unsuspecting faithful succumbed to the duplicitous charms of salvation by faith and the unapproved theological-linguistic renderings of the Gospels and Pauline letters.

In interrogations before the inquisitors, the accused heretics from Hawkins's crew were frequently asked whether they had brought any books with them to the Gulf of Mexico. The trial in 1573 of the Englishman William Calens — accused, convicted, and sentenced for Lutheran heresy — is a case in point. He confessed that his shipmates had prayed the Our Father and Creed and read the Psalms in English, prompting the censors to remark that while such works (like the Psalms) had inherent religious value, their translation into English made them immediately suspect. Chapter 7 of the indictment handed down by then-prosecutor Bonilla noted that the corsairs in Hawkins's ship had brought many Lutheran books as well as the Gospels and Pauline letters in English, which the shipmates were required to hear daily.[6]

While inquisitors and theorists viewed the issue of book distribution with considerable gravity, in practice, those charged with enforcing the Index in New Spain only inconsistently upheld its rules. The result was a contingent application of power and religious authority. Whereas inquisitors strove to ban autochthonous Mexican literature deemed unorthodox, inquisitional comisarios and inquisitors in theory engaged in an effort to remove from circulation books that appeared on the Index.

In terms of the everyday regulation of books, comisarios were charged with the recall and removal from circulation of all prohibited books outside the immediate geographic reach of the inquisitors themselves in Mexico City. On the gulf coast, Veracruz was the officially approved port of entry for ships entering New Spain with merchandise through the Spanish transatlantic mercantile trade routes. The inquisitors appointed a comisario there with the mandate to review incoming ships for potential intellectual contraband. But the efficacy of this control was blunted by the distaste of individual comisarios in Veracruz for certain components of the Index as well as by the widespread disdain it elicited among Spaniards. Unlike Veracruz, places like Zacatecas and Guatemala saw a vigorous regulation of books within the jurisdictions of comisarios who were active defenders of the Index.

All of New Spain was, in theory, subject to the recall efforts of the Index and the inquisitional apparatus. In application, however, the book censorship project varied widely. Attendance at the annual Lent edict of the faith was enforced with difficulty. Copies of pronouncements banning books or prayers were routinely torn off the front doors of churches and cathedrals. Others claimed that inquisitional decrees were useful only to wipe their asses. People used copies of the Gospels as amulets against lightning and painful childbirth. Friars refused to relinquish books prohibited by the Index or by decree. The overall picture of censorship as a tool of control was haphazard and ad hoc rather than complete and effective.

Print Controls

Censorship of print in the early modern Hispanic world was divided, in practice and by law, between pre- and postproduction regulation. Through the Council of Castile the Crown exercised preproduction control of the book trade through licenses to print books. In theory the Council of Castile could prevent the publication of virtually any book simply by refusing a license for its publication. In practice, however, this rarely happened, since it tended to issue licenses to printers whose individual books received minimal oversight from the Crown. Consequently, there was little prepublication censorship in the Hispanic world from the Crown.[7] Likewise authors often enlisted high-ranking clerics to compose an approval, called a *nihil obstat* (nothing stands in the way) in an attempt to block postproduction censorship.

The Crown did attempt on various occasions to assert its rights and prerogatives concerning censorship of publications. A notable effort was a series of royal edicts banning the transatlantic shipment of popular chivalric, knights-errant novels such as *El Cid, Amadís de Gaula, Primaleón,* or generically titled "romanceros" or "libros de caballería."[8] By all appearances, however, the royal effort was a colossal failure. Even inquisitional authorities did not take such bans seriously, placing in jeopardy the efforts of the Crown at controlling literary taste. The Crown was effective, however, when it acted as a kind of final arbiter of specific high-profile issues. For example, Philip II banned the manuscripts by Sahagún that formed the Florentine Codice. But the Crown tended to steer away from vigorous censorship endeavors, leaving them to its Inquisition.

While the Crown regulated the licensing of print, the Inquisition laid claim to censor any book after its publication if it contained anything deemed worthy of censure. The result was that censorship operated on two levels: the

Crown controlled the initial printing licenses, but the Inquisition could censure anything after that initial approval even if the Crown had authorized its publication. This meant, in effect, that the Spanish Inquisition, or its satellite courts like the one in Mexico, could prohibit or order expurgated or removed from circulation any book that had already been published. This assertion of ecclesiastical and legal power was impressive, since prior to 1559 only local ecclesiastical and university censures or specific Church council or papal decrees had been undertaken. The papacy and general councils of the Church had asserted their legal authority to ban works for centuries, but there had never been any systematic attempt to compile these efforts into a single Index.[9] By the 1540s various universities, like Louvain and Paris, had begun to issue Indexes, but the issue was one of jurisdiction and even of anti-Gallic sentiment. Many Spanish theologians and canon lawyers viewed Indexes of Prohibited Books issued by universities as local and not universally binding. But the Spanish Inquisition would assert its legal right to prohibit any book on the grounds that its jurisprudential precedent derived from the papacy itself and was endorsed by the Crown. The result was, of course, the infamous Index issued by the Spanish Inquisition in 1554 and 1559; subsequently (much amplified and expanded) editions were issued in 1583, 1612, 1632, and 1640.[10]

Among the offenses for which the Inquisition threatened excommunication was the reading, possession, distribution, or even knowledge of books on the Index. After the reading of the edict of the faith, those who did not come forward to denounce any prohibited books could be prosecuted by the Inquisition. While in theory the edict enjoined the populace to relinquish its prohibited books annually, the practice was to make a concerted effort to recall and remove from circulation books that appeared in recently issued Indexes. This meant that there were specific time frames in which the edicts stressed the recall of books — as in the early 1560s (in Spain though not in Mexico), 1584–87, 1613–16, and so on.

These purges, like the review of ships in Veracruz, had varied results. In some jurisdictions the enforcement was vigorous while in others the comisario charged with the task was himself found to possess prohibited books in defiance of the Index. But the success of this approach was often predicated on the belief of the citizenry. Many comisarios avoided entering private homes or engaging in widespread invasions of personal libraries to root out prohibited books. Rather, the mere threat of excommunication for possessing a book banned by the Inquisition was enough. Books were relinquished, though grudgingly, and people came forth to deposit them with their local comisario. In many cases books were simply left anonymously in the cathedral for the comisario to find. Many of the people who possessed prohibited books feared that their neighbors, family, or friends would denounce them to the Inquisition. By voluntarily relinquishing their books they avoided stiffer penalties. If a book was only recently banned, by relinquishing it one incurred no penalty, whereas to be discovered with the same book ex post facto resulted in inquisitional prosecution and punishment.

But prosecution for the actual possession of prohibited books was a pretty rare event in Mexico. In some instances individuals accused of heresy were questioned about their books, and in other cases charges for reading or possessing prohibited books were folded into heresy trials. But overall there was no vigorous prosecution of the sole act of possessing prohibited books. Indeed, there were only eight trials in over a century for the specific crime of possessing prohibited books. The question of prohibited books was inseparable from the general question of heterodoxy and heresy both in theory and in inquisitional prosecution.

The first orchestrated purge of prohibited books in Mexico occurred in the winter of 1571–72. Among the efforts of the new inquisitor general Moya de Contreras was a general purge of prohibited books in line with the 1559 Index. The result of the purge was a *memoria,* or an inventory, unsigned but in Ledesma's hand.[11] Geographic features indicate that the removal from circulation of books on the 1559 Index was relatively local, suggesting that Moya de Contreras had commissioned Ledesma to conduct a general visita in the immediate surroundings of Mexico City. There was ample correspondence to the inquisitional comisarios in other parts of New Spain, ordering them, in the 1570s, to conduct visitas of mendicant and private libraries. In the Ledesma purge, all of the notable Spaniards who had books taken were citizens of Mexico-Tenochtitlan. Numerous conventual libraries were inspected, all of which were Franciscan and located in the densely populated area surrounding Mexico City, including houses at Tepeyac (likely Santa Cruz de Tlatelolco), Xochimilco, Tepeapulco, Tula, Xilotepec, Huexotla, and Cuauhtitlan.[12]

One can draw some general features of the purge of 1571–72 by Ledesma that highlighted both the inefficacy of port controls in Veracruz and the popular nature of certain types of prohibited works. Ledesma confiscated a high number of books, 727, though this also reflected the higher literacy rates and population of Mexico-Tenochtitlan. This number was larger than most other such efforts throughout the sixteenth and seventeenth centuries in Mexico, though in 1588 the comisario in Puebla, the cathedral canon Alfonso Ruiz Hernández de Santiago, confiscated 555 books during a purge.[13] Other purges tended to be more limited in scope given the smaller populations of the areas outside the Valley of Mexico. For example, under relatively strong enforcement in Yucatán, the comisario Cristóbal Miranda confiscated 74 books in

1574.[14] In 1586 the purge undertaken by the comisario of Yucatán, the Franciscan Hernando de Sopuerta, yielded some 136 books.[15]

In the Ledesma purge, scripture was by far the most common work removed from owners. He confiscated nearly 200 scriptural editions: 109 complete Bibles, 39 editions of Gospels and Pauline letters, 30 New Testaments, 11 Gospels and letters specifically in Spanish, 2 Psalms, 2 books of Proverbs, and 2 editions (presumably manuscript) of Gospels and letters in Indian languages (probably the Ecclesiastes or Parables of Solomon manuscripts), for a total of 195 books. Since vernacular Bibles were specifically banned in their entirety by the 1559 Index, there were sure to be more than a few of these among the 178 editions in which the language was not stated. Numerous Latin scriptural editions were also banned by the Index for a variety of reasons ranging from typographical errors to commentary by heretics to being the fruit of a heretical press in a place like Germany. Among the educated classes in Mexico, scripture was popular reading. Even high-ranking officials of empire and Church did not necessarily share the extreme views of the inquisitors and theologians who fashioned the 1559 Index. For example, the Audiencia judge Vasco de Puga was forced to relinquish a copy of the Gospels in Spanish.[16]

In addition to scripture, Ledesma confiscated large numbers of books of hours, or prayer books for daily use: 135 in all, 128 of which did not specify language. Like scripture, all hours in Spanish and vernacular tongues were prohibited en masse by the 1559 Index. Ledesma would have handed over these hours to a censor to review their language and content, and, if deemed legal, they would be returned to their owners. On the other hand, all Spanish hours were to be destroyed. But flummoxing the inquisitional efforts to rid the Catholic world of vernacular books of hours was the obduracy of virtually the entire Spanish world. Jerónimo de Aguilar, the Spaniard marooned in Cozumel who, along with Cortés's mistress Malinche, facilitated the very conquest of Mexico with his knowledge of Maya, had held on desperately to the one book he possessed during his period away from Spanish culture: a Spanish book of hours. If the inquisitors in Mexico viewed prohibited books in the context of theories about infection and heresy, they understood their duties in practical terms. So popular and so important were such books of hours that inquisitors in Mexico repeatedly warned their comisarios of the dire social consequences of burning such books in public, given their traditional place in lay spiritual practice among Spaniards. For example, on November 8, 1577, the inquisitors Bonilla and Dávalos ordered their comisario in the Yucatán to "burn the [Pauline] Letters, Gospels and Hours in Spanish in a secret place so that no one can observe this, given the scandal it would create for people to see such popular books burned by the Church."[17]

The most frequently confiscated individual author in Ledesma's purge was Erasmus. He impounded thirty-six editions of Erasmus in his purge, twelve of them being the *Chiliads* (or, the *Adagia*). Like Spanish hours and scripture, Erasmus continued to be widely popular in Mexico despite the efforts to ban the vast majority of his works. Esteban de Portillo, the provisor of the archdiocese and former inquisitor ordinary for Montúfar, was forced to relinquish a copy of Erasmus's *Chiliads*.[18] The irony was surely not lost on Portillo, who could not have claimed ignorance of the law. Prohibited works of Erasmus were also routinely found by Ledesma in Franciscan houses. In many instances, these works were kept in private cells of friars or even in the order's library, either through the deliberate resistance to their prohibition or with a wink and a nod from the guardian. Alonso Cabello, for example, enjoyed free access to Erasmus by permission of his guardian in Cholula: the infuriated conservatives of the house denounced him for his nativity sermon.[19]

The best-selling author of the entire sixteenth century in the Hispanic world was the Dominican Luis de Granada.[20] Despite being considered a perfectly orthodox man and theologian, his hugely popular *Libro de oración y meditación* — a guide to spiritual discovery for the laity — was banned by the 1559 Index as being dangerously close to the alumbrado heresy. In 1561 an approved, "corrected" edition was issued, but the ban on the pre-1561 editions remained. But like bans on Spanish hours and Bibles, the ban on Granada's work was ignored, and it circulated freely between Seville and Veracruz. Yet it does not appear in Ledesma's purge. There are various potential explanations for the absence: it was not circulating in Mexico City; or Ledesma ignored the ban. Given the evidence of its widespread circulation between Seville and Veracruz from 1572 to 1640, it seems likely Ledesma looked the other way, but, like contraband in general, this is conjecture based on negative evidence. The question, though, is why Ledesma would have ignored such a ban, given his alliance with enemies of Dominican reform. It is possible that Ledesma inspected the Dominican houses and the report appeared in the now-lost first two pages of the memoria.

Authors besides Erasmus who did appear with regularity in Ledesma's purge were John Wild, Zumárraga, and Alonso de Molina — Franciscans all. Their unapproved additions were found in every Franciscan residence Ledesma visited during his purge. Zumárraga's Erasmian *Doctrina* had been banned by Montúfar, and Ledesma was eager to seek out copies of it, confiscating fifteen copies of the work. Molina was a noted Nahuatl expert whose *Vocabulario* had been banned once, forcing him to produce a revised edition acceptable for print in 1571. Ledesma confiscated fifteen copies of the work, either in an attempt to ascertain the edition or simply out of spite.

John Wild was revered as one of the Franciscan order's most popular German preachers of the 1540s and 1550s, having been cathedral preacher of Mainz.[21] After he died in 1554 his sermons and commentaries were widely published and, as Ledesma discovered in his purge, found their way to numerous Mexican Franciscan houses.[22] His works were staggeringly popular. By 1600, his homiletic works went through some 194 different editions, and 388,000 copies were printed. These same posthumous editions were banned later by the 1583 and 1612 Indexes, unless they were the officially approved versions — editions that did not seem to circulate at all. Some modern scholars have argued that Lutheran printers altered Wild's original sermons and exegeses and that the resulting publications were intended to besmirch the good name of a loyal Catholic.[23] But printers whose Catholic orthodoxy could hardly be challenged produced many of Wild's works. For example, William Desboys, who had also printed works by Chrysostom, a Latin Bible by the University of Paris theologian Jean Benoit, and the *Decretum,* printed Wild's exegesis on the letter of Romans in Paris in 1559.[24] The exegesis was consistently condemned for its discussion of works and faith.[25] Wild and his posthumous printers were also intimately connected with John Cochläus, the virulent enemy of and preacher against Luther, also of Mainz.[26] Ledesma's fellow Salamanca Dominican, Domingo de Soto, an intimate of Melchor Cano, attacked Wild's exegesis of the Gospel of John as heretical. Wild's works ended up on the 1583 Index not from the deliberate corruption of his works but from a deep Dominican hostility to Franciscan spiritualism and discussions of the value of faith and works. In the end Ledesma confiscated nineteen works by Wild, all biblical exegeses and sermons, ten of which were his exegesis on the Gospel of John. In the aftermath he seems to have been successful in convincing Moya de Contreras to issue a ban on his works, much as the Salamancan Dominicans were successful in placing many of Wild's works on the 1583 Index.

Besides these works by Franciscans and Erasmus, Ledesma confiscated a wide range of spiritual, confessional, and legal books. Not all of these works were necessarily banned by the Index, demonstrating the exacting and precise nature of this visita. Many of the works Ledesma confiscated were works known to have one banned edition, like the *Flos Sanctorum* (of which he confiscated two). In other cases Ledesma may have felt that the books simply looked a bit suspicious, and he probably ordered them reviewed to verify that they did not contain any heresies. For example, he confiscated ten editions of Jerome in an effort to discern the edition and place of publication, since humanists had employed Jerome's works and Melanchthon had published editions of Jerome with his own commentaries. Ledesma also confiscated more than a dozen copies of works by Chrysostom, whose works had been edited by heretics in Germany.

The purge of 1571–72 demonstrated that both lay and clerical Spaniards in Mexico read and possessed a wide range of prohibited works between 1559 and 1572. Scripture, prayer books, Erasmus, and spiritual works continued to be read despite the Index's prohibition. While there was virtually no presence of or popularity for Luther or Calvin, many Spaniards in Mexico viewed the prohibition of otherwise orthodox authors with distrust. In other cases the deep distrust of the humanist-Erasmian Franciscans in Mexico for the Index and its rules was refracted in their intransigence over the bans on works by their own order's authors as well as on works by Erasmus.

The Problem of Port Controls

In addition to the general visita of 1571–72, there were other methods for the enforcement of the Index in Mexico in this period. The Inquisition aimed to establish a kind of *cordon sanitaire* in Veracruz in keeping with the idea espoused by Peña, Simancas, Castro, and Páramo that ports were sites of viral infection of heresy. The Inquisition's comisario in Veracruz was required to board all incoming ships in the mercantile fleets and search them for book imports as well as to conduct a general visita, which meant interviewing the people on board. By both of these methods the results of enforcing the Index were inconsistent at best.

There appears to have been almost no regulation of the book trade through Veracruz before 1572.[27] Veracruz was part of the diocese of Puebla and fell under the jurisdictional claims of Puebla's diocesan Inquisition, which was operative as early as 1536 but generally not very active until the 1550s, when it began to adjudicate cases.[28] None of the diocesan officials appears to have engaged in regulating the book trade or inspecting ships. In 1563 the diocesan prosecutor did investigate a case of potential book smuggling, but this was an isolated case.[29]

In 1572 Francisco López de Rebolledo was named comisario of the Holy Office in Veracruz, a position he held until his death in 1591. Thereafter the office of comisario in Veracruz was held by Franciscans for twenty-five uninterrupted years until 1617. During this forty-five-year period, regulation of books was lax in Veracruz. So unsalubrious is Veracruz's climate that before the eighteenth century the port existed primarily as an unpacking area. The majority of traders who dealt with merchandise coming through Veracruz lived in Xalapa or Mexico City and went to Veracruz only when the mercantile fleet from Seville had arrived, fleeing the port when finished. In theory, the resident Franciscan comisarios were also running the Franciscan house in the port, though it is unclear if López de Rebolledo was a resident of the port. Assuming that the comisarios were in fact undertaking visitas regularly, even the results of those visitas reflect lassitude in enforcing the Index. The first way in which the comisarios rejected the law was in their method of conducting the visitas themselves. They were required to interview all passengers and *gente de mar* (i.e., sailors) on board every ship. This was clearly stated in the numerous instructions written to them by inquisitors and reiterated in all the standard legal discussions of the Inquisition.

Despite the clarity of the law and the theory of the Inquisition, the comisarios of Veracruz interviewed not a single bishop, priest, viceroy, Audiencia judge, a single woman and only a small handful of passengers in their visitas. The first extant visita undertaken took place over a three-month period between October and December 1572. López de Rebolledo interviewed at least sixty-three individuals of whom only five were not sailors.[30] This incidence of nonsailors was actually one of the highest of any of the visitas of ships undertaken in Veracruz in seven decades. Moreover, in this first formal visita, López de Rebolledo made no effort to ask the sailors about books or inspect the ship for book imports. Instead of vigorously enforcing the inquisitional law concerning licenses from the Seville Inquisition and the strict rules about book transport, comisarios in Veracruz interviewed almost exclusively sailors. That the sailors were always headed back to Spain and the passengers were those who were most likely to bring their personal books with them underscored the legal rejection of the Index by the comisarios. For example, on August 26, 1580, *maese* Juan de Atibar stated during the visita before López de Rebolledo that there were several Dominican friars on board the transatlantic journey, yet not a single one of them figured among the thirty-five men interviewed by the comisario.[31] A flood of both legally acceptable and forbidden books thus entered Mexico.

The comisarios of Veracruz did on occasion take depositions and inventories of individuals coming into Mexico with the express purpose of selling books or when individual citizens from Spain offered an inventory of books. For example, in 1605 Diego de Sossa brought a large shipment of books for the captain García de Quadros. Sossa had brought some one hundred books, presumably for sale, from Spain. Among his inventory one finds primarily spiritual guides: three dozen prayer books (*oratorios*), unidentified hours of Our Lady, thirty copies of prayer books by Luis de Granada (presumably the *Libro de oración y meditación*), the potentially prohibited *Historia pontifical* by Gonzalo Illescas, three *Flos Santorums,* and a smattering of confessional, sacramental, and missal guides. Even in this case there did not seem to be much attempt to avoid declaring possession of questionable editions or illegal books, since the editions of Luis de Granada and *Historia pontifical* were not specified.[32]

In September 1619 Hernando Mexía declared his merchandise before the newly appointed comisario of Veracruz Mateo Carvajal: books he had brought from Seville for the book dealer Diego Garrido in Mexico. As was the case with Sossa and with most book transactions, the lion's share of the editions was composed of spiritual works, along with grammars and light literature. He had brought a copy of Ribadeneira's *Flos Santorum*, Luis de Granada's prayer book, Nebrija's Spanish grammar, and *Don Quijote*. Among the other secular works were some unidentified books by Cortés (perhaps his *Cartas de relación*) and comedies of Lope de Vega. He also had brought works by Bellarmine and theological summaries by various authors.[33]

But these declarations of merchandise were the exception. In general few dealers or merchants declared their goods, and in virtually no instance did the comisarios interview noncommercial bearers of books. Likewise, if the inquisitional law was clear that all members of the Church were subject to doctrinal oversight, the Index was occasionally overly complex, which was one of its principal bureaucratic failings. In many cases the Index prohibited only certain editions of a book. This was the case with the *Flos Santorum*, a book that had only certain approved editions. The same held for certain classical works in Latin that were banned in translation and for Cicero (any editions with commentaries by heretics like Melanchthon were banned). But the comisarios of Veracruz neglected to investigate these important legal details. The detailed visita documents routinely failed to mention the specific edition of a *Flos Santorum* or the language of books of hours. In many cases hours in Spanish were mentioned, but the comisario did not mention whether he had confiscated the illegal work or not.

One can consult the visitas to gain a fuller picture of the transatlantic books — both legal and illegal — circulating around and through Veracruz. The first extant visita with information on books, from the summer of 1575, shows that even at that point there were substantial structural deficiencies in the censorship apparatus. López de Rebolledo did not record the edition or language of the books. Many were potentially illegal, such as the hours and the *Historia pontifical*, depending on the edition, and the knights' tales, like *Amadís*, which the Crown attempted to ban. Spiritual books, especially prayer books, were among the most popular works, along with the *Flos Santorum* and a variety of adventure tales. Forty-six men were interviewed, and the numbers below (table 9.1) represent not the numbers of editions on board ships but the number of times the individual book was mentioned, which still provides a good estimate of the relative popularity of the book.

The ineffective apparatus of visitas continued through the end of the sixteenth century and into the seventeenth. Throughout the visitas of López de

Table 9.1. Visita de navíos, *July–August 1575, Veracruz*

Horas, latín	14
Horas [no language stated]	1
Horas de nuestra señora según el resado nueuo	1
Flos Sanctorum [no author or edition given]	7
La historia pontifical	5
Libros de caballerías	4
Coplas [poetry]	3
Orlando [furioso]	2
Boscán	2
Carlo magno	2
[un libro de] don Antonio de Guevara	1
Las epístolas de Guevara	1
La propalabia	1
Diana	1
Brebiarios de lo nuevo romano	1
Libros de estudio	1
Diurno de letanías, latín	1
Libros de geografía y cosmografía por nabegación	1
La creación del mundo	1
Un libro del marqués de [. . .]	1
Un libro de Quiñones	1
Calvario	1
Libros de pasatiempo en lengua italiana	1
La torre de David	1
Un confesionario	1
[un libro de] fray Luis de Granada	1
El tormento y agonía de la muerte	1
Contentus mundi	1
Primaleón	1
Renolido	1
Un libro italiano	1
Marco aurelio	1
Pauligovio	1
Amadís	1
Oliveros	1

Source: AGN, Inq., vol. 72, exp. 24, vol. 80, exp. 1

Rebolledo and the Franciscans, nonspecific books of hours, the *Amadís,* nonspecific editions of the *Flos Santorum* and the *Historia pontifical* continued to circulate widely. The epic tale of Chile *La Araucana* by Alonso Ercilla became quite popular, going through nineteen editions between 1569 and 1598, as did other exploits of the conquests of the New World, which circulated frequently in Veracruz.[34] In the autumn of 1581 during his visita, López de Rebolledo recorded that of twenty-seven sailors he interviewed, thirteen mentioned that there were Spanish books of hours on board their ships.[35] A decade later, in May 1590, López de Rebolledo recorded three mentions of Spanish hours after interviewing nine sailors. In both of these cases nothing seems to have transpired either in Veracruz or Mexico City to stop the circulation of these illegal books.[36]

The Franciscan comisarios who succeeded López de Rebolledo were no stricter. In 1591 in the first visita recorded by the new comisario, Diego de Bobadilla, the flood of banned books continued unabated. Among the forty-five sailors he interviewed, Spanish and nonspecific hours and the *Flos Santorum* circulated widely along with the ever-popular works of Luis de Granada, knights' tales, and comedies (table 9.2).

While the comisarios continued not to enforce the bans by not confiscating potentially prohibited books, in the early decades of the seventeenth century the popularity of hours, in Latin and Spanish, continued unabated. The popularity of the works of Luis de Granada even began to increase, and with each visita these two types of books were consistently the most popular. Likewise, libros de caballería remained immensely popular, but the very fact that the comisarios did not bother to discover the title or edition was telling. Generically titled "devotional" books also met this same lack of investigation.[37] In one such visita in 1600 the Franciscan comisario Francisco Carranco interviewed thirty-four individuals, thirteen of whom mentioned Spanish devotional books, six nonspecific books of hours, and five copies of Luis de Granada. He also noted four mentions of *Guzmán de Alfarache,* which had only just been published in 1599 and which was so popular that it went through twenty-six editions in its first six years, from 1599 to 1604.[38] In the summer of 1608 the Dominican García Guerra arrived in Mexico as the archbishop, bringing with him the author of *Guzmán,* Mateo Alemán, which may suggest a good deal about the continuing lax enforcement of controls of that book and others in Veracruz, given Guerra's well-known fondness for *la dolce vita.*[39] In any case Carranco oversaw other equally lax visitas, like the one in October 1601 (table 9.3). In the autumn of 1602 he oversaw one of the most flagrantly incomplete visitas of the port's already lax standards, one in which he interviewed seventy-seven men. The comisario recorded no fewer than thirty-nine

Table 9.2. Visita de navíos, *October–December 1591, Veracruz*

Horas [no language given]	6
Horas, romançe	4
Horas, latín	3
Flos Sanctorum	5
Libros de caballerías	3
(una parte del) pontifical [La historia pontifical]	2
un libro de fray Luis de Granada	1
un libro pequeño de fray Luis de Granada de oraciones y exercicios	1
Contentis mundi	2
Espejo de la bida humana	1
Araucana	1
La austriada	1
Reglón por la instructión de España	1
Un libro de Santa Catarina de Sena	1
La çimsa de Inglaterra	1
La estada del príncipe don Felipe en italia	1
Don beliano	1
Guzmán casado	1
Oraciones en romançe	1
La corónica de España	1
un libro de Antonio de Gueuara	1
un libro de la conversión de la Magdalena	1

Source: AGN, Inq., vol. 172, exp. 4, vol. 173, exp. 2a

mentions of hours (with no language given), seventeen Spanish hours, fifteen nonspecific *Flos Santorums,* and ten copies of Luis de Granada. The ever-popular *Historia pontifical,* which went through forty-six editions between 1565 and 1630, continued to come through Veracruz despite the ban on certain editions.[40]

There was little change into the seventeenth century in the nonapplication or disregard for the Index on the part of the Franciscan comisarios in Veracruz. The major shift was the increasing popularity of the work of Cervantes, especially *Don Quijote,* which was mentioned by five sailors out of thirty-two in the visita of September 1605 undertaken in Veracruz by Carranco. The famous novel had arrived in Mexico within months of its publication and would continue to remain popular.[41] But a change of comisarios did not bring a change in the broader picture. The Franciscan comisario Baltasar Morales reported dozens of books of hours circulating, including ninety-one hours of no particular language and twenty-one Spanish hours out of 131 individuals

Table 9.3. Visita de navíos, *October 1601, Veracruz*

Horas en latín	15
Horas [no language given]	15
Horas en romançe	2
Libros de cauallerías	18
Devocionarios en romançe	12
Devocionarios [no language given]	2
Historias [no title given]	11
Devocionarios de fray Luis de Granada	5
Libros de fray Luis de Granada [no title given]	2
Romanceros	4
Flos Sanctorum [no author given]	3
La cisma de Inglaterra	1
Libro de cauallerías de Febo	1
Exerçiçios espirituales	1
Rosario de nuestra señora	1
Dichos y sentençias agudas	1
El rreyno de Dios por un padre de la Compañía de Jesús [no name given]	1

AGN, Inq., vol. 265, exp. 4

interviewed in September 1608.[42] Overall, there was a long tradition of non-enforcement of the Index in Veracruz over several decades.

There are a variety of potential explanations for the procedural shortcomings in Veracruz. Irving Leonard, for one, attributes them to the stifling heat of the gulf coast and to the sloth and ineptitude of the comisarios. It is tempting to explain this in climatologic ways, but this does not explain why friars endured equally hellish conditions in other parts of Mexico. There is no shortage of stories of friars in Mexico enduring extreme physical privation. Augustinian friars traveled through the stifling heat of lowland Michoacán in rough habits. Domingo de Betanzos supposedly walked barefoot from Guatemala to Mexico City.[43] Graft and corruption, however, are hardly illogical explanations for the state of port controls in Veracruz. López de Rebolledo was accused, though exculpated, of trading in contraband. His successor, the Franciscan Diego de Bobadilla, was accused of soliciting sexual favors in the confessional at the end of his tenure in 1597.[44]

In the end there was more at work than peculation and the seduction of young girls in Veracruz as a site of book censorship. There was widespread disdain for the rules of the visita and the details of the Index. This was most manifest in the distrust of the Franciscans for the Index. They had been singled out time and again by the Dominicans and other inquisitors. The Franciscans, still smarting over the devastation wrought on their mendicant libraries by Ledesma, probably distrusted the extreme measures of the 1583 Index. Over-all, the enforcement of one of the central components of censorship—port controls—was a failure in early Mexico. Prior to 1571 diocesan officials of Puebla did not appear to have placed much emphasis on installing a vicar in the port to screen the book trade. By the late sixteenth century, both López de Rebolledo and the Franciscan comisarios simply did not enforce the controls expected both by the rules of the Index or by theorists like Peña and Castro, who saw port controls as central to the success of censorship efforts. The result was that much of urban Mexico was a place of considerable exposure to European theological controversies. The debates over humanism, Erasmus, Trent, Catholic reform, and grace were given wide purchase through the gap-ing hole in the barrier to the diffusion of books that was Veracruz. The avail-ability of numerous prohibited works in urban markets can be traced directly to the lack of enforcement of the Index in the entry port of Veracruz.

Urban and Rural Control of Books

As in Spain and Italy, enforcement of the Index in Mexico was most effective in cities.[45] In contrast to ports, where the interests of merchants were strong and tied to commerce, cities in both colonial Mexico and early modern Spain that were not ports tended to be more easily (and closely) regulated. On the one hand, urban citizens had more to lose from appearing to be heterodox than sailors. Simultaneously, cities tended to have a much higher concentra-tion of the personnel associated with the social control of ideas, like inquisi-tors, bishops, a cathedral chapter, and university professors. Comisarios in Mexico tended to live in cities that had cathedral chapters, large conventual houses, and colleges. As late as 1600, there were few comisarios located out-side of such areas in New Spain, though on occasion missionaries in rural Indian areas (like Chiapas) performed double duty as comisarios. In general the rural areas of colonial Mexico tended to be far less regulated by royal or religious officials.

The enforcement of the Index tended to vary considerably from one city to another. In some cases the comisarios were vigilant and strict in their enforce-ment of the Index; in others, they were lax, owing perhaps to an ideological distrust of the Index. In other places the comisarios were foot-draggers who had little interest in enforcing the directives of the Inquisition. For example, Melchor Gómez de Soria had been the diocesan inquisitor ordinary in Zacate-cas before being nominated comisario in Guadalajara. On March 14, 1571, he wrote to Ledesma as governor of the archdiocese of Mexico to inform him of his personal library, noting that "if some [books] or others are prohibited, please inform me so that I can send them to your reverence later."[46] In the same letter, he informed the archdiocese that among his books were the New Testament letters and Gospels in Spanish, and he asked the inquisitor "to inform me if they can be read because I have a good deal of them."[47] It boggles the imagination that one of the central components of the 1559 Index—the prohibition of the scripture in vernacular—was unknown to Gómez de Soria, a man who had been dean of the Michoacán cathedral chapter and later cathedral canon in Guadalajara.

Gómez de Soria's strategy of pretending not to know the contents of the Index seems to have worked. On May 22, 1572, he wrote to the new inquisitor general, Moya de Contreras, to say that he had not received a response from the Holy Office concerning the Gospels and letters in Spanish.[48] Alas, in 1586 the other comisario of Guadalajara, the cathedral chantre Francisco Martínez Tinoco de Segura, conducted a purge of books—presumably in the private libraries of citizens—and reported his findings of both the books recalled and their owners. Gómez de Soria was found to have the *Adagia* of Erasmus and Wild's commentary on the Gospel of John, both of which were prohibited in the 1583 Index.[49]

Gómez de Soria was hardly the only inquisitional comisario and urban resident not to enforce the Index. While his disobedience regarding the Index may have been theological, in other cases it appears to have been personal. Often, comisarios simply did not fulfill any of their censorial duties. For example, in 1567 the provisor of Puebla, Pedro Ortiz de Zúñiga, was the diocesan Inquisition's vicar. He was prosecuted for concubinage by the diocesan Inquisition for which he previously worked. Convicted, he was sentenced to two months' loss of pension from the administration of sacraments, 220 pesos in fines (about the average annual salary of a parish priest), and the costs of the trials; in addition, he was ordered not to have any contact, social or otherwise, with his two presumed mistresses, María de Rivera and Magdalena Rodríguez.[50] In the late 1570s Cristóbal de Badillo, comisario of Michoacán and former professor of law at the University of Mexico, passed much of his time buying expensive silk suits, playing cards, and engaging in fights. Ultimately, his commission was revoked for gambling.[51] In other cases, comisarios were tried for doctrinal offenses. The cathedral canon and comisario of Puebla (1578–1606) Alfonso Ruiz Hernández de Santiago was prosecuted and convicted by the Inquisition itself for blasphemy and sentenced to six months' exile in 1605.[52] Overall, the strict legal, theological, and moral orthodoxy of the Inquisition was faced with the problems of everyday disregard for the immutable quality of the law.

In contrast to the examples given above, other cities hosted vigorous defenders and enforcers of the Index, notably in Zacatecas and Guatemala. As early as the 1560s Juan de las Ribas was operating as the vicar of the mining city of Zacatecas. In 1574 he undertook a purge of prohibited books as the inquisitional comisario, confiscating many books of hours—because "they lack beginning and ends and need to be corrected"—and Spanish Bibles. He also confiscated a copy of Wild's commentaries on Matthew because they did not bear the censura of the University of Salamanca. In a strange move, he reported that a licenciado Sotomayor had a copy of Torquemada, though Ribas incorrectly recorded the title as the *Reportorium Inquisitorum,* noting that he did not understand the rule of the Index concerning inquisitional manuals.[53]

Diego de Sepúlveda was the cura and vicar of Zacatecas after Ribas from 1575 to about 1585 and later comisario of Zacatecas from 1586 to 1605. He demonstrated acumen for his job markedly different from that of others. In his correspondence with the inquisitors in 1586 and 1587 in his efforts to enforce the new Index of 1583, Sepúlveda showed attention to detail often absent in the other comisarios' correspondence, always noting the publication date or edition of a book. Sepúlveda had recalled copies of the *Flos Sanctorum* only when they were prohibited editions. He may very well have had a better grasp of the Index than the inquisitor Bonilla. In letters dated November 12, 1586, and February 12, 1587, Sepúlveda notified the inquisitors in Mexico City that he had confiscated copies of the *Historia pontifical* because they were editions from 1569.[54] The 1583 Index had prohibited all editions of the *Historia pontifical* printed before 1573, yet in the margin of the letter of February 1587 Bonilla had written, "Return to owner because it is not prohibited."[55] But even Sepúlveda was not, it seems, immune to the charms of his female penitents. He had been accused in 1591 (though there was no trial) for having solicited doña María Pérez in the confessional in 1575 when she was a young bride.[56]

If enforcement of the Index in urban centers with resident comisarios owed much to the idiosyncrasies of human nature, the enforcement of censorship in rural Mexico was a function of logistics. There is abundant evidence that there were logistical problems in enforcing the Index. In numerous instances there was no Index locally available for a comisario to consult (this was true at times even in cities). On October 12, 1585, the inquisitors Bonilla and Santos García wrote to the comisario of Veracruz that they were still waiting for a copy of the new 1583 Index and that they had not received the edition in the shipment from Seville in the most recent merchant fleet.[57] The inquisitors shortly thereafter possessed copies of the new Index; but the same cannot be said for inquisitors in other parts of the viceroyalty.

Much of rural Mexico lacked for Indexes. On September 22, 1587, the inquisitors sent out lists of commonly circulating prohibited books to those comisarios "in those parts [of New Spain] where the General Catalogue had not yet arrived," suggesting that the absence of the Index was quite common.[58] In such a letter to the comisario of Guadalajara, the inquisitors wrote that because "in some parts of that diocese there was no notice of the Index and because in some towns of Spaniards it would be possible for some prohibited books to circulate; we therefore send with this the list of those books which are most likely to continue to circulate."[59] Likewise, on March 14, 1588, Bonilla and Santos García sent a list of the prohibited books "which tend to" continue to circulate to the comisario in Guatemala.[60]

The situation compelled the inquisitors in 1587 to compose a generalized list of the most commonly circulating prohibited works for comisarios "in those areas where a General Catalogue had not yet arrived."[61] This was a blanket admission that the Index was physically lacking in much of Mexico. The prohibited books viewed as most likely to be circulating and therefore most in need of purgation included, among others,

- every type of hours in Spanish
- small hours called Crown of Our Lady
- various manuals of conscience
- Bouquet of Spiritual Flowers (*Ramillete de flores espirituales*)
- all letters and Gospels in Spanish
- all letters and Gospels in Indian vernacular languages
- The Papal History (*La historia pontifical*)

These were the books considered both most dangerous and whose ban was most likely to be ignored by the populace unless vigorously reminded. Authorities in Chiapas confronted similar circumstances. In October 1586, the inquisitors wrote to Noreña, explaining that "so few or no Indexes had arrived in this flota that we have no other [copy] to send to your reverence and thus you need to make do with what you have there [in Chiapas]."[62] Similar problems continued in other sparsely populated regions. In Acapulco, the comisario Alonso Muñoz wrote that he inspected a ship coming from Peru in late 1586 but that in order to complete the inspection it was "necessary to have here the Catalogue or memoria of prohibited books."[63] This was not Muñoz's last request for an Index. He made similar requests in letters of March 10, 1587, and April 8, 1587.[64]

In urban areas the enforcement of the Index may have counted on a better apparatus for control, but that same enforcement also encountered a better educated population, one more likely to distrust certain strands of conservative thinking. By and large, the everyday enforcement of the Index varied considerably between city and countryside and from city to city depending on the ideology and temperament of the local comisario. In the end, despite all the high-flown theories about the need to protect doctrinally isolated regions, those who were charged with this task, much to the horror of the theorists, more often than not balked at their duties or even opposed them openly.

Conclusion

Jurists and theologians considered the control of transregional book movement and the regulation of reading to be extremely important components of the spiritual health of the faithful and of the Church itself. Likewise, the concerns about incursion, infection, and doctrinal movement were central to inquisitional censure. On one level this discourse was abstruse and theoretical, as in the work of Aquinas and Castro, or specific, as in the inquisitional instructions. On another level this discourse was translated into the prosecutorial activity of the Inquisition and codified in the Index itself. Yet if the theorization of the inherent connections between heresy, books, and censorship tended to promote the Index and the Inquisition as central components of defense, the application of censorship rules and the Index varied considerably in Mexico. A great deal depended on individual views of the law, dissident theology, competing ideologies, geography, and the availability of the Index itself.

But can this variable enforcement be attributed solely to idiosyncrasy? Was it part of a much larger pattern in Spanish America that social historians have described for some time now? For example, it is a commonplace to argue that the ancient formula *Obedezco pero no cumplo* (I obey but do not enforce the law) was the standard legal attitude of Spanish administrators in the Indies. But what if the law itself was physically absent, as in the case of the Index?

What could jurists or theologians do when that very law was never entirely clear? The concept of positive law operating in opposition to cultural attitudes does not entirely explain the flexibility of legal applications in the colonial system when it comes to censorship. For example, even the very quality and force of the law were fluid. Were the commentaries of Peña or Covarrubias binding and did they possess the force of actual law itself? The doctrinal works of glossators and theorists did not specifically legislate. For example, Eimeric, though viewed as an authority, did not actually define the compulsory quality of the law but instead outlined the ideological justification of inquisitional law and procedure. Technically speaking, only the legislation of the Suprema and the rulings of the papacy carried the full force of the law itself for inquisitional censorship. But even then that supposed immutable quality was unclear. Castro argued that papal fiats without proper review by councils or cardinals were useless.

So where exactly was the law located for censorship in Mexico? In many ways, it could never be precisely located because Hispanic law was not circumscribed to a discrete body of legislation. Even the presumption of which legislation was legitimate was always debated. The difference between codified law as contained, for example, in the *Decretales,* and the commentaries on the canon law as contained in the works of Peña, Covarrubias, Simancas, and Torquemada was blurred. For many inquisitors the distinction between the force of legislation and jurisprudential commentary was unimportant in the application of case law itself. As was the case in Guatemala in 1608 and 1609 even the ostensibly concrete nature of positive law was not enough to resolve fundamental differences in the interpretation of censorship and inquisitional law, since competing legislation was at odds with it.

As was often the case, the law had to answer to custom. *Ad abolendam* may have represented concrete, codified papal law, but even the censors and inquisitors admitted that customary concerns could trump positive law. And, taking a page right out of Melchor Cano and other conservatives, inquisitors and censors would point to the collective force of tradition as carrying the same authority as written law itself. But even within the written law and commentary philosophy deep divisions emerged over definitions of heresy, the need for censorship, and the jurisdiction of the Inquisition. Castro said that Erasmus was a great scholar even as Montúfar and Cano were demanding a ban on his works. Juan de Torquemada viewed papal legislation as infallible and therefore possessing the incontrovertible force of law, whereas Villadiego and Castro had a considerably weaker papal personality in mind. Even Raymond of Peñafort, the patron saint of canon law, considered the person of the pope fallible and subject to review or disenfranchisement if necessary. Simancas stuck to the dual bailiwick of censure as regulating pertinacious expression of inner doubt, while Suárez exempted inner conscience from the Church's oversight. So even if one presumes that written law in the form of commentary could compel obedience, that same written law was not uniform. Add customary concerns, and the waters were muddied further. Confession was an expression of custom eventually codified. But how often should it take place and should Indians, for example, be allowed to receive the Eucharist? No single legislative fiat could solve the riddle of the competing forces of custom and law.

In addition to the overlapping claims of custom, tradition, codified law, and scholarly commentary, there were other reasons for the relative inefficacy of inquisitional censorship in early Mexico. Broad disdain and distrust of the extremely conservative ideology of the fashioners of the Index—and especially of the Dominicans who crafted the 1583 Index under the aegis of Inquisitor General Quiroga—burrowed deeply into religious consciousness at the highest levels. The peninsular Spaniards and criollos who comprised the laity in Mexico as well as the growing mestizo population developed their own sense of rules about the Church. This laity was not formally schooled in theology and had only a rudimentary exposure to major theologians and works. Nevertheless, the books found regularly entering Veracruz, in private libraries, and relinquished to the Inquisition after the Edict of the Faith show that the laity read spiritual works with great interest. This meant that the average person, whether literate or not, would have been exposed to some of the major trends in religion in Spain as well as in Mexico. Likewise, blaspheming disregard for the tithe, diocesan censure, and even of many sacraments, especially confession and the Eucharist, was commonplace.

While only a small fraction of the population was literate (perhaps as low as 5 percent), the public reading of books was extremely common. The Indian practices of public bathing (in *temazcales*) and drinking in *pulquerías* (bars where mildly alcoholic pulque was served) were adopted by Spaniards, especially men.[1] Mexico City alone boasted of more than 300 taverns of varying style and clientele by the 1620s.[2] These spaces became fertile ground not only for romantic, sexual, and social encounters but also for political debate and discussion, readings of books, and reenactments of literary scenes. Even though Indians were often legislatively banned from selling pulque, the collective massive popularity of pulque and pulquerías made it virtually impossible for alcaldes or others to shut them down entirely. And all along the circulation of prohibited books and manuscripts and of seditiously heretical discussions continued unabated in the confines of social spaces where the Inquisition would have liked to insert itself but in which it could not necessarily always succeed in operating—in bedrooms, whether in prayer or fornication; in bars, in public readings of novels or clandestine debate; and in privately written satires of priests, bishops, and politicians.

And Spaniards in Mexico, lay and clerical, did not always share the more conservative theology of friars or pious jurists. For example, the laity in particular viewed sexual sins as relatively minor. This led to the backpedaling of inquisitional censure of fornication to prosecute only statements about fornication. Jesuits' views of the cultural context of statements about sex and sexual innuendo also undercut the absolute views of more conservative censors, who interpreted sexual sins in light of the Sixth Commandment and the sacrament of marriage. But even if the laity were relatively impious in relation to sexuality, there appears to have been a real concern on the part of the laity for their spiritual health. Spiritual works advising them on their inner spirituality were extremely popular, as were the moral theology of Antonio Diana and the moral novels of Antonio de Guevara, like the *Libro aureo de Marco Aurelio* (The Golden Book of Marcus Aurelius) and *El reloj de príncipes* (The Dial of Princes). Likewise, Luis de Granada's *Libro de oración y meditación* and the *Historia pontifical* remained a staple in many libraries, despite the fact that some editions were banned. The ban on books of hours seems to have been ignored wholesale. And the continued popularity of tales like *Guzmán de Alfarache, Amadís de Gaula,* and *Don Quijote* shows that despite the vigorous efforts of clerical moralists, the laity continued to view such forms of entertainment as orthodox and acceptable. Moreover, in addition to the laity, a substantial portion of Augustinian and Franciscan friars appears to have distrusted and disobeyed the extremely conservative vision of orthodoxy of the Index.

But this does not mean that the laity rejected the entirety of that counter-reform tendency. The 1559 Index, for example, was notable for formalizing the bans on the works of major heretics like Calvin and Luther and for making official the prohibition of vernacular translations of scripture. Either the laity in Mexico appears to have agreed with the condemnation of Luther and others or the ban on his works was so effective that his works were never available in Mexico. The voluminous documentation of formal inquisitional book censorship in Mexico up to 1640 includes only two mentions of someone having possessed a book by Luther — Alonso Calderón, the alcalde of Acapulco, who had a copy of Luther's *De potestate papae* in 1568, and the censor Rodrigo Moriz, who read Luther.[3] Comparing Luther with the roughly two hundred copies of scripture confiscated by Ledesma in Mexico City in 1572, one quickly sees that Spaniards in Mexico had no particular interest in Luther while they saw fit to disobey many other facets of the Index.

Nevertheless, when the inquisitors dealt with the issues facing them not as theorists but as practitioners of law and colonial authority, they came directly up against the deep cultural unpopularity of much of the Index. When the inquisitors of Mexico wrote to their comisario in 1577 to warn him of the dangers of public book burning they left a much deeper mark on their legacy than they may have suspected. By their admonition they admitted that while they could force people to relinquish their books, they failed to convince them that such a policy was necessary to protect Catholicism.

The relationship between formal ecclesiological theory and its placement in a new context — in Mexico — brings to mind the cultural adaptation not only of the laity but of the censors themselves. The sociologist Howard Becker defines the sacred society as one that possesses an impermeable value system and is marked by isolation.[4] Likewise, Marcel Bataillon explains the reaction to Erasmianism in Spain after the 1550s in terms of cultural, intellectual, and linguistic isolation.[5] This was the goal, as well, of the port controls for the Mexican Inquisition as much as it was for Innocent III when he explained the effects of heresy as infectious and poisonous in *Vergentis*.[6]

Becker proposes various subtypes of the sacred society, one of which applies to Mexico: the imposed-prescribed. According to Becker a prescribed sacred society is marked by a dogmatic control of ideas.[7] This may very well be the case in some instances, but Becker's further distinction of an imposed and prescribed sacred society is apropos of Mexico. The imposed sacred society derives from a previously existing prescribed sacred society and is imposed by conquest. The destruction of the value systems and material props of the conquered society is common, as is the replacement of the value system and language with the exogenous victor's system. In some instances one could make this point for Mexico — many indigenous rites and ceremonies were outlawed. In other instances, this does not apply to Mexico, as when Franciscan missionaries endeavored to catechize and preach in indigenous languages.[8] But in 1577 the Inquisition proved itself a staunch defender of the exogenous, imposed sacred system when it banned Indian language translations of scripture. Thus there was a debate about the extent of the dogmatic control of ideas and about just how far the sacred society of Catholic Spain should go in imposing its orthodoxy and replacing the pre-Hispanic order. Just how much imposition and replacement could work? Should the ostensibly victorious Catholic order impose Hispanicization as a way of controlling the continued dogmatic control of ideas? or would that control be more effective if it was assuaged with cultural or linguistic adaptation? Even those who endeavored to impose this sacred social structure could not decide as a group on the extent of that imposition.

Becker divides the sacred society into indigenous and exogenous, with various subtypes. The indigenous is characterized by the preservation of isolation and the entrusting of value transmission to a specific class. In Catholic society, this role was assigned to the priesthood, and the censors and inquisitors of the Inquisition were the elite members of that class. But in the case of Mexico, that class was operating in the dual context of Indian and Spanish "republics." While the missionaries, in their work among Indian communities, could be better characterized as operating in an imposed and exogenous sacred society, the inquisitors and censors held no jurisdiction over Indians and thus continued to operate in their ostensibly indigenous (Spanish) culture. Becker explains such a scenario as one of transplanted and exogenous sacred society, marked by segregation and incomplete participation in the host culture. Moreover, the transplanted, exogenous, prescribed sacred society "immediately before the transplantation . . . existed as part of a larger indigenous [i.e., peninsular Spanish] society."[9] Therefore, the "contrast with the 'host' society results in some measure of isolation which continues as long as the smaller society patterns itself along the lines of its earlier 'home' culture."[10]

The censors were thus in many ways caught between two worlds. Ideologically, they had deep bonds with the religious value systems of their original culture — Catholic Spain and Salamanca. At the same time censors and other inquisitional functionaries involved in censorship began to be deeply integrated within a transplanted Spanish culture. This was the case when don Felipe Ruiz de Corral was placed in the upper crust of the conquistador class of Guatemala. The irony was that a man deeply tied to the original Spanish Catholic culture, bishop Juan Ramírez, who had been raised at San Esteban in Salamanca, would come up against the shifting social context of the Inquisition when he challenged the power of the criollo elites who, in Guatemala, held the reins of inquisitional power.

Censors of early Mexico possessed a clear identity as defenders of Spanish Catholic thought and order. But they were also deeply divided over the very definitions of that order. The Dominicans continued to see themselves as the bulwarks against an eroding conservatism, especially in the face of the increasingly flexible view of blasphemy and heresy championed by Pedro de Hortigosa and the Jesuits more generally. So while Becker's categorization is instructive, in some ways the categories broke down in Mexico, because the dogmatic control of ideas was challenged not only by the laity but from within the imposed sacred society. Likewise, the isolation of that imposed sacred society became increasingly more porous as the Inquisition in Mexico began to be permeated at all levels by the criollo elite and by competing visions of the reach of inquisitional censure.

Instead, the Inquisition's overall activity in Mexico produced a porous sa-

cred society, one with a dogmatic control of ideas which allowed for considerable adaptation based on local customs and circumstances. Recall the often
futile efforts of the Franciscan comisario of rural Michoacán, Diego Muñoz.
Time and again he corresponded with the inquisitors about folk magic, sexual
deviance, and even the frequent eating of meat on Fridays and during Lent.
For example, on June 14, 1616, Muñoz wrote to the inquisitors about Diego
Romero, who had eaten pheasant on a Friday. In response to the admonition
of his neighbor, Tomás de Morales, that this was a heretical act, Romero said
that his "life was boring" and for that reason he liked to eat pheasant on
Fridays.[11] The inquisitors never even bothered to answer their comisario's
letter, much less prosecute Romero. During the zealous thirteenth-century
Inquisitions and even during the Montúfar and Moya de Contreras periods in
Mexico, such crimes were dealt with swiftly. Peña said such actions were to be
punished by inquisitors. But by the seventeenth century the permeation of
local customs and a more flexible inquisitional apparatus began to result in
lesser punishment of such offenses.

Likewise, other examples elucidate the problems of viewing a complete
isolation of the sacred social dogma of Spanish Catholicism as an outgrowth
of an imposed doctrinal system. Maturino Gilberti promoted an adaptive
approach to the integration of Catholicism as much as any missionary. For
him the Indians of Michoacán would be best converted and encouraged to join
the Catholic orbit if they were discouraged from worshipping their old gods.
But this assumed that friars liberated from diocesan oversight could engage in
this sort of program. Gilberti came up squarely against the universalist aspirations of Montúfar and Bishop Quiroga, who viewed their charge in terms that
fit within Becker's rubric, as bearers of an imposed and exogenous sacred
system which does not adapt, since to adapt was to admit lack of universality
in that doctrinal system.

Two processes were at work. First, there was the ostensibly universalist and
immutable ideological foundation of inquisitional censorship and control. This
was associated with the hard-line defense of Dominican privilege, the development of inquisitional procedure and rigorism of the medieval period, and the
primacy of Salamanca as a theological force. Censors and inquisitors in Mexico
were all either directly or indirectly influenced by this trajectory. They had read
Aquinas, Eimeric, Peña, Simancas, and Torquemada. The earliest censors were
from Salamanca; their successors were taught by Salamanca-trained professors. And the concrete expression of this inquisitional ideology was found in
the manuals and treatises by inquisitional and ecclesiological theorists.

But even the ostensible imposition of this exogenous sacred society was
fractured. The imposition was never complete because the architects of that

sacred society could not agree on the form to be imposed. The very definition of orthodoxy and the purview of the regulation of orthodoxy by Inquisition and censure were forever debated and disputed. Moreover, the extent of that imposition was debated. Should bigamy be punished severely? Should inner conscience be regulated? Should fornicators be prosecuted by the Inquisition? Should blasphemy, if it did not reflect inner doubt, fall under the jurisdiction of the Inquisition? Was Erasmus a heretic? Should the ban on vernacular Bibles be mitigated or ignored in Mexico for the catechesis of the Indians? In the face of divisions on these questions and so many others, the ability to impose a monolithic sacred value system and doctrinal orthodoxy would always be incomplete.

These broad thematic questions about the relationship of law and custom and of the ability of the Inquisition to impose orthodoxy imply methodological issues. I have provided a view from the inside of the inquisitional mind as opposed to a study of the effects of that inquisitional mind on the laity. This book is less about the cultural impact of the Inquisition and its censorship apparatus than about the internal logic of that apparatus. This focus led me to consider both traditional intellectual history sources — treatises — as well as the quotidian expressions of doctrinal mentality in the form of debates within the Inquisition found not in print but in archival material. From a methodological point of view, the work of theologians and jurists collectively represents a traditional source of inquiry for intellectual history. I have combined analysis of this philosophical discourse with that of the mentality of the censors as expressed in their daily operations. While they were deeply involved in that formal ideology, their expression of the way in which censorship would be applied offers a different source for intellectual historians, one that has gone largely unmined. To date most attention to the workings of the Inquisition in Mexico which has involved the nonelites has focused on the ways in which vaguely defined "popular" classes have been impacted by the Inquisition. Likewise, the study of the content of ideology, ideas, and mentality has been shifted predominantly to the ways in which ideas are culturally managed and deployed.

I have placed the ideas at the center of attention and place the issue of their cultural impact to the side, but not entirely offstage. An assessment of the ideas' contents is the way in which the mental world of the censor and the theologian can be understood. Some will find this unsatisfactory, but in offering a sustained discussion of that ideological world I hope to have demonstrated the seriousness with which the censors took up the challenge of defending, in their minds, the order of Catholic thought or adapting it to allow for chocolate before the Mass or cohabitation if the sinners did not promote it as beneficial. Peyote may have been banned by the Mexican Holy Office, but who was going to enforce the ban if its use was limited to certain occasions?

I have focused on the content of the ideas even if I have placed those ideas in the context of a transplanted doctrinal system, operating in the context of America and not the home site of Spain. A shift in analysis — from the specific cultural management of ideas to the content of those ideas as the practitioners attempted to make sense of those ideas — does not necessarily mean a shift in historical methodology. This may seem surprising to those who have grown accustomed to associating intellectual history with analysis of important philosophical trends and cultural history with the history of mentality and of the popular classes. But this denies the potential for challenging intellectual history. One can employ archival material in tracing the development of ideas, even elite ideas, in the early modern world. The interstices of archival documentation hold some of the most fruitful new avenues for intellectual history precisely because no one has previously thought them worthy as sources for the history of philosophy, whether religious, political, or social philosophy. This offers the potential to bridge the gap between the high-end, treatise-writing version of intellectual history and the low-end history of mentality that for the past twenty years have been placed in an artificial dichotomy.

Erasmus imagined a republic of letters some five centuries ago. Some would see in Erasmus and his ideas an assault on the collective traditions of Catholic thought. Others, like Castro, who agreed with many conservatives that Luther was a menace and that Spanish Bibles were a recipe for feeding new heresies, considered Erasmus one of the great intellectuals of the day. The irony is that theorists as widely different in their views of Catholic order and governance as Cano and Castro would both occupy the same Iberian intellectual world that informed the way that a new, American religious order in Mexico would struggle to define and understand its relationship to that republic of letters. *Don Quijote* landed on the Mexican gulf shore within months of its publication at the same time that Torquemada and Eimeric were deeply entrenched in the intellectual world of the Mexican capital. Peyote and the Virgin of Guadalupe, fornication and attendance at the Mass, medieval law and customary interpretations of intellectual control would exist in uneasy parallel.

It was an especially hot May in 1626 in Mexico-Tenochtitlan and for months Hortigosa's asthma was making it nearly impossible for him to breathe. He was nearly eighty years old and he knew he would die soon.[12] On the evening of May 10, the city still warm and dusty, the cathedral maestrescuela, returning from a visit to the nuns of San Jerónimo, walked along Mesones Avenue, lined with prostitutes. He contemplated the lessons he had received from

Hortigosa on sin and grace, and wondered what to make of the free will of both those women and the men who sought them out and decided that in the end, only they could decide. The next morning he, along with his colleagues of the cathedral chapter, would receive the news that the Jesuit had expired. Meanwhile, a Dominican friar crossed the street from the Inquisition's shoddily constructed offices and wiped the sweat from his brow, returning from a meeting with the inquisitor; he fumed that the jurist would not prosecute a case of witchcraft which had been sent by a comisario from the mountains of Puebla.

Despite his agony, Hortigosa had celebrated Mass that morning and shortly thereafter received the last rites. Later that evening, he put down his edition of Horace and said a prayer for the soul of the woman who sold tamales outside the front door of the Colegio de San Pedro y San Pablo where he had lived nearly all of the last fifty years. The sounds of his adopted city were dying down and it would be the last time he would fall asleep to their familiar dirge. The next morning the residents of San Pedro y San Pablo accompanied him as he prepared for his death. One of them asked him what was his fondest memory in life and he replied "now, with this aridity and heat—the gardens, the flowers, and the fountains, but for this the Lord tells me where I am going: 'the beauty of the field is with me.'" These words from Psalm 50 may have been his last and for two more hours the death rattle continued, each moment growing more agonizing, his breathing more labored with each inhalation. And then the Jesuit closed his eyes for the last time.

Appendix 1:
Inquisitional Trials

Previous quantitative studies of the Spanish Inquisitions, such as those by Alberro, Henningsen, and Henningsen and Contreras relied principally on *relaciones de causas,* or summaries of inquisitional cases sent from local Inquisitions to the Suprema. Alberro employed relaciones as well as *nóminas* (personnel lists) and deposition summaries, which can be used like relaciones but were usually kept in Mexico rather than forwarded to Madrid. These approaches have both advantages and disadvantages. The primary advantage of using lists of the available cases is expediency. There is no need to wade through the volumes of trials to determine the caseload of a specific local Inquisition that has a mostly complete archive, like Mexico's or Cuenca's. In places where the original case files are lost, as in Seville, using relaciones de causas is one of the few ways to reconstruct inquisitional activity. Because few inquisitional archives are extant, relaciones and nóminas are especially valuable investigative tools in any attempt to make a global assessment of the overall nature of the Spanish Inquisition. Henningsen and Contreras specifically sought to compare the stereotypical visions of the Spanish Inquisition as murderous and sanguine with the actual data. Their findings represented the first systematic attempt to show that in reality the various Spanish Inquisitions executed in person only a small percentage of the accused (about 1.8 percent of convictions from 1540 to 1700).[1] Others, who had fled the jurisdiction, were executed in effigy and in occasional cases individuals were convicted post mortem and their disinterred bodies were immolated in autos-de-fe. The rate of execution in person in Spain is almost identical to the 1.7 percent rate in Mexico for the period between 1528 and 1630 considered in this study: 26 executions out of 1563 adjudicated trials.

The primary disadvantage of using relaciones and lists of caseloads is that they are inevitably incomplete. Reliance on nóminas and relaciones led Alberro to include thousands of proceedings that were never adjudicated. Thus there were thousands of cases in which only a deposition was taken and with no further action by either the local comisario or the inquisitors in Mexico City. Henningsen's and Contreras's goal was global and widespread, and by definition they were incapable, given archival losses, of finding all the cases. This is not the case for Mexico: Mexico's inquisitional archive is relatively complete. For this reason I opted for comprehensiveness over expediency. Consequently, the database below is much more extensive and accurate than those preceding it. Nevertheless, like all such quantifications, it remains incomplete. My goal, however, was different from the goals of previous studies as well, and so my numbers differ.

First, I was interested in determining the frequency of the use of censors in inquisitional procedure in Mexico, so I undertook an examination of the contents of material in the Inquisition section of the Mexican National Archive before 1640. I reviewed 470 volumes of the archival material and found 1,607 complete trials for which there was evidence that the Inquisition adjudicated the case.[2] Among these trials are 229 individual cases of calificación, as well as several sets of calificación which cannot be definitively identified with a trial. There were undoubtedly cases for which complete documentation is missing, but from 1527 to 1639 there were at least that many trials.

The purpose of this methodology was both quantitative and qualitative. In terms of sheer numbers the preponderance or absence of theological review can go a long way toward demonstrating the power the censors held. Qualitatively I have used the content of the reviews as the core of my study of intellectual trends with the Holy Office. Combined, these approaches allow for a relatively comprehensive vision of the world of the censors both in terms of their everyday presence in censorship decisions as well as the ideological content of those decisions.

Finally, a note on the databases of the Inquisition caseload which I have used in this study. I included all complete trials that contained a sentence and interviews, since sentencing patently answers the question as to the existence of the trial, even when other portions are not included or are missing. Complete trials include denunciations, witness testimonies, arrest warrants, interrogations of the accused, indictments from the prosecutor, sometimes torture, calificación, votes, and sentencing as well as judicial back and forth between lawyers and occasional correspondence. In cases where it was apparent that substantial portions of the trial were missing, especially the sentence itself, I did not include the trial in the database since it was not clear if a trial took place. On the other hand, since I was attempting to determine the extent to which censors were used, I made certain exceptions. For example, in any case where a censor was called and the review or the order for review and other elements of a trial are extant I included it in the database. I did so because the question Was a censor called or not? was patently answered. But I excluded those cases where the trial transcript was incomplete and no review appeared because I could not be certain that a censor was not called. I also excluded stand-alone censor reviews when their associated trial record is today lost even though it is clear a trial transpired. I also included some incomplete trials in the database. These were cases in which the archival record preserved only testimonies and the review but not the prosecutor's report or the sentence. Even though these reports were missing it is known that there was a trial in which a censor was called. Moreover, the inquisitors did not call censors in cases they did not adjudicate. In some cases the inquisitors absolved the accused. But in any instance the presence of interviews in Mexico City and censors' reviews proves that there was a trial even if today some parts of it are missing.

In the table below, as in the tables found throughout the manuscript, I have differentiated trials of propositions, blasphemy, and heresy, though in many instances the final judgments of the court found heresy or blasphemy to be the final charge in cases of propositions. The result is that nearly half (46.7 percent) of all Inquisition trials adjudicated in this period involved heterodoxy in a broad sense.

Accusation	Number of cases	Number of cases with censors	Percentage of caseload	Percentage of cases with censors
Propositions	296	89	18.0	30.1
Bigamy	263	1	16.0	0.4
Blasphemy	258	36	15.7	13.9
Heresy	214	53	13.0	24.8
Judaizing	108	1	6.6	0.9
Superstition, witchcraft, etc.	89	19	5.4	21.3
Desacato	75	4	4.6	5.3
Solicitation during confession	54	3	3.3	5.5
Querella	52	2	3.2	3.8
Processes of office	42	0	2.6	0.0
Apostasy	39	3	2.4	7.7
Imitating priest or inquisitor	35	3	2.1	8.6
Flight	23	0	1.4	0.0
Cohabitation	18	3	1.1	16.7
Sacrilege	18	5	1.1	27.8
Idolatry	16	1	1.0	6.3
False testimony	9	0	0.5	0.0
Possessing prohibited books	8	2	0.5	25.0
Sanbenitos	7	0	0.4	0.0
Inhábil	7	0	0.4	0.0

(continued)

Accusation	Number of cases	Number cases with censors	Percentage of caseload	Percentage of cases with censors
Revelations	4	3	0.2	75.0
Islam	3	1	0.2	33.3
Incest	2	0	0.1	0.0
Total Trials	1607[3]	223		13.9
Total Charges	1640	229[4]	100.0	14.0

Source: AGN, Inq., vols.: 1, 1A, 2–54, 54bis, 55–59, 68–72, 74–85, 88–140, 143–61, 163–68, 174–78, 180–88, 206–19, 221, 224, 226, 232, 234, 238–40, 242, 244, 246–49, 251A, 253, 254, 254A, 255–64, 266–76, 278, 279, 282, 287, 288, 291, 292, 294, 298–300, 303, 304, 306, 307, 309–11, 313–15, 317, 319–22, 325–33, 337, 338, 340–42, 344–50, 352, 353, 355, 357–59, 361–64, 366, 367, 370–75, 377–80, 382, 384, 386–89, 452, 454, 455, 463, 464, 466, 469–72, 474, 477–83, 486, 488, 489, 491, 493, 495, 508–10, 558, 601, 636, 640, 659, 683, 695, 823, 916, 927, 977, 1487, 1489, 1490–95, 1529, 1530, 1547, 1552–54, caja 161.

Notes

1. Alberro, *La actividad del Santo Oficio de la Inquisición*; Contreras and Henningsen, "Forty-Four Thousand Cases"; Henningsen, "La elocuencia de los números."

2. See appendix 3 below.

3. While I noted 1,607 trials the number of charges is higher, as there were 33 added charges (i.e., cases with double or triple accusations).

4. Calificaciones occurred in trials with more than one charge (four trials with two charges and one trial with three charges), resulting in an inflated total number of calificaciones.

Appendix 2:
Censors

Calificador	Date	Origin	Class background	Location	Order	Source
maestro Martín de Perea	1571	P	upper administrative	Mexico	OSA	[1]
maestro Bartolomé de Ledesma	1572	P	laboring; administrative elite; academic	Mexico, Oaxaca	OP	[2]
dr. Pedro Sánchez	1572	P	academic; administrative elite	Mexico	SJ	[3]
dr. Rodrigo de Barbosa	1572	P	hidalgo; upper administrative	Mexico	sec	[4]
Domingo de Salazar	1572	P	upper administrative	Oaxaca, Mexico, Philippines	OP	[5]
Antonio de Quixada	1572	P	middle administrative	Yucatán, Mexico	OFM	[6]
Diego Ordóñez	1572	P	hidalgo; middle administrative	Mexico	OFM	[7]
Pedro de Pravia	1572	P	upper administrative	Mexico	OP	[8]

Calificador	Date	Origin	Class background	Location	Order	Source
Alonso de Noreña	1573	P	upper administrative	Chiapas	OP	[9]
Tomás de Cárdenas	1573		administrative elite	Guatemala	OP	[10]
Juan de Castro	1573		upper administrative	Guatemala	OP	[11]
Lope de Montoya	1577		upper administrative	Guatemala	OP	[12]
Rodrigo de Seguera	1577	P	upper administrative		OFM	[13]
Rodrigo de Sopuerta	1579		upper administrative	Yucatán	OFM	[14]
maestro Juan Ramírez	1585	P?	hidalgo; upper administrative	Mexico, Guatemala	OP	[15]
maestro Agustín Dávila Padilla	1591	C	administrative elite; academic	Mexico	OP	[16]
dr. Pedro de Hortigosa	1592	P	upper administrative; academic	Mexico	SJ	[17]
Juan Dávila	1592				OP	[18]
dr. Hernando Ortiz de Hinojosa	1592	C	upper administrative; academic	Mexico	sec	[19]
Juan de San Sebastián	1592				friar	[20]
Sancho de Meras	1593	P	upper administrative	Mexico	OFM	[21]
dr. don Juan de Cervantes	1594	C?	hidalgo; administrative elite	Mexico	sec	[22]
maestro Pedro de Agurto	1594	C	upper administrative	Mexico, Cebu	OSA	[23]
Cristóbal Guerrero Góngora	1594		administrative elite		OP	[24]
maestro Diego de Contreras	1594	C	administrative elite; academic		OSA	[25]
Diego Martínez	1596	P			OFM	[26]
Tomás de Sant Juan	1596	P?	upper administrative	Coyoacán	OP	[27]
Miguel Agia	1596	P	academic		OFM	[28]
Francisco de Vera	1597	P	upper administrative		Mcd	[29]
Juan Maldonado	1598	P	hidalgo	Manila	OP	[30]

Calificador	Date	Origin	Class background	Location	Order	Source
maestro don Agustín de Carvajal	1598	C	hidalgo; upper administrative		OSA	31
Gabriel Baptista	1599	P	upper administrative		OFMd	32
Juan de Salas	1600	P	upper administrative	Mexico	OFM	33
dr. Pedro Morales	1600	P	upper administrative	Mexico	SJ	34
Pedro de la Cruz	1600	P	upper administrative	Zacatecas, Mexico	OFM	35
Luis Vallejo	1603		academic	Mexico	OP	36
Juan de Contreras	1604	C	upper administrative		OSA	37
Pedro de Montes	1604	P?	upper administrative	Philippines	SJ	38
maestro Pedro Solier	1605	P	administrative elite; academic	Puerto Rico, Santo Domingo, Manila	OSA	39
Diego Arellano	1605	P			OFM	40
Francisco Coronel	1605	P			OSA	41
dr. Diego de León Plaza	1605	P	administrative elite	Mexico	sec	42
maestro Cristóbal de la Cruz	1605		upper administrative		OSA	43
Juan de la Cieza	1605	P	upper administrative		OFM	44
maestro Luis de Solórzano	1609				OP	45
Baltasar Maldonado Márquez	1610	C?	middle administrative	Tecamachalco	OFM	46
Juan de Elormendi	1611	P	upper administrative	Zacatecas	OFM	47
maestro Francisco de Villanueba Guzmán	1611	C	hidalgo		OP	48
Juan de Zurita	1611	C	hidalgo; upper administrative		OFM	49
Rodrigo Cabredo	1612	P	upper administrative		SJ	50

Calificador	Date	Origin	Class background	Location	Order	Source
Juan de Santa Anna	1613	P	upper administrative	Puebla, Pachuca	OFMd	[51]
maestro Francisco de Orea	1613	P?	middle administrative	Guatemala	Mcd	[52]
maestro Francisco Ximénez	1614	P	upper administrative	Guatemala, Mexico	Mcd	[53]
maestro Francisco Muñoz	1615	C	upper administrative	Mexico	OSA	[54]
maestro Miguel García Serrano	1615		upper administrative	Manila	OSA	[55]
Juan López	1616	P	middle administrative	Michoacán	OFM	[56]
Gastón de Peralta	1616		hidalgo; upper administrative	Oaxaca	OFM	[57]
Diego Agúndez	1616	C	middle administrative		OFM	[58]
maestro Diego de Carvajal	1616	C	hidalgo	Guadalajara	OSA	[59]
maestro Bartolomé Gómez	1617	C	middle administrative		OP	[60]
Baltasar de Morales	1617	P	middle administrative	Veracruz	OFM	[61]
Francisco Durán	1617	C	undistinguished		OFM	[62]
maestro Juan Morillo	1617	C	hidalgo		OSA	[63]
Rodrigo Moriz	1617		upper administrative		OSAd	[64]
maestro Antonio del Pozo	1617	P	rural laboring	Oaxaca	OP	[65]
Gerónimo Bazán	1618	C	hidalgo; administrative elite		OFM	[66]
Miguel de la Cruz	1618	P	upper administrative		OFM	[67]
dr. Bartolomé González Soltero	1619	C	administrative elite	Mexico	sec	[68]
Gabriel Arias	1619	P	undistinguished		OFM	[69]
Juan Márquez Maldonado	1619	C?	upper administrative	Puebla	OFM	[70]
maestro Cristóbal de Aguilera y Vélez	1619				OP	[71]
Juan de Salazar	1619				OFM	[72]

Calificador	Date	Origin	Class background	Location	Order	Source
Alonso de Salazar	1619				OP	[73]
Diego de Santisteban	1619		academic		SJ	[74]
maestro Lázaro de Prado	1620	P	upper administrative	Mexico	OP	[75]
maestro Martín de Vergara	1620	P	hidalgo; middle administrative	Michoacán	OSA	[76]
Antonio Gutiérrez	1620		upper administrative	Philippines	OP	[77]
Cristóbal Ángel	1621	P	middle administrative	Mexico	SJ	[78]
Bartolomé de Burguillos	1622	P	upper administrative	Mexico	OFMd	[79]
Juan Cornejo	1622		upper administrative	Mexico/ Tlatelolco	OFM	[80]
Andrés Bravo	1622				OFM	[81]
Antonio Ocampo	1622			Manila	OSA	[82]
maestro Alonso de Valdés	1623	C	hidalgo; upper administrative	Mexico	OSA	[83]
Francisco Velasco	1623	C	hidalgo, titled; upper administrative		OFM	[84]
Antonio Hinojosa	1623	C	hidalgo; administrative elite		OP	[85]
maestro Vicente Mixangos	1623		middle administrative	Culiacán	OSA	[86]
Joseph Morán de la Cerda	1624	C	hidalgo; middle administrative	Jalisco	OFM	[87]
don licenciado Juan Vásquez de Cisneros	1625		hidalgo		sec	[88]
Alonso Vásquez de Cisneros	1625		hidalgo		OFM	[89]
Juan Enríquez	1625	C	middle administrative	Oaxaca	OP	[90]
Rodrigo Alonso Barreña	1625	P	middle administrative	Mexico/ Tlatelolco	OFM	[91]
Agustín Aldrete	1625	P?	academic; upper administrative		OP	[92]
Luis Zapata	1625	C	hidalgo; upper administrative	Teotihuacan	OFM	[93]

Calificador	Date	Origin	Class background	Location	Order	Source
Juan Díaz Arce	1626	P	upper administrative	Mexico	OP	[94]
dr. Alonso Muñoz	1626		upper administrative	Mexico	sec	[95]
dr. Nicolás de la Torre	1626		upper administrative	Mexico	sec	[96]
Luis Gutiérrez	1626	C	undistinguished		OFM	[97]
Juan de Ygueribar	1626	C	undistinguished	Guadalajara	OFM	[98]
Domingo de Portú	1626	P	hidalgo; upper administrative		OFM	[99]
maestro Jacinto de Hoces	1626	P?	upper administrative		OP	[100]
Nicolás de San Lorenzo	1626	C	middle administrative	Jalisco	OFM	[101]
maestro Pedro García Serrano	1626		upper administrative	Philippines	OSA	[102]
maestro Miguel García Serrano	1626		upper administrative	Philippines	OSA	[103]
Pedro Álvarez	1626		middle administrative	Guatemala	OP	[104]
Gaspar de la Figuera	1626				SJ	[105]
Pedro de Aguilar	1627		middle administrative	Querétaro	OFM	[106]
maestro Francisco de Arébalo	1627	P	upper administrative	Mexico, Zacatecas, Guadalajara	OP	[107]
Juan de Carrascosa	1627		middle administrative	Guadalajara	OFM	[108]
Pedro Pacheco	1627		middle administrative	Guatemala	OP?[109]	[110]
Francisco de Lugo	1627				SJ	[111]
Juan de Ledesma	1627	C	academic	Mexico	SJ	[112]
maestro Juan de Noval	1628			Oaxaca	OP	[113]
Gabriel de Morillo	1628		hidalgo	Michoacán	OFM	[114]
Gerónimo Castellete	1628	P		Michoacán	OSA	[115]
Francisco de la Cruz	1628	P	upper administrative	Mexico	OFMd	[116]
Francisco Silvestre Magallón	1628	P		Campeche	OFM	[117]

Calificador	Date	Origin	Class background	Location	Order	Source
Alonso del Rincón	1628	P?	middle administrative	Manila	OSA	[118]
Juan de San Pedro	1628				OFMd	[119]
Esteban Tamayo	1628			Tulticlan	OFM	[120]
Joseph Durán	1628		middle administrative	Texcoco	OFM	[121]
Francisco Rodríguez	1628		academic; upper administrative	Mexico	OFM	[122]
Diego Delgado	1628			Trujillo	Mcd	[123]
maestro Félix Barrientos	1629	P	undistinguished	Guatemala, Yucatán	OP	[124]
Francisco Calderón	1629	P	academic		SJ	[125]
maestro Juan de Herrera	1629		upper administrative; academic		Mcd	[126]
Gaspar de Torres	1630	P	hidalgo		OFMd	[127]
Hernando Martín Calvo	1630				OP	[128]
Pedro de Montenegro	1631				OP	[129]
Jacinto de Cabaña	1631	P	academic; upper administrative	Guatemala	OP	[130]
Francisco Mazuelos	1632		middle administrative	Chiapas	OFM	[131]
Andrés de Valencia	1632		academic	Mexico	SJ	[132]
Juan Antonio Suárez	1632		academic	Mexico	SJ	[133]
Alonso Guerrero	1633					[134]
Gregorio Maldonado	1634		academic	Yucatán	OFM	[135]
Martín de Peralta	1634	C	hidalgo; upper administrative		OSA	[136]
Luis de Castilla	1634	C	hidalgo		OP	[137]
Francisco de Areizaga	1635		upper administrative		OFM	[138]
Cristóbal de Rivera	1635	P	hidalgo; middle administrative	Yucatán	OFM	[139]
maestro Jacinto de la Cajica	1636	C	middle administrative	Izúcar	OP	[140]
Antonio de Chinchilla	1637	P	middle administrative		OFM	[141]
Felipe de Elexalde y Vergara	1637	P	hidalgo; middle administrative	Michoacán	OSA	[142]

Calificador	Date	Origin	Class background	Location	Order	Source
Martín de Elexalde y Vergara	1637	P	hidalgo	Michoacán	OSA	[143]
maestro Andrés de Morales	1637	P	hidalgo; upper administrative	Guatemala	Mcd	[144]
Diego de los Ríos	1638	C	hidalgo; academic		OSA	[145]
Juan de Vallecillo	1638		academic	San Luis Potosí, Puebla	SJ	[146]
Juan de Prada	1639	P?			OFM	[147]
Luis de Molina	1639		middle administrative	San Luis Potosí	SJ	[148]
dr. don Cristóbal Millán	1640		hidalgo	Mexico	sec	[149]
dr. don Antonio de Peralta	1640		hidalgo; upper administrative		sec?	[150]
Francisco de Arista	1640			Guatemala	SJ	[151]
Pedro de Prado	1640			Guatemala	SJ	[152]

Abbreviations:
C=criollo
d=*descalzo* (barefoot friars)
P=peninsular
Mcd=Mercedarian
OFM=Ordo Fratrum Minorum (Franciscans)
OP=Ordo Praedicorum (Dominicans)
OSA=Ordo Sancti Augustini (Augustinians)
SJ=Societatis Jesu (Jesuits)
sec=secular
$N=151$
By Origin
95=data available; 56=no data
peninsular   n=54–62; 36–41 percent of total; 57–65 percent of those with data
criollo   n=30–33; 20–22 percent of total; 32–35 percent of those with data
By Class
126=data available; 25=no data

hidalgo[153]	n=32; 21 percent of total;	25 percent of those with data
administrative elite[154]	n=12; 8 percent of total;	10 percent of those with data
upper administrative[155]	n=60; 40 percent of total;	48 percent of those with data
middle administrative[156]	n=27; 18 percent of total;	21 percent of those with data
academic[157]	n=21; 14 percent of total;	17 percent of those with info
laboring/undistinguished[158]	n=7; 5 percent of total;	6 percent of those with data

By religious order

OFM	n=54; 36 percent
OP	n=36; 24 percent
OSA	n=25; 17 percent
SJ	n=17; 11 percent
Sec	n=9; 6 percent
Merced	n=6; 4 percent
Mendicant of uncertain order	n=1; 1 percent
Unclear/no data	n=3; 2 percent

Notes

1. AGN, Inq., vol. 60, exp. 3; as visitador de libros: AGN, Inq., vol. 1486, exp. s/n, f. 30.

2. AGN, Inq., vol. 60, exp. 4. Officially named visitador de libros in 1575, AGN, Inq., vol. 1486, exp. s/n, f. 52.

3. AGN, Inq., vol. 61, exp. 6.

4. AGN, Inq., vol. 62, exp. 1.

5. AGN, Inq., vol. 62, exp. 5; and as visitador de libros, AGN, Inq., vol. 1486, exp. s/n, f. 34.

6. AGN, Inq., vol. 63, exp. 18.

7. AGN, Inq., vol. 65, exp. 5.

8. AGN, Inq., vol. 65, exp. 6, vol. 1486, exp. s/n, f. 30.

9. AGN, Inq., vol. 65, exp. 10.

10. AGN, Inq., vol. 76, exp. 10, vol. 90, exp. s/n, fs. 29–30.

11. AGN, Inq., vol. 76, exp. 10, vol. 90, exp. s/n, fs. 29–30.

12. AGN, Inq., vol. 76, exp. 48, vol. 119, exp. 6. In a calificación from Guatemala in 1580, fray Lope de Montoya joined Dominican fray Juan de Castro. In general, friars who signed the same calificación came from the same order when it was not part of a junta de calificadores of the 1570s. Also in 1591 he penned a calificación as prior in Santo Domingo in Guatemala. See AGN, Inq., vol. 239, exp. s/n, f. 92.

13. AGN, Inq., vol. 59, exp. 4, vol. 85, exp. 26, vol. 189, exp. 3; Gómez, "Nómina," 490.

14. AGN, Inq., vol. 85, exp. 26.

15. AGN, Inq., vol. 1486, exp. s/n, fs. 63–64; García Granados, *El deán turbulento*, 16.

16. AGN, Inq., vol. 194, exp. 8. Mentioned as "visitador de libros de su orden" in 1592 in AGN, Inq., vol. 1486, exp. s/n, f. 64. Also see Eubel and van Gulik, eds., *Hierarchia Catholica*, 4: 176.

17. AGN, Inq., vol. 206, exp. 2, vol. 206, exp. 3, vol. 223, exp. 31.

18. Gómez, "Nómina," 490–91.

19. AGN, Inq., vol. 195, exp. 2. His commission as censor was revoked soon after his appointment for having an "unclean" genealogy.

20. AGN, Inq., vol. 239, exp. s/n, f. 228.

21. AGN, Inq., vol. 197, exp. 7.

22. AGN, Inq., vol. 203, exp. 8, vol. 1486, exp. s/n, f. 78.

23. AGN, Inq., vol. 66, exp. 5. In 1573, named as "teólogo de asistir en las causas de la fe," in AGN, Inq., vol. 1486, exp. s/n, f. 37, and in 1585 as visitador de libros for Augustinian houses in AGN, Inq., vol. 636, exp. s/n, f. s/n. As a student of De la Veracruz in Mexico he was more than likely a criollo, and this is supported by González Dávila in *Teatro eclesiástico*, 69.

24. AGN, Inq., vol. 199, exp. 4.

25. AGN, Inq., vol. 205, exp. 7, vol. 1486, exp. s/n, f. 79; Eubel and van Gulik, eds., *Hierarchia Catholica*, 4: 176. Named visitador de libros, as was his brother, the Augustinian Juan de Contreras, in 1603: AGN, Inq., vol. 1486, exp. s/n, f. 98.

26. AGN, Inq., vol. 201, exp. 2A.

27. AGN, Inq., vol. 201, exp. 10, vol. 242, exp. s/n, f. 145, vol. 1486, exp. s/n, f. 87.

28. AGN, Inq., vol. 187, exp. 13; Gallegos Rocafull, *El pensamiento mexicano*, 262.

29. AGN, Inq., vol. 202, exp. 1, vol. 1486, exp. s/n, fs. 89–90.

30. AGN, Inq., vol. 203, exp. 10.

31. AGN, Inq., vol. 203, exp. 7, vol. 1486, exp. s/n, f. 90; Eubel and van Gulik, eds., *Hierarchia Catholica*, 4: 199.

32. AGN, Inq., vol. 223, exp. s/n, f. s/n, vol. 1486, exp. s/n, f. 96.

33. AGN, Inq., vol. 203, exp. 5, vol. 203, exp. 12, vol. 223, exp. s/n, f. 251.

34. AGN, Inq., vol. 255, exp. 1, vol. 1486, exp. s/n, f. 95; García Icazbalceta, "El padre Pedro de Morales."

35. AGN, Inq., vol. 261, exp. 4, vol. 261, exp. 5, vol. 1486, exp. s/n, f. 96.

36. AGN, Inq., vol. 269, exp. s/n.

37. AGN, Inq., vol. 347, exp. s/n, f. 402, vol. 368, exp. s/n, f. 507.

38. AGN, Inq., vol. 454, exp. 2, vol. 1486, exp. s/n, f. 102; Gómez, "Nómina," 493.

39. AGN, Inq., vol. 275, exp. 10, vol. 1486, exp. s/n, f. 104; Eubel and van Gulik, eds., *Hierarchia Catholica*, 4: 176, 286.

40. AGN, Inq., vol. 347, exp. s/n, f. 358.

41. AGN, Inq., vol. 347, exp. s/n, f. 367.

42. AGN, Inq., vol. 276, exp. 4.

43. AGN, Inq., vol. 1486, exp. s/n, fs. 103–4; Gómez, "Nómina," 493.

44. AGN, Inq., vol. 1486, exp. s/n, f. 104; Gómez, "Nómina," 493–94.

45. AGN, Inq., vol. 1486, exp. s/n, f. 106.

46. AGN, Inq., vol. 375, exp. 6, vol. 1486, exp. s/n, f. 112.

47. AGN, Inq., vol. 291, exp. 2, vol. 478, exp. s/n, f. 262, vol. 1486, exp. s/n, fs. 112–13.

48. AGN, Inq., vol. 291, exp. 6, vol. 1486, exp. s/n, f. 113.

49. AGN, Inq., vol. 823, exp. 6; Gómez, "Nómina," 495.

50. AGN, Inq., vol. 287, exp. 1, vol. 1486, exp. s/n, fs. 113–14.

51. AGN, Inq., vol. 300, exp. 7, vol. 373, exp. 19, vol. 1486, exp. s/n, fs. 117–18.

52. AGN, Inq., vol. 1486, exp. s/n, f. 119.

53. AGN, Inq., vol. 305, exp. 9, vol. 1486, exp. s/n, f. 120.

54. AGN, Inq., vol. 310, exp. 1.

55. AGN, Inq., vol. 1486, exp. s/n, f. 128; Gómez, "Nómina," 496.

56. AGN, Inq., vol. 307, exp. 3, vol. 1486, exp. s/n, fs. 123–24.

57. AGN, Inq., vol. 61, exp. 8, vol. 1486, exp. s/n, f. 119.

58. AGN, Inq., vol. 305, exp. 12.

59. AGN, Inq., vol. 846, exp. s/n, vol. 1486, exp. s/n, f. 126.

60. AGN, Inq., vol. 484, exp. 1.

61. AGN, Inq., vol. 484, exp. 11.

62. AGN, Inq., vol. 318, exp. 3.

63. AGN, Inq., vol. 1486, exp. s/n, f. 127.

64. AGN, Inq., vol. 1486, exp. s/n, fs. 130–31; Gómez, "Nómina," 497. In 1618 he was found prosecuted for possessing prohibited books, including by Luther, convicted, and consequently had his commission of calificador revoked: AGN, Inq., vol. 320, exp. 6.

65. AGN, Inq., vol. 319, exp. 3, vol. 1486, exp. s/n, f. 128. He was named "corrector de libros" in 1618. See AGN, Inq., vol. 1486, exp. s/n, fs. 131–32.

66. AGN, Inq., vol. 60, exp. 6, vol. 221, exp. 11, vol. 307, exp. 8.

67. AGN, Inq., vol. 320, exp. 8, vol. 1486, exp. s/n, fs. 132–33.

68. AGN, Inq., vol. 314, exp. 4.

69. AGN, Inq., vol. 324, exp. 2.

70. AGN, Inq., vol. 289, exp. 9j, vol. 375, exp. 6.

71. AGN, Inq., vol. 1486, exp. s/n, f. 138.

72. AGN, Inq., vol. 309, exp. s/n, f. 34.

73. AGN, Inq., vol. 306, exp. 9.

74. AGN, Inq., vol. 306, exp. 9.

75. AGN, Inq., vol. 289, exp. 2.

76. AGN, Inq., vol. 286, exp. 4, vol. 1486, exp. s/n, f. 139.

77. AGN, Inq., vol. 1486, exp. s/n, f. 140; Gómez, "Nómina," 498–99.

78. AGN, Inq., vol. 337, exp. 11, caja 165, carpeta 3, exp. 3, f. 8.

79. AGN, Inq., vol. 341, exp. 1, vol. 1486, exp. s/n, f. 144, caja 165, carpeta 3, exp. 39, f. 101.

80. AGN, Inq., vol. 1486, exp. s/n, f. 149; Gómez, "Nómina," 499.

81. AGN, Inq., vol. 347, exp. s/n, f. 479.

82. AGN, Inq., vol. 347, exp. s/n, fs. 443–44.

83. AGN, Inq., vol. 489, exp. 9, vol. 724, exp. s/n, f. 38.

84. AGN, Inq., vol. 341, 2a parte, exp. 6; Gómez, "Nómina," 499.

85. AGN, Inq., vol. 195, exp. 2; Gómez, "Nómina," 500–01.

86. AGN, Inq., vol. 1486, exp. s/n, f. 153.

87. AGN, Inq., vol. 349, exp. 16.

88. AGN, Inq., caja 165, carpeta 3, exp. 51, f. 132.

89. AGN, Inq., caja 165, carpeta 3, exp. 51, f. 132.

90. AGN, Inq., vol. 351, exp. 8, vol. 1486, exp. s/n, fs. 168–69, 172.

91. AGN, Inq., vol. 221, exp. 10, vol. 1486, exp. s/n, fs. 165–66, caja 165, carpeta 3, exp. 54, f. 137.

92. AGN, Inq., vol. 352, exp. [4].

93. AGN, Inq., vol. 352, exp. 6, vol. 1486, exp. s/n, f. 167.

94. AGN, Inq., vol. 223, exp. s/n, f. 260, vol. 357, exp. 8.

95. AGN, Inq., vol. 357, exp. 8.

96. AGN, Inq., vol. 357, exp. 8.

97. AGN, Inq., vol. 490, exp. 1.

98. AGN, Inq., vol. 356, exp. 4.

99. AGN, Inq., vol. 356, exp. 7, vol. 1486, exp. s/n, f. 176.

100. AGN, Inq., vol. 356, exp. 8.

101. AGN, Inq., vol. 357, exp. 11.

102. AGN, Inq., vol. 307, exp. 6.

103. AGN, Inq., vol. 1486, exp. s/n, f. 174.

104. AGN, Inq., vol. 1486, exp. s/n, f. 173.

105. AGN, Inq., vol. 659, exp. 6, vol. 1552, exp. s/n, fs. 195–96.

106. AGN, Inq., vol. 823, exp. s/n, fs. 340–41.

107. AGN, Inq., vol. 640, exp. 6, vol. 1486, exp. s/n, f. 179; Medina, *La imprenta en México,* 2: 146.

108. AGN, Inq., vol. 360, 2a parte, exp. 2, vol. 373, exp. 19.

109. In AGN, Inq., vol. 361, exp. 3, he is listed as Franciscan but in Gómez, "Nómina," as Dominican. Intuitively, it would be more logical that he were a Dominican, given the strong presence of that order in Guatemala and the relative weak presence of the Franciscans there.

110. AGN, Inq., vol. 361, exp. 3.

111. AGN, Inq., vol. 221, exp. 1, vol. 659, exp. 6.

112. AGN, Inq., vol. 362, exp. 2, vol. 362, exp. 17, vol. 364, exp. 7, vol. 659, exp. 6; Gallegos Rocafull, *El pensamiento mexicano,* 237.

113. AGN, Inq., vol. 365, exp. 19.

114. AGN, Inq., vol. 365, exp. 16, vol. 1486, exp. s/n, f. 183.

115. AGN, Inq., vol. 365, exp. 31; Gómez, "Nómina," 505.

116. AGN, Inq., vol. 365, exp. 34, vol. 724, exp. s/n, f. 41, vol. 1486, exp. s/n, f. 183.

117. AGN, Inq., vol. 364, exp. 12, vol. 1486, exp. s/n, f. 183.

118. AGN, Inq., vol. 494, exp. 5.

119. Gómez, "Nómina," 503.

120. AGN, Inq., vol. 373, exp. 19; Gómez, "Nómina," 503–4.

121. AGN, Inq., vol. 1486, exp. s/n, f. 159.

122. AGN, Inq., vol. 379, exp. 5, vol. 1486, exp. s/n, f. 182; Gómez, "Nómina," 504.

123. AGN, Inq., vol. 363, exp. 28, f. 220.

124. AGN, Inq., vol. 495, exp. s/n, f. 116.

125. AGN, Inq., vol. 362, exp. 2, exp. 17; *Diccionario Porrúa,* 6ª ed. (Mexico, 1995), 532.

126. AGN, Inq., vol. 362, exp. 2, vol. 362, exp. 17.

127. AGN, Inq., vol. 370, exp. 7.

128. Gómez, "Nómina," 505.

129. AGN, Inq., vol. 372, exp. 4.

130. AGN, Inq., vol. 372, exp. 6, vol. 482, exp. s/n, f. 196.

131. AGN, Inq., vol. 372, exp. 28.

132. AGN, Inq., vol. 695, exp. s/n, f. 285; Gómez, "Nómina," 507–8.

133. AGN, Inq., vol. 695, exp. s/n, f. 285; Gómez, "Nómina," 508.

134. AGN, Inq., vol. 375, exp. 10.

135. AGN, Inq., vol. 379, exp. 7.

136. Gómez, "Nómina," 506.

137. Gómez, "Nómina," 506.

138. AGN, Inq., vol. 379, exp. 10.

139. AGN, Inq., vol. 495, exp. 19.

140. AGN, Inq., vol. 377, exp. 18.

141. AGN, Inq., vol. 493, exp. s/n, fs. 45–53.

142. AGN, Inq., vol. 374, exp. 1; Gómez, "Nómina," 507.

143. AGN, Inq., vol. 374, exp. 1; Gómez, "Nómina," 507. This fray Martín was the brother of fray Felipe de Lexalde y Vergara. Both were nephews (via their mother) of the maestro fray Martín de Vergara mentioned above.

144. AGN, Inq., vol. 493, exp. 2.

145. AGN, Inq., vol. 352, exp. [5].

146. AGN, Inq., vol. 386, exp. 12.

147. AGN, Inq., vol. 387, exp. 5.

148. AGN, Inq., vol. 387, exp. 15, vol. 454, exp. 4.

149. Gómez, "Nómina," 508.

150. Ibid.

151. AGN, Inq., vol. 390, exp. s/n.

152. AGN, Inq., vol. 390, exp. s/n.

153. Since censors often lacked titles, sons or direct relatives of don/doña or titled hidalgos.

154. Inquisitors; censors of the Suprema; archbishops of metropolitan sees (except Manila); presidents of major Councils or Audiencias; viceroys; rectors of major universities; direct relatives of same.

155. Those with high level positions within one's order, such as guardian, prior, in a major house, like Mexico City; rector of a college; provincial of major province; cathedral canon in a major city; inquisitional comisario of a major city; comisario/vicar general of the order; bishop of suffragen see; oidores; regidores of major cities; direct relatives of same; relatives of familiares in major cities.

156. Those with a middling position within order, such as guardian, prior in a provincial house; comisario in a minor city; relatives of middling administrators, like regidores of provincial cities, alguaciles, alcaldes, notaries, familiares in minor cities. In cases where there was further data on the censor's biography, I have counted them as both hidalgo and some other status.

157. University professors, lectors of theology within one's order, writers of treatises — a somewhat deceptive category, since to rise to a high administrative level within the regular orders, one usually served the order in an academic capacity first. In some cases censors have been classified as both academic and some other status if data was available.

158. Given the importance of status and class in colonial/early modern Hispanic society, it is safe to assume that when a censor in his genealogy did not specifically outline his good family status that he likely came from low/working class/rural background. Entry into an order offered an opportunity for education. One notices that in the case of these men, they very rarely achieved much status within their order, though being appointed a calificador offered considerable prestige in itself. Testimonial profiles also suggest class background. Their witnesses for limpieza de sangre were limited largely to rural, or working-class professions, like barbers, cobblers, tailors, labradores, etc.

Appendix 3:
Inquisitors

Tenure	Inquisitor	Other positions held
1571–74	dr. don Pedro Moya de Contreras	cathedral maestrescuela, Canaries inquisitor, Murcia, 1569 viceroy, New Spain, 1573 archbishop, Mexico, 1573–91†
1573–93	dr. Alfonso Fernández de Bonilla	fiscal, Inquisition, Mexico, 1571–74 visitador general, Peru, 1586 archbishop elect, Mexico 1592– c.1601†
1574–77	licenciado Alfonso Granero Dávalos	visitador, Inquisition, Canaries, <1573[1] fiscal, Inquisition, Mexico 1573–74 bishop, La Plata (Bolivia), 1579– c.1587†
1580–91	licenciado [don?] Francisco Santos García[2]	cathedral canon, Mexico, 1540–53 provisor, archdiocese, Mexico, 1553–66 cathedral treasurer, Mexico, 1562–6 fiscal, Inquisition, Mexico, 1575–80 bishop, Guadalajara 1592–98†

'enure	Inquisitor	Other positions held
593–98	dr. don Bartolomé Lobo Guerrero	fiscal, Inquisition, Mexico, 1581–93
		bishop, Santa Fe de Bogotá, 1596–1607
		archbishop, Lima 1607–23†
594–1609	licenciado don Alonso de Peralta	bishop elect, Charcas, 1609[3]
599–1618	licenciado Gutierre Bernardo de Quiroz	inquisitor, Toledo 1618–27
		bishop, Puebla, 1627–38†
609–11†	dr. Gonzalo Martos de Bohórquez	fiscal, Inquisition, Mexico, 1593–1609
613–25	dr. Juan Gutiérrez Flores	fiscal, Inquisition, Sicily, 1600–1602
		inquisitor, Mallorca, 1605–13
		visitador general, Audiencia of Lima, 1625
		coadjustor, diocese, La Paz 1631†
617–33†	dr. don Francisco Bazán de Albornoz	fiscal, Inquisition, Cartagena de Indias, <1617
623–25†	licenciado Gonzalo Messía Lobo	inquisitor, Canaries <1623
627	licenciado don Martín Carrillo y Aldrete	visitador general, New Spain
		inquisitor, General Council of the Inquisition
628–39†	don Gaspar de Valdespina	fiscal, Inquisition, Lima, 1611–1628
631–39	dr. Bartolomé González Soltero	calificador, Inquisition, Mexico, 1619–24
		fiscal, Inquisition, Mexico, 1624–34
		bishop, Guatemala, 1641–c.1651†
638–62†	licenciado Domingo Vélez de Asas y Argos	inquisitor, Cartagena de Indias <1637
642–	dr. don Francisco de Estrada y Escobedo	fiscal, Inquisition, Mexico, 1634–42
		bishop, Havana
		bishop, Guatemala
		bishop elect of Puebla†

N=16
Hidalgos   7 (44 percent)
Doctores   8 (50 percent)
Licenciados   7 (44 percent)
Bishops   5 (or 6?) or archbishops, 3 (50 or 56 percent)
Former fiscals   10 (63 percent)
Sources: AGN, Inq., vols. 1–63; 65–72; 74–85; 88–169; 172–285; 287–92; 294–335; 337–38; 340–91; 449–50; 452–55; 458; 463–64; 466–67; 469–86; 488, exps. 4, 5; 489–96; 498; 499, exp. s/n, fs. 148–93; 508–10; 558–60; 636; 640; 659; 670; 673, exps. 48–54; 674, exp. 32; 683, exp. 2, exp. 4; 705, exp. 3; 823; 846; 916, exp. 8; 927, exp. 11; 977, exp. 18; 1111;

1175, exp. 44; 1311; 1487–95; 1529–30; 1547; 1550; 1552–54; cajas 154; 161; 163–65; 167–68.

Eubel and van Gulik. *Hierarchia Catholica Medii et Recentioris Aevi.*
Gómez. "Nómina."
Medina, *Historia del santo oficio de México.*
Páramo, *De origine et progressv.*
Pavón Romero, "Doctores en la Universidad de México."
Poole, Stafford, *Pedro Moya de Contreras.*

Notes

1. This was noted in the letter of July 14, 1573, sent by the Suprema to the Inquisition in Mexico with instructions that Dávalos be appointed fiscal in place of Bonilla, who was promoted to inquisitor. It was received in Mexico on August 23, 1574. See AGN, Inq., vol. 223, 1a parte, exp. s/n, f. 22v.

2. On November 8, 1571, don Francisco [Rodríguez?] Sanctos, treasurer of the Mexico City cathedral, testified before the new inquisitor Moya de Contreras. The deposition was not signed, so while it is likely that this was the same future inquisitor, it is not entirely conclusive. See AGN, Inq., vol. 226, exp. s/n, f. 319.

3. In a letter dated April 1609 from the inquisitors in Mexico to the Guatemala comisario don Felipe Ruiz de Corral, the inquisition notary wrote that the letter was from licenciado don Alonso de Peralta, "electo de la yglesia de las Charcas." See AGN, Inq., vol. 470, exp. s/n, f. 552.

Notes

Abbreviations

ACSE	Archivo del Convento de San Esteban, Salamanca
AGN	Archivo General de la Nación (Mexico)
ar.	article
c.	capitulum (chapter)
disp.	disputatio (argument)
exp.	expediente (file)
f.	foja (page)
Inq.	Inquisición (as a section of archive)
lib.	liber (book)
qu.	question
§	section
s/n	sin número (unfoliated)
ST	*Summa theologiae* of Thomas Aquinas. Citations are by section (e.g., 2.2), article and question.
tit.	title
vol.	volume

For Eimeric, I have relied on Nicolau Eimeric, *Directorium Inquisitorum . . . cum comentariis Francisci Pegñae* (Venice, 1595). Commentaries by Peña are given as "Peña, comment." and then specify the part of the *Directorium* (first, second, or third) from which they are taken. Citations of the Canon Law are given according to volume (e.g.,

Decretum, Decretales, Sextus), book (lib.), title (tit.), chapter (c.) or question (qu.). Likewise for the canonist commentators and theologians I have given citation by location rather than by page number since page numeration varies between volumes, whereas location by book, section, article, disputation, and so on does not vary as much between volumes. Scriptural citations are from the Oxford NRSV unless otherwise specified.

Introduction

1. Horace, *Epistulae* 1.18.71: "Semel emissum volat irrevocabile verbum."

2. Simancas, *De catholicis institutionibus*, tit. 38, nu. 10: "Multae autem sunt causae, propter quas libri haereticorum in ignem mittendi sunt . . . Deinde, semel emissum volat irrevocabile verbum; at scripta per multa secula durant et posteros etiam inficere queunt. Denique voces haereticorum civitatem unam replere vix possunt; libri vero de Populo in Populum, de Regno in Regnum per facile transeunt." Most theorists and scholars of the early modern period cited and noted their sources, as do modern-day scholars, and jurists in particular tended to be a bit obsessive in citations as a manner of legal proof, though it was hardly uncommon to crib or blatantly plagiarize in these works.

3. *Decretum,* causa 24, qu. 3, c. 16: "resecandae sunt putridae carnes: et scabiosa ouis a caulis repellenda, ne tota domus, massa corpus et pecora ardeat, corrunpatur, putrescat, intereant."

4. León Pinelo, *Qvestión moral.*

5. The ban was issued June 19, 1620: AGN, Inq., vol. 333, exp. 35. For Vergara's request, see AGN, Inq., vol. 486, 2a parte, exp. s/n, f. 417.

6. AGN, Inq., vol. 90, exp. 42.

7. AGN, Inq., vol. 16, exp. 9.

8. AGN, Inq., vol. 16, exp. 9, f. 368: "debía muy grabemente ser castigado por escandaloso y que las proposiçiones tenían por escandalosas como quiera que fuesen dichas en espeçial en tierra nueba y gente nueba en la fee y en tiempos tan peligrosos."

9. AGN, Jesuitas, III-26, exp. 22, f. 7v.

10. AGN, Inq., vol. 139, exp. 62.

11. Expressed most notably in his study *Local Religion in Sixteenth-Century Spain.*

12. The historiography of the Inquisition is extremely dense and extensive, and a full treatment here would be impossible. Indeed, so dense is the scholarship that the history of the historiography is itself a genre unto itself, as can be seen in Ricardo García Cárcel's intellectual history of the Black Legend, *La leyenda negra.* For a recent discussion, see Moreno, *La invención de la Inquisición.* For examples of scholarship which has examined the Inquisition from an institutional perspective, see, among others, Contreras, *El santo oficio de la inquisición en Galicia;* Da Costa Pôrto, *Nos tempos do visitador;* Escudero, ed., *Perfiles jurídicos de la inquisición española;* Escudero, "Los orígenes del 'Consejo de la Suprema Inquisición' "; Espinosa, "Conflictos políticos y jurisdiccionales"; Greenleaf, *Zumárraga and the Mexican Inquisition;* Medina, *Historia del santo oficio en México;* Monter, *Frontiers of Heresy.*

13. E.g., Luque Muriel, "Los abecedarios"; Palacios Alcalde, "Legislación inquisitorial"; Pérez Martín, "La doctrina jurídica y el proceso inquisitorial"; Tomás y Valiente, *El derecho penal;* idem, *Gobierno e instituciones.*

14. Lea, *History of the Inquisition in Spain,* and idem, *The Inquisition in the Spanish Dependencies.*

15. Kamen, *The Spanish Inquisition;* Peters, *Inquisition.*

16. For some general studies in this vein, see Alberro, *Del gachupín al criollo;* Alcalá-Zamora, ed., *La vida cotidiana;* Carrato, *Igreja, iluminismo e escolas mineiras coloniais;* Corcuera de Mancera, *El fraile, el indio, y el pulque;* Curcio-Nagy, *Great Festivals of Colonial Mexico City;* Few, *Women Who Lead Evil Lives;* Lewis, *Hall of Mirrors;* Monter, *Frontiers of Heresy;* Nalle, *Mad for God;* Quezada, *Enfermedad y maleficio;* Quezada, Rodríguez, and Suárez, eds., *Inquisición novohispana.* On the relationship between the Inquisition and the repression or regulation of various forms of sexual behavior, see Behar, "Sex and Sin, Witchcraft and the Devil"; Bennassar, "Le modèle sexuel"; Boyer, *Lives of the Bigamists;* Carrasco, *Inquisición y represión sexual;* Garza Carvajal, *Butterflies Will Burn;* Mott, *Escravidão, homossexualidade e demonologia,* and idem, *O sexo proibido;* Núñez Roldán, *El pecado nefando del Obispo de Salamina;* Quezada, *Sexualidad, amor y erotismo;* Schwartz, "Pecar en las colonias." For discussions of the broader relationship between the Church and the regulation of sex, see Corcuera de Mancera, *Del amor al temor;* Gruzinski "Los cenizos del deseo"; Herrera Puga, *Sociedad y delincuencia;* Núñez Roldán, *Vida cotidiana en la Sevilla del Siglo de Oro;* Ortega, ed., *De la santidad a la perversión;* Seminario de Historia de las Mentalidades, *El placer de pecar y el afán de normar;* Tomás y Valiente, "El crimen y el pecado contra natura"; Tomás y Valiente et al., *Sexo barroco;* Tortorici, " 'Heran Todos Putos' "; Vainfas, *Trópico dos pecados.* For excellent discussions of the issue of sexual solicitation in the confessional and the Inquisition's response, see Alejandre García, *El veneno de Dios,* and Haliczer, *Sexuality in the Confessional.* For some offerings on the Mexican Inquisition as it dealt with peoples of African descent, see Bristol, *Christians, Blasphemers, and Witches;* Cárdenas, *Hechicería, saber y transgresión,* and portions of Villa-Flores, *Dangerous Speech,* and idem, "Voices from a Living Hell." While the Inquisition did not, after 1571, have authority over the Indians, there were some notorious inquisitional proceedings in the period before that (notably against don Carlos of Texcoco and in the Yucatán). See Clendinnen, *Ambivalent Conquests; Proceso inquisitorial del cacique de Tetzcoco.* After 1571 special tribunals called *provisoratos de indios* were established to regulate and prosecute idolatry in Mexico. See Chuchiak, "La inquisición Indiana y la extirpación de idolatrías"; Durán, *Historia de las Indias de Nueva España;* Tavárez, "La idolatría letrada," and idem, "Idolatry as an Ontological Question." In Peru the archdiocesan court itself prosecuted widespread extirpation campaigns. See Duviols, *La lutte contre les religions autochtones dans le Péru colonial;* MacCormick, *Religion in the Andes;* Mills, *Idolatry and Its Enemies.* In other cases royal officials or alcaldes prosecuted idolatry cases. See Scholas and Adams, eds., *Proceso contra Tzintzicha Tangaxoan, el Cantzontzin;* Tavárez, "Autonomy, Honor, and the Ancestors."

17. These are all extensive and well-developed subfields of the Inquisition, and I offer here only a highly abbreviated listing of the available scholarship. For scholarship on Judaism and conversos and the relationship to the Inquisition, see Alpert, *Criptojudaísmo e Inquisición;* Blázquez Miguel, *Inquisición y criptojudaísmo;* Carrete Parrondo, *El judaísmo español y la Inquisición;* Gil, *Los conversos y la inquisición sevillana;* Graizbord, *Souls in Dispute;* Lazar and Haliczer, eds., *Jews of Spain and the Expulsion of*

1492; Liebman, *Jews in New Spain;* Netanyahu, *Origins of the Inquisition,* and idem, *Toward the Inquisition;* Starr-LeBeau, *In the Shadow of the Virgin;* Toro, ed., *Los Juo- díos en la Nueva España.* On witchcraft, see Caro Baroja, *Las brujas y su mundo;* Congreso Nacional de San Sebastián, *Brujología;* Ebright and Hendricks, *The Witches of Abiquiu;* Gil del Río, *La Santa Inquisición;* Ginzburg, *The Night Battles;* Henningsen, *The Witches' Advocate;* Mello e Souza, *O diabo e a terra de Santa Cruz;* Norgueira, "A migração do Sabbat"; Pavia, *Drama of the Siglo de Oro;* Rodríguez-Vigil Rubio, *Bruxas, lobos e Inquisición.* On alumbradismo, see Giordano, *María de Cazalla;* Jaffery, *False Mystics;* Llamas Martínez, *Santa Teresa de Jesús y la Inquisición española;* Pastore, *Un'eresia spagnola;* Ramírez L., ed., *María Rita Vargas, María Lucía Celis;* Santonja, *La herejía de los alumbrados;* Sarrión Mora, *Beatas y endemoniadas.*

18. For an abbreviated listing on *derecho indiano,* see Barrientos Grandón, *La cultura jurídica;* Manzano Manzano, *Historia de las recopilaciones de Indias;* Ots y Capdequí, *Manual de historia de derecho español;* Pérez Fernández, *El derecho hispano-indiano;* Sánchez Bella et al., *Historia del derecho indiano.*

19. López Vela, "El calificador"; Pinto Crespo, "La censura"; Roldán Pérez, "Reflex- iones sobre la producción literaria de los funcionarios inquisitoriales." For the discussion of Núñez, see Méndez, *Secretos de Oficio,* 165–228. Also, Méndez, along with Cas- tellanos, Fernando del Mar, and Morales, has provided a valuable catalogue of books and manuscripts censored by the Mexican Inquisition, in *Catálogo de textos marginados novohispanos.*

20. Bujanda, *Index des livres interdits;* Cavarra, ed., *Inquisizione e Indice;* De los Reyes Gómez, *El libro en España y América;* López-Vidriero and Cátedra, eds., *El libro antiguo español.*

21. Alcalá, ed., *Inquisición española y mentalidad inquisitorial,* and idem, ed., *Proceso inquisitorial de Fray Luis de León;* Asensio, "Censura inquisitorial"; Borromeo, "In- quisizione spagnola e libri proibiti"; Cerrón Puga, "La censura literaria"; Gacto, "Inquisi- ción y censura en el Barroco"; Guibovich Pérez, *Censura, libros e inquisición.*

22. See Alcalá, *Literatura y ciencia;* Baudot and Méndez, *Amores prohibidos;* Méndez et al., *Catálogo de textos marginados novohispanos,* and Peña, *La palabra amordazada.*

23. Bollème, *La Bibliothèque bleue;* Dadson, *Libros, lectores y lecturas;* Defourneaux, *L'Inquisition espagnole et les livres français;* Domínguez Guzmán, *La imprenta en Sevilla en el siglo XVII;* Furet et al., *Livre et société;* García Oro and Portela Silva, *Monarquía y los libros en el Siglo de Oro;* Grendler, *The Roman Inquisition and the Venetian Press;* Griffin, *Journeymen-Printers, Heresy, and the Inquisition;* Guibovich Pérez, *La inquisi- ción y la censura de libros,* and idem, *Censura, libros e inquisición;* Hernández González, "Suma de inventarios de bibliotecas del siglo XVI"; Leonard, *Baroque Times in Old Mexico,* and idem, *Books of the Brave;* Mandrou, *De la culture populaire;* Martínez Millán, "Aportaciones a la formación del estado moderno"; Morón Arroyo, "La inquisi- ción y la posibilidad de la gran literatura barroca española"; Pardo Tomás, *Ciencia y censura;* Ramos Soriano, "Criterios inquisitoriales"; Ruiz y Torres, "A puerta cerrada"; Rundine, *Inquisizione spagnola: Censura e libri proibiti;* Schons, *Book Censorship in New Spain;* Sharrer, "Juan de Burgos"; Tellechea Idígoras, "Biblias publicadas fuera de España."

24. There is extensive scholarship on these subfields. An excellent comprehensive treat-

ment of ideological intolerance in broad context is found in Escudero, ed., *Intolerancia e Inquisición*. Other excellent studies include Avilés, *Erasmo y la Inquisición;* Bataillon, *Erasmo y España;* Fragnito, *La Bibbia al rogo;* Fernández, *Panorama social del humanismo español;* Goñi Gaztambide, "El impresor Miguel de Eguía"; Homza, "Erasmus as Hero, or Heretic?" and idem, *Religious Authority in the Spanish Renaissance;* Longhurst, *Luther's Ghost in Spain,* and idem, *Luther and the Spanish Inquisition;* Menéndez Pelayo, *Historia de los heterodoxos españoles;* Miranda, *El erasmista mexicano;* Nieto, *Juan de Valdés;* Oberman, *Luther;* Rodríguez, *El Catecismo Romano ante Felipe II y la Inquisición española;* Serrano y Sanz, "Pedro Ruiz de Alcaraz"; Tellechea Idígoras, *El arzobispo Carranza y su tiempo.*

25. Bennassar, avec Dedieu et al., *Inquisition espagnole;* Contreras, *El santo oficio en Galicia;* Maravall, *La cultura del Barroco.*

26. For general discussions of these historiographic trends, see Burke, *The French Historical Revolution,* and Lockhart, "The Social History of Colonial Spanish America."

27. Alberro, *Inquisición y sociedad en México;* Contreras, *El santo oficio en Galicia;* García Cárcel, *Herejía y sociedad en el siglo XVI;* Greenleaf, *The Mexican Inquisition;* Millar Carvacho, *Inquisición y sociedad.*

28. Pérez Villanueva and Escandell Bonet, eds., *Historia de la Inquisición en España y América.*

29. E.g., Blázquez Miguel, *La Inquisición en Albacete,* and idem, *La Inquisición en Cataluña;* Bombín Pérez, *La Inquisición en el País Vasco;* Borromeo, "Inquisizione spagnola e libri proibiti in Sicilia ed in Sardegna"; Braga, *A Inquisição nos Açores;* Chinchilla Aguilar, *La Inquisición en Guatemala;* Contreras, *El santo oficio de la inquisición en Galicia;* Coronas Tejada, *La Inquisición en Jaén;* Costa Pôrto, *Nos tempos do visitador;* Dedieu, *L'Administration de la foi;* Deive, *Heterodoxia e inquisición en Santo Domingo;* García Cárcel, *Herejía y sociedad en el siglo XVI;* Medina, *La inquisición en Cartagena de Indias.*

30. Ginzburg, *The Cheese and the Worms;* Ladurie, *Montaillou.*

31. Notably Chartier, *The Cultural Uses of Print;* Darnton, *The Great Cat Massacre.*

32. Alberro, *La inquisición y sociedad en México,* and idem, *El águila y la cruz* and *Del gachupín al criollo.*

33. For Pinto Crespo, see note 19 above. Also see Prosperi, *Tribunali della coscienza.*

34. See Albaret, *Les Inquisiteurs,* and Prado Moura, *Inquisición e inquisidores en Castilla.*

35. *Processus in causa fidei.*

36. Godman, *Saint as Censor.*

37. See Alejandre García and Torquemada, *Palabra de hereje,* and Torquemada, "Censura de libros y barreras aduaneras."

38. Prosperi, "L'Arsenale degli inquisitori."

39. See Vovelle, *Ideologies and Mentalities.* Also see discussion in LeGoff, "Mentalities."

40. Hordes, "The Inquisition as Economic and Political Agent."

41. Greenleaf, "The Great Visitas of the Mexican Holy Office."

42. Especially in *De legibus.*

43. For the discussion that follows in this paragraph and in some other areas and for

putting me on to the trail of the work of historians of customary law, I am thankful to William Christian, Jr., who indirectly led me to this material and the discussions of consuetidinary concerns in derecho indiano.

44. Tau Anzoátegui, *La ley en América hispana*, 8: "El complejo orden jurídico indiano se integra principalmente con tres Fuentes: la ley, la costumbre, y la doctrina de los autores. No operaban dichas Fuentes de modo uniforme ni exclusive, ni tampoco respondían a una jerarquía establecida."

45. Cited in Fernández Arruti, "La costumbre en la nueva codificación canónica," 1:165.

46. Ferdinand Tönnies called *gesellschaft* a "planned, bureaucratic" or "associational" society in which he compared various attempts to structure society either as responding to law as custom or to impose law from above. Thomas Hobbes famously concluded that minus social order man lived in a state of war of all against all in which life was "solitary, poor, nasty, brutish and short." Tönnies, on the other hand, responded to the classic Hobbesian line by arguing that gesellschaft could be understood historically, to which he contrasted *gemeinschaft* as "unity prior to the rise of individuality." In the early twentieth century, Tönnies reacted to the so-called historical school of law, which conceived of law not as a system of codification but of "slow 'organic' growth out of custom and usage." See Cahnman, "Max Weber and the Methodological Controversy in the Social Sciences."

Chapter 1. Longue Durée *Concerns*

1. A good overview as well as collection of documents on the late classic and medieval ecclesiological discussions can be found in Peters, ed., *Heresy and Authority*.

2. For an overview of Augustine's life, see Brown, *Augustine of Hippo*.

3. Many of these documents and stories are related in Peters, ed., *Heresy and Authority*. For an excellent intellectual history of medieval Europe, see Colish, *Medieval Foundations of the Western Intellectual Tradition*.

4. The bull is reproduced in Peters, ed., *Heresy and Authority*, 170–73. For a discussion of penal law and the distinction between civil and ecclesiastical courts and punishments, see Tomás y Valiente, *La tortura judicial*.

5. A recent study has shown that the *Decretum* was a process rather than a simple onetime redaction: Winroth, *The Making of Gratian's* Decretum.

6. There is an extensive scholarship on Innocent III. For some basic discussions, see Moore, *Pope Innocent III*; Pennington, *Pope and Bishops*; Powell, *Innocent III*; Ullmann, "The Significance of Innocent III's *Vergentis*."

7. For a concise biography, see Bustos, *Santo Domingo de Guzmán*.

8. For some well-known and reliable discussions, see Albaret, *Les Inquisiteurs*; Given, *Inquisition and Medieval Society*; Ladurie, *Montaillou*; Weis, *The Yellow Cross*.

9. For a discussion of the emerging rules on confession, see Tentler, *Sin and Confession*.

10. *Historia de la Inquisición en España y América*, 1:249–67; and Gregory IX, *Declinate iam mundi* (May 26, 1232) and Innocent IV, *Inter alia desiderabilia cordis nostris* (October 20, 1249), both in Martínez Díez, ed., *Bulario de la inquisición española*, 28–35.

11. In Martínez Díez, ed., *Bulario de la Inquisición española*, 38–39: "Nec per hoc, quod fidei negotium generaliter in ipsis partibus vobis committimus, commissiones a

praefata Sede diocoesanis eisdem factas, si forsan illarum seu etiam ordinaria velint auctoritate procedere, intendimus reuocare."

12. In *Ne Inquisitionis* and *Ut negotium fidei*. See Martínez Díez, ed., *Bulario de la inquisición española*, 50–53.

13. A standard biography is that by his contemporary and fellow Dominican Thomas Agni da Lentino, archbishop of Cosenza, later primate of Jerusalem, and is reproduced in *Acta sanctorum*. Also see discussion in Del Col, *L'Inquisizione in Italia*, 87–88. A modern discussion can be found at www.domcentral.org/trad/disciples/o1petver.htm, the Web site of the Dominicans from the Province of St. Albert the Great in Chicago. The canonization was confirmed on April 29, 1253, by Innocent IV in the bull *Magnis et crebis*.

14. See Pasamar Lázaro, *La cofradía de San Pedro Mártir de Verona*.

15. *Sextus*, lib. 5, tit. 2, c. 17. For discussions of the legal controversies of Boniface VIII's papacy, see Giles of Rome, *On Ecclesiastical Power*; John of Paris, *On Royal and Papal Power*; Leclercq, *Jean de Paris et l'ecclésiologie du XIIIe siècle*; Wood, ed., *Philip the Fair and Boniface VIII*.

16. For an overview of the controversies, see Mundy and Woody, eds., *Council of Constance*, and Stump, *Reforms of the Council of Constance*.

17. In his *Tractatus factus contra avisamentum Basiliensium quod non liceat appellare a Concilo ad Papam* (1436) as well as in *Summa ecclesiastica* (1450).

18. For a good overview of the concerns and issues surrounding conciliarism, see Tierney, *Foundations of the Conciliar Theory*.

19. The only full-length biography of which I am aware is Brugada i Gutiérrez-Ravé, *Nicolau Eimeric*. The *Directorium Inquisitorum* also contains autobiographical information.

20. I discuss Eimeric at length in chapters 2 and 3. Bernard Gui's manual was not printed in the sixteenth century and while he was an active and well-known inquisitor in fourteenth-century Toulouse, Carcassone, and the Languedoc, after the medieval period his work on procedure fell into general disuse in the Hispanic world and was never printed in the early modern era. His manual was published in Paris in 1886. For some discussions, see Delisle, *Notice sur les manuscrits de Bernard Gui*; Dondaine, "Le manuel de l'inquisiteur"; Douais, "Préface."

21. For discussions of Fournier, see Ladurie, *Montaillou*, and Weis, *The Yellow Cross*.

22. For an overview of the issue, see Peters, *Torture*.

23. See Contreras and Henningsen, "Forty-Four Thousand Cases," and Henningsen, "La elocuencia de los números."

24. A comprehensive overview of the legal and jurisdictional history of the Iberian medieval inquisitions is given in Páramo, *De origine et progressv*. Despite its age and Latin prose, it remains one of the best legal histories of the medieval inquisitions. One may also consult Lea, *History of the Inquisition in Spain*.

25. See his monumental work of intellectual history, *Origins of the Inquisition*.

26. For general discussion of the period, see Edwards, *The Spain of the Catholic Monarchs*.

27. For concise discussion of the early years of the newly formed Inquisition, see Starr-LeBeau, *In the Shadow of the Virgin*.

28. For a good discussion of the early development of the Suprema and the conciliar administrative structure of the Spanish Inquisition, see Escudero, "Inquisidor General y Consejo de la Suprema," and idem, "Los orígenes del 'Consejo de la Suprema Inquisición'"; Palacios Alcalde, "Legislación inquisitorial (1478–1504)." For discussions of the emergent physical plant of the Inquisition, see Martínez Millán, *La hacienda de la Inquisición.*

29. For magisterial and classic studies of the topic, see Bataillon, *Erasmo y España,* and Fernández, *Panorama social del humanismo español,* among others.

30. Bataillon's discussion is extensive in *Erasmo y España.* Also see "Actas originales de las congregaciones celebradas en 1527"; Avilés, *Erasmo y la Inquisición;* Homza, "Erasmus as Hero or Heretic?"

31. For Cano's biography and his role in the Valdés Inquisition, see Caballero, *Vida de Melchor Cano,* and González Novalín, *Fernando de Valdés.* On Cano's (central) role in the Carranza trial, see Tellechea Idígoras, *El arzobispo Carranza y su tiempo.* For a good overview of Cano's notorious hatred of the Jesuits, see Cano, "Censura y parecer," and O'Reilly, "Melchor Cano and the Spirituality of St. Ignatius Loyola."

32. Rueda Ramírez, *Negocio e intercambio cultural,* 331.

33. Discussed in Tellechea Idígoras, *El arzobispo Carranza y su tiempo.* The Roman trial of Carranza is discussed at length in Tellechea Idígoras, *El proceso romano del Arzobispo Carranza.* Simancas relates his monomaniacal hatred of Carranza in his autobiography, "La vida y cosas notables del señor Obispo de Zamora."

Chapter 2. Medieval and Early Modern Precedents

1. Simancas, *De catholicis institutionibus,* tit. 30, nu. 7: "Ad summam, haeresibus vera et Catholica Fides et Religio labefactur, anime et corpora occiditur, tumultus et seditiones commoventur; pax et tranquilitas publica perturbatur; denique totius Reipublicae Christianae status et forma in pejus commatatur et nonnumquam subvertitur etiam et extinguitur. Sed haeresim omnium pessimae haereticorum hujus temporis sunt, quia non portionem aliquam laedere, sed ipsa Christianae Religionis conantur fundamenta destruere." For an excellent discussion of Simancas and Páramo, their careers, and their approaches to inquisitional theory, see Hossain, "Was Adam the First Heretic?" For a fuller discussion, see her Johns Hopkins doctoral thesis, "Arbiters of Faith, Agents of Empire" (2006).

2. For a general discussion of Hawkins, see Kelsey, *Sir John Hawkins.*

3. Páramo, *De origine et progressv,* preface: "ab haereticas pestes Oficii Sancti ferrum et ignem admouerint eos silentio praetermittere noluimus, nec quidem regna, Respublicas, nationes, regiones, oppida et urbae quae, vel salubri hoc remedio ad repellendum morbum tam periculosum usae sint, vel in sui pernicem illud reciecerint."

4. Ibid., lib. 3, tit. 3, c. 6, nu. 17. On Nestor: "Vermes linguam eius corrserunt ipse tamen allisus humo periit." On Marcus Ephesinus: "cholico morbo laborans (ex ore enim eructabat stercora) diris cruciatibus afflictus interiit."

5. Ibid., lib. 3, tit. 3, c. 6, nu. 31: "Caluinus cum quatuor annos nouem morbis dirissimis excruciaretur atque tabesceret . . . nempe cholica, dolore articulorum, calculo, haemorrhoidibus, febri iasthmate, capitis dolore, pituita, sanguinis vomitatione, denique pediculi undique scantentibus exersus, infelicissime ac foedissime obiit."

6. It begins, "Vergentis in senium saeculi corruptelam" meaning, loosely, "The corruption of a world advances unto its old age."

7. *Decretales,* lib. 5, tit. 7, c. 10, *Vergentis:* "nondum tamen usque adeo pestis potuit mortificari mortifera, quin, sicut cancer, amplius serperet in occulto et iam in aperto suae virus iniquitatis effundat."

8. Ibid.: "vulpes demolientes vineam Domini . . . lupos ab ovibus videamur . . . canes muti non valentes latrare."

9. Leo X: "Exurge Domine et iudica causam tuam, memor esto improperiorum tuorum, eorum quae ab insipientibus siunt tota die: inclina aurem tuam ad preces nostras, quoniam surrexerunt vulpes quaerentes demoliri vineam, cuis tu torcular calcasti solus . . . Exterminare nititur eam aperde sylva et singularis ferus depascitur eam." Cited and redacted in Páramo, *De origine et progressv,* lib. 2, tit. 2, c. 1, nu. 7. I have partially relied on the translation in Bainton, *Here I Stand,* 114.

10. *Decretales,* lib. 5, tit. 7, c. 12: "Laici non praedicent, nec occulta conventicula faciant, nec sacerdotes reprehendant."

11. *Decretales,* lib. 5, tit. 7, c. 10.

12. AGN, Inq., vol. 252, exp. s/n, fs. 197–274. Maturino Gilberti (discussed below in chapter 5), expressed the line of Joachim of Fiore, that only certain holy men would be saved when the Beast arrived. See AGN, Inq., vol. 43, exp. 6, exp. 30.

13. I Cor. 3:1–2.

14. *Decretales,* lib. 5, tit. 7, c. 12: "Tanta est enim divinae scripturae profunditas, ut non solum simplices et illiterati, sed etiam prudentes et docti non plene sufficient ad ipsius intelligentiam indagandam."

15. Fernández, *Panorama social del humanismo español,* 406. The biblical line is from Romans 12:3: "For by the grace given to me I say to everyone among you not to think of yourself more highly than you ought to think, but to think with sober judgment, each according to the measure of faith that God has assigned." The Latin Bible uses the verb *sapere,* translated into the NRSV and the New American Bible ("the official Catholic Bible") as "to think." There are, however, multiple meanings of sapere, none of which would have been lost on Innocent III or on future scholars citing Romans 12:3. Besides to know, sapere means to taste of, smack of, to have the flavor of. Jerome's Latin could also be translated as, "Do not taste what is forbidden." One of the principal divisions of religious error-crimes under the jurisdiction was "sapit haeresim" which means, literally, smacks of heresy. Slightly lower in gravity than outright heresy, the use of the verb sapere in this context adds further meaning to the use of Romans 12:3, precisely because sapere was a verb used generally in discussion of heresy and tasting what is forbidden, and rarely as its secondary meaning, to know, by theologians and canonists.

16. AGN, Inq., vol. 71, exp. 6.

17. Tomás y Valiente, *Gobierno e instituciones,* 19.

18. Dondaine, "Le manuel de l'inquisiteur."

19. See Wakefield, "Notes on Some Antiheretical Writings."

20. Dondaine, "Le manuel de l'inquisiteur."

21. On Spanish "Instructions," see González Novalín, "Las instrucciones de la Inquisición española."

22. For a good overview of the development of Spanish inquisitional law and practice, especially as found in manuals, see Errera, *Processus in causa fidei,* and Pérez Martín, "La

doctrina jurídica y el proceso inquisitorial." While not necessarily always dealing with inquisitional law, the best overall treatment of penal law for early modern Spain can be found in Tomás y Valiente, *El derecho penal.*

23. For Eimeric's biography, see Brugada i Gutiérrez-Ravé, *Nicolau Eimeric.*

24. See, among many, Delisle, *Notice sur les manuscrits de Bernard Gui;* Dondaine, "Le manuel de l'inquisiteur"; Given, *Inquisition and Medieval Society.*

25. Discussed at length in Errera, *Processus in causa fidei.*

26. Errera, *Processus in causa fidei,* 303.

27. See Errera, *Processus in causa fidei.* It was also printed in 1485 in Rome, followed by Salamanca editions of 1496, 1497, 1514, and 1519.

28. See Errera, *Processus in causa fidei,* and Van der Vekene, *Biblioteca bibliographica historiae sanctae inquisitionis,* 1:14–15, 43.

29. For biographical information on Castro, see the extensive intellectual history and paean to Tridentine Catholicism, Olarte, *Alfonso de Castro.*

30. Castro's *Aduersus omnes haereses* went through twenty printed editions (Paris, 1534, 1541, 1543 [twice], 1560; Cologne, 1539, 1540, 1543, 1549, 1558; Salamanca, 1541; Lyon, 1546, 1555; Venice, 1546, 1555; Antwerp, 1556, 1557, 1560, 1565, 1568), and his *De justa haereticorum punitione,* while not as widely printed, nevertheless went through several editions (Salamanca, 1547; Venice, 1549; Lyon, 1556, 1566; Antwerp, 1568; Rome, 1625). See Olarte, *Alfonso de Castro;* Van der Vekene, *Biblioteca bibliographica historiae sanctae inquisitionis,* 1:16–24. For further discussions of Castro's philosophy of penal law, see Castillo, *Alfonso de Castro y el problema de las leyes penales,* and Rodríguez Molinero, *Origen español de la ciencia del derecho penal.*

31. Van der Vekene, *Biblioteca bibliographica historiae sanctae inquisitionis,* 1:20–26. Gui's manual remained in manuscript until Célestin Douais revived it in the nineteenth century as a source of historiographic and theological inquiry. See Douais, "Préface," ix–xii. Douais found two manuscripts in Toulouse, one in the British Museum, which was considered inferior, and an apparent fraud or incorrect seventeenth-century manuscript in the French National Library. For an overview of Gui's works, see Delisle, *Notice sur les manuscrits de Bernard Gui.*

32. Castro's presumed treatise is cited in Pavia, *Drama of the Siglo de Oro,* 19, n. 55, and in the Espasa Calpe *Enciclopedia* (Madrid, 1911), 12:377. Pavia cites the work as appearing in 1540, Espasa Calpe as being published in Lyon in 1568. Olaechea Labayen in "Opinión de los teólogos españoles," 15–16, also says the treatise was printed in Lyon in 1568. Castro's awareness of the witchcraft investigations is discussed further in Norgueira, "A migração do Sabbat."

33. Alfonso de Castro, *De potestate legis poenalis,* quoted in Errera, *Processus in cause fidei,* 152: "Nam tam frequens et tam prolixa legum et canonum et doctorum citatio ad solam proficit memoriae ostentationem, non autem ad meliorem interpretationem, aut maiorem confirmationem aut legentibus generare fastidium et saepe illorum perturbare memoriam."

34. For biographical sketches of Peña's career, see Godman, *Saint as Censor,* 90–94; Peters, "Francisco Peña and the 'Directorium Inquisitorum.'"

35. Godman, *Saint as Censor,* 90.

36. Godman provides a transcription of Peña's appointment to the Congregation of the

Index from the Archivo della Congregazione per la Dottrina della Fede, Vatican City, Indice, Diarii I, fol. 16v. This is a particularly valuable contribution of Godman's study because the Archivo della Congregazione was only opened in 1998 and hitherto was closed to research. Tedeschi predicted in the 1980s that if the archives of the Roman Inquisition were suddenly thrown open to historians, as they now have been, their use would not change our understanding of that institution—a claim that does not seem to be borne out by Godman's study. See Tedeschi, "The Dispersed Archives of the Roman Inquisition."

37. His decisions were included in Santa María, *Relación del martyrio.*

38. Godman, *Saint as Censor,* 90–93. For further discussion of Peña, see Peters, "Francisco Peña and the 'Directorium Inquisitorum.' "

39. Godman, *Saint as Censor,* 92–93.

40. 1579 in Rome.

41. For detail on editions of the *Directorium,* see Gacto, "Aproximación al Derecho penal de la Inquisición"; Godman, *Saint as Censor,* 90–93; Peters, "Francisco Peña and the 'Directorium Inquisitorum' "; and Van der Vekene, *Biblioteca bibliographica historiae sanctae inquisitionis,* 1:15, 31–43. The *Directorium* was published by itself in Rome in 1587 and 1595 and with commentaries by Peña (Rome, 1578, 1583, 1585, 1587; Venice, 1595 [twice], and 1607).

42. AGN, Inq., vol. 581, exp. 3.

43. Medina, *La imprenta en México,* 1:cxxix–cxxx. For the accounts of the autos de fe, see Bocanegra, *Avto General de la Fee,* and *Avto General de la Fee* (1659). For further discussion of the 1659 auto, see García-Molina Riquelme, "El Auto de Fe de México de 1659." For a general discussion of inquisitional autos de fe, see Domínguez Ortiz, *Autos de la inquisición de Sevilla.*

44. AGN, Inq., vol. 581, exp. 3, f. 359.

45. AGN, Inq., vol. 438, exp. 49, f. 494, exp. 67, f. 569.

46. Hampe Martínez, *Santo Oficio e historia colonial,* 77–84.

47. AGN, Inq., vol. 455, exp. s/n, fs. 256–57.

48. Jerome, "On the Letter to the Galatians," in *The Jerome Biblical Commentary.*

49. See H. G. Liddell and R. Scott, *Greek-English Lexicon* (Oxford, 1996).

50. *Decretum,* causa 24, qu. 3, c. 27.

51. *ST,* 2.2, qu. 11, ar. 1.

52. *Decretum,* causa 24, qu. 3, c. 29.

53. The quotation in the Canon Law may very well have been a conglomerate quotation. Augustine had two principal written attacks on the Manicheans. One treatise is titled *Contra Faustum Manichaeum,* which is found in the *Patrologia Latina,* vol. 42, is part of the *De civitate Dei,* and is referenced by Aquinas in *ST,* 2.2, qu. 11, ar. 1, quoting "Qui in Ecclesia Christi morbidum aliquid pravumque quid sapient, si correcti ut sanum rectumque sapient, resistant contumaciter, suaque pestifera et mortifera dogmata emendare nolunt, sed defendere persistun, haeretici sunt." This was a standard discussion of pertinacity. The other treatise is *Contra manicheos* and contains nearly identical wording as above and as found in the *Decretum*'s incorporation.

54. *Decretum,* causa 24, qu. 3, c. 31: "Haeretici sunt qui quod praue sapient contumaciter defendunt." Also see Augustine, *Contra manicheos.*

55. Augustine, *De vera religione,* c. 11: "saepe etiam sinit diuina prouidentia per nonnullas nimium turbulentas carnalium hominum seditiones expelli de populo Christiano etiam bonos uiros."

56. Augustine, *De fide et symbolo,* c. 1: "Quoniam scriptum est et apostolicae disciplinae robustissima auctoritate firmatum, Quia iustus ex fide vivit (Hab. 2,4; Gal 3,11); eaque fides officium a nobis exigit et cordis et linguae; ait enim Apostolus, Corde creditur ad iustitiam, ore autem confessio fit ad salutem (Rom. 10,10)."

57. Eimeric, *Directorium,* 1a pars, c. 1.

58. Quoted in Eimeric, *Directorium,* 2a pars, c. 1.

59. Peña, comment. 1, 2a pars.

60. Ibid.: "pertinax is dicitur, qui persistit in errorem, quem sub reatu culpae deserere tenetur, cum nec is solum dicatur pertinax, qui falsam asserit."

61. Castro, *De justa haereticorum punitione,* lib. 1, c. 1.

62. Castro, *Aduersus omnes haereses,* lib. 1, c. 1

63. The scholarship on Suárez is extensive. See, e.g., Aguilera González, *Concepto de teología en el padre Francisco Suárez;* Barcia Trelles, *Internacionalistas españoles del siglo XVI;* Bastit, *Naissance de la loi moderne;* Coujou, *Suárez et la refondation de la métaphysique comme ontologie;* Giovanni, *Diritto naturale della Riforma cattolica;* Ippolito, *Analogia dell'essere;* Molina Meliá, *Iglesia y Estado en el siglo de oro español;* Rábade Romeo, *Francisco Suárez;* Scott, *Catholic Conception of International Law.*

64. Suárez, *De censuris,* disp. 1, § 1, nu. 5: "Censura est poena spiritualis et medicinalis, privans usu aliquorum spiritualium bonorum, pero Ecclesiasticam potestatem ita imposita, ut per eamdem ordinarie absolvi possit."

65. Ibid., disp. 1, § 1, nu. 6 : "Tum etiam quia haec censura non privat hominem spiritualibus bonis habitualibus seu permanentibus et internis, ut sunt in primis character, quia indelebilis est et ideo non potest censura privare potestate ordinis."

66. Ibid., disp. 4, § 1, nu. 3: "actus potestatis ligandi atque solvendi a Christo datae."

67. AGN, Inq., vol. 455, exp. s/n, fs. 256–57.

68. Matthew 18:18.

69. Quoted in Suárez, *De censuris,* disp. 1, § 2, nu. 14: "Hominem malum et perniciosum a vobis separate per excommunicationem." Taken from Augustine's *Retractiones,* in which he discussed I Cor. 5:13.

70. Suárez, *De censuris,* disp. 2, § 3, nu. 3: "nam Ecclesia militans et visbilis, per ministros in ea militantes, ac visibiles, gubernari debet."

71. Covarrubias, *In Bonifacii Octavi Constitutionum,* 1a pars, § 1, nu. 9: "Secundo hinc constat, impiam esse Lutheri assertionem et plane haereticam, qua asseuerat excommunicationem poenam tantum externam esse, atque ideo non priuare hominem communibus spiritualibus orationibus."

72. Covarrubias, *In Bonifacii Octavi Constitvtionum,* 1a pars, § 1, nu. 11: "Igitur ad extirpandam prauam istam argumentatione, oportet expendere, qua ratione excommunicatio sit medicinalis."

73. Suárez, *De censuris,* the title topic of disp. 4, § 2: "Utrum censura ferri possit propter peccatum mere internum."

74. "sed tamen uerbo, uel facto externius non ostendunt."

75. Suárez, *De censuris,* disp. 4, § 2, nu. 1: "Propter actum mere internum non potest ferri censura."

76. *ST,* 1.2, qu. 91, ar. 4.

77. Simancas, *De catholicis institutionibus,* tit. 42, nu. 3, tit. 42, nu. 11.

78. Ibid., nu. 2: "Nam quod haereticus pure intellectualis, qui nunquam haeresim protulit, non indicat in sententiam excommunicationis, neque ob eam rem subjacet judicio Ecclesiae, aut jurisdictioni civili" and "Ecclesia non habet potestatem super actus solos interiores, neque illos sua jurisdictione dirigere, prohibere, aut punieri potest."

79. Ibid., nu. 11.

80. Suárez, *De censuris,* disp. 4, § 2, nu. 5: "qui generatim docerunt habere Ecclesiam jurisdictionem directam in actus pure internos et consequenter posse illos praecipere vel prohibere etiam sub censura."

81. Ibid., disp. 4, § 2, nu. 14. It is instructive to see Suárez's conclusion at length: "There is not a single decree in the entire positive law by which censure can be brought against the transgressors of a precept by only an internal act. . . . It must be stated as true that censura cannot be brought by the law itself for a purely internal sin, because it is entirely outside the judgment of the Church. For the Church is visible and perceptible; likewise, it does not have direct power except in sensible men or in souls unless united by bodies; thus it has no direct power in purely internal acts but only in those which are united in the external from the internal." ("Nullum ergo est in toto positivo jure Decretum, quo censura feratur contra transgredientes praeceptum per solum actum internum . . . Dicendum est vero etiam censuram ipso jure latam non posse cadere in peccatum pure internum, quia omnino est extra forum Ecclesiae. Est enim Ecclesia visibilis ac sensibilis; et ideo, sicut directe non habet potestatem nisi in homines sensibiles et in animas non nisi ut corporibus unitas, ita non habet directam potestatem in actus pure internos, sed edo, qui ex internis et externis componuntur.")

82. Castro, *De justa haereticorum punitione,* lib. 2, c. 18: "Et hoc est quod communis Theologorum sententia dicit, Ecclesiam non posse obligar ad actus interiores."

83. Castro, *De justa haereticorum punitione,* lib. 2, c. 18: "Et (ut ingenue loquar) non bene illius Clementinae litteram intellexit, nec bene illius sensum consideravit. Illa enim Clementina non punit solos actus animae interiores, in quos nullum (ut diximus) Ecclesia habet forensem jurisdictionem, sed punit actus exteriores, qui ab illis interioribus procedunt."

84. Eimeric, *Directorium,* 1a pars, c. 2.

85. *ST,* 2.2, qu. 2, ar. 5.

86. Ibid., ar. 6.

87. Ibid.

88. Extensive commentary in Peña, comments. 20–26, 1a pars.

89. Castro, *Aduersus omnes haereses,* lib. 1, c. 9.

90. Ibid.: "Non enim omnes aequa lege tenetur ad credendum."

91. Ibid.: "At non idem est in praelatis et praedictoribus, quos ignorantia non excuset, eo que tenentur scire ea quae ad officium suum petinent, vt nihil praedicent quod non sit eis perfecte exploratum."

92. Eimeric, *Directorium,* 1a pars, qu. 10: "Disputandum ne sit publice de fide." Taken from *ST,* 2.2, qu. 10, ar. 7.

93. Villadiego, *Tractatus contra hereticam prauitatem,* qu. 11: "An si heretici in errore persistent et volunt publice disputare confirmantes errores suos: sit cum eis disputandum." Also see *Sextus,* lib. 5, tit. 2, c. 2, *Quicunque,* § 1: "Inhibemus quoque, ne cuiquam laicae personae liceat publice vel privatim de fide catholica disputare. Qui vero contra fecerit, excommunicationis laqueo innodetur."

94. *ST,* 2.2, qu. 10, ar. 7.

95. Ibid.: "Coram sapientibus in fide firmis nullum periculum est disputare de fide."

96. Ibid.: "Si coram simplicibus, est distinguendum."

97. Ibid.: "Necessarium est publice disputandum dummodo inueniantur aliqui ad hoc sufficientes et idonei, qui errores confutare possint."

98. Peña, comment. 25, 1a pars: "de causis disputare de fide clericis literatis licet, laicis autem et praesertim illiteratis non licet."

99. Peña, comment. 3, 2a pars: "Hic videtur indicari non potuisse Episcopum et Inquisitorem condemnare hos libros nisi mandatum habuissent speciale a Sede Apostolica."

100. Ibid.: "Rursus Episcopi et Inquisitores prohibere etiam possunt in suis dioecesibus libros de haeresi suspectos ob quamcumque haeresis suspicionem, tametsi sint a catholicis auctoribus editi."

101. AGN, Inq., vol. 139, exp. 60.

102. AGN, Inq., vol. 141, exp. 79, vol. 141, exp. 86, vol. 142, exp. 43

103. Matthew 7:16–19.

104. Peña, comment. 2, 2a pars: "cum manifestum sit arbore damnata ob pestilentes fructus, ipsos etiam fructus interdici, ne venenum instillent; fructus vero doctrinarum haereticorum, in libris eorum in primis contineri exploratissimum est."

105. Peña, comment. 52, 2a pars: "qui vivae haereticorum voces vix unam civitatem replere possunt, libri autem cum facile hinc et inde transuebantur, non modo vnam civitatem, sed et regna et prouincias inficiunt." This line was stolen from Simancas without acknowledgment, which leads one to wonder, since Peña, in general, cited his sources extensively. See notes 1 and 2 above from the introduction.

106. Peña, comment. 52, 2a pars: "de libris habentibus ancipites, dubias, seu ambiguas propositiones, quae duplicem sensum habere possunt: haereticum vnum, alterum catholicum."

107. Fragnito, *La Bibbia al rogo,* and idem, ed., *Church, Censorship and Culture.* For the Spanish Indexes, see Bujanda, *Index de l'inquisition espagnole, 1551, 1554, 1559,* vol. 5 of 11 in *Index des livres interdits.*

108. Peña, comment. 52, 2a pars: "de libris et tractatibus quorumdam inutilibus et infrugiferis, aut qui de rebus leuibus, vel ridiculis tractant."

109. Augustine, *De catechizandis rudibus,* c. 6, nu. 10: "Si enim fictas poetarum fabulas et ad voluptatem excogitates animorum, quorum cibus nugae sunt, tamen boni qui habentur atque appelantur grammatici, ad aliquam utilitatem referre conantur, quamquam et ipsam vanam et avidam saginae saecularis: quanto nos decet esse cautiores, ne illa quae vera narramus, sine suarum cassarum redditione digesta, aut inani suavitate, aut etiam perniciosa cupiditate credantur?"

110. Plato, *Gorgias.*

111. Peña, comment. 17, 2a pars: "sed haec severitas ab Ecclesiae tribunali, quae sanguine non fundit, longe abest."

112. Eimeric, *Directorium,* 2a pars, c. 4, and Peña, comment. 3, 2a pars.

113. AGN, Inq., vol. 289, exp. 9j, vol. 320, exp. 6, vol. 1486, exp. s/n, fs. 130–31.

114. Peña, ed., *Litterae apostolicae,* 115–16, 129–30. He reproduced the two bulls: *Cum meditatione cordis* (1550) by Julius IV and *Cum pro munere* (1564) by Pius IV.

115. Delbene, *De officio S. Inquisitionis circa haeresim,* 1a pars, dubitatio 46, petitio 23, "An Episcopi et Inquisitores concedere possint licentiam legendi libros prohibitos?"

116. Castro, *De justa haereticorum punitione,* lib. 1, c. 19: "Quia absente populi applausu, facile cessabit ventus superbiae."

117. Ibid.: "In materia de praedestinatione et praescientia Dei, quilibet sutor et sartor argumentari novit et nervos adhibere argumentis; illis tamen vix poterit respondere doctissimus vir, qui cuique alteri viro erudito facile responderet."

118. Ibid.: "coram viris doctis et in fide constantibus."

119. Castro, *Aduersus omnes haereses,* lib. 1, c. 9: "non possum stomachari in eso qui ut suum institutum laudent, non verentur coram populo iactare et dicere, eum qui semel habitum illius ordinis susceperet, non posse in fide errare aut deficere . . . Nonne hoc aperta est blasphemia, cum pero hoc magis tribuere videatur habitui quod induitur, quam fidei aut gratiae Dei?"

120. Castro, *De justa haereticorum punitione,* lib. 1, c. 19.

121. See Olaechea Labayen, "Opinión de los teólogos españoles," 126.

122. Castro, *Aduersus omnes haereses,* lib. 1, c. 13: "Secunda haeresum causa est defectus praedicationis verbi Dei."

123. Ibid.

124. Ibid.: "Difficile certe est creditu, vt indoctum vulgus legens id intelligat, quod doctissimi viri longo studio, diurturna examinatione vix capere possunt."

125. Castro, *De justa haereticorum punitione,* lib. 2, c. 3: "Quamvis haereses crimen sit adeo pestilens . . . quod toti Christianae reipublicae magis nocere possit."

126. Castro, *Aduersus omnes haereses,* lib. 1, c. 9: "Non enim mones aequa lege tenetur ad credendum."

127. Ibid., lib. 1, c. 13: "vnde euenit vt si forte haereticus aliquis suum venenum spargere populo coeperit."

128. Ibid.

129. AGN, Inq., vol. 4, exp. 2.

130. Castro, *De justa haereticorum punitione,* lib. 2, c. 15: "Necessarium est igitur, ut omnes haereticorum libri comburantur, ne pestilens aliqua maneat radix, quae novos quotidie valeat ex se gignere haereticos."

131. AGN, Inq., vol. 77, exp. 25.

132. AGN, Inq., vol. 90, exp. 13.

133. Castro, *Aduersus omnes haereses,* lib. 1, c. 12: "In libris gentilium multa reperies quae cum fide catholica velut ex diametro pugnant . . . Ibi fratrum discordias irreconciliables reperies, ibi parentum in filios acerbissimas animaduersiones, ibi filiorum pertinacissimas inobedientias, ibi deorum obscoenissimos amores, adulteria, strupra et rapti Ganymedis honores." The line about Ganymede is an obtuse reference to homosexuality. Zeus fell in love with a boy, Ganymede, whom he made his cupbearer, and, presumably, lover. Ganymede became a standard synonym for a passive homosexual or young male in a sexual relationship with an older man.

134. AGN, Inq., vol. 353, exp. 26, f. 372.

135. Castro, *Aduersus omnes haereses,* lib. 1, c. 12: "Propter quod non inmerito Plato huiusmodi poetas a sua Republica abigit."

136. AGN, Inq., vol. 337, exp. 12.

137. See Mott, *Escravidão, homossexualidade e demonologia.*

138. AGN, Inq., vol. 510, exp. 33.

139. Covarrubias, *In Bonifacii Octavi Constitutionum,* 1a pars, § 1, nu. 11: "eius finis est mederi peccatori, morbo peccati laboranti."

Chapter 3. Theories of Adjudication

1. Vitoria, "I: On the Power of the Church," in *Political Writings,* 84.

2. For discussion of Vitoria's academic training in Paris, see García Villoslada, *La universidad de París durante los estudios de Francisco de Vitoria.* For more general, comprehensive discussion of the "School of Salamanca" as a site of reinvigorated Thomist scholasticism, see Belda Plans, *La escuela de Salamanca.*

3. Vitoria, "I: On the Power of the Church," in *Political Writings,* 86.

4. For a good overview of the issue in the Spanish context, see Alcalá, "Herejía y jerarquía."

5. Eimeric, *Directorium,* 3a pars, intro.: "a Sede Apostolica deputatus."

6. Ibid., 3a pars, qu. 1, "De conditione Inquisitoris": "sacra doctrina fidei eminenter eruditus."

7. Peña, comment. 51, 3a pars: "Ordinarii, vt summus Romanus Pontifex et Episcopi locorum, qui cum ordinantur, seu consecrantur, iure diuino in haereticos accipiunt potestatem et iurisdictionem . . . Alii sunt iudices delegati, quibus a sede Apostolica hoc munus iudicandi haereticos in specie datum est, quos iura, Inquisitores, vocant."

8. Ibid.: "adsit per doctrinam fidei vere et proprie theologiae cognitionem accipere debemus: iuris prudentia enim non dicitur fidei doctrina."

9. Simancas, *De catholicis institutionibus,* tit. 41, nu. 3: "ut Inquisitores eliganter Jurisperiti, quam Theologi: quidquid Theologaster ille deliret Occam."

10. Peña, comment. 51, 3a pars: "Veruntamen hoc est certum, quod solus theologus, aut solus iurisperitus non facile dirimet hanc litem."

11. Ibid.: "ut in illis ciuitatibus, in quibus duo sunt Inquisitores, unus eligatur probatissimus et doctissimus theologus, alius constituatur iurisconsultissimus et canonum pertissimus: grauia enim sunt fidei negotia et res, quas tractant, magnae; et propterea per iudices integerrimos et doctissimos esse peragenda."

12. Eimeric, *Directorium,* 3a pars, qu. 5, "De comparatione Episcopi et Inquisitoris."

13. See discussion below in part 2.

14. Peña, comment. 79, 3a pars: "Quod si manifestissima esset inquisitoris haeresis et malitia effrenis: ut si contra fidem pradicarent, aut scriberet, aut praedicari et scribi permitteret, aut haereticos captos impunitos dimitteret et his similia perpetraret, quae in manifestum fidei detrimentum conuerterentur, nec facile summus Pontifex posset consuli et interea fides periclitaretur; liceat tunc Episcopo in inquisitorem agere."

15. Castro, *Aduersus omnes haereses,* lib. 1, c. 8: "Iudex ergo requiritur, qui sententiam dicat, cui ob temperare oportet. Talis autem iudicandi potestas non est in aliquo inferiori episcopo, aut in collegio cui praeest."

16. Ibid.: "Non enim est canonistarum munus de haeresi aut de fide iudicare, sed theologorum, quibus diuinum ius committitur."

17. Simancas, *De catholicis institutionibus,* tit. 41, nu. 11.

18. Simancas, "La vida y cosas notables," 162. The title was given in Spanish in the autobiography, though the book was never translated out of Latin.

19. Suárez, *De censuris,* disp. 2, § 1, nu. 3: "institutio censurae non fit, nisi quando in particulari praescribitur modus talis poenae," and disp. 3, § 1, nu. 1: "nulla est autem censura, quae feratur, nisi sit conjuncta, vel annexa alicui praecepto humano."

20. Ibid., disp. 2, § 2, nu. 5: "In aliis etiam potest esse haec potestas."

21. Ibid., disp. 2, § 6, nu. 1: "hujusmodi enim intentio vitiat actum moralem, ut per se notum est et praesertim actum judicandi, ut eleganter docet Ambrosius, in cap. Judicet, 3, quaest. 7; et Gregorius, in cap. Judicare, 11, quaest. 3 . . . Quod ideo addo, quia interdum talis intentio potest ita praecipitem agere judicem in censura ferenda, ut substantialem defectum committat."

22. Quoted in López Vela, "El calificador," 349.

23. See chapter 5 for further discussion.

24. "Copilación de las Instrucciones en Toledo," 199.

25. See Prado Moura, *Inquisición e inquisidores.*

26. Peña, comment. 126, 3a pars: "Caeterum quamuis hodie inquisitores sint iurisperiti ut in Hispania, eosdem nihilominus peritos vocare possunt, ac debent: in primis uero theologos, quorum est propositionum gradus et qualitates expendere."

27. Eimeric, *Directorium,* title topic of 3a pars, qu. 78: "An de consilio peritorum ferenda sit ad Episcopo et Inquisitore sententia",and Peña, comment. 127, 3a pars.

28. Peña, comment. 127, 3a pars: "Inquisitores non coguntur sequi peritorum consilium."

29. Quoted in Eimeric, *Directorium,* 3a pars, qu. 78.

30. AGN, Inq., vol. 3, exp. 2.

31. Peña, comment. 127, 3a pars: "Non tamen audacter a peritorum consilio discedent."

32. Villadiego, *Tractatus contra hereticam pravitatem,* qu. 15: "Modum autem qui debet observari est: qui antequae sententia ferant: inquisitores praefati et episcopus faciant secum convenire viros sapientes et doctos deum timentes: cum quorum consilio procedere habent ad sententiam ferendae."

33. Simancas, *De catholicis institutionibus,* tit. 54, "De propositionum qualitate."

34. Albertinus, *De agnoscendis,* qu. 10, nu. 8, nu. 9; Del Río, *Disquisitionum magicarum,* lib. 5, § 15.

35. *Historia de la Inquisición en España y América,* 1:881–85. The title of Rojas's treatise is problematic on many levels, and I have not been able to determine a decent translation. One possibility is "On the Singular Successes against the Heretics in Favor of the Faith," which seems to express the general sense, but it is not consistent with the corrupted noun declensions and grammar of the title. "De succesionibus" can mean "on the successes" or "on the successors" and "de haereticis" means "of/on the heretics." But the "et" (and) implies that the rest of the title is linked to the first two phrases, but "singularia in fidei favorem" is a corruption, since "singularia" is an adjective describing a feminine singular nominative noun, which does not exist anywhere in the title, or a single feminine ablative noun, which also does not exist in the title. If "singularia" is left

out, the title could mean literally "On the Successions and on the Heretics in Favor of the Faith," which is equally poor, since usually the preposition "contra" (against) is used or the noun "haereticis" is left without a preposition to imply ablative case "against the heretics." In the end, the best bet is that the noun forms are a kind of corrupted or Hispanicized Latin. I am thankful to Hugh Thomas for his help and advice with this particularly troublesome bit of Latin grammar.

36. Rojas, *De succesionibus,* nu. 384: "In exponendis vero Verbis dubiis, agnoscendique factis vel Catholicis dictis, aut suspectis vel haereticis, periti Sacrae Theologiae professores sunt vocandi, qui vulgo Qualificatores nuncupantur, quorum assertionibus omnimodam Inquisitores adhibeant fidem."

37. Ibid., nu. 409, nu. 423.

38. AGN, Inq., vol. 116, exp. 9.

39. Cano, *De locis theologicis,* lib. 12, c. 6, outlines this formula and is redacted and in turn glossed by Peña, comment. 27, 2a pars.

40. Peña, comment. 27, 2a pars, glossing Cano: "Catholicae veritates illae habendae sunt: quae in scriptura sacra veteris, aut novi testamenti continentur; ipse enim apertus scripturae sensus certum praesefert catholicae veritatis iudicium."

41. Ibid., again using Cano: "Quidquid Doctores et Pastores Ecclesiae in Concilio legitime congregati fidelem populum docent, quo ad Christi fidem attinet, id plane verissimum est et pro catholica veritate accipiendum."

42. *Decretum,* causa 24, qu. 1, c. 2: [Gratian's gloss] "Non est retractandum quod semel sinodus statuit contra unamquamque heresim."

43. Peña, comment. 27, 2a pars: "Erit ergo eius iudicium certissimum, stabile et infalibile."

44. Cano, *De locis theologicis,* lib. 12, c. 6.

45. AGN, Inq., vol. 32, exp. 9.

46. AGN, Inq., vol. 32, exp. 9, f. 237.

47. AGN, Inq., vol. 273, exp. 7.

48. AGN, Inq., vol. 111, exp. 6.

49. Quoted by Peña in comment. 27, 2a pars: "Si scholastici theologici aliquam itidem conclusionem firmam et stabilem uno ore omnes statuerint, atque ut certum theologiae Decretum fidelibus amplectendum contanter et perpetuo docuerint, illam ut catholicam ueritatem fideles sane amplectantur."

50. Castro, *Aduersus omnes haereses,* lib. 1, c. 8: "Quamobrem recte dici solet, articulos Parisiensis non transire montes."

51. See Maguire, *John of Torquemada,* and Netanyahu, *Origins of the Inquisition.*

52. Torquemada, *Summae ecclesiasticae,* lib. 4, c. 9. There were variant spellings for his work, which originally appeared as *Summa de ecclesia,* though variants like the one in the edition on which I relied (in the Biblioteca Nacional de Chile) as well as *Summa ecclesiae* exist.

53. Castro, *De justa haereticorum punitione,* lib. 1, c. 4: "A multis enim non solum idiotis et ignorantibus: sed viris etiam alioqui doctis, hac in parte erratum est, cum multas propositiones in suis scriptis velut haereticas diffamaverunt, quae nihil minus, quam haereticae dici merenbantur."

54. Ibid.

55. Ibid., lib. 1, c. 5: "Non est ergo veritas aliqua catholica censenda a sola pontificis aut Ecclesiae definitione."

56. Ibid., lib. 1, c. 4.

57. For a discussion of Boniface VIII in the context of the law and its traditions, see Muldoon, "Boniface VIII's Forty Years of Experience."

58. Wood, ed., *Philip the Fair and Boniface VIII.* For much more extensive discussion of the controversy among Boniface's contemporaries, see Giles of Rome, *On Ecclesiastical Power;* John of Paris, *On Royal and Papal Power.*

59. Bainton, *Here I Stand,* 128.

60. AGN, Inq., vol. 117, exp. 18.

61. Raymond of Peñafort, *Summa,* lib. 1, tit. 5, § 2: "Punitur autem haereticus excommunicatione, depositione, rerum ablatione et militari persecutione . . . quia indistincte sive sit clericus, sive Papa, vel quilibet inferior debet deponi ab omni dignitate."

62. For his conciliarism, see Castro, *De justa haereticorum punitione,* esp. lib. 1, c. 4, c. 5.

63. Peña, comment. 3, 1a pars.

64. Castro, *De justa haereticorum punitione,* lib. 1, c. 3: "Sed difficultas est non parva agnoscere, quo pacto inter se different, haeresis et error in fide."

65. Torquemada, *Summae eclesiasticae,* lib. 4, c. 8, c. 9.

66. Castro, *De justa haereticorum punitione,* lib. 1, c. 3: "Et istae tales propositiones non sunt proprie objectum fidei: cum naturali ratione comprehenduntur. Nam (ut beatus Gregorius ait) fides non habet meritum, cui humana ratio praebet experimentum. Assertio ergo talis, quae est contra credibilia, quae naturali ratione probari possunt, erronea in fide dicetur . . . quod haeresis proprie dicta est contra credibilia, quae superant omnem virtutem intellectus. Error vero in fide est contra credibilia, quae ratione naturali probari possunt."

67. Ibid.

68. AGN, Inq., vol. 261, exp. 9a.

69. AGN, Inq., vol. 117, exp. 5.

70. For this study I have relied on the Venice edition of 1754. While editions as early as 1671 seem to exist, they are extremely rare, and I have as yet to encounter a first edition from 1642.

71. Alberghini, *Manuale qualificatorum,* the title topic of c. 12: "De variis propositionum censuris, seu qualificationibus."

72. Ibid., c. 12, § 2: "Propositio haeretica est illa, quae habet omnimodam contrarietatem cum objecto fidei."

73. Ibid.: "vel propositio haeretica dicitur, quae aperte alicui Catholicae veritati de fide definitae, contraria est." Also see Albertinus, *De agnoscendis,* qu. 6, nu. 1; Simancas, *De catholicis institutionibus,* tit. 54, nu. 3; Suárez, *De fide,* disp. 16, § 2, nu. 2.

74. Alberghini, *Manuale qualificatorum,* c. 12, § 3: "Quidam autem putant non sufficere hanc directam contradictionem fidei, aut Catholicae veritati, ut propositio haeretica dicatur, nisi accedat pertinacia in proferente, seu ab haeretico prolata sit; quod si ab alio dicta fuerit, dicetur propositio contraria fidei, sed haeretica proprie non erit."

75. See Beltrán de Heredia, *Domingo Báñez y las controversias sobre la gracia;* Salaverri de la Torre, "La noción de Iglesia del Padre Luis de Molina"; Smith, *Freedom in Molina.*

76. Alberghini, *Manuale qualificatorum,* c. 12, § 4: "sed melior et communior sententia est, quod omnis propositio contraria fidei, haeretica proprie est."

77. Ibid.: "ad propositionem haereticam objectivam, seu ad objectum haeresis, pertinacia non requiritur, quia hoc objectum in sola contradictione cum objecto fidei consistito."

78. Ibid., c. 12, § 8: "propositio haeresim sapiens . . . dicitur ea, quae non per evidentem consequentiam, sed per consequentias probabilissimas et moraliter certas."

79. "Más vale estar bien amancebado(a) que mal casado(a)."

80. AGN, Inq., vol. 275, exp. 1.

81. Alberghini, *Manuale qualificatorum,* c. 12, § 12.

82. Ibid.

83. AGN, Inq., vol. 11, exp. 4, f. 304.

84. Alberghini, *Manuale qualificatorum,* c. 12, § 15.

85. Castro, *Aduersus omnes haereses,* lib. 1, c. 13.

86. Ibid., lib. 1, c. 9.

87. Castro, *De justa haereticorum punitione,* lib. 1, c. 3.

88. Castro, *Aduersus omnes haereses,* lib. 1, c. 9.

89. AGN, Inq., vol. 188, exp. 4.

90. While careful not to defend Joachim of Fiore or his fellow Franciscans who followed his ideas, Castro may nevertheless have had their chiliasm in mind when he "demoted" this idea from heresy to temerarity. For a discussion of this strand of thought, see Baudot, *Utopia and History,* and Phelan, *The Millennial Kingdom.*

91. Eimeric, *Directorium,* 2a pars, qu. 41, "De blasphemis": "De ergo turbatio et commotione ex metu mortis et trucidatione corporis proprii non excuscat idolum, seu daemonem adorantem ad haeresi, quia est contra primum articulum fidei; quo excusabit turbatio et commotione ex perditione unius denarii uel consimilis rei ab haeresi, contra articulum fidei, haeresis enomentem?"

92. AGN, Inq., vol. 366, exp. 3.

93. AGN, Inq., vol. 267, exp. 7.

94. AGN, Inq., vol. 325, exp. 1.

95. Peña, comment. 66, 2a pars.

96. Simancas, *De catholicis institutionibus,* tit. 8, nu. 1: "Blasphemare est maledicere; non tamen quaelibet maledictio blasphemia solet appelari, sed ea dumtaxet, quae est execratio, aut convicium impium contra Deum, vel contra Divos . . . sunt et aliae plures . . . verbi gratia, si quis juraverit per membra pudenda Divorum."

97. AGN, Inq., vol. 186, exp. 5a. The phrase used was "bujarrón."

98. Castro, *De justa haereticorum punitione,* lib. 1, c. 12: "Nam Theologi non computant blasphemiam inter peccata infidelitatis, ac proinde negant blasphemiam ad haeresim pretiñere."

99. Augustine, *De fide et symbolo,* c. 1. Also see chapter 2, above.

100. Castro, *De justa haereticorum punitione,* lib. 1, c. 12: "Ex quo manifeste colligitur blasphemiam non esse vitium oppositum fidei, sed esse vitium contra confessionem fidei."

101. *ST,* 2.2., qu. 13, ar. 1, summarized generally in Covarrubias, *In constitvtionibis secvndae,* 1a pars, § 7, nu. 11 as: "Est autem blaphemus qui negat aliquid de Deo, quod ei

conuenit: aut tribuit Deo aliquid, quod ei nequaquam conuenit, quemadmodum S. Thom. explicat."

102. Leviticus 24:10–16.

Chapter 4. The Salamanca Connection

1. For a good biographical overview, see García Icazbalceta, "Fr. Bartolomé de Ledesma."

2. ACSE, *Libro de profesiones*, includes the vows of the convent of the sixteenth century, listing date and sponsor. There is an extensive literature on Salamanca, San Esteban, and the University of Salamanca. For some standard discussions, see Belda Plans, *La escuela de Salamanca*; Carro, *La teología y los teólogos-juristas españoles*; Cortés Vázquez, *La vida estudiantil*; Esperabé de Arteaga, *Historia interna y pragmática de la Universidad de Salamanca*; Espinel, *San Esteban de Salamanca*; Fernández Álvarez, *La Universidad de Salamanca*; Gallegos Rocafull, *El hombre y el mundo de los teólogos españoles*; O'Meara, "The Dominican School of Salamanca"; Ramírez González, *Grupos de poder clerical*; Ramos et al., *Francisco de Vitoria y la escuela de Salamanca*; Rodríguez Cruz, *Salmantica docet*.

3. For information on Betanzos, see Carreño, *Fr. Domingo de Betanzos*, and García Icazbalceta, "La orden de predicadores en México."

4. AGN, Inq., vol. 3, exp. 2, vol. 31, exp. 3, vol. 43, exp. 4, vol. 43, exp. 24.

5. See Beltrán de Heredia, *Domingo Báñez y las controversias sobre la gracia*, and Esperabé de Arteaga, *Historia interna y pragmática de la Universidad de Salamanca*. On Salazar, see AGN, Inq., vol. 10, exp. 4, vol. 62, exp. 5

6. ACSE, *Libro de profesiones*; AGN, Inq., vol. 146, exp. s/n, fs. 63–64; García Granados, *El deán turbulento*, 16.

7. This according to his limpieza de sangre statement for his formal appointment as calificador in 1572: AGN, Inq., vol. 60, exp. 4.

8. AGN, Inq., vol. 484, exp. 1.

9. AGN, Inq., vol. 65, exp. 6, vol. 1486, exp. s/n, f. 30.

10. *Efemérides de La Real y Pontificia Universidad de México*, 57, 61, 70, 78, 82.

11. AGN, Inq., vol. 65, exp. 6.

12. Saranyana, "La eucaristía en la teología sacramentaria Americana."

13. AGN, Inq., vol. 59, exp. 4, vol. 60, exp. 3, vol. 60, exp. 4, vol. 61, exp. 6, vol. 62, exp. 1, vol. 62, exp. 5, vol. 63, exp. 18, vol. 65, exp. 5, vol. 65, exp. 6, vol. 65, exp. 10, vol. 76, exp. 10, vol. 76, exp. 48, vol. 85, exp. 26, vol. 119, exp. 5, vol. 119, exp. 6, vol. 189, exp. 3, vol. 194, exp. 8, vol. 239, exp. s/n, f. 92, vol. 1486, exp. s/n, fs. 63–64; García Granados, *El deán turbulento*, 16; R. Gómez, "Nómina," 490.

14. For biographical information, see *Historia de la Inquisición en España y América*, 1:692–93; Ricard, "Notes sur la biographie de Montúfar"; Ricard, *Études et documents pour l'histoire missionaire*, 66–71.

15. ACSE, *Libro de profesiones*, and AGN, Inq., vol. 60, exp. 4.

16. The year of Montúfar's death has been a subject of controversy for some time, though Lundberg, in his doctoral thesis (2004), brought to light definitive evidence. Some, like Ricard, argue that Montúfar died in 1572. The debate concerns the date of his

birth and later statements about the time he spent in various offices, like that of archbishop of Mexico. Montúfar's signature does not appear after 1569 in any documentation I have seen. We know that he was in very poor health at least as early as 1569 and
possibly much earlier, though the exact nature of the illness is unclear. Montúfar died,
according to a letter from Ledesma to King Phillip II, on March 7, 1572, something that is
reiterated in a letter from Viceroy Enríquez to the king shortly after Montúfar's death.
For elaboration see Lundberg, "Unity and Conflict," 221–29.

17. AGN, Inq., vol. 223, 1a parte, exp. s/n, f. 24. The letter reads in part: "muy bien fue
ynbiarnos los dos quadernos de las qualificaçiones y censura que ay [allí?] se hizo de las
Biblias y luego se ymbiaron de aquí a Salamanca para el cathálogo que allí se ua orde-
nando."

18. See Pinto Crespo, *Inquisición y control ideológico*.

19. Ledesma, *De septem nouae legis sacramentis summarium*, 213–17.

20. It is unclear whether Barbosa obtained his doctorate in Salamanca or Mexico. In
AGN, Inq., vol. 62, exp. 1, he is said to have obtained it in Salamanca, but in a trial in
1562 (AGN, Inq., vol. 17, exp. 17) he signed himself licenciado, implying that he received
a doctorate after 1562 and his arrival in Mexico.

21. AGN, Inq., vol. 31, exp. 3, vol. 117, exp. 18; Gómez, "Nomina," 307; Pavón
Romero, "Doctores en la Universidad de México," 256.

22. AGN, Inq., vol. 15, exp. 1, vol. 15, exp. 7. Also see Schwaller, *The Church and
Clergy in Sixteenth-Century Mexico*, 34.

23. For biographical and intellectual information on De la Veracruz, see Ennis, *Fray
Alonso de la Vera Cruz*. For De la Veracruz's influence broadly speaking, one may also
consult the excellent general intellectual history of colonial Mexico: Gallegos Rocafull, *El
pensamiento mexicano*.

24. AGN, Inq., vol. 66, exp. 5, vol. 203, exp. 7, vol. 846, exp. s/n, vol. 1486, exp. s/n, f.
90, vol. 1486, exp. s/n, f. 126; *Efemérides de La Real y Pontificia Universidad de México*;
Pavón Romero, "Doctores en la Universidad de México," 256, 266. For biography of
Agurto, see García Icazbalceta, "Fr. Pedro de Agurto."

25. Ruiz Fidalgo, *La imprenta en Salamanca*, 1: 30, 2: 541–44.

26. García Icazbalceta, "El P. Pedro de Morales"; Martínez Ferrer, *La penitencia en la
primera evangelización de México*.

27. AGN, Inq., vol. 255, exp. 1, vol. 1486, exp. s/n, f. 95.

28. AGN, Inq., vol. 63, exp. 18.

29. AGN, Inq., vol. 65, exp. 5, vol. 78, exp. 7.

30. Gallegos Rocafull, *El pensamiento mexicano*, 251.

31. For a concise biography, see García Granados, *El deán turbulento*. For discussion
of the Remesal case, see MacLeod, *Las Casas, Guatemala, and the Sad but Inevitable
Case of Antonio Remesal*.

32. For a broad general discussion of early Guatemala, see Jones, *Guatemala in the
Spanish Colonial Period*, and Martínez Peláez, *La patria del criollo*.

33. AGN, Inq., vol. 65, exp. 10, vol. 76, exp. 10, vol. 90, exp. s/n, fs. 29–30.

34. AGN, Inq., vol. 285, exp. s/n, fs. 28–29.

35. The drama runs on and on in AGN, Inq., vols. 509 and 510, among others. Also see
AGN, Inq., vol. 283, exp. s/n, fs. 475–478, vol. 285, exp. s/n, fs. 28–29.

36. See the still classic study by Ots y Capdequí, *El estado español en las Indias*.

Chapter 5. The Early Inquisitions, 1525–71

1. González de San Segundo, "Tensiones y conflictos de la Inquisición en Indias," 607.

2. Used as the title in Medina, *La inquisición primitiva Americana.*

3. For a more general discussion of the issue of jurisdiction and conflicts between state, Church, and Inquisition in the Americas, see Maqueda Abreu, *Estado, Iglesia e Inquisición en Indias.*

4. González de San Segundo, "Tensiones y conflictos de la Inquisición en Indias."

5. See discussions in García Gutiérrez, *Bulario de la Iglesia mejicana.*

6. The literature is vast. For some standard works, see Carreño, *Fr. Domingo de Betanzos;* Corcuera de Mancera, *El fraile, el indio, y el pulque;* D'Olwer, *Fray Bernardino de Sahagún;* Kobayashi, *La educación como conquista;* Phelan, *The Millennial Kingdom;* Ricard, *Spiritual Conquest.*

7. Greenleaf, *Mexican Inquisition,* 10.

8. For the early period, see Greenleaf, *Zumárraga and the Mexican Inquisition.*

9. Carreño, *Fr. Domingo de Betanzos;* Espinel, *San Esteban de Salamanca.*

10. A memoria of sanbenitos records their immolations: AGN, Inq., vol. 77, exp. 35. Also see the excellent discussion of the cases in Greenleaf, *Mexican Inquisition,* 26–37.

11. AGN, Inq., vols. 1, 1A, 14, 40, 42.

12. Carreño, *Fr. Domingo de Betanzos.*

13. AGN, Inq., vol. 1, exp. 17.

14. AGN, Inq., vol. 1, exp. 8, vol. 1, exp. 29, vol. 40, exp. 4, vol. 42, exp. 14.

15. AGN, Inq., vol. 1, exp. 8.

16. AGN, Inq., vol. 14, exp. 2.

17. *Historia de la Inquisición en España y América,* 1:690–92.

18. The trial is reproduced in *Proceso inquisitorial del cacique de Tetzcoco.*

19. AGN, Inq., vol. 2, exp. 2.

20. The trial can be found in AGN, Inq., vol. 2, exp. 10.

21. An internal 1630 memoria drawn up by the Inquisition's archivist lists twenty-five executions for 1527–1630, but we also know that don Carlos de Texcoco had been executed on Zumárraga's orders in 1539, though he is not listed in the 1630 memoria: AGN, Inq., vol. 77, exp. 35. By 1630 the Mexican Inquisition had adjudicated 1,563 cases, for which I derived the information of rates of execution (see appendix 3). It remains unclear exactly how many people were executed in person by the Mexican Inquisition, but all the available evidence — internal memos from inquisitors, contemporary descriptions, case law, and secondary scholarship — suggests that around forty-five were executed. García-Molina (below) finds evidence for thirty-nine executions for the period 1571–1820, and the 1630 memoria includes four more for the period 1527–70, to which don Carlos de Texcoco can be added, for a total of forty-four. There is no evidence that there were any other executions, though a handful may have been lost or forgotten; given the notoriety and fanfare of autos de fe, however, and the fact that the executions were never hushed up, it is extremely unlikely that the total number of executions was higher than fifty. After the 1659 auto de fe only a smattering of individuals were executed, though there were notorious executions of José Ma. Morelos and Miguel Hidalgo during the independence movement in the 1810s. For figures on the 1659 auto and for the total of executions, see García-Molina Riquelme, "El Auto de Fe de México de 1659," and the

Relación del Avto General de la Fee (1659). Also see Alberro, *La actividad del Santo Oficio,* and idem, *Inquisición y sociedad en México;* Bocanegra, *Avto General de Fee.* There is, of course, controversy about the numbers. García Icazbalceta argues for a total of forty-one executions by the Mexican Inquisition in *Bibliografía mexicana del siglo XVI,* but he does not include punishments meted out beyond the scope of autos de fe. Liebman argues against these figures in his article "The Abedeciario and a Check-List of Mexican Inquisition Documents," but he provides no new evidence for this claim. He shows that the Abedeciario of the Inquisition (a registry of cases and sentences) records forty-nine executions from 1528 to 1704. Liebman correctly notes that dozens or possibly hundreds of persons convicted by the Inquisition died as a result of other punishments — notably, service in the galleys — but the point here is that in terms of actual public executions, there is no evidence for more than fifty persons publicly executed on the bonfire, even according to Liebman's interpretation. Contreras and Henningsen produced a now-famous discussion of the overall composition of the Spanish Inquisitions' various trials and executions, concluding that just under 2 percent of the convicted were executed, which is the same as for Mexico. See their essay "Forty-Four Thousand Cases."

22. *Historia de la Inquisición en España y América,* 1:688–90.

23. See Ruiz Medrano, "Los negocios de un arzobispo," 73.

24. AGN, Inq., vol. 1A, exp. 35, vol. 3, exp. 10, vol. 5, exp. 1, vol. 5, exp. 2, vol. 5, exp. 6, vol. 5, exp. 7, vol. 5, exp. 8, vol. 5, exp. 11, vol. 5, exp. 17, vol. 6, exp. 1, vol. 7, exp. 11, vol. 17, exp. 17, vol. 18, exp. 6, vol. 18, exp. 10, vol. 18, exp. 11, vol. 18, exp. 17, vol. 19, exp. 2, vol. 19, exp. 4, vol. 19, exp. 9, vol. 20, exp. 6, vol. 25, exp. 3, vol. 25, exp. 5, vol. 25, exp. 6, vol. 26, exp. 3, vol. 26, exp. 4, vol. 26, exp. 6, vol. 27, exp. 1, vol. 27, exp. 2, vol. 27, exp. 3, vol. 28, exp. 1, vol. 29, exp. 2, vol. 31, exp. 1, vol. 32, exp. 17, vol. 39, exp. 1, vol. 41, exp. 3, vol. 43, exp. 24, vol. 45, exp. 20, vol. 68, exp. 2, vol. 71, exp. 8, vol. 80, exp. 7, vol. 95, exp. 4, vol. 96, exp. 2, vol. 97, exp. 1, vol. 98, exp. 4, vol. 112, exp. 3, vol. 114, exp. 3, vol. 184, exp. 3

25. AGN, Inq., vol. 60, exp. 4, vol. 62, exp. 1.

26. Also see Schwaller, *The Church and Clergy in Sixteenth-Century Mexico,* 20–21.

27. Notably outlined in Clendinnen, *Ambivalent Conquests.*

28. AGN, Inq., vol. 15, exp. 12, vol. 35, exp. 1, vol. 40, exp. 36.

29. AGN, Inq., vol. 40, exp. 35.

30. AGN, Inq., vol. 40, exp. 35.

31. AGN, Inq., vol. 15, exp. 12.

32. AGN, Inq., vol. 32, exp. 9.

33. The words of Otáñez: "niega el poder espiritual y temporal del sumo pontífice y cabeza de la yglesia de Dios," AGN, Inq., vol. 32, exp. 9, f. 240.

34. AGN, Inq., vol. 32, exp. 9, f. 237.

35. AGN, Inq., vol. 10, exp. 4, f. 147r: "no es pecado dormir un hombre con muger agena."

36. AGN, Inq., vol. 10, exp. 4, f. 147: "quando en el acusado no se siente contumaçia ny maliçia siempre se a de usar mas de misericordia que de rrigor . . . por tanto dezimos que el juez desta causa no deve sentençiar al dicho por el rrigor del derecho ny según la pena ordinaria."

37. AGN, Inq., vol. 3, exp. 5.

38. AGN, Inq., vol. 3, exp. 5, f. 142: "dezimos que nos pareçe, ser la dicha proposición herética, contra la sagrada escriptura, y determinación de la sancta madre yglesia cathólica. Aunque el que la dixo no es hereje, como pareçe por su confesión en la qual sintiendo como cathólico dize y conoçe la dicha proposición, ser herética y mala, y que el no la dixo con intento de affirmarla, sino que el enojo que quando la dixo, tenía, no le dio lugar, a considerar lo que dezía."

39. AGN, Inq., vol. 16, exp. 12.

40. AGN, Inq., vol. 16, exp. 12, f. 22r: "para entender la grabedad que tiene esta proposiçión avemos de tratalla desde su principio porque no se podrá saber el deffecto que tiene de otra manera."

41. AGN, Inq., vol. 16, exp. 12, f. 22r: "sobre el qual como piedra biva está hedificada nuestra santa madre yglesia de Roma."

42. AGN, Inq., vol. 16, exp. 12, f. 22r: "cuerpo desta yglesia militante."

43. Quoted by the Dominican friars in Spanish in AGN, Inq., vol. 16, exp. 12, f. 22r.

44. AGN, Inq., vol. 16, exp. 12.

45. AGN, Inq., vol. 16, exp. 12, fs. 26–28.

46. AGN, Inq., vol. 16, exp. 12, f. 26r.

47. AGN, Inq., vol. 16, exp. 12, f. 28r: "no puede errar determinando cosa que directa o indirectamente toque a la fee."

48. AGN, Inq., vol. 16, exp. 12, fs. 24–25.

49. AGN, Inq., vol. 16, exp. 12, f. 24v: "aquella proposición solamente es herética que verdadera y propiamente es contraria a alguna proposición revelada por Dios en la sagrada escritura tocante a la religión xpiana y contra la determinación de la yglesia."

50. AGN, Inq., vol. 16, exp. 12, f. 24r: "con más claridad y brevedad las ponen los theólogos."

51. AGN, Inq., vol. 16, exp. 12, f. 25r.

52. Fernández del Castillo, *Libros y libreros en el siglo XVI*, 37.

53. AGN, Inq., vol. 29, exp. 3.

54. AGN, Inq., vol. 40, exp. 12.

55. AGN, Inq., vol. 40, exp. 12, f. 159: "culpado especialmente siendo hombre docto."

56. AGN, Inq., vol. 8, exp. 1. Also see Bujanda, *Index de l'inquisition espagnole*.

57. See, among others, the trial against Alonso Calderón, alcalde mayor of Acapulco, for having a copy of Luther's *De potestate papae* in 1568, AGN, Inq., vol. 9, exp. 5; and against María de la Concepción for blasphemy, having read fray Luis de León, in 1574, AGN, Inq., vol. 48, exp. 4.

58. AGN, Inq., vol. 4, exp. 2.

59. Gomes Moreira, "Don Vasco de Quiroga"; Krippner-Martínez, *Rereading the Conquest*; León, *Don Vasco de Quiroga*; Miranda Godínez, *Don Vasco de Quiroga*; Moreno, *Don Vasco de Quiroga*; Ramírez Montes, *La catedral de Vasco de Quiroga*; Warren, *Vasco de Quiroga y sus hospitales-pueblo*.

60. AGN, Inq., vol. 43, exp. 4.

61. See Bataillon, *Erasmo y España*, 807–32; Greenleaf, *Zumárraga and the Mexican Inquisition*. Zumárraga's Erasmianism is seen best in his *Doctrina*.

62. The proposition that had caused scandal among numerous people (at least according to Montúfar) was that "speaking of the unions that occurred in the holy resurrection

of our redeemer Christ" Zumárraga had concluded that "the blood of the tree [cross] was reintegrated by divine potential, or at least that amount necessary for the body and was thus reunited with divinity." In AGN, Inq., vol. 43, exp. 4, f. 119, the calificación reads in part: "hablando de las huniones que se hizieron en la santa resureçión de nuestro redentor Christo (que la sangre de Ramada fue recogida por la potençia diuina a lo menos la que hera nescesaria para el cuerpo y fue unida a la diuinidad)."

63. Good discussions of these issues can be found in Bataillon, *Erasmo y España.*

64. See, among others, Alcalá, ed., *Proceso inquisitorial de Fray Luis de León,* and Tellechea Idígoras, *El arzobispo Carranza.*

65. The events of the Tlazazalca rivalry and encounters are described in detail by Carrillo Cázares in *Vasco de Quiroga,* 1:125–66.

66. The censorship trials of Gilberti's works are found in AGN, Inq., vol. 43, exp. 6, exp. 20, and vol. 72, exp. 35, and have been transcribed in Fernández del Castillo, *Libros y libreros en el siglo XVI,* 4–37. His broader movements can be found in León Alanís, *Los orígenes del clero y la iglesia en Michoacán,* which offers an overview of the missionary projects in sixteenth-century Michoacán.

67. Baudot, *Utopia and History,* offers excellent discussions of this for the Mexican context. For Spain, the classic study remains Bataillon, *Erasmo y España.*

68. Good overviews of Tlatelolco and the Franciscan humanist project there can be found in Kobayashi, *La educación como conquista,* and León-Portilla, *Bernardino de Sahagún.*

69. Castro, "Utrum indigenae."

70. The discussions have been transcribed in Fernández del Castillo, *Libros y libreros en el siglo XVI,* 4–44.

71. AGN, Inq., vol. 43, exp. 6.

72. AGN, Inq., vol. 43, exp. 6, exp. 20.

73. Discussions on the debates concerning Indians and the sacraments can be found in Martínez Ferrer, *La penitencia en la primera evangelización de México,* and Saranyana, "La eucaristía en la teología sacramentaria Americana."

74. Ennis, *Fray Alonso de la Vera Cruz.*

75. Their rivalry is discussed at length in Ennis, *Fray Alonso de la Vera Cruz.* The original can be found in Archivo Histórico Nacional (Madrid), Inq., legajo 4437, exp. 5.

76. For discussions of the conflict between De la Veracruz and Montúfar, see Ennis, *Fray Alonso de la Vera Cruz.*

77. See Medrano, "Los negocios de un arzobispo."

78. Flint, "The Martín Cortés Conspiracy Reexamined."

79. Lundberg, "Unity and Conflict," 182–89.

80. AGN, Inq., vol. 3, exp. 2, fs. 62, 64.

81. AGN, Inq., vol. 3, exp. 2. The trial and its broader political context are discussed at greater length in Greenleaf, *Mexican Inquisition,* 140–48.

82. The censors consulted in the trial included the Augustinians maestro fray Antonio de San Ysidro, prior of San Agustín in Mexico City, and fray Joseph de Herrera, lector in theology; the Dominicans Osorio, Ledesma, maestro fray Domingo de la Cruz, former prior of Santo Domingo in Mexico City who had previously given his opinion on Zumárraga's *Doctrina,* and Juan de Ozpina; fray Cristóbal de la Cruz (his order is unknown);

fray Joan Baptista (possibly the same Franciscan Baptisa who wrote a famous confessional manual); the Franciscan fray Juan Focher; licenciado Juan Márquez (a canon lawyer and cathedral canon of Michoacán); as well as the friars Juan de Escalante, Juan Nafarmendi, Fernando de Paz, and Juan Martínez (whose corporate identities are not given); dr. Rafael de Cervantes, treasurer of the Mexico archdiocesan cathedral chapter and former prosecutor for the Zumárraga inquisition.

83. Suárez, *De censuris,* disp. 2, § 6, nu. 1: "Quid necessarium ut censura recte moraliter feratur. Non debet ferri ex pravo affectu."

84. AGN, Inq., vol. 3, exp. 2, fs. 84–85.

85. AGN, Inq., vol. 3, exp. 2, f. 63.

86. AGN, Inq., vol. 3, exp. 2, f. 65.

87. AGN, Inq., vol. 3, exp. 2, f. 66.

88. Galatians 3:27.

89. AGN, Inq., vol. 3, exp. 2, f. 73.

90. Contained most notably in Session 7, canons 6, 7, and 8 of Trent. Quoted by Ledesma in AGN, Inq., vol. 3, exp. 2, f. 68: "Hoc nanque est quod concilia Floren. et Trinden. diffiniunt cum dicunt Sacramenta nouae legis et continere et conferre gratiam digne suscipientibus, seu non ponentibus obicem."

91. AGN, Inq., vol. 3, exp. 2, f. 68: "Eisdem rationibus censeo haereticam esse quartam partem secundae propositionis."

92. AGN, Inq., vol. 3, exp. 2, f. 70. Also see *ST,* 2.2, qu. 2, ar. 6, qu. 3, ar. 3 and qu. 10, ar. 7, and *Decretales,* lib. 5, tit. 7, c. 10, *Vergentis.*

93. AGN, Inq., vol. 3, exp. 2, f. 73: "dico esse scandalosam praesertim hoc tempore cum vergat in contemptum sacramentorum et avertat homines a devotione et participatione eorum."

94. AGN, Inq., vol. 3, exp. 2, f. 71: "qui fideles sic scandalizari possunt et turbari in fide." On this propinquity: "hodiernis diebus periculose qui ex eis heretici suos possent confirmare errores" and "haeretici suos defendant errores."

95. AGN, Inq., vol. 3, exp. 2, f. 72: "illi propinqua vim haereticorum errori."

96. See discussions in Brown, *Augustine of Hippo.*

97. AGN, Inq., vol. 3, exp. 2, fs. 71–72. I have paraphrased since Focher wrote two similar opinions, both of which said the same thing but in slightly different wording. "Assertor in nullo in praefatis errauit quetum capio ut probatum est [. . .] non statim se declarauerit et circo pro his propositionibus nulla tenus potest puniri. Et praelatus eius ad cuius praesentia hoc negocium [sic] latum est tenetur declarare eum esse innocentum et ab imposito sibi crimine absoluere." And: "Ex his omnibus dictis puto satis apparere qui praelatarum assertor propositionum ni nullo quod ni eis asseruit, errauit [. . .] et omnio nullatenque pro his a se sic assertis potest puniri."

98. AGN, Inq., vol. 3, exp. 2, f. 94.

99. AGN, Inq., vol. 3, exp. 2, f. 92.

100. Greenleaf, *Zumárraga and the Mexican Inquisition,* 17.

101. Ramírez González, *Grupos de poder clerical,* 2:81.

102. Lundberg, "Unity and Conflict," 186.

103. AGN, Inq., vol. 4, exp. 9.

104. AGN, Inq., vol. 4, exp. 9.

105. AGN, Inq., vol. 4, exp. 9, f. 280: "el dicho deán está tenido en toda esta tierra por mi enemigo mortal."

106. AGN, Inq., vol. 4, exp. 9, f. 272: "don Alonso Chico de Molina a dicho y publicado ante muchas personas afirmando que yo he dicho ciertas proposiciones heréticas y malsonantes en púlpito o fuera del contra nuestra sancta fe cathólica . . . por tanto pido y supplico a V.S. mande parecer ante sí al dicho deán Chico que con juramento declare que proposiciones he dicho y si las tiene escriptas las exhiba."

107. AGN, Inq., vol. 4, exp. 9, f. 289.

108. AGN, Inq., vol. 4, exp. 6. Also see Greenleaf, *Mexican Inquisition,* 150.

109. Ramírez, *Grupos de poder clerical,* 2:103.

110. Lundberg, "Unity and Conflict," 191.

111. AGN, Inq., vol. 3, exp. s/n, fs. 96–97.

112. AGN, Inq., vol. 112, exp. 3.

113. Lundberg, "Unity and Conflict," 221–29.

114. See Nesvig, "Pearls Before Swine," Appendix 3.

Chapter 6. The Holy Office Established, 1571–90

1. For biographical information on Moya de Contreras, I have relied on Poole, *Pedro Moya de Contreras.*

2. In many cases the formal appointment of the inquisitor is not found in the Mexican inquisitional archive even if their activity is. As in chapter 8, where I provide a collective biography of the personnel of the Mexican Inquisition, I have relied on extensive archival appearances of the inquisitors in the case law as well as biographical information found in some printed sources. See appendixes 1 and 2 for further detail.

3. Ramírez Cruz, *Salmantica Docet;* Ramírez González, *Grupos de poder clerical;* Zúñiga y Ontiveros, *Catálogo de los Colegiales.*

4. The same trend occurred contemporaneously in Spain. See Prado Moura, *Inquisición e inquisidores.*

5. AGN, Inq., vol. 59, exp. 4, vol. 60, exp. 3, vol. 60, exp. 4, vol. 61, exp. 6, vol. 62, exp. 1, vol. 62, exp. 5, vol. 63, exp. 18, vol. 65, exp. 5, vol. 65, exp. 6, vol. 65, exp. 10, vol. 76, exp. 10, vol. 76, exp. 48, vol. 85, exp. 26, vol. 119, exp. 5, vol. 119, exp. 6, vol. 189, exp. 3, vol. 239, exp. s/n, f. 92, vol. 1486, exp. s/n, fs. 30, 34, 52, 63–64. Also see García Granados, *El deán turbulento,* 16, and Gómez, "Nómina," 490.

6. See the still-reigning principal study, Tellechea Idígoras, *El arzobispo Carranza.*

7. AGN, Inq., vol. 10, exp. 4, vol. 60, exp. 4, vol. 62, exp. 5, vol. 65, exp. 6, vol. 76, exp. 10, vol. 90, exp. s/n, fs. 29–30, vol. 1486, exp. s/n, fs. 63–64.

8. AGN, Inq., vol. 65, exp. 10, vol. 76, exp. 10, vol. 90, exp. s/n, fs. 29–30.

9. AGN, Inq., vol. 60, exp. 3, vol. 74, exp. 40, vol. 116.

10. AGN, Inq., vol. 65, exp. 6.

11. AGN, Inq., vol. 35, exp. 2, vol. 63, exp. 18.

12. AGN, Inq., vol. 62, exp. 1, vol. 74, exp. 40

13. AGN, Inq., vol. 61, exp. 6.

14. AGN, Inq., vol. 76, exp. 10.

15. AGN, Inq., vol. 76, exp. 31.

16. AGN, Inq., vol. 142, exp. 41.

17. The commission can be found in Moya de Contreras's letter of March 6, 1573: AGN, Inq., vol. 90, exp. s/n, fs. 29–30.

18. There are numerous trials. Many of them have been transcribed in the volume *Corsarios franceses e ingleses en la Inquisición de la Nueva España.*

19. AGN, Inq., vol. 1111, exp. s/n, f. 88: "el delito de los casados dos bezes es bien frequente en estas partes y ésto como es hecho y que de suyo se está qualificado no ai para que los theólogos lo qualifiquen sino estando el reo conbençido del delito con el dicho paresçer."

20. AGN, Inq., vol. 112, exp. 4: "el reo creía que aunque un hombre se echase con una muger soltera y se lo pagase no hera pecado mortal y que él lo auía leydo en un libro."

21. AGN, Inq., vol. 112, exp. 4.

22. See Socolow, *The Women of Colonial Latin America,* 53–55.

23. AGN, Inq., vol. 117, exp. 6.

24. AGN, Inq., vol. 117, exp. 6.

25. AGN, Inq., vol. 74, exp. 40.

26. AGN, Inq., vol. 78, exp. 3, f. 90.

27. AGN, Inq., vol. 46, exp. 17: "que en la ostia consagrada no estaua más que Jesu Christo y no estaua allí el padre ni el espírictu sancto."

28. AGN, Inq., vol. 46, exp. 17, f. 459.

29. AGN, Inq., vol. 116, exp. 10, f. 334.

30. AGN, Inq., vol. 116, exp. 10.

31. AGN, Inq., vol. 114, exp. 5.

32. AGN, Inq., vol. 114, exp. 5, f. 388.

33. AGN, Inq., vol. 112, exp. 7: "a mí no me consuelan sino tostones."

34. AGN, Inq., vol. 112, exp. 7.

35. AGN, Inq., vol. 112, exp. 3: "valía más una confesión hecha a Dios que diez a un sacerdote." A copy of this charge is found in AGN, Inq., vol. 74, exp. 40, f. 179.

36. Cf. AGN, vol. 74, exp. 40, f. 223.

37. AGN, Inq., vol. 117, exp. 1.

38. AGN, Inq., vol. 117, exp. 18.

39. See Henningsen, *The Witches' Advocate.*

40. Simancas, *De catholicis institutionibus,* tit. 30, nu. 18: "Facere autem sortilegia et imagines cereas, vel alias observationes vanas ad provocandum et aliciendum animum ad amorem; si modo non misceantur sacra profanes, superstitiosa sunt magis quam haeretica" and tit. 30, nu. 20: "cum incertum est, utrum divinationes et sortilegia sapient manifestam haeresim et propterea de jurisdictione amgibitur, Inquisitores de eo cognoscere nequeunt."

41. AGN, Inq., vol. 128, exp. 12, f. 258.

42. AGN, Inq., vol. 128, exp. 12, f. 294.

43. AGN, Inq., vol. 128, exp. 14, fs. 459–60.

44. AGN, Inq., vol. 128, exp. 14, f. 494.

45. For further discussion of this question, see Schwartz, *All Can Be Saved.*

46. AGN, Inq., vol. 112, exp. 13.

47. AGN, Inq., vol. 187, exp. 2.

48. AGN, Inq., vol. 49, exp. 6.

49. AGN, Inq., vol. 49, exp. 6, f. 151.

50. AGN, Inq., vol. 119, exp. 6, f. 119: "los lutheranos no son tan malos como los haçen; algunas cosas buenas tienen."

51. AGN, Inq., vol. 119, exp. 6, f. 208.

52. Drawn from the same data set used in tables 6:1 and 6:2.

53. Pravia's calificación: AGN, Inq., vol. 114, exp. 5, f. s/n.

54. His trials are in AGN, Inq., vol. 88, exp. 1, and vol. 116, exp. 1. For a biography, see Miranda, *El erasmista mexicano.* For the sermon he preached in Cholula which led to his second heresy trial, see Nesvig, "El sermón de un erasmista olvidado."

55. AGN, Inq., vol. 91, exp. s/n, f. 294

56. See Pinto Crespo, *Inquisición y control ideológico.*

57. Such correspondence abounds in AGN, Inq., vol. 142. For specific examples, see AGN, Inq., vol. 139, exp. 55, vol. 139, exp. 74.

58. AGN, Inq., vol. 139, exp. 7, vol. 139, exp. 61, vol. 139, exp. 72, vol. 141, exp. 88, vol. 141, exp. 95, vol. 142, exp. 7, vol. 142, exp. 8.

59. AGN, Inq., vol. 1A, exp. 41.

60. AGN, Inq., vol. 450, exp. s/n, fs. 575–76.

61. See Baudot, *Utopia and History,* and Phelan, *The Millennial Kingdom.*

62. For an overview of the project at Tlatelolco, see Kobayashi, *La educación como conquista,* and Mathes, *Santa Cruz de Tlatelolco.* On the Franciscan missionary and educational projects, also see Burkhart, *Holy Wednesday;* Cifuentes, con García, *Letras sobre voces;* Gonzalbo Aizpuru, *Historia de la educación en la época colonial: El mundo indígena;* León-Portilla, *Bernardino de Sahagún;* Osorio Romero, *La enseñanza del latín a los indios.*

63. For his defense of Indian intellect and education, see Castro, "Utrum indigenae." For further discussion, see Olaechea Labayen, "Opinión de los teólogos españoles sobre dar estudios mayores a los Indios."

64. On the decline of Tlatelolco, see Kobayashi, *La educación como conquista.* On the controversy and subsequent ban on the *Historia general,* see León-Portilla, *Bernardino de Sahagún,* 161–80.

65. I am grateful to Barry Sell for bringing this to my attention. For evidence that Carochi relied on Sahagún, see Carochi, *Grammar of the Mexican Language,* 375, 420–21, 424, 436, 458 (in the explanatory notes by Lockhart).

66. AGN, Inq., vol. 1A, exp. 41, f. 198.

67. AGN, Inq., vol. 90, exp. 42.

68. See Clendinnen, *Ambivalent Conquests.*

69. AGN, Inq., vol. 1A, exp. 41, f. 106 [198] [189]. Confounding this date is a copy of the questionnaire found in a different volume of the inquisitional archive with a date of 1570 written across the top but in a different hand. Given that the questionnaire was in the hand of the inquisitional notary, Pedro de los Ríos, appointed in late 1571, this date seems inaccurate and is likely the result of poor paleography.

70. AGN, Inq., vol. 43, exp. 4, fs. 133–36: "Presupuesta que por el Santo offiçio se prohibe un libro de mano que pareçe ser el Ecclesiastés traduzido en lengua yndia y otro qualquier de la sagrada scriptura en la dicha lengua o en otra vulgar se pregunta lo primero:

que libros ai de la sagrada scriptura traduzidos en lengua de los yndios

item si de la execuçión desta prohibiçión resultará alguna deminuçión y falta a la doctrina de los yndios

item en caso que uuiese la dicha falta que libros de los dichos son preçisamente necesarios a los ministros para administraçión de la dicha doctrina

item si es bueno prohibir a los mesmos yndios in totum que no tengan cosa alguna de molde ni de mano traduzido en su vulgar vista su capaçidad y bejeza de su yngenio."

71. AGN, Inq., vol. 43, exp. 5.

72. While not specifically about the missionary endeavor, for a good overview of the alphabetization of Mixtec (Ñudzahui) language, see Terraciano, *The Mixtecs of Colonial Oaxaca.*

73. AGN, Inq., vol. 43, exp. 4, f. 133: "excelente lengua mexicana . . . con su exposición en la dicha lengua, muy útil y prouechoso para los ministros que predican a estos naturales."

74. AGN, Inq., vol. 43, exp. 4, f. 133: "no es justo que sean priuados de tan gran favor que con los dichos libros deuotos tiene para consolación espiritual de sus almas y saluación dellas."

75. AGN, Inq., vol. 43, exp. 4, fs. 136–37.

76. AGN, Inq., vol. 43, exp. 4, f. 132.

77. AGN, Inq., vol. 90, exp. 67, f. 199.

78. AGN, Inq., vol. 140, exp. 15.

79. AGN, Inq., vol. 450, exp. s/n, fs. 575–76.

80. AGN, Inq., vol. 140, exp. 15.

81. AGN, Inq., vol. 78, exp. 18, vol. 84, exp. s/n.

82. AGN, Inq., vol. 84, exp. s/n.

83. AGN, Inq., vol. 585, exp. 54. Bujanda, *Index de l'inquisition espagnol; Index de Quiroga.*

84. AGN, Inq., vol. 139, exp. 61, vol. 139, exp. 64, vol. 141.

85. Their trials are transcribed in Fernández del Castillo, *Libros y libreros en el siglo XVI,* 85–244.

86. See Griffin, *Journeymen-Printers, Heresy, and the Inquisition.*

87. For elaboration on the Ocharte and Ortiz trials, see Donahue-Wallace, "Prints and Printmakers in Viceregal Mexico City," 179–81 and Ward, " 'Estos cuentos son sin cuenta.' "

Chapter 7. The Ebb of the Holy Office, 1591–1640

1. AGN, Inq., vol. 466, exp. 1.

2. AGN, Inq., vol. 466, exp. 1, f. 5: "Las palabras que aquel hombre dixo conforme a la qualidad de la persona y ocasión en que se dixeron, solo parecen desconcertadas y viciosas como pullas que suelen echar labradores, pero no traen sospecha de sentir mal de la fe."

3. AGN, Inq., vol. 466, exp. 1, f. 23: "que sea absuelto attenta su poca capaçidad."

4. AGN, Inq., vol. 267, exp. 5: "estando çierto hombre açotando a un esclabo suio dixo

el dicho esclabo reniego de los sanctos y diziéndole el dicho su amo, que dizes perro, respondió el dicho esclabo que el Diablo lo había engañado que no había sabido lo que se había dicho." For a discussion of the ways black slaves were treated in the Mexican Inquisition, see Villa-Flores, *Dangerous Speech,* 127–47.

5. AGN, Inq., vol. 267, exp. 5: "aquella proposición dicha en tal occasión y reportándose incontinenti, no pareçe de mucha consideración."

6. For overviews of this debate, see Beltrán de Heredia, *Domingo Báñez y las controversias sobre la gracia;* Flint, *Divine Providence;* Luis de Molina, *On Divine Foreknowledge;* Salaverri de la Torre, "La noción de la Iglesia del Padre Molina"; Smith, *Freedom in Molina.*

7. *Decretum,* causa 24, qu. 1, c. 1: "Achatius non est inuentor factus noui erroris, sed ueteris imitator." See also *Decretum,* causa 24, qu. 3, c. 16, *Resecandae sunt.*

8. The archival citations for the appointments are extensive and are compiled in appendix 1b of Nesvig, "Pearls Before Swine."

9. There is extensive discussion of Lobo Guerrero in his role as extirpator and archbishop of Lima. See, e.g., Duviols, *La lutte contre les religions autochtones dans le Péru colonial;* Mantilla Ruiz, *Don Bartolomé Lobo Guerrero;* Mills, *Idolatry and Its Enemies.*

10. See appendix 2 for his tenure.

11. Medina, *Historia del santo oficio en México.*

12. González Dávila, *Teatro eclesiástico,* 69.

13. Argued generally in Alberro, *Inquisición y sociedad en México.*

14. Here, as in other places, I am deeply grateful to Bob Ferry, who allowed me to review his work in progress on the physical plant of the Mexican Inquisition, which outlines the many structural problems of the tribunal in the 1620s and 1630s, especially regarding the jail and the tribunal's courthouse.

15. AGN, Inq., vol. 1486, exp. 2.

16. See, among others, Hordes, "The Inquisition as Economic and Political Agent," and Netanyahu, *The Origins of the Inquisition.*

17. Hordes, "The Inquisition as Economic and Political Agent."

18. Greenleaf, "The Great Visitas of the Mexican Holy Office."

19. For biographical information, see Beristáin de Souza, *Biblioteca hispanoamericana,* 2:108–9; Zambrano, *Diccionario bio-bibliográfico,* 7:563–626. Also see Virgil, *Aeneid,* trans. Theodore C. Williams (Boston, 1910).

20. Zambrano, *Diccionario bio-bibliográfico,* 7:597–99.

21. Poole, *Pedro Moya de Contreras,* 45, 145, 150, 205.

22. AGN, Inq., vol. 206, exp. 2, vol. 206, exp. 3, vol. 223, exp. 31.

23. Gonzalbo Aizpuru, *Historia de la educación en la época colonial: Los criollos.*

24. Cano, "Censura y parecer."

25. For an excellent discussion of the issue in the Spanish context, see Alcalá, "Herejía y jerarquía."

26. AGN, Inq., vol. 283, exp. s/n, fs. 475–78.

27. See AGN, Inq., vol. 509 and vol. 510, among others. For a good overview of the story, see García Granados, *El deán turbulento.*

28. AGN, Inq., vol. 283, exp. s/n, f. 448.

29. AGN, Inq., vol. 283, exp. s/n, fs. 449–50.

30. AGN, Inq., vol. 283, exp. s/n, f. 450: "no ay quien pueda negar que el commissario es official de la sede appostólica. cap. inquisitores lib. 6 uidelicet episcopum non posse contra inquisitorem procedere durante officio. Ergo neque contra eius subdelegatum."

31. AGN, Inq., vol. 283, exp. s/n, f. 450: "de manera que el aver puesto excomunión el obispo al commisario fue temeridad por estarle prohibido en derecho . . . y teniendo obligación de faborecer las causas y ministros del Santo officio a dado sospecha de impedimento que es grave delicto en los que presumen impedir el libre ministerio del santo officio."

32. AGN, Inq., vol. 283, exp. s/n, fs. 338, 451–452. It begins: "Quaerit an episcopus in hac nova Hispania possit publicare edictum de fide? Ratio dubitandi est qui episcopus est inquisitor ordinarius, ad quem ex proprio officio pertinet ut propaget fides et haereses extirpet — ergo post publice praecipere ut ad ipsum haeretici deferant et contra ipsos inquirere."

33. AGN, Inq., vol. 283, exp. s/n, f. 450. The Jesuits' citation is as follows: "Simancas, de inst. Cath. tit. 25, nu. 3, tit. 34, nu. 39; Albertinus lib. De agnos. assert. qu. 11, un. 11; Diego Pérez, lib. 8 ordin. tit. 4; Villadiego de haeresibus, qu. 7, 8; Silvest. Verbo de haeresis 2 f a nu. 10; Magister Azor lib. 8 moral inst. c. 18."

34. AGN, Inq., vol. 283, exp. s/n, f. 450: Relying on Rojas, *De successionibus*, nu. 415, nu. 445.

35. AGN, Inq., vol. 283, exp. s/n, f. 451.

36. AGN, Inq., vol. 283, exp. s/n, f. 452: their proof for this: "Francisco Suárez, tom. 5 disput. 5, sec. 4, nu. 44; Juan de Rojas, 1 parte de haereticis, nu. 443."

37. AGN, Inq., vol. 283, exp. s/n, fs. 457–74.

38. The exchange can be found in AGN, Inq., vol. 284, exp. s/n, fs. 124–32.

39. AGN, Inq., vol. 284, exp. s/n, f. 131v: "los calificadores de México que no vieron esto, estuvieron muy ciegos, o muy negligentes en verlo . . . los calificadores de México no acertaron esta vez engañados por la falsa relación."

40. See MacLeod, *Las Casas, Guatemala, and the Sad but Inevitable Case of Antonio Remesal.*

41. AGN, Inq., vol. 339, exp. 11, vol. 339, exp. 58.

42. For good studies, see Martínez, *Jaque mate al obispo virrey;* De la Torre Villar, *Don Juan de Palafox y Mendoza.*

43. AGN, Inq., vol. 278, exp. 2, vol. 278, exp. 3.

44. AGN, Inq., vol. 278, exp. 3.

45. Peña, comment. 1, 2a pars.

46. AGN, Inq., vol. 341, 1a parte, exp. 1.

47. AGN, Inq., vol. 332, exp. 5.

48. AGN, Inq., vol. 209, exp. 7.

49. See Giordano, *María de Cazalla;* Jaffary, *False Mystics;* Pastore, *Un'eresia spagnola.*

50. As related in the trial records.

51. AGN, Inq., vol. 210, exp. 2.

52. AGN, Inq., vol. 210, exp. 3.

53. AGN, Inq., vol. 266, exp. s/n, fs. 176–77.

54. AGN, Inq., vol. 288, exp. 1, f. 4v.

55. AGN, Inq., vol. 322, exp. s/n, f. s/n: "estando çierto hombre seglar moço y distraido valentón y usado, a jurar, hablando con çiertas personas víspera de la expetaçión de nuestra señora oyendo repicar las campanas preguntó que fiesta era, a que respondió una de las dichas personas que era nuestra señora de la O y entonçes dixo el dicho hombre estas palabras nuestra señora de la hodida."

56. AGN, Inq., vol. 322, exp. s/n, f. s/n: "una gran blasfemia y sacrilegio . . . como advirtió bien el Obispo Simancas en su libro de catholicis institutionibus."

57. AGN, Inq., vol. 322, exp. s/n, f. s/n: "aquellas palabras son malsonantes . . . pero no contienen blasphemia ni indicio de sentir mal de nuestra señora."

58. Again, I am grateful to Bob Ferry, for allowing me to review his work in progress on the physical plant of the Mexican Holy Office.

59. AGN, Inq., vol. 311, exp. 2: "los inquisidores heran unos borrachos y locos que no sabían lo que se hazían ni miraban a sus viçios y vellaquerías."

60. AGN, Inq., vol. 311, exp. 2: "las palabras son escandalosas y ofensivas a las pias orejas y desacatadas contra el santo oficio de la inquisición y sus mandatos."

61. AGN, Inq., vol. 311, exp. 2: "los inquisidores auiendo visto pleyto y su calificación mandaron que se suspenda."

62. AGN, Inq., vol. 300, 2a parte, exp. 9.

63. AGN, Inq., vol. 368, exp. s/n, f. 507.

64. AGN, Inq., vol. 338, exp. 6. A similar case in 1628 appears in AGN, Inq., vol. 454, exp. 4.

65. AGN, Inq., vol. 471, exp. [64], fs. 231–35.

66. AGN, Inq., vol. 471, exp. [64], fs. 235–38.

67. Similar examples can be found throughout AGN, Inq., vol. 302, exp. 13, vol. 322, exp. s/n, fs. 372–83, vol. 471, exp. [64].

68. Greenleaf, "The Great Visitas."

Chapter 8. Lucre and Connections

1. Contreras and Henningsen, "Forty-Four Thousand Cases," 115.

2. AGN, Inq., vol. 1A, exp. 34, vol. 3, exp. 4, vol. 3, exp. 5, vol. 3, exp. 13, vol. 7, exp. 4, vol. 7, exp. 7, vol. 10, exp. 4, vol. 14, exp. 50, vol. 15, exp. 2, vol. 15, exp. 3, vol. 15, exp. 4, vol. 16, exp. 8, vol. 16, exp. 9, vol. 16, exp. 14, vol. 17, exp. 5, vol. 17, exp. 7, vol. 17, exp. 11, vol. 24, exp. 3, vol. 24, exp. 6, vol. 32, exp. 3, vol. 34, exp. 7, vol. 36, exp. 9bis, vol. 43, exp. 5, vol. 43, exp. 8, vol. 46, exp. 7, vol. 46, exp. 8, vol. 46, exp. 9, vol. 71, exp. 4, vol. 71, exp. 5, vol. 92, exp. 1, vol. 187, exp. 1.

3. AGN, Inq., vol. 35, exp. 1, vol. 40, exp. 35.

4. See Nesvig, "Heterodoxia popular e Inquisición diocesana en Michoacán."

5. AGN, Inq., vol. 31, exp. 3, vol. 36, exp. 11, vol. 46, exp. 11.

6. AGN, Inq., vol. 45, exp. 4, vol. 109, exp. 1, vol. 110, exp. 8, vol. 111, exp. 3.

7. AGN, Inq., vol. 11, exp. 2.

8. AGN, Inq., vol. 10, exp. 1, vol. 25, exp. 4.

9. AGN, Inq., vol. 2, exp. 15, vol. 15, exp. 12, vol. 15, exp. 14, vol. 31, exp. 2, vol. 35, exp. 1, vol. 40, exp. 35, vol. 143, exp. 1.

10. AGN, Inq., vol. 7, exp. 5, vol. 7, exp. 6, vol. 12 (in toto), vol. 13, exp. 1, vol. 13, exp. 2, vol. 18, exp. 13, vol. 19, exp. 7, vol. 33, exp. 1, vol. 45, exp. 2A, vol. 1547, exp. 1.

11. AGN, Inq., vol. 35, exp. 1, vol. 40, exp. 35.

12. AGN, Inq., vol. 40, exp. 35.

13. AGN, Inq., vol. 62, exp. 1, vol. 74, exp. 40.

14. See Clendinnen, *Ambivalent Conquests.*

15. AGN, Inq., vol. 35, exp. 1, vol. 40, exp. 35.

16. See Chinchilla Aguilar, *La Inquisición en Guatemala,* and Nesvig, "Heterodoxia popular e Inquisición diocesana."

17. For information and background on Moya de Contreras, see Poole, *Pedro Moya de Contreras.*

18. Ibid.

19. AGN, Inq., vol. 314, exp. 4.

20. Lea, *History of the Inquisition in Spain,* 2:235.

21. Caro Baroja, "El señor inquisidor"; Contreras, *El santo oficio de la inquisición en Galicia.*

22. AGN, Inq., vol. 1486, exp. 2.

23. See Aiton, "Real Hacienda in New Spain."

24. For a good study of the economic workings of the Inquisition in general, see Martínez Millán, *La hacienda de la Inquisición.* By the 1540s, the bishops of Oaxaca and Michoacán were receiving salaries of 500,000 maravedies.

25. Aiton, "Real Hacienda in New Spain."

26. González Dávila, *Teatro eclesiástico,* 40, 67.

27. For sources and biographical data for the inquisitors, see appendix 2. On Bonilla, see Poole, *Pedro Moya de Contreras,* 207.

28. Contreras, *El santo oficio en Galicia;* Prado Moura, *Inquisición e inquisidores en Castilla.*

29. Thomas, *Who's Who of the Conquistadors,* 252–53.

30. See AGN, Inq., vol. 60, exp. 6, vol. 195, exp. 8, vol. 221, exp. 1, vol. 386, exp. 10. Vázquez de Tapia wrote an account of his role in the conquest of Tenochtitlan and as Cortés's partisan. See his *Relación de méritos y servicios.*

31. Eubel and van Gulik, eds., *Hierarchia Catholica,* 4:199. For discussions of the conquistador and criollo elite connections among inquisitional functionaries, especially the Albornoz, Bazán, Carvajal, Cervantes, Peralta, and Vázquez de Tapia, I have relied on various archival sources: AGN, Bienes Nacionales, vol. 661, exp. 20, vol. 824, exp. 31, vol. 1147, exp. 9; AGN, General de Parte, vol. 3, exp. 38, vol. 6, exp. 399, vol. 6, exp. 565; AGN, Inq., vol. 128, exp. 10, vol. 195, exp. 8, vol. 221, exp. 11, vol. 307, exp. 8, vol. 320, exp. 9, vol. 320, exp. 12, vol. 366, exp. 14, vol. 446, exp. s/n, vol. 493, exp. s/n, vol. 510, exp. 20; AGN, Mercedes, vol. 2, exp. s/n; AGN, Ordenanzas, vol. 1, exp. 108; AGN, Reales Cédulas, vol. 1, exp. 161, vol. 1, exp. 289, vol. 11, exp. 115, vol. 12, exp. 336, vol. 16, exp. 589, vol. 48, exp. 243; AGN, Tierras, vol. 2955, exp. 109, vol. 2984, exp. 11. For more on Francisco Verdugo, see González Dávila, *Teatro eclesiástico,* 62.

32. Thomas, *Who's Who of the Conquistadors,* 277–80.

33. AGN, Inq., vol. 203, exp. 7; Eubel and van Gulik, eds., *Hierarchia Catholica,* 4:198.

34. Archival data for the consultores has been gleaned from the collective case law (in which they appear in the trial transcript), though they also appear in more specific locations, such as: AGN, Inq., vol. 11, exp. 3bis, vol. 48, exp. 5, vol. 52, exp. 5, vol. 63, exp.

2, vol. 63, exp. 7, vol. 66, exp. 6, vol. 86, exp. 96, vol. 92, exp. 2bis, vol. 116, exp. 6, vol. 117, exp. 18, vol. 121, exp. 2, vol. 124, exp. 6, vol. 143, exp. 7, vol. 147, exp. 6, vol. 165, exp. 4, vol. 180, exp. 1, vol. 189, exp. 15, vol. 190, exp. 4, vol. 190, exp. 5, vol. 202, exp. 9, vol. 205, exp. 3, vol. 206, exp. 3, vol. 209, exp. 9, vol. 220, exp. 10, vol. 221, exp. 4, vol. 273, exp. 6, vol. 274, exp. 6, vol. 274, exp. 10, vol. 279, exp. 12, vol. 307, exp. 5, vol. 325, exp. 6, vol. 332, exp. 5, vol. 341, exp. 1, vol. 347, exp. s/n, fs. 348–50, 354, 421–22, 480–84, vol. 356, exp. 1, vol. 364, exp. 13, vol. 366, exp. 41, vol. 379, exp. 13, vol. 385, exp. 2, vol. 387, exp. 1, vol. 452, exp. 5, vol. 466, exp. 13, vol. 466, exp. 14, vol. 480, exp. 1, vol. 490, exp. 3, vol. 491, exp. s/n, vol. 659, exp. 7, vol. 683, exp. 5, vol. 823, exp. 1, vol. 846, exp. 16, vol. 1486, exp. s/n, fs. 34, 122. Among printed material, see Gómez, "Nómina"; Poole, *Pedro Moya de Contreras.*

35. For his marriage, see AGN, Inq., vol. 279, exp. 12. For his involvement in trials, see, among others, AGN, Inq., vol. 279, exp. 12, vol. 307, exp. 5, vol. 466, exp. 13, vol. 480, exp. 1, vol. 823, exp. s/n.

36. Poole, *Pedro Moya de Contreras.*

37. Pérez Puente, "Los canónigos catedráticos de la Universidad de México." For inquisitional salaries, see AGN, Inq., vol. 1486, exp. 2.

38. *Efemérides de La Real y Pontificia Universidad de México,* 32, 40; Ramírez González, *Grupos de poder clerical,* 2:38.

39. Archivo de la Universidad de Salamanca (hereafter AUS), libros de grados mayores, vol. 774, fs. 89–90; *Efemérides de La Real y Pontificia Universidad de México,* 40.

40. Poole, *Pedro Moya de Contreras.*

41. AGN, Inq., vol. 66, exp. 6.

42. Chinchilla Aguilar, *La Inquisición en Guatemala,* 141.

43. For a detailed list and information on the comisarios, see Nesvig, "Pearls Before Swine," appendix 1f.

44. Pérez Puente, "Los canónigos catedráticos de la Universidad de México."

45. León Alanís, *Los orígenes del clero y la iglesia en Michoacán,* 283–85.

46. Archivo del Cabildo de la Catedral de Morelia, Ramo Colegio de San Nicolás, leg. 4, exp. 20.

47. See notes 30 and 31 above for more detailed archival citations relating to the Cervantes Carjaval, Vázquez de Tapia, and other clans.

48. See appendix 1 for detailed listings of the censors. I have relied on this collective information for this section rather than provide extensive citations.

49. Enumerated at length in Nesvig, "Pearls Before Swine," appendix 1.

50. AGN, Inq., vol. 16, exp. 9, vol. 31, exp. 3; *Efemérides de La Real y Pontificia Universidad de México,* 12.

51. The *Historia de la Fundación y discurso de la provincia de Santiago de México.*

52. For example, in many of the likely peninsular cases, the limpiezas were drawn up in Spain, with witnesses stating that they knew the subject in Spain. Likewise in four cases depositions for limpieza were given in Mexico with criollo witnesses stating that they knew the subject from infancy or childhood. While not definitive, these were likely criollos.

53. This number would be higher if further data existed. For example, many of the nominations of censors in the 1620s and 1630s came by legislative fiat from the Suprema

in Madrid. While it is possible that they nominated criollos from afar, it is more likely that these nominees were men whom the members of the Suprema knew by family connection or by their participation in peninsular religious life. Moreover, if one could extract the birth data from the early unofficial censors, one would surely find that the vast majority of them were peninsulars, since the first criollos did not reach adulthood until the 1540s and did not reach the age at which they could act as censors until the 1550s or later.

54. Castañeda Delgado and Fernández, *La jerarquía de la Iglesia en Indias*, 42–43.

55. Ibid., 72–73.

56. Discussed at length in Ramírez González, *Grupos de poder clerical*.

57. ACSE, Libro de profesiones, and AGN, Inq., vol. 60, exp. 4, vol. 62, exp. 5.

58. AGN, Inq., vol. 60, exp. 4.

59. Gonzalbo Aizpuru, *Historia de la educación en la época colonial: Criollos.*

60. Pavón Romero, "Doctores en la Universidad de México."

61. AGN, Inq., vol. 269, exp. s/n; Ramírez González, *Grupos de poder clerical*, 2:106.

62. AGN, Inq., vol. 341, 2a parte, exp. 6, vol. 364, exp. 7; Gómez, "Nómina," 499.

63. For this period, of 109 censors (87 for which there is information), 39 came from the administrative upper class, or 36 percent of the total sample, and nearly half (45 percent) of those for whom there is data.

64. AGN, Inq., vol. 194, exp. 8, vol. 205, exp. 7, vol. 275, exp. 10, vol. 1486, exp. s/n, fs. 64, 79, 104; Eubel and van Guilk, eds., *Hierarchia Catholica*, 4:176–77.

65. AGN, Inq., vol. 1486, exp. s/n, fs. 63–64.

66. AGN, Inq., vol. 60, exp. 4, vol. 62, exp. 5, vol. 203, exp. 8, vol. 1486, exp. s/n, f. 78; Eubel and van Gulik, eds., *Hierarchia Catholica*, 3:111, 4:85.

67. AGN, Inq., vol. 314, exp. 4.

68. AGN, Inq., vol. 60, exp. 3, vol. 60, exp. 6, vol. 65, exp. 6, vol. 74, exp. 40, vol. 197, exp. 7, vol. 223, exp. s/n, f. 260, vol. 261, exp. 4, vol. 261, exp. 5, vol. 267, exp. 10, vol. 289, exp. 2, vol. 289, exp. 9j, vol. 291, exp. 2, vol. 338, exp. 1, vol. 341, 2a parte, exp. 6, vol. 364, exp. 7, vol. 379, exp. 5, vol. 1486, exp. s/n, fs. 96, 112–13, 182; Gómez, "Nómina," 499, 504.

69. AGN, Inq., vol. 349, exp. 16.

70. AGN, Inq., vol. 1486, exp. s/n, f. 149; Gómez, "Nómina," 499.

71. Gómez, "Nómina," 506.

72. AGN, Inq., vol. 341, exp. 1, vol. 1486, exp. s/n, f. 144, caja 165, carpeta 3, exp. 39.

73. AGN, Inq., vol. 352, exp. [4].

74. AGN, Inq., vol. 195, exp. 2; Gómez, "Nómina," 500–01.

75. AGN, Inq., vol. 364, exp. 7; Carreño, *La Real y Pontificia Universidad de México;* Pavón Romero, "Doctores en la Universidad de México"; Plaza y Jaén, *Crónica de la real y pontificia universidad de México;* Ramírez González, *Grupos de poder clerical;* Saranyana, "La eucaristía en la teología sacramentaria Americana."

76. AGN, Inq., vol. 16, exp. 9, vol. 31, exp. 3; *Efemérides de la real y pontificia universidad*, 12.

77. AGN, Inq., vol. 276, exp. 4, vol. 314, exp. 4; Pavón Romero, "Doctores en la Universidad de México," 261.

78. Pavón Romero, "Doctores en la Universidad de México," 250.

79. AUS, vol. 1028, fs. 3–11.

80. León Alanís, *Los orígenes del clero y la iglesia en Michoacán*, 283–85.

81. AGN, Inq., vol. 276, exp. 4.

82. AGN, Inq., vol. 201, exp. 10, vol. 1486, exp. s/n, f. 87.

83. AGN, Inq., vol. 289, exp. 9j, vol. 362, exp. 2, vol. 362, exp. 17, vol. 364, exp. 7, vol. 659, exp. 6.

84. AGN, Inq., vol. 61, exp. 6.

85. Saranyana, "La eucaristía en la teología sacramental Americana."

86. Ibid.

87. Ibid. For his role as theological advisor at the Council, see Martínez Ferrer, *La penitencia en la primera evangelización de México*, and Poole, *Pedro Moya de Contreras*, 131, 145.

88. For discussion of Ortiz de Hinojosa and his memorials to the Council, see Poole, *Pedro Moya de Contreras*, 141–43.

89. One can find Hortigosa's manuscripts in the Biblioteca Nacional de México, Fondo Reservado (hereafter BN, FR): "De sacramentis poenitentiae et confirmationis," mss. 881–882 v. 2, and "In 2.am 2.ae quaestionae divi Thomae commentarii de Fide: spe et charitate," ms. 554.

90. BN, FR, ms. 524, fs. 272–424.

91. BN, FR, ms. 881. Also see Beristáin, *Biblioteca hispanoamericana*, 2:108–9.

92. BN, FR, ms. 559.

93. See Gallegos Rocafull, *El pensamiento mexicano*, 239. The manuscripts are found in BN, FR, ms. 672.

94. The discussions on sacraments are found in BN, FR, ms. 882, fs. 1–125, those on baptism in BN, FR, ms. 882, fs. 128–269, and those on the Eucharist in BN, FR, ms. 882, fs. 311–515. The analysis of the Trinity is found in BN, FR, ms. 524.

95. Reproduced in Mariscal, *Carta*.

96. See Gallegos Rocafull, *El pensamiento mexicano*, 255, and García Icazbalceta, "El P. Pedro de Morales."

97. Gallegos Rocafull, *El pensamiento mexicano*, 237.

98. BN, FR, ms. 485.

99. Gallegos Rocafull, *El pensamiento mexicano*, 245.

100. Ibid.

101. BN, FR, ms. 871.

102. *Monástica theología* (Mexico, 1618). See Medina, *La imprenta en México*, 2:80–81.

103. Gallegos Rocafull, *El pensamiento mexicano*, 252. The manuscript is part of a larger project, "In divi Thomae questiones," produced in 1596 by the Convento de San Agustín in Mexico City, found today in BN, FR, ms. 317.

104. Gallegos Rocafull, *El pensamiento mexicano*, 254.

105. Ibid., 262, 264.

106. *Sermón . . . a la Dedicación del Ilustre y Real Templo de Iesus María de México* (Mexico, 1621). See Medina, *La imprenta en México*, 2:98–99.

107. *Sermón . . . día del Angélico Doctor Sancto Thomás de Aquino siete de março 1632* (Mexico, 1632). See Medina, *La imprenta en México*, 2:146.

Chapter 9. Cordon Sanitaire

1. Pulque is a mildly alcoholic drink made by fermenting the *aguamiel* (liquid) inside the heart of the agave plant. Pulque had considerable ritual importance in pre-Hispanic Mexico, and in the colonial period it became a standard drink among a wide range of Indians, mestizos, urban working and middle classes, and rural communities. *Pulquerías,* bars where pulque was served (often illegally), drew their customers from a wide range of social groups.

2. See Medina, *La imprenta en México,* 2:67.

3. Medina, *Historia del santo oficio en México.* Bohórquez was only ordained on his nomination as inquisitor.

4. Quoted in Zambrano, *Diccionario bio-bibliográfico,* 7:601: "¿Donde está mi Viejo, que no me hallo sin él? Ni puede este tribunal pasar sin su consejo." It is not clear who said this line, though according to Zambrano it was an inquisitor. We do know that Hortigosa held considerable sway with Moya de Contreras and was the favored censor of the Mexican Inquisition for three decades. Chapter 7 discusses him in greater detail.

5. For general discussion of the global political context of the issue, see Kelsey, *Sir John Hawkins.*

6. AGN, Inq., vol. 52, exp. 5, f. 350.

7. For overviews, see De los Reyes Gómez, *El libro en España y América;* Pinto Crespo, *Inquisición y control ideológico.*

8. For discussions, see Leonard, *Books of the Brave.*

9. Overviews of this authority are discussed in Castro, *De justa haeriticorum punitione,* and Eimeric, *Directorium* among other places. For a broader overview in a lengthy global context, see Bujanda, *Index des livres interdits.*

10. Chronological histories of the Index are best discussed in Bujanda, *Index des livres interdits,* and De los Reyes Gómez, *El libro en España y América.*

11. AGN, Jesuitas, III-26, exp. 22. Evidence in this section is gleaned from this document unless otherwise noted. I have footnoted specific pages but otherwise I rely on this document generally for this discussion. The original order to undertake this task has apparently been lost, but the result (the memoria) remains today in the Jesuit section of the Mexican National Archive. It lacks its first two pages and begins paginated number 3, which leaves to speculation the content of the first two pages, though the formula of book inventories of this sort suggests that there would have been a brief statement of the nature of the inventory followed simply by lists. The remaining document represents lists of books identified with the owners or the mendicant houses in which they were found. A careful reading of its entries allows one to make some conclusions about its timing despite the absence of notarized signatures and dates. The oidor of the Audiencia of Mexico, Vasco de Puga, was listed as having relinquished a handful of books, so this automatically places the document between 1559, when Puga arrived in Mexico as oidor of the Audiencia, and 1576, when he died. In 1563 Puga published in Mexico one of the first summaries of derecho indiano and was shortly thereafter recalled to Spain, only to return to Mexico in 1568. See Puga, *Prouisiones cédulas Instrucciones.* Pedro Martín, son of Pero Martín, "who lives in front of the houses of Vasco de Puga," also relinquished books, corroborating these dates. One can further limit the date for this document with references to other inquisitional officials. Frequently mentioned as part of the purge was the 1571 edition of

the *Vocabulario* (a Nahuatl-Spanish dictionary) of fray Alonso de Molina — like Zumár-raga and Gilberti, a Franciscan and a target of the Montúfar Inquisition's censorship. Since Puga was removed from office as oidor in September 1572 as a result of a royal investigation into corruption by the royal inspector Valdés de Cárcamo, the document and attendant purge occurred between late 1571 and the summer of 1572.

12. AGN, Jesuitas, III-26, exp. 22, f. 8r. For location of these convents, see Gerhard, *Historical Geography of New Spain*.

13. AGN, Inq., vol. 82, exp. 15A.

14. AGN, Inq., vol. 77, exp. 43, f. 274

15. AGN, Inq., vol. 141, exp. 86.

16. AGN, Jesuitas, III-26, exp. 22, f. 7v.

17. AGN, Inq., vol. 84, exp. 31, f. 161: "las Epístolas y euangelios en Romançe y las oras en romançe las quemara en lugar secreto que nadie lo vea por el escándalo que se podría reçiuir de ver quemar libros de que por tan tiempo usa la yglesia."

18. AGN, Jesuitas, III-26, exp. 22, f. 6r. On Portillo's various positions of authority, see AGN, Inq., vol. 48, exp. 5, vol. 274, exp. 6. See chapter 5 above for further discussion.

19. AGN, Inq., vol. 88, exp. 1, vol. 116, exp. 1.

20. Rueda Ramírez, *Negocio e intercambio cultural*, 331.

21. For biographical information on Wild, see *Enciclopedia cattolica* (Vatican City, 1950), 5:1210; *Oxford Encyclopedia of the Reformation* (New York, 1996), 4:273–74; Zawart, *History of Franciscan Preaching*, 419–23.

22. AGN, Jesuitas, III-26, exp. 22.

23. Zawart, *Franciscan Preaching*.

24. E.g., Jean Benoit, *Biblia sacra iuxta vulgate quam dicunt editionem . . .* , 2d ed. (Paris, 1552), and John Chrysostom, *Ennaratio in Esaiam prohetam,* trans. Godefridus Tilmannus (Paris, 1555). For biographical information on Benoit, see *Archives biographiques françaises,* microform, ed. Susan Bradley (London, 1988–90), fiche 83.

25. Ferus, *Exegesis in Epistolam Beati Pauli ad Romanos*.

26. For examples of Cochläus's attacks on Luther and Hus, see his *Historiae Hussitarum, Adversus cucullatum Minotaurum Vuittenbergensem,* and *Zweyn sermon*.

27. In *Books of the Brave* Irving Leonard suggested that a strong censorship apparatus was established in Veracruz much before 1571, though there is no documentation confirming the claim.

28. There was one trial, for bigamy, adjudicated in Veracruz in 1541 by licenciado Antonio de Sopuerta as the visitador of the diocese. See AGN, Inq., vol. 23, exp. 5. This, however, appears to be something of an anomaly, as the next complete trial in the diocese of Puebla appears in 1552: AGN, Inq., vol. 96, exp. 5.

29. AGN, Inq., vol. 4, exp. 2.

30. AGN, Inq., vol. 75, exp. 14.

31. AGN, Inq., vol. 169, exp. 2.

32. AGN, Inq., vol. 471, exp. 36, f. 112.

33. AGN, Inq., vol. 326, exp. 6.

34. AGN, Inq., vol. 83, exp. 10, vol. 83, exp. 11, vol. 85, exp. 19, vol. 169, exp. 2, vol. 171, exp. 1. For editions of the *Araucana,* see Palau y Dulcet, *Manual del libro hispanoamericano,* 5:79–80.

35. AGN, Inq., vol. 43, exp. 12, vol. 172, exp. 3.

36. AGN, Inq., vol. 172, exp. 2.

37. AGN, Inq., vol. 172, exp. 12, vol. 172, exp. 13, vol. 172, exp. 14, vol. 172, exp. 15, vol. 173, exp. 1, vol. 173, exp. 3, vol. 173, exp. 4, vol. 173, exp. 5, vol. 173, exp. 6, vol. 173, exp. 7.

38. AGN, Inq., vol. 257, exp. 2.

39. Leonard, *Baroque Times in Old Mexico,* 1–20.

40. Palau y Dulcet, *Manual del librero hispano-americano,* 7:30.

41. AGN, Inq., vol. 276, exp. 13, vol. 291, exp. 6a.

42. AGN, Inq., vol. 470, 1a parte, exp. s/n, fs. 170–308.

43. For the personal hell that would have been the missionary efforts in the *tierra caliente* in the sixteenth century, see León Alanís, *Los orígenes del clero y la iglesia en Michoacán.* For the austerity of Betanzos, see Carreño, *Fr. Domingo de Betanzos.*

44. AGN, Inq., vol. 160, exp. 8.

45. See, e.g., Borromeo, "Inquisizione spagnola e libri proibiti in Sicilia ed in Sardegna"; Fragnito, "The Central and Peripheral Organization of Censorship"; Pinto Crespo, *Inquisición y control ideológico;* Schons, *Book Censorship in New Spain;* Torquemada, "Censura de libros y barreras aduaneras."

46. AGN, Inq., vol. 74, exp. 24: "si alguno o algunos se hallare prohibidos se me auisen porque los embiaré a V.M. luego."

47. AGN, Inq., vol. 74, exp. 24: "me auise V.M. si se puede leer porque tengo para mí ay muchos."

48. AGN, Inq., vol. 74, exp. 35.

49. AGN, Inq., vol. 141, exp. 79. See *Index de Qurioga.*

50. AGN, Inq., vol. 34, exp. 8.

51. AGN, Inq., vol. 83, exp. 1.

52. AGN, Inq., vol. 274, exp. 4.

53. AGN, Inq., vol. 78, exp. 20, f. 334.

54. AGN, Inq., vol. 141, exp. 88, vol. 142, exp. 7.

55. AGN, Inq., vol. 142, exp. 7, f. s/n.

56. AGN, Inq., vol. 225A, exp. s/n, fs. 333–34.

57. AGN, Inq., vol. 139, exp. 62.

58. AGN, Inq., vol. 140, exp. 15.

59. AGN, Inq., vol. 142, exp. 27: "en algunas partes de ese obispado no se tiene notiçia del cathálogo General y porque en algunas poblaçiones de españoles sería possible auer algunos libros prohibidos por él se le embía con ésta la memoria de los que verissímilmente puede auer."

60. AGN, Inq., vol. 142, exp. 40.

61. AGN, Inq., vol. 140, exp. 15.

62. AGN, Inq., vol. 141, exp. 106: "an venido también en esta flota tan pocos o ningunos cathálogos que no tenemos otro que embiar a Vuestra Reverencia y así se deue contentar con hazer lo que pudiere con el que allá tiene."

63. AGN, Inq., vol. 169, exp. 3.

64. AGN, Inq., vol. 169, exp. 3.

Conclusion

1. See, e.g., Alberro, *Del gachupín al criollo.*

2. David F. Marley, *Historic Cities of the Americas: An Illustrated Encyclopedia* (Santa Barbara, 2005), 1: 255.

3. AGN, Inq., vol. 9, exp. 5, vol. 289, exp. 9j, vol. 320, exp. 6.

4. Becker, *Through Values to Social Interpretation.*

5. Bataillon, *Erasmo y España.*

6. *Decretales,* lib. 5, tit. 7, c. 10, *Vergentis.*

7. Becker, *Through Values to Social Interpretation.*

8. Ibid.

9. Ibid. 271.

10. Ibid., 271–72.

11. AGN, Inq., vol. 312, exp. s/n, f. 29.

12. His death is related in Zambrano, *Diccionario bio-bibliográfico,* 7: 604–6.

Bibliography

Archives

Archivio Segreto Vaticano, Vatican City
 Nunziature Diverse
Archivo del Convento de San Esteban, Salamanca
 Libro de profesiones
Archivo General de la Nación, Mexico City
 Bienes Nacionales
 Edictos de la Inquisición
 General de Parte
 Inquisición
 Jesuitas
 Mercedes
 Ordenanzas
 Reales Cédulas
 Tierras
 Universidad
Archivo de la Universidad de Salamanca, Salamanca
 Libros de grados mayores
 Libros de salarios

Libraries

Beinecke Rare Book and Manuscript Library, New Haven, Connecticut
Biblioteca del Antiguo Colegio de San Nicolás de Hidalgo, Morelia, Mexico
Biblioteca Eusebio Francisco Kino, Mexico City
Biblioteca Nacional de Chile, Santiago
Biblioteca Nacional de España, Madrid
Biblioteca Nacional de México, Mexico City
British Library, London
Centro de Estudios de Historia de México, Condumex, Mexico City
John Carter Brown Library, Providence, Rhode Island

Primary Printed Sources

"Actas originales de las congregaciones celebradas en 1527 para examinar las doctrinas de Erasmo." Análisis y extractos de Antonio Paz y Meliá y Manuel Serrano y Sanz. *Revista de Archivos, Bibliotecas y Museos* 6 (1902).

Agni da Lentino, Thomas. "Vita S. Petri Martyris." In *Acta sanctorum*. Vol. 12 of 69. Paris, 1866 [1274].

Alberghini, Giovanni. *Manuale qualificatorum Sanctae Inquisitionis in quo omnia qua ad illud Tribunal ac haeresum censuram pertinent, brevi methodo addunctur.* Venice, 1754.

Albertinus, Arnaldus. *De agnoscendis assertionibvs catholicis et haereticis tractatus.* Rome, 1572.

Alcalá, Ángel, ed. *Proceso inquisitorial de Fray Luis de León.* Salamanca, 1991.

Alemán, Mateo. *Guzmán el alfarache.* Madrid, 1983 [c. 1599].

Almandoz Garmendía, José Antonio, ed. *Fray Alonso de Veracruz O.S.A. y la encomienda indiana en la historia eclesiástica novohispana (1522–1556): Edición crítica del texto.* De dominio infidelium et iusto bello. Foreword by Ernest J. Burrus. Madrid, 1971–77.

Aquinas, Thomas. *Summa Theologiae.* General ed. Thomas Gilby. 60 vols. Cambridge, 1964–76.

Aristotle. *Politics.* Translated by with intro., notes, and appendices Ernest Barker. Oxford, 1958.

Augustine, St., Bishop of Hippo. *De fide et symbolo.* In *Sancti Aurelii Augustini Hipponensis Episcopi Opuscula.* Edited by Antonio Merino. Madrid, 1800.

——. *De utilitate credendi ad Honoratum.* In *Sancti Aurelii Augustini Hipponensis Episcopi Opuscula.* Edited by Antonio Merino. Madrid, 1800.

——. *De catechizandis rudibus.* In *Sancti Aurelii Augustini Hipponensis Episcopi Opuscula.* Edited by Antonio Merino. Madrid, 1800.

——. *De vera religione.* In *Sancti Aurelii Augustini Hipponensis Episcopi Opuscula.* Edited by Antonio Merino. Madrid, 1800.

Biblia sacra vulgatae editionis Sixti V. pontificis maximi jussu recognita, et Clementis VIII. auctoritate edita. Lyon, 1827.

Bocanegra, Mathías de. *Avto General de Fee.* Mexico, 1649.

Calvin, Jean. *Institutes of the Christian Religion.* 2 vols. Philadelphia, 1960.

Cano, Melchor. "Cénsura y parecer que dio contra el Instituto de los Padres Jesuitas." British Library ms. Cod. Eg. 453. N.p., n.d.

——. *De locis theologicis.* Salamanca, 1563.

Canones et decreta sacrosancti oecvmenici et generalis Concilii Tridentini svb Pavlo III, Ivlio III, Pio IIII pontificibvs max. Venice, 1564.

Canons and Decrees of the Council of Trent. Edited and trans. by H. J. Schroeder. Rockford, Ill., 1978.

Cárdenas, Juan de. *Los problemas y secretos marauillosos de las Indias.* Mexico, 1591.

Carochi, Horacio. *Grammar of the Mexican Language with an Explanation of Its Adverbs (1645).* Translated and edited by, with commentary by James Lockhart. Stanford, 2001.

Castillo, Hernando de. *Cancionero general nueuamente añadido.* Toledo, 1520.

Castro, Alfonso de. *Aduersus omnes haereses.* Cologne, 1549.

——. *De justa haereticorum punitione.* Madrid, 1773.

——. "Utrum indigenae novi orbis instruendi sint in mysteriis theologicis et artibus liberalibus" [ms., Salamanca, 1543]. Edited by Juan B. Olaechea Labayen. *Anuario de estudios americanos* 15 (1958).

Cervantes, Miguel de. *Don Quijote.* Madrid, 2005 [1605].

Ciruelo, Pedro. *Reprouación de las supersticiones y hechizerías.* Edited by Alva V. Ebersole. Valencia, 1978 [1530].

Cochlaeus, Johannes. *Adversus cucullatum Minotaurum Vuittenbergensem.* S. Victor bei Mainz, 1548.

——. *Historiae Hvssitarvm libri dvodecim.* S. Victor bei Mainz, 1549.

——. *Zweyn sermon, von Mari der muter Gottes, Einer S. Jeronymi, zu irem Job, Der Ander Mart. Lutheri, zu ihrer Schmach, Mit Göttlicher schrifft verantworter und widergelegt.* S. Victor bei Mainz, 1548.

"Copilación de las Instrucciones del Oficio de la Santa Inquisición hechas en Toledo, año mil y quinientos y setenta y uno." In *Introducción a la inquisición española.* Edited by Miguel Jiménez Montserín. Madrid, 1980.

Cortés, Hernán. *Cartas de relación.* Edited by Ángel Delgado Gómez. Madrid, 1993.

Covarrubias y Leyva, Diego de. *In Bonifacii Octavi Constitvtionvm, quae incipit, alma mater, svb titvl. de sentient. Excommunicat. Lib. 6 Comentarii.* In *Opera.* Vol. 1 of 2. Antwerp, 1610–14.

——. *In constitvtionibis secvndae ex rvbrica de pactis lib. VI. cvivsqve initvm, quamuis pactum.* In *Opera.* Vol. 1 of 2. Antwerp, 1610–14.

——. *Qvatvor libros variarvm resolvtionvm.* In *Opera.* Vol. 2 of 2. Antwerp, 1610–14.

Cuervo, Justo, ed. *Historiadores del Convento de San Esteban de Salamanca.* 3 vols. Salamanca, 1915.

Decrees of the Ecumenical Councils. Edited by Norman P. Tanner. Washington, D.C., 1990.

Decretales Gregorii IX. Lyon, 1671.

Decretum Magistri Gratiani. Lipsia, 1922.

Delbene, Thomas. *De officio S. Inquisitionis circa haeresim.* Lyon, 1680.

del Río, Martín. *Disquisitionum magicarum.* Louvain, 1600.

Díaz del Castillo, Bernal. *Historia verdadera de la conquista de Nueva España*. Mexico, 1939.

Durán, Diego. *Historia de las Indias de Nueva España e Islas de la Tierra Firme*. Edited by Ángel Ma. Garibay K. Mexico, 1984.

Efemérides de la Real y Pontificia Universidad de México según sus libros de claustros. Edited by Alberto María Carreño. Vol. 1 of 2. Mexico, 1963.

Erasmus, Desiderius. *The Education of a Christian Prince*. Edited by Lisa Jardine. Cambridge Texts in the History of Political Thought. Cambridge, 1997.

———. *Ten Colloquies*. Translated by Craig R. Thompson. New York, 1986.

Ercilla, Alonso. *La Araucana*. Santiago, 1910 [1578].

Eimeric, Nicolau. *Directorium Inquisitorum . . . cum commentariis Francisci Pegñae*. Venice, 1595.

Fernández del Castillo, Francisco, ed. *Libros y libreros en el siglo XVI*. Mexico, 1914.

Foster, Kenelm, trans., ed. and intro. *The Life of Saint Thomas Aquinas: Biographical Documents*. London, 1959.

Garcés, Julián. "Carta a la Santidad de Paulo III." In *Bulario de la Iglesia mejicana: Documentos relativos a erecciones desmembraciones, etc., de Diócesis mejicanas*. Edited by Jesús García Gutiérrez. Mexico, 1951.

García Gutiérrez, Jesús, ed. *Bulario de la Iglesia mejicana: Documentos relativos a erecciones desmembraciones, etc. de Diócesis mejicanas*. Mexico, 1951.

Giles of Rome. *On Ecclesiastical Power/De ecclesiastica potestate*. Translated with intro. by Arthur P. Monahan. Texts and Studies in Religion. Vol. 41. Lewiston; Queenston; Lampeter, 1990.

Gómez, R. "Nómina del Tribunal de la Inquisición de Nueva España, 1571–1646." *Boletín del Archivo General de la Nación* [Mexico] 36 (1955).

Gonsalves de Mello, José Antônio, ed. *Confissões de Pernambuco, 1594–1595: Primeira visitação do Santo Ofício ás partes do Brasil*. Recife, 1970.

González de Cossío, Francisco, ed. *Crónicas de la Compañía de Jesús en la Nueva España*. Mexico, 1979.

González Dávila, Gil. *Teatro eclesiástico de la primitiva iglesia de las Indias occidentales, vidas de svs arzobispos, obispos, y cosas memorables de svs sedes*. Madrid, 1649.

Gui, Bernard. *Practica inquisitionis hereticae pravitatis*. Paris, 1886.

Hobbes, Thomas. *Leviathan: Or the Matter, Forme and Power of a Commonwealth, Ecclesiasticall and Civil*. Edited with intro. by Michael Oakeshott. Oxford, 1946.

Index et cathologus librorum prohibitorum, mandato . . . Gasparis a Qurioga . . . in regnis Hispaniarum Generalis Inquisitoris denuo editus. Madrid, 1583.

Index Librorvm Prohibitorvm, cvm regvlis confectis per Patres a Tridentina Synodo delectos, auctoritate Pij IV. primum editus . . . Rome, 1593.

Index Librorvm Prohibitorvm, cvm regvlis confectis per Patres a Tridentina Synodo delectos, auctoritate Sanctifs. D. N. Pii IIII, Pont. Max. comprobatus. Venice, 1564.

Index Librorvm Prohibitorvm et Expvrgatorvm . . . Bernardi de Sandoval et Roxas . . . Madrid, 1612.

Jerome, St. *The Jerome Biblical Commentary*. 2 vols. Edited by Raymond E. Brown et al. Foreword by Augustin Cardenal Bea. Englewood Cliffs, N.J., 1968.

John of Paris. *On Royal and Papal Power*. Translated with intro. by J. A. Watt. Toronto, 1971.

Las Casas, Bartolomé de. *Brevíssima relación de la destrucción de las Indias.* Seville, 1552.

Lazarillo de Tormes. Madrid, 1987 [c. 1554].

Ledesma, Bartolomé de. *De septem nouae legis sacramentis summarium.* Mexico, 1566.

León [Pinelo], Antonio de. *Epítome de la Biblioteca Oriental i Occidental, Náutica i Geográfica...* Madrid, 1629.

———. *Qvestión moral Si el Chocolate quebranta el ayuno Eclesiástico.* Madrid, 1636.

Liber Sextus Decretalium Bonifacij VIII, Clementinas, Extrauagantes communes, et cetera. Venice, 1615.

Lorenzana, Francisco Antonio de, ed. *Concilios provinciales primero, y segundo, celebrados en la muy noble, y muy leal ciudad de México, presidiendo el Illmo. y Rmo. Señor D. Fr. Alonso de Montúfar, en los años de 1555, y 1565.* Mexico, 1769.

———. *Concilium mexicanum provinciale III. Celebratum mexici anno MDLXXXV. praeside D.D. Petro Moya, et Contreras archiepiscopo ejusdem urbis etc.* Mexico, 1770.

Luis de Granada. *Libro de oración y meditación.* Madrid, 1999 [c. 1561].

———. *Meditaciones muy devotas, sobre algvnos passos y mysterios principales de la vida de nuestro Saluador...* Salamanca, 1579.

Luis de León. *De los nombres de Cristo.* Edited by Cristóbal Cuevas. Madrid, 1997.

Luther, Martin. *The Babylonian Captivity of the Church.* In *Martin Luther's Basic Theological Writings.* Edited by Timothy F. Lull. Minneapolis, 2005.

———. *Freedom of a Christian.* In *Martin Luther's Basic Theological Writings.* Edited by Timothy F. Lull. Minneapolis, 2005.

Mariscal Hay, Beatriz, ed. *Carta del padre Pedro de Morales de la Compañía de Iesús. Para el muy reverendo Padre Everardo Mercuriano, general de la misma Compañía. En que se da relación de la festividad que en esta insigne Ciudad de México se hizo este año de setenta y ocho, en la collocación de las sanctas reliquias que nuestro muy santo Padre Gregorio XIII les embió.* Mexico, 2000.

Martínez Díez, Gonzalo, ed. *Bulario de la Inquisición española: Hasta la muerte de Fernando el Católico.* Madrid, 1998.

Molina, Luis de. *On Divine Foreknowledge: Part IV of the* Concordia. Translated with intro. and notes by Alfred J. Freddoso. Ithaca, 1988.

Monteiro, Pedro. "Catalogo dos revedores dos livros e qualificadores do Santo Officio, que tem servido nas tres inquisições." In *Noticia geral das Santas Inquisições deste reino.* Lisbon, 1750.

Muñoz, Diego. *Descripción de la provincia de San Pedro y San Pablo de Michoacán, en las Indias de la Nueva España.* Introduction by José Ramírez Flores. Guadalajara, 1965 [c. 1588].

Páramo, Luis de. *De origine et progressv oficii sanctae inquisitionis.* Madrid, 1598.

Peña, Francisco. "De expurgendis juris consultorum libris abolendisque falsis eorum dogmatibus. Facilis et breuis methodus." Archivio Segreto Vaticano, Nunziature Diverse 264. [Rome], 1577.

———, ed. *Litterae apostolicae diversorvm svmmorvm pontificvm Pro Officio Sanctissimae Inquisitionis.* Venice, 1595.

Peters, E. M., ed. and trans. *Heresy and Authority in Medieval Europe: Documents in Translation.* Philadelphia, 1980.

Pius V. *Bvlla confirmationis et novae concessionis priuilegiorum Mendicantium.* Mexico, 1568.

Plato. *Gorgias.* Translated by Robin Waterfield. Oxford, 1994.

Plaza y Jaén, Cristóbal Bernardo de la. *Crónica de la real y pontificia universidad de México.* Paleographic version with preface, notes and appendix by Nicolás Rangel. Mexico, 1931.

Proceso inquisitorial del cacique de Tetzcoco, don Carlos Ometochtzin, (Chichimeca-tecotl). Mexico, 1980.

Puga, Vasco de. *Prousiones cédulas Instruciones de su Magestad: ordenanças de difuntos y audiencia, para la Buena expedición de los negocios y administración de justicia: y gouernación desta nueua España: y para el buen tratamiento y obseruación de los yndios.* Mexico, 1563.

Quevedo, Francisco de. *El buscón.* Madrid, 1990.

Ramírez L., Edelmira, ed. *María Rita Vargas, María Lucía Celis: Beatas embaucadoras de la colonia: de un cuaderno que recogió la Inquisición a un iluso, Antonio Rodríguez Colodrero, solicitante de escrituras y vidas.* Mexico, 1988.

Raymond of Peñafort. *Summa ad manuscriptorum fidem recognita et emendate.* Verona, 1744.

Relación del Avto General de la Fee. Mexico, 1659.

Repertorium Inquisitorum pravitatis haereticae. Valencia, 1494.

Reusch, Heinrich, ed. *Die Indices Librorum Prohibitorum des Sechzenten Jahrhunderts.* Tübingen, 1886.

Ribadeneyra, Pedro de. "Historia del cisma de Inglaterra." In *Historias de la contrar-reforma.* Introduction and notes by Eusebio Rey. Madrid, 1945 [1588].

Rojas, Juan de. *De succesionibus, de haereticis et singularia in fidei favorem.* Salamanca, 1581.

Santa María, Juan de. *Relación del martyrio qve seys padres Descalços Franciscos y veynte Iapones christianos padecieron en Iapón . . . hecha por Fr. Iuan de Santa María Prouincial de la Prouincia de S. Ioseph de los Descalços; van añadidos en esta impres-sión tres capítulos de Francisco Peña, Auditor de Rota, donde se muestra que aquella muerte fue verdadero martyrio.* Rome, 1599.

Scholes, Frances V., and Eleanor B. Adams, eds. *Proceso contra Tzintzicha Tangaxoan, el Caltzontzin,formado por Nuño de Guzmán, año de 1530.* Mexico, 1952.

Simancas, Diego de. *De catholicis institutionibus, Liber ad praecauendus, et extirpandas haereses admodum necessarius.* Ferrara, 1692 [1552].

———. "La vida y cosas notables del señor Obispo de Zamora don Diego de Siman-cas . . . " In *Autobiografías y memorias.* Edited by M. Serrano y Sanz. Madrid, 1905.

Suárez, Francisco. *Defensio fidei catholicae et apostolicae adversvs Anglicanae sectae errores . . .* Cologne, 1614.

———. *Disputationes de censuris in communi, excommunicatione, suspensione et inter-cito, itemque de irregularitate.* In *Opera omnia.* Vol. 23 of 28. Edited by Carlos Bertón. Paris, 1856–78.

———. *Lectiones de Fide: Anno 1583 in Collegio Romano.* Edited by Kart Deuringer. Granada, 1967.

Toro, Alfonso, ed. *Los Judíos en la Nueva España: Documentos del siglo XVI, corre-spondientes al ramo de Inquisición.* 2d ed. Mexico, 1982.

Torquemada, Juan de. *Summae ecclesiasticae.* Salamanca, 1560 [c. 1450].

———. *Tractatus factus contra avisamentum Basiliensium quod non liceat appellare a Concilo ad Papam.* N.p., c. 1436.

Valdés, Juan de. *Diálogo de doctrina cristiana.* With biographical and critical notes by B. Foster Stockwell. Buenos Aires, 1946 [1529].

Vallejo, Luis. *Sermón que predicó . . . a la Beatificación de la Bienauenturada Madre Sancta Theresa de Iesús.* Mexico, 1614.

Vázquez de Tapia, Bernardino. *Relación de méritos y servicios del conquistador Bernardino. Vázquez de Tapia, vecino y regidor de esta gran ciudad de Tenustitlán, México.* Edited by Jorge Gurría Lacroix. Mexico, 1953.

Vignate, Ambrosius de. *Tractatvs de haeresi . . . cum commentarijs Francisci Pegnae sacrae theologiae et iuris vtriusque doctoris.* Rome, 1581.

Villadiego, Gonzalo. *Tractatus contra hereticam prauitatem.* Salamanca, 1519.

Vitoria, Francisco de. *Political Writings.* Edited by Anthony Pagden and Jeremy Lawrance. Cambridge, 1991.

Wild (Ferus), Johann. *Exegesis in Epistolam Beati Pauli ad Romanos.* Paris, 1559.

Zumárraga, Juan de. *La doctrina breue muy prouechosa.* Mexico, 1543.

Secondary Printed Sources

Aguilera González, Francisco María. *Concepto de teología en el padre Francisco Suárez.* Mexico, 2000.

Aiton, Arthur Scott. "Real Hacienda in New Spain under the First Viceroy." *Hispanic American Historical Review* 6 (1926).

Albaret, Laurent, ed. *Les Inquisiteurs: Portraits de défenseurs de la foi en Languedoc (XIIIe–XIVe siècles).* Toulouse, 2001.

Alberro, Solange. *La actividad del Santo Oficio de la Inquisición en Nueva España, 1571–1700.* Mexico, 1981.

———. *El águila y la cruz: Orígenes religiosos de la conciencia criolla: México, Siglos XVI–XVII.* Mexico, 1999.

———. *Del gachupín al criollo: O de cómo los españoles de México dejaron de serlo.* Mexico, 1992.

———. *Inquisición y sociedad en México, 1571–1700.* Mexico, 1988.

Alberro, Solange, and Serge Gruzinski. *Introducción a la historia de las mentalidades.* Seminario de Historia de las Mentalidades y Religión en el México Colonial. Mexico, 1979.

Alcalá, Ángel. "Control inquisitorial de humanistas y escritores." In *Inquisición española y mentalidad inquisitorial.* Edited by Ángel Alcalá. Barcelona, 1984.

———. "Herejía y jerarquía: La polémica sobre el Tribunal de Inquisición como desacato y usurpación de la jurisdicción episcopal." In *Perfiles jurídicos de la inquisición española.* Edited by José Antonio Escudero. Madrid, 1989.

———. *Literatura y ciencia ante la Inquisición Española.* Madrid, 2001.

———, ed. *Inquisición española y mentalidad inquisitorial.* Barcelona, 1984.

Alcalá-Zamora, José N., ed. *La vida cotidiana en la España de Velázquez.* Madrid, 1999.

Alejandre García, Juan Antonio. *El veneno de Dios: La Inquisición de Sevilla ante el delito de solicitación en confesión.* Madrid, 1994.

Alejandre García, Juan Antonio, and María Jesús Torquemada. *Palabra de hereje: La inquisición de Sevilla ante el delito de proposiciones.* Seville, 1998.

Alpert, Michael. *Criptojudaísmo e Inquisición en los siglos XVII y XVIII: La ley en la que quiere vivir y morir.* Barcelona, 2001.

Altman, Ida. *Emigrants and Society: Extremadura and America in the Sixteenth Century.* Berkeley, 1989.

Ambrosetti, Giovanni. *Il diritto naturale della Riforma cattolica: Una giustificazione storica del sistema di Suárez.* Milan, 1951.

Asensio, Eugenio. "Censura inquisitorial de libros en los Siglos XVI y XVII. Fluctuaciones. Decadencia." In *El libro antiguo español.* 5 vols. General eds. María Luisa López-Vidriero and Peter M. Cátedra. Salamanca, 1988–99.

Avilés, Miguel. *Erasmo y la Inquisición: El libelo de Valladolid y la Apología de Erasmo contra los frailes españoles.* Madrid, 1980.

Bacigalupo, Marvyn Helen. *A Changing Perspective: Attitudes toward Creole Society in New Spain (1521–1610).* London, 1981.

Bailey, F. G. *The Witch Hunt, or, The Triumph of Morality.* Ithaca, 2000.

Bainton, Roland H. *Here I Stand: A Life of Martin Luther.* New York, 1950.

Bakhtin, Mikhail. *Rabelais and His World.* Translated by Hélène Iswolsky. Bloomington, 1984.

Barcia Trelles, Camilo. *Internacionalistas españoles del siglo XVI, Francisco Suárez (1546–1617).* Valladolid, 1938.

Barlow, R. H. *Tlatelolco, fuentes e historia.* Edited by Jesús Monjarás-Ruiz, Elena Limón, María de la Cruz Paillés H. Mexico, 1989.

Barrientos Grandón, Javier. *La cultura jurídica en la Nueva España: Sobre la recepción de la tradición jurídica europea en el virreinato.* Mexico, 1993.

Bastit, Michel. *Naissance de la loi moderne: La pensée de la loi de saint Thomas à Suarez.* Paris, 1990.

Bataillon, Marcel. *Erasmo y España: Estudios sobre la historia espiritual del siglo XVI.* Translated by Antonio Alatorre. Mexico, 1966.

———. "Honneur et Inquisition: Michel Servet poursuivi per l'inquisition espagnole." *Bulletin Hispanique* 27 (1925).

Baudot, George. *Utopia and History: The First Chroniclers of Mexican Civilization (1520–1569).* Translated by Bernard R. Ortiz de Montellano and Thelma Ortiz de Montellano. Niwot, Colo., 1995.

Baudot, George, and María Águeda Méndez. *Amores prohibidos: La palabra condenada en el México de los virreyes: antología de coplas y versos censurados por la Inquisición de México.* Foreword by Elías Trabulse. Mexico, 1997

Bécares Botas, Vicente. "Compras de libros para la biblioteca universitaria salmantina del renacimiento." In *El libro antiguo español.* 5 vols. General eds. María Luisa López Vidriero and Peter M. Cátedra. Salamanca, 1988–99.

Becker, Howard. *Through Values to Social Interpretation: Essays on Social Contexts, Actions, Types, and Prospects.* Durham, 1950.

Behar, Ruth. "Sex and Sin, Witchcraft and the Devil in Late-Colonial Mexico." *American Ethnologist* 14 (1987).

Belda Plans, Juan. *La escuela de Salamanca y la renovación de la teología en el siglo XVI.* 2 vols. Madrid, 2000.

Beltrán de Heredia, Vicente. *Domingo Báñez y las controversias sobre la gracia: Textos y documentos.* Madrid, 1968.

Bennassar, Bartolomé. "Le modèle sexuel: L'Inquisition d'Aragon et la repressión des péchés 'abominables.' " In Bartolomé Bennassar, avec Jean-Pierre Dedieu et al. *Inquisition espagnole: XVIe–XIXe siècle.* Paris, 1979.

Bennassar, Bartolomé, avec Jean-Pierre Dedieu et al. *Inquisition espagnole: XVIe–XIXe siècle.* Paris, 1979.

Beristáin de Souza, José Mariano. *Biblioteca hispanoamericana septentrional.* 3 vols. Mexico, 1981 [1810–16].

Bertrán i Roigé, Primo. *Catálogo del Archivo del Colegio de España.* Bologna, 1981.

Bilinkoff, Jodi. *The Avila of Saint Teresa: Religious Reform in a Sixteenth-Century City.* Ithaca, 1989.

Blázquez Miguel, Juan. *Inquisición y criptojudaísmo.* Madrid, 1988.

———. *La Inquisición en Albacete.* Albacete, 1985.

———. *La Inquisición en Cataluña: El tribunal del Santo Oficio de Barcelona, 1487–1820.* Foreword by Henry Kamen. Toledo, 1990.

Bollème, Geneviève. *La Bibliothèque bleue: Littérature populaire en France du XVIIe au XIXe siècle.* Julliard, 1971.

Bombín Pérez, Antonio. *La Inquisición en el País Vasco: El tribunal de Logroño (1570–1610).* Bilbao, 1997.

Borromeo, Agostino. "The Inquisition and Inquisitorial Censorship." In *Catholicism in Early Modern Europe: A Guide to Research.* Reformation Guides to Research. Vol. 2. Edited by John O'Malley. St. Louis, 1988.

———. "Inquisizione spagnola e libri proibiti in Sicilia ed in Sardegna durante il XVI secolo." *Annuario dell'istituto storico italiano per l'età moderna e contemporanea* 35–36 (1983–84).

Bourdieu, Pierre. *Homo Academicus.* Translated by Peter Collier. Stanford, 1988.

Bouza, Fernando. *Comunicación, conocimiento y memoria en la España de los siglos XVI y XVII.* Salamanca, 2000.

Boyd-Bowman, Peter. *Índice geobiográfico de cuarenta mil pobladores españoles de América en el siglo XVI.* Bogotá, 1964.

Boyer, Richard. *Lives of the Bigamists: Marriage, Family, and Community in Colonial Mexico.* Albuquerque, 1995.

Brading, D. A. *The First America: The Spanish Monarchy, Creole Patriots, and the Liberal State, 1492–1867.* Cambridge, 1991.

Braga, Paulo Drumond. *A Inquisição nos Açores.* Ponta Delgada, Azores, 1997.

Bravo Ugarte, José. *Diócesis y obispos de la iglesia mexicana (1519–1965).* Mexico, 1965.

Bristol, Joan Cameron. *Christians, Blasphemers, and Witches: Afro-Mexican Ritual Practice in the Seventeenth Century.* Albuquerque, 2007.

Brown, Peter. *Augustine of Hippo.* Berkeley, 1967.

Brugada i Gutiérrez-Ravé, Josep. *Nicolau Eimeric (1320–1399) i la polèmica inquisitorial.* Barcelona, 1998.

Bruno, Cayetano. *Derecho público de la Iglesia en Indias: Estudio histórico-jurídico.* Salamanca, 1967.

Bujanda, J. M. de. *Index des livres interdits.* 11 vols. Sherbrooke, Quebec; Geneva, 1984.

Burke, Peter. *The French Historical Revolution: The* Annales *School, 1929–1989.* Stanford, 1990.

Burkhart, Louise M. *Holy Wednesday: A Nahua Drama from Early Colonial Mexico.* Philadelphia, 1996.

Bustos, Tomás de. *Santo Domingo de Guzmán: Predicador del Evangelio.* Salamanca, 2000.

Caballero, Fermín. *Conquenses ilustres.* Vol. 2: *Vida de Melchor Cano.* Madrid, 1871.

Cabrero de Anta, Marcelino, Arturo Alonso Lobo, and Sabino Alonso Morán. *Comentarios al derecho canónico.* Vol. 1 of 4. Foreword by Francisco Barbado Viejo. Madrid, 1963.

Cahnman, Werner J. *Weber and Toennies: Comparative Sociology in Historical Perspective.* Edited [and trans.] with intro. by Joseph B. Maier, Judith Marcus, and Zoltán Tarr. New Brunswick, 1995.

Cárdenas, Alejandra. *Hechicería, saber y transgresión: Afromestizas ante la inquisición (Acapulco: 1621–1622).* Chilpancingo, Mexico, 1997.

Carías, Marcos. *Crónicas y cronistas de la conquista de Honduras.* Tegucigalpa, Honduras, 1998.

Caro Baroja, Julio. *Las brujas y su mundo.* 2 vols. Madrid, 1968.

———. *El Señor Inquisidor y otras vidas por oficio.* Madrid, 1968.

Carrasco, Rafael. *Inquisición y represión sexual en Valencia: Historia de los sodomitas, 1565–1785.* Barcelona, 1985.

Carrato, José Ferreira. *Igreja, iluminismo e escolas mineiras coloniais (notas sôbre a cultura da decadência setecentista).* São Paulo, 1968.

Carreño, Alberto María. *Fr. Domingo de Betanzos: Fundador en la Nueva España de la venerable orden dominica.* Mexico, 1924.

———. *La Real y Pontificia Universidad de México 1536–1865.* Mexico, 1961.

Carrete Parrondo, Carlos. *El judaísmo español y la Inquisición.* Madrid, 1992

Carrillo Cázares, Alberto. *Vasco de Quiroga: La pasión por el derecho: El pleito con la Orden de San Agustín (1558–1562).* 2 vols. Zamora, Morelia, 2003.

Carro, Venancio P. *La teología y los teólogos-juristas españoles ante la conquista de América.* 2 vols. Madrid, 1944.

Castañeda Delgado, Paulino, and Juan Marchena Fernández. *La jerarquía de la Iglesia en Indias: El episcopado americano, 1500–1850.* Madrid, 1992.

Castillo, Santiago. *Alfonso de Castro y el problema de las leyes penales: O la obligatoriedad moral de las leyes humanes.* Salamanca, 1941.

Cavarra, Angela Adriana, ed. *Inquisizione e Indice nei secoli XVI–XVIII: Testi e immagini nelle raccolte casanatensi.* Rome, 1998.

Cerrón Puga, Ma. Luisa. "La censura literaria en el *Index* de Quiroga (1583–1584)." In *Actas del IV Congreso Internacional de la Asociación Internacional Siglo de Oro.* Edited by María Cruz García and Alicia Cordón Mesa. Alcalá, 1998.

Cervantes, Fernando. *The Devil in the New World: The Impact of Diabolism in New Spain.* New Haven, 1994.

Chartier, Roger. *Cultural History: Between Practices and Representations.* Translated by Lydia G. Cochrane. Ithaca, 1988.

———. *The Cultural Uses of Print in Early Modern France.* Translated by Lydia Cochrane. Princeton, 1988.

Châtellier, Louis. *The Europe of the Devout: The Catholic Reformation and the Formation of a New Society.* Translated by Jean Birrell. Cambridge, 1987.

Chinchilla Aguilar, Ernesto. *La Inquisición en Guatemala.* Guatemala, 1953.

Chocano Mena, Magdalena. *Fortaleza docta: Élite letrada y dominación social en México colonial (Siglos XVI–XVII).* Barcelona, 2000.

Chodorow, Stanley. *Christian Political Theory and Church Politics in the Mid-Twelfth Century: The Ecclesiology of Gratian's Decretum.* Berkeley, 1972.

Chrisman, Miriam Usher. *Lay Culture, Learned Culture: Books and Social Change in Strasbourg, 1480–1599.* New Haven, 1982.

Christian, William, Jr. *Local Religion in Sixteenth-Century Spain.* Princeton, 1981.

Chuchiak, John, IV. "La inquisición Indiana y la extirpación de idolatrías: El castigo y la represión en el Provisorato de Indios en Yucatán, 1570–1690." In *Nuevas perspectivas sobre el castigo de la heterodoxia indígena en la Nueva España, siglos XVI–XVIII.* Edited by Ana de Zaballa Beascoechea. Bilbao, 2005.

Cifuentes, Bárbara, con la colaboración de Lucina García. *Letras sobre voces: Multilingüismo a través de la historia.* Mexico, 1998.

Clendinnen, Inga. *Ambivalent Conquests: Maya and Spaniard in Yucatan, 1517–1570.* Cambridge, 1987.

Cline, Sarah. "The Spiritual Conquest Reexamined: Baptism and Christian Marriage in Early Sixteenth-Century Mexico." In *The Church in Colonial Latin America.* Jaguar Books on Latin America, no. 21. Edited by John W. Schwaller. Wilmington, Del., 2000.

Cohen, Thomas M. *Fire of Tongues: António Vieira and the Missionary Church in Brazil and Portugal.* Stanford, 1998.

Colish, Marcia L. *Medieval Foundations of the Western Intellectual Tradition, 400–1400.* New Haven, 1997.

Congreso Nacional de San Sebastián. *Brujología: Congreso de San Sebastián: ponencias y comunicaciones.* Madrid, c. 1975.

Contreras, Jaime. "La infraestructura social de la inquisición: Comisarios y familiares." In *Inquisición española y mentalidad inquisitorial.* Edited by Ángel Alcalá. Barcelona, 1984.

———. *El santo oficio de la inquisición en Galicia, 1560–1700: Poder, sociedad y cultura.* Madrid, 1982.

Contreras, Jaime, and Gustav Henningsen. "Forty-Four Thousand Cases of the Spanish Inquisition (1540–1700): Analysis of a Historical Data Bank." Translated by Anne Bonn. In *The Inquisition in Early Modern Europe.* Edited by Gustav Henningsen and John Tedeschi in assoc. with Charles Amiel. De Kalb, Ill., 1986.

Corcuera de Mancera, Sonia. *Del amor al temor: Borrachez, catequesis y control en la Nueva España, 1555–1771.* Mexico, 1994.

———. *El fraile, el indio, y el pulque: Evangelización y embriaguez en la Nueva España (1523–1548).* Mexico, 1991.

Coronas Tejada, Luis. *La Inquisición en Jaén.* Jaén, 1991.

Corsarios franceses e ingleses en la Inquisición de la Nueva España, Siglo XVI. Mexico, 1945.

Cortés Vázquez, Luis. *La vida estudiantil en la Salamanca clásica.* Salamanca, 1996.

Costa Pôrto, José da. *Nos tempos do visitador: Subsídio ao estudo da vida colonial pernambucana, nos fins do século XVI.* Recife, 1968.

Coujou, Jean-Paul. *Suárez et la refondation de la métaphysique comme ontologie: Étude et traduction de l'Index détaillé de la métaphysique d'Aristote de F. Suárez.* Louvain, 1999.

Cowan, Alexander. *Urban Europe, 1500–1700.* London, 1998.

Cressy, John. "Literacy in Seventeenth-Century England: More Evidence." *Journal of Interdisciplinary History* 8 (1974).

Crosby, Alfred W. *The Columbian Exchange: Biological and Cultural Consequences of 1492.* Foreword by Otto von Mering. Westport, 1973.

Cuevas, Mariano. *Historia de la Iglesia en México.* 5 vols. Mexico, 1927.

Cutter, Charles R. *The Legal Culture of Northern New Spain, 1700–1810.* Albuquerque, 1995.

Curcio-Nagy, Linda. *Great Festivals of Colonial Mexico City: Performing Power and Identity.* Albuquerque, 2004.

Dadson, Trevor J. "La librería de Cristóbal López (1606): Estudio y análisis de una librería madrileña de principios del siglo XVII." In *El libro antiguo español.* 5 vols. General eds. María Luisa López-Vidriero and Peter M. Cátedra. Salamanca, 1988–99.

———. *Libros, lectores y lecturas: Estudios sobre bibliotecas particulares españolas del Siglo del Oro.* Madrid, 1998.

Darnton, Robert. *The Great Cat Massacre, and Other Episodes of French Cultural History.* New York, 1984.

———. *The Literary Underground of the Old Regime.* Cambridge, Mass., 1980.

Davis, Natalie Zemon. *Fiction in the Archives: Pardon Tales and Their Tellers in Sixteenth-Century France.* Stanford, 1987.

———. "Printing and the People." In *Society and Culture in Early Modern France.* Stanford, 1975.

de la Cruz de Arteaga y Falguera, Cristina. *Una mitra sobre dos mundos: La de don Juan de Palafox y Mendoza, Obispo de Puebla de los Ángeles y de Osma.* Puebla, 1992.

de la Fuente, Vicente. *La retención de Bulas en España ante la historia y el derecho.* 2 vols. Madrid, 1865.

de la Torre, Antonio. "La Universidad de Alcalá. Datos para su estudio. Cátedras y catedráticos desde la inauguración del Colegio de San Ildefonso hasta San Lucas de 1519." *Revista de Archivos, Bibliotecas y Muesos* 20 (1909) and 21 (1909).

———. "La Universidad de Alcalá: Estado de la enseñanza según las visitas de cátedras de 1524–25 a 1527–28." In *Homenaje a Menéndez Pidal.* Madrid, 1925.

de la Torre Villar, Ernesto. *Breve historia del libro en México.* Mexico, 1999.

———. *Don Juan de Palafox y Mendoza: Pensador político.* Mexico, 1997.

de los Reyes, Jesús Aguado. *Fortuna y miseria en la Sevilla del siglo XVII.* Sevilla, 1996.

de los Reyes Gómez, Fermín. *El libro en España y América: Legislación y censura, siglos XV–XVIII.* 2 vols. Madrid, 2000.

Dealy, Ross. *The Politics of an Erasmian Lawyer: Vasco de Quiroga.* Malibu, 1976.

Deane, Herbert A. *The Political and Social Ideas of St. Augustine.* New York, 1963.

Dedieu, Jean-Pierre. *L'Administration de la foi: L'Inquisition de Tolède (XVIe–XVIIIe siècle).* Madrid, 1989.

———. "The Archives of the Holy Office of Toledo as a Source for Historical Anthropology." In *The Inquisition in Early Modern Europe: Studies on Sources and Methods.* Edited by Gustav Henningsen and John Tedeschi, in assoc. with Charles Amiel. De-Kalb, Ill., 1986.

Defourneaux, Marcelin. *L'Inquisition espagnole et les livres français au XVIIIe siècle.* Paris, 1963.

Deive, Carlos Esteban. *Heterodoxia e inquisición en Santo Domingo, 1492–1822.* Santo Domingo, 1983.

Del Col, Andrea. *L'Inquisizione in Italia: Dal XII al XXI secolo.* Milan, 2006.

Deleito y Piñuela, José. *La mala vida en la España de Felipe IV.* Foreword by Gregorio Marañón. Madrid, 1948.

Delisle, Léopold. *Notice sur les manuscrits de Bernard Gui.* Paris, 1879.

Delumeau, Jean. *Catholicism between Luther and Voltaire: A New View of the Counter-Reformation.* Introduction by John Bossy. London, 1977.

Díaz, José Simón. "La literatura medieval castellana y sus ediciones españoles de 1501 a 1560." In *El libro antiguo español.* 5 vols. General eds. María Luisa López-Vidriero and Peter M. Cátedra. Salamanca, 1988–99.

D'Olwer, Luis Nicolau. *Fray Bernardino de Sahagún (1499–1590).* Translated by Mauricio J. Mixco. Foreword by Miguel León-Portilla. Salt Lake City, 1987.

Domínguez Guzmán, Aurora. *La imprenta en Sevilla en el siglo XVII (Catálogo y análisis de su producción) 1601–1650.* Seville, 1992.

Domínguez Ortiz, Antonio. *Autos de la inquisición de Sevilla (Siglo XVII).* Seville, 1994.

Donahue-Wallace, Kelly Thomas. "Prints and Printmakers in Viceregal Mexico City, 1600–1800." Ph.D. diss., University of New Mexico, 2000.

Dondaine, Antoine. "Le manuel de l'inquisiteur (1230–1330)." *Archivum Fratrum Praedicatorum* 18 (1947).

Douais, Célestin. "Préface." *Practica inquisitionis hereticae pravitatis.* Bernard Gui. Paris, 1886.

Douglas, Mary. *Purity and Danger: An Analysis of Concepts of Pollution and Taboo.* New York, 1966.

Duby, Georges. "The Diffusion of Cultural Patterns in Feudal Society." *Past and Present* 39 (1968).

Duffy, Eamon. *Saints and Sinners: A History of the Popes.* New Haven, 1997.

Duviols, Pierre. *La lutte contre les religions autochtones dans le Péru colonial: "L'extirpation de l'idolâtrie," entre 1532 et 1660.* Lima, 1971.

Ebright, Malcolm, and Rick Hendricks. *The Witches of Abiquiu: The Governor, the Priest, the Genízaro Indians, and the Devil.* Albuquerque, 2006.

Edwards, John. *The Spain of the Catholic Monarchs, 1474–1520.* Oxford, 2000.

Eire, Carlos M. N. *From Madrid to Purgatory: The Art and Craft of Dying in Sixteenth-Century Spain.* Cambridge, 1995.

———. *War Against the Idols: The Reformation of Worship from Erasmus to Calvin.* Cambridge, 1986.

Eisenstein, Elizabeth L. *The Printing Revolution in Early Modern Europe.* Cambridge, 1983.

Elliott, J. H. *Empires of the Atlantic World: Britain and Spain in America, 1492–1830*. New Haven, 2006.

——. *Imperial Spain, 1469–1716*. New York, 1963.

——. *Spain and Its World, 1500–1700*. New Haven, 1989.

Ennis, Arthur. *Fray Alonso de la Vera Cruz, O.S.A. (1507–1584): A Study of His Life and His Contributions to the Religious and Intellectual Affairs of Early Mexico*. Louvain, 1957.

Errera, Andrea. *Processus in causa fidei: L'evoluzione dei manuali inquisitoriali nei secoli XVI–XVII e il manuale inedito di un inquisitore perugino*. Bologna, 2000.

Escudero, José Antonio. "Inquisidor General y Consejo de la Suprema: Dudas sobre competencias en nombramientos." In *Perfiles jurídicos de la inquisición española*. Edited by José Antonio Escudero. Madrid, 1989.

——. "Los orígenes del 'Consejo de la Suprema Inquisición.'" In *Inquisición española y mentalidad inquisitorial*. Edited by Ángel Alcalá. Barcelona, 1984.

——, ed. *Intolerancia e Inquisición*. 3 vols. Madrid, 2005.

——, ed. *Perfiles jurídicos de la inquisición española*. Madrid, 1989.

Esperabé de Arteaga, Enrique. *Historia interna y pragmática de la Universidad de Salamanca*. 2 vols. Salamanca, 1914–17.

Espinel, José Luis. *San Esteban de Salamanca: Historia y guía (Siglos XIII–XX)*. Salamanca, 1995.

Espinosa, Ma. del Carmen. "Conflictos políticos y jurisdiccionales en la inquisición Episcopal a mediados del siglo XVI." In *Inquisición novohispana*. Edited by Noemí Quezada, Martha Eugenia Rodríguez, and Marcela Suárez. Mexico, 2000.

Eubel, Conradus, and Guillelmus van Gulik, eds. *Hierarchia Catholica Medii et Recentioris Aevi*. 5 vols. Regensburg, 1923–35.

Febvre, Lucien. *The Problem of Unbelief in the Sixteenth Century: The Religion of Rabelais*. Translated by Beatrice Gottlieb. Cambridge, Mass., 1982.

Febvre, Lucien, and Henri-Jean Martin. *The Coming of the Book: The Impact of Printing 1450–1800*. Translated by David Gerard. London, 1976.

Fernández, Luis Gil. *Panorama social del humanismo español, 1500–1800*. Madrid, 1997.

Fernández Álvarez, Manuel, ed. *La Universidad de Salamanca*. Vol. 2: *Atmósfera intelectual y perspectivas de investigación*. Salamanca, 1990.

Fernández Arruti, José Ángel. "La costumbre en la nueva codificación canónica." In *Le Nouveau Code de Droit Canonique/The New Code of Canon Law. Proceedings of the 5th International Congress of Canon Law*. Edited by M. Thériault and J. Thorn. Ottawa, 1986.

Fernández de Recas, Guillermo S. *Aspirantes americanos a cargos del Santo Oficio*. Foreword by Manuel Romero de Terreros. Mexico, 1956.

Few, Martha. *Women Who Lead Evil Lives: Gender, Religion, and the Politics of Power in Colonial Guatemala*. Austin, 2002.

Flint, Shirley Cushing. "The Martín Cortés Conspiracy Reexamined." *Sixteenth Century Journal* 39 (2008).

Flint, Thomas P. *Divine Providence: The Molinist Account*. Ithaca, 1998.

Flores, Jesús Romero. *Iconografía colonial*. Mexico, n/d.

Florescano, Enrique. *Memoria mexicana: Ensayo sobre la reconstrucción del pasado: Época prehispánica–1821.* Mexico, 1994.

Fragnito, Gigliola. *La Bibbia al rogo: La censura ecclesiastica e i volgarizzamenti della Scrittura (1471–1605).* Bologna, 1997.

———. "The Central and Peripheral Organization of Censorship." In *Church, Censorship and Culture in Early Modern Italy.* Edited by Gigliola Fragnito. Translated by Adrian Belton. Cambridge, 2001.

———, ed. *Church, Censorship and Culture in Early Modern Italy.* Translated by Adrian Belton. Cambridge, 2001.

Furet, François, et al. *Livre et société dans la France du XVIIIe siècle.* 2 vols. Paris, 1965–70.

Gacto, Enrique. "Aproximación al Derecho penal de la Inquisición." In *Perfiles jurídicos de la Inquisición española.* Edited by José Antonio Escudero. Madrid, 1989.

———. "Inquisición y censura en el Barroco." In *Sexo barroco y otras transgresiones premodernas.* Francisco Tomás y Valiente et al. Madrid, 1990.

Gallegos Rocafull, José Manuel. *El hombre y el mundo de los teólogos españoles de los siglos de oro.* Mexico, 1946.

———. *El pensamiento mexicano en los siglos XVI y XVII.* Mexico, 1951.

García Aguilar, Idalia. *Miradas aisladas, visiones conjuntas: Defensa del patrimonio documental mexicano.* Mexico, 2001.

García Cárcel, Ricardo. *Herejía y sociedad en el siglo XVI: La inquisición en Valencia 1530–1609.* Barcelona, 1979.

———. *La leyenda negra: Historia y opinión.* Madrid, 1998.

García Granados, Jorge. *El deán turbulento.* Guatemala, 1962.

García Icazbalceta, Joaquín. *Bibliografía mexicana del siglo XVI: Catálogo razonado de libros impresos en México de 1539 a 1600.* Mexico, 1954 [1886].

———. "La destrucción de antigüedades." In *Obras.* Vol. 2 of 10. Mexico, 1896.

———. *Don Fray Juan de Zumárraga, primer obispo y arzobispo de México.* Mexico, 1881.

———. "Fr. Bartolomé de Ledesma." In *Obras.* Vol. 3 of 10. Mexico, 1896.

———. "Fr. Pedro de Agurto." In *Obras.* Vol. 3 of 10. Mexico, 1896.

———. "La orden de predicadores en México." In *Obras.* Vol. 2 of 10. Mexico, 1896.

———. "El P. Pedro de Morales." In *Obras.* Vol. 3 of 10. Mexico, 1896.

García Ivars, Flora. *La represión en el Tribunal Inquisitorial de Granada, 1550–1819.* Madrid, 1991.

García-Molina Riquelme, Antonio. "El Auto de Fe de México de 1659: El saludador loco, López de Aponte." *Revista de la Inquisición* 3 (1994).

García Oro, José, and María José Portela Silva. *Monarquía y los libros en el Siglo de Oro.* Alcalá, 1999.

G[arcía] Villoslada, Ricardo. *La universidad de París durante los estudios de Francisco de Vitoria, O.P., 1507–1522.* Rome, 1938.

———, ed. *Historia de la Iglesia en España.* 5 vols. Madrid, 1976–80.

Geertz, Clifford. *Local Knowledge: Further Essays in Interpretive Anthropology.* New York, 1983.

Gerhard, Peter. *Historical Geography of New Spain, 1519–1821.* Cambridge, 1972.

Gibson, Charles. *The Aztecs under Spanish Rule: A History of the Indians of the Valley of Mexico, 1519–1810*. Stanford, 1964.

Gil, Juan. *Los conversos y la inquisición sevillana*. Seville, 2000.

Gil del Río, Alfredo. *La Santa Inquisición: Sus principales procesos contra la brujería en España*. Madrid, 2002.

Ginzburg, Carlo. *The Cheese and the Worms: The Cosmos of a Sixteenth-Century Miller*. Translated by John and Anne Tedeschi. Baltimore, 1980.

——. *The Night Battles: Witchcraft and Agrarian Cults in the Sixteenth and Seventeenth Centuries*. Translated by John and Anne Tedeschi. New York, 1985.

Giordano, María Laura. *María de Cazalla (1487–?)*. Madrid, 1998.

Given, James B. *Inquisition and Medieval Society: Power, Discipline, and Resistance in Languedoc*. Ithaca, 1997.

Godman, Peter. *The Saint as Censor: Robert Bellarmine between Inquisition and Index*. Leiden, 2000.

Gomes Moreira, José Aparecido. "Don Vasco de Quiroga. Pensamiento indígena y jurídico-teológico." Tesis de Maestría, Escuela Nacional de Antropología e Historia [Mexico], 1989.

Gonzalbo Aizpuru, Pilar. *Historia de la educación en la época colonial: La educación de los criollos y la vida urbana*. Mexico, 1999.

——. *Historia de la educación en la época colonial: El mundo indígena*. Mexico, 1990.

González Casanova, Pablo. "El pensamiento perseguido." In *Inquisición novohispana*. Edited by Noemí Quezada, Martha Eugenia Rodríguez, and Marcela Suárez. Mexico, 2000.

González de Cossío, Francisco. *La imprenta en México, 1594–1820: Cien adiciones a la obra de don José Toribio Medina*. Foreword by Agustín Millares Carlo. Mexico, 1947.

González de San Segundo, Miguel Ángel. "Tensiones y conflictos de la Inquisición en Indias: La pre-Inquisición o Inquisición primitiva (1493–1569)." In *Perfiles jurídicos de la Inquisición española*. Edited by José Antonio Escudero. Madrid, 1989.

González González, Enrique, with collaborator Víctor Gutiérrez Rodríguez. *Una república de lectores: Difusión y recepción de la obra de Juan Luis Vives*. Mexico, 2007.

González González, Enrique, and Leticia Pérez Puente, eds. *Colegios y universidades*. 2 vols. Mexico, 2001.

González Novalín, José. *El inquisidor general Fernando de Valdés*. Oviedo, 1971.

——. "Las instrucciones de la Inquisición española. De Torquemada a Valdés (1484–1561)." In *Perfiles jurídicos de la Inquisición española*. Edited by José Antonio Escudero. Madrid, 1989.

González Obregón, Luis. *D. Guillén de Lampart: La Inquisición y la independencia en el siglo XVII*. Mexico, 1908.

Goñi Gaztambide, J. "El impresor Miguel de Eguía, procesado por la Inquisición." *Hispania Sacra* 1 (1948).

Grahn, Lance. *The Political Economy of Smuggling: Regional Informal Economies in Early Bourbon New Granada*. Boulder, 1997.

Graizbord, David L. *Souls in Dispute: Converso Identities in Iberia and the Jewish Diaspora, 1580–1700*. Philadelphia, 2004.

Greenleaf, Richard. "The Great Visitas of the Mexican Holy Office, 1645–1669." *The Americas* 44 (1988).

———. *The Mexican Inquisition in the Sixteenth Century.* Albuquerque, 1969.

———. *Zumárraga and the Mexican Inquisition, 1536–1543.* Washington, D.C., 1961.

Grendler, Paul F. *The Roman Inquisition and the Venetian Press, 1540–1605.* Princeton, 1977.

Griffin, Clive. *The Crombergers of Seville: The History of a Printing and Merchant Dynasty.* Oxford, 1988.

———. "Un curioso inventario de libros de 1528." In *El libro antiguo español.* 5 vols. General eds. María Luisa López-Vidriero and Peter M. Cátedra. Salamanca, 1988–99.

———. *Journeymen-Printers, Heresy, and the Inquisition in Sixteenth-Century Spain.* Oxford, 2005.

Gruzinski, Serge. "Los cenizos del deseo." In *De la santidad a la perversión: O de por qué no se cumplía la ley de Diós en la sociedad novohispana.* Edited by Sergio Ortega. Mexico, 1986.

———. *The Conquest of Mexico: The Incorporation of Indian Societies into the Western World, 16th–18th Centuries.* Translated by Eileen Corrigan. Cambridge, 1993.

Guibovich Pérez, Pedro. *Censura, libros e inquisición en el Perú colonial, 1570–1754.* Seville, 2003.

———. *La inquisición y la censura de libros en el Perú virreinal (1570–1813).* Lima, 2000.

Haliczer, Stephen. *Sexuality in the Confessional: A Sacrament Profaned.* Oxford, 1996.

———, ed. *Inquisition and Society in Early Modern Europe.* London, 1986.

Hall, David D. *Cultures of Print: Essays in the History of the Book.* Amherst, 1996.

———. *The Faithful Shepherd: A History of the New England Ministry in the Seventeenth Century.* Chapel Hill, 1972.

Hamilton, Earl J. *American Treasure and the Price Revolution in Spain, 1501–1650.* Harvard Economic Studies. Volume 43. New York, 1965.

Hampe Martínez, Teodoro. *Santo Oficio e historia colonial: Aproximaciones al Tribunal de la Inquisición de Lima, 1570–1820.* Lima, 1998.

Harline, Craig E. *A Bishop's Tale: Mathias Hovius among His Flock in Seventeenth-Century Flanders.* New Haven, 2000.

Haring, C. H. *Spanish Empire in America.* New York, 1947.

———. *Trade and Navigation between Spain and the Indies in the Time of the Hapsburgs.* Cambridge, Mass., 1918.

Hasker, William, David Basinger, and Eef Dekker, eds. *Middle Knowledge: Theory and Applications.* New York, 2000.

Henningsen, Gustav. "The Archives and the Historiography of the Spanish Inquisition." Translated by Lawrence Scott Rainey. In *The Inquisition in Early Modern Europe.* Edited by Gustav Henningsen and John Tedeschi in assoc. with Charles Amiel. De Kalb, Ill., 1986.

———. "La elocuencia de los números: Promesas de las 'relaciones de causas' inquisitoriales para la nueva historia social." In *Inquisición española y mentalidad inquisitorial.* Edited by Ángel Alcalá. Barcelona, 1984.

———. *The Witches' Advocate: Basque Witchcraft and the Spanish Inquisition, 1609–1614.* Reno, 1980.

Henningsen, Gustav, and John Tedeschi, in assoc. with Charles Amiel, eds. *The Inquisition in Early Modern Europe: Studies on Sources and Methods.* DeKalb, Ill., 1986.

Hernández González, Ma. Isabel. "Suma de inventarios de bibliotecas del siglo XVI (1501–1560)." In *El libro antiguo español*. 5 vols. General eds. María Luisa López-Vidriero and Peter M. Cátedra. Salamanca, 1988–1999.

Herrera Puga, Pedro. *Sociedad y delincuencia en el Siglo de Oro*. Foreword by José Cepeda Adán. Madrid, 1974.

Hoberman, Louisa Schell. *Mexico's Merchant Elite, 1590–1660: Silver, State, and Society*. Durham, 1991.

Holt, M. P. *The French Wars of Religion, 1562–1629*. Cambridge, 1996.

Homza, Lu Ann. "Erasmus as Hero, or Heretic?: Spanish Humanism and the Valladolid Assembly of 1527." *Renaissance Quarterly* 50 (1997).

———. *Religious Authority in the Spanish Renaissance*. Baltimore, 2000.

Hordes, Stanley. "The Inquisition as Economic and Political Agent: The Campaign of the Mexican Holy Office against the Crytpo-Jews in the Mid-Seventeenth Century." *The Americas* 39 (1982).

Hossain, Kimberly Lynn. "Arbiters of Faith, Agents of Empire: Spanish Inquisitors and Their Careers, 1550–1650." Ph.D. diss., Johns Hopkins University, 2006.

———. "Was Adam the First Heretic? Diego de Simancas, Luis de Páramo, and the Origins of Inquisitorial Practice." *Archiv für Reformationsgeschichte* 97 (2006).

Hsia, R. Po-Chia. *The World of Catholic Renewal, 1540–1770*. Cambridge, 1998.

Hunt, Lynn, ed. *The New Cultural History*. Berkeley, 1989.

Ippolito, Benedetto. *Analogia dell'essere: La metafisica di Suàrez tra onto-teologia medievale e filosofia moderna*. Preface by Marta Cristiani and Giacomo Marramao. Milan, 2005.

Jaffery, Nora. *False Mystics: Deviant Orthodoxy in Colonial Mexico*. Lincoln, Neb., 2004.

Jiménez Moreno, Wigberto. "Nota preliminar." In *Historia general de las cosas de Nueva España*. Bernardino Sahagún. Mexico, 1934.

Jobe, Patricia H. "Inquisitorial Manuscripts in the Biblioteca Apostolica Vaticana: A Preliminary Handlist." In *The Inquisition in Early Modern Europe: Studies on Sources and Methods*. Edited by Gustav Henningsen and John Tedeschi in assoc. with Charles Amiel. DeKalb, Ill., 1986.

Jones, Oakah L. *Guatemala in the Spanish Colonial Period*. Norman, 1994.

Kamen, Henry. *The Phoenix and the Flame: Catalonia and the Counter-Reformation*. New Haven, 1993.

———. *The Spanish Inquisition: A Historical Revision*. New Haven, 1997.

Keen, Benjamin. *Essays in the Intellectual History of Colonial Latin America*. Boulder, 1998.

Kelley, Donald R. *The Writing of History and the Study of Law*. Aldershot, UK, 1997.

Kelsey, Harry. *Sir John Hawkins: Queen Elizabeth's Slave Trader*. New Haven, 2003.

Kicza, John E. *Colonial Entrepreneurs: Family and Business in Bourbon Mexico*. Albuquerque, 1983.

Kobayashi, José María. *La educación como conquista (empresa franciscana en México)*. Mexico, 1974.

Krippner-Martínez, James. *Rereading the Conquest: Power, Politics, and the History of Early Colonial Michoacán, 1521–1565*. University Park, Pa., 2001.

Ladero Quesada, Miguel Ángel. "Spain, circa 1492: Social Values and Structures." In *Implicit Understandings: Observing, Reporting, and Reflecting on the Encounters Between Europeans and Other Peoples in the Early Modern Era.* Edited by Stuart B. Schwartz. Cambridge, 1994.

Ladurie, Emmanuel LeRoy. *Carnival in Romans.* Translated by Mary Feeney. New York, 1979.

———. *Montaillou: The Promised Land of Error.* Translated by Barbara Bray. New York, 1978.

Lanning, John Tate. *Academic Culture in the Spanish Colonies.* Oxford, 1940.

Lazar, Moshe, and Stephen Haliczer, eds. *Jews of Spain and the Expulsion of 1492.* Lancaster, Calif., 1997.

Lea, Henry Charles. *History of the Inquisition in Spain.* 4 vols. New York, 1906–1907.

———. *The Inquisition in the Spanish Dependencies.* London, 1908.

Leclercq, Jean. *Jean de Paris et l'ecclésiologie du XIIIe siècle.* Paris, 1942.

LeGoff, Jacques. "Mentalities: A History of Ambiguities." In *Constructing the Past: Essays in Historical Methodology.* Edited by Jacques LeGoff and Pierre Nora. Introduction by Colin Lucas. New York, 1985.

León, Nicolás. *Don Vasco de Quiroga: Grandeza de su persona y de su obra.* Mexico, 1984.

León Alanís, Ricardo. *Los orígenes del clero y la iglesia en Michoacán, 1525–1640.* Morelia, 1997.

León-Portilla, Miguel. *Bernardino de Sahagún: Pionero de la antropología.* Mexico, 1999.

Leonard, Irving A. *Baroque Times in Old Mexico: Seventeenth-Century Persons, Places, and Practices.* Ann Arbor, 1959.

———. *Books of the Brave: Being an Account of Books and of Men in the Spanish Conquest and Settlement of the Sixteenth-Century World.* Ann Arbor, 1949.

Lewis, Laura. *Hall of Mirrors: Power, Witchcraft, and Caste in Colonial Mexico.* Durham, 2003.

Liebman, Seymour B. "The Abedeciario and a Check-List of Mexican Inquisition Documents at the Henry E. Huntington Library." *Hispanic American Historical Review* 44 (1964).

———. *The Jews in New Spain: Faith, Flame, and the Inquisition.* Coral Gables, Fla., 1970.

Llamas Martínez, Enrique. *Santa Teresa de Jesús y la Inquisición española.* Madrid, 1972.

Lockhart, James. *The Nahuas after the Conquest: A Social and Cultural History of the Indians of Central Mexico, Sixteenth through Eighteenth Centuries.* Stanford, 1991.

———. "The Social History of Colonial Spanish America: Evolution and Potential." *Latin American Research Review* 7 (1972).

Longhurst, John E. *Luther and the Spanish Inquisition: The Case of Diego de Uceda, 1528–1529.* Albuquerque, 1953.

———. *Luther's Ghost in Spain, 1517–1546.* Lawrence, Kan., 1969.

López Cervantes, Gonzalo, and Rosa María García García. *Ensayo bibliográfico del período colonial de México.* Mexico, 1989.

López Vela, Roberto. "El calificador en el procedimiento y la organización del Santo Oficio: Inquisición y órdenes religiosas en el siglo XVII." In *Perfiles jurídicos de la inquisición española*. Edited by José Antonio Escudero. Madrid, 1989.

López-Vidriero, María Luisa, and Pedro M. Cátedra, eds. *El libro antiguo español*. 5 vols. Salamanca, c. 1988–99.

Luhmann, Niklas. *Religious Dogmatics and the Evolution of Societies*. Translated and with introduction by Peter Beyer. Studies in Religion and Society. Vol. 9. New York, 1984.

Lundberg, Magnus. "Unity and Conflict: The Church Politics of Alonso de Montúfar, O.P., Archbishop of Mexico, 1554–1572." Ph.D. diss., Lund University, 2004.

Luque Muriel, Francisco. "Los abecedarios como fuente para el estudio de la legislación." In *Perfiles jurídicos de la inquisición española*. Edited by José Antonio Escudero. Madrid, 1989.

MacCormick, Sabine. *Religion in the Andes: Vision and Imagination in Early Colonial Peru*. Princeton, 1991.

MacLeod, Murdo J. *Las Casas, Guatemala, and the Sad but Inevitable Case of Antonio Remesal*. Pittsburgh, 1970.

Maguire, William Edward. *John of Torquemada, O.P.: The Antiquity of the Church*. Washington, D.C., 1957.

Mandrou, Robert. *De la culture populaire aux 17e et 18e siècles: La Bibliothèque bleue de Troyes*. Paris, 1964.

Mantilla Ruiz, Luis Carlos. *Don Bartolomé Lobo Guerrero: Inquisidor y tercer arzobispo de Santa Fé de Bogotá (1599–1609)*. Bogotá, 1996.

Manzano Manzano, Juan. *Historia de las recopilaciones de Indias*. 2 vols. 3d ed. Madrid, 1991.

Maqueda Abreu, Consuelo. *Estado, Iglesia e Inquisición en Indias: Un permanente conflicto*. Madrid, 2000.

Maravall, José Antonio. *La cultura del Barroco: Análisis de una estructura histórica*. Barcelona, 1975.

Martínez, Gregorio Bartolomé. *Jaque mate al obispo virrey: Siglo y medio de sátiras y libelos contra Don Juan de Palafox y Mendoza*. Mexico, 1991.

Martínez Ferrer, Luis. *La penitencia en la primera evangelización de México (1523–1585)*. Mexico, 1998.

Martínez Millán, José. "Aportaciones a la formación del estado moderno y a la política española a través de la censura inquisitorial durante el período 1480–1559." In *La inquisición española: Nuevas visiones, nuevos horizontes*. Edited by J. Pérez Villanueva. Madrid, 1980.

———. *La hacienda de la Inquisición, 1478–1700*. Madrid, 1984.

Martínez Peláez, Severo. *La patria del criollo: Ensayo de interpretación de la realidad colonial guatemalteca*. Guatemala, 1970.

Mathes, Michael. *Santa Cruz de Tlatelolco: La primera biblioteca académica de las Américas*. Mexico, 1982.

McKenzie, D. F. *Bibliography and the Sociology of Texts*. Cambridge, 1999.

Medina, José Toribio. *Historia del tribunal del santo oficio de la inquisición en México*. Expanded by Julio Jiménez Rueda. Mexico, 1905.

———. *La imprenta en México*. 8 vols. Santiago, 1908–12.

———. *La inquisición en Cartagena de Indias*. Foreword by Pedro Gómez Valderrama. Bogotá, 1978.

———. *La inquisición primitiva Americana*. Santiago, c. 1914.

Mello e Souza, Laura de. *O diabo e a terra de Santa Cruz: Feitiçaria e religiosidade popular no Brasil colonial*. São Paulo, 1986.

Méndez, María Águeda. *Secretos del Oficio: Avatares de la inquisición novohispana*. Mexico, 2001.

Méndez, María Águeda, Ricardo Camarena Castellanos, Fernando del Mar, and Ana María Morales, eds. *Catálogo de textos marginados novohispanos. Inquisición: Siglo XVII*. Archivo General de la Nación. Mexico, 1997.

Menéndez Pelayo, Marcelino. *Historia de los heterodoxos españoles*. Madrid, 1880.

Millar Carvacho, René. *Inquisición y sociedad en el virreinato peruano: Estudios sobre el tribunal de la Inquisición de Lima*. Lima, 1998.

Millares Carlo, Agustín. *El Epítome de Pinelo, primera bibliografía del nuevo mundo*. Washington, D.C., 1958.

Millares Carlo, Agustín, and Julián Calvo. *Juan Pablos, primer impresor que a esta tierra vino*. Mexico, 1953.

Miller, Perry. *Orthodoxy in Massachusetts, 1630–1650*. Gloucester, Mass., 1965.

Mills, Kenneth R. *Idolatry and Its Enemies: Colonial Andean Religion and Extirpation, 1640–1750*. Princeton, 1997.

Miranda, José. *El erasmista mexicano: Fray Alonso Cabello*. Mexico, 1958.

Miranda Godínez, Francisco. *Don Vasco de Quiroga y su Colegio de San Nicolás*. Morelia, 1972.

Molina Meliá, Antonio. *Iglesia y Estado en el siglo de oro español: El pensamiento de Francisco Suárez*. Valencia, 1977.

Monter, William. *Frontiers of Heresy: The Spanish Inquisition from the Basque Lands to Sicily*. Cambridge, 1990.

Moore, Barrington, Jr. *Moral Purity and Persecution in History*. Princeton, 2000.

Moore, John C. *Pope Innocent III (1160/61–1216): To Root Up and to Plant*. Leiden, 2003.

Moreno, Doris. *La invención de la Inquisición*. Madrid, 2004.

Moreno, Juan Joseph. *Don Vasco de Quiroga, Primer Obispo de Michoacán: Fragmentos de la vida y virtudes de . . .* Morelia, 1965.

Morera, Jaime. *Pinturas coloniales de ánimas del purgatorio: Iconografía de una creencia*. Mexico, 2001.

Morón Arroyo, Ciriaco. "La inquisición y la posibilidad de la gran literatura barroca española." In *Inquisición española y mentalidad inquisitorial*. Edited by Ángel Alcalá. Barcelona, 1984.

Mott, Luiz. *Escravidão, homossexualidade e demonologia*. São Paulo, 1988.

———. *O sexo proibido: Virgens, gays e escravos nas garras da Inquisição*. Campinus, 1988.

Muir, Edward, and Guido Ruggiero, eds. *History from Crime*. Translated by Corrado Biazzo Curry, Margaret A. Gallucci, and Mary M. Gallucci. Baltimore, 1994.

Muldoon, James. "Boniface VIII's Forty Years of Experience in the Law." *The Jurist* 31 (1971).

———. *Canon Law, the Expansion of Europe, and World Order*. Aldershot, UK, 1998.

———. *"Extra ecclesiam non est imperium:* The Canonists and the Legitimacy of Secular Power." *Studia Gratiana* 9 (1966).

———, ed. *The Spiritual Conversion of the Americas*. Gainesville, 2004.

Mundy, John Hine, and Kennerly M. Woody, eds. *Council of Constance: The Unification of the Church*. New York, 1961.

Muriel, Josefina. *Los recogimientos de mujeres: Respuesta a una problemática social novohispana*. Mexico, 1974.

Nalle, Sara T. "Literacy and Culture in Early Modern Castile." *Past and Present* 125 (1989).

Nesvig, Martin Austin. "Heterodoxia popular e Inquisición diocesana en Michoacán, Siglo XVI." *Tzintzun* 39 (2004).

———. "Pearls before Swine: Theory and Practice of Censorship in New Spain, 1527–1640." Ph.D. diss., Yale University, 2004.

———. "El sermón de un erasmista olvidado." *Boletín del Archivo General de la Nación* [Mexico], 6a época, no. 5 (2004).

———, ed. *Local Religion in Colonial Mexico*. Albuquerque, 2006.

Netanyahu, Benzion. *The Origins of the Inquisition in the Fifteenth Century*. New York, 1995.

———. *Toward the Inquisition: Essays on Jewish and Converso History in Late Medieval Spain*. Ithaca, 1997.

Nieto, José C. *Juan de Valdés and the Origins of the Spanish and Italian Reformation*. Geneva, 1970.

Norgueira, Carlo Roberto. "A migração do Sabbat: A presença 'estrangeira' das bruxas européias no imaginário ibérico." *Espado, Tiempo y Forma*, serie 4, vol. 5 (1992).

Núñez Roldán, Francisco. *La vida cotidiana en la Sevilla del Siglo de Oro*. Madrid, 2004.

———. *El pecado nefando del Obispo de Salamina: Un hombre sin concierto en la corte de Felipe II*. Seville, 2002.

Oberman, Heiko A. *Luther: Man between God and the Devil*. New York, 1992.

O'Gorman, Edmundo. *Idea del descubrimiento de América: Historia de esa interpretación y crítica de sus fundamentos*. Mexico, 1951.

———. *Invención de América: El universalismo de la cultura de Occidente*. Mexico, 1958.

Olaechea Labayen, Juan B. "Opinión de los teólogos españoles sobre dar estudios mayores a los Indios." *Anuario de estudios americanos* 15 (1958).

Olarte, Teodoro. *Alfonso de Castro (1495–1558): Su vida, su tiempo y sus ideas filosóficas-jurídicas*. San José, Costa Rica, 1946.

O'Malley, John W. *The First Jesuits*. Cambridge, Mass., 1993.

———. *Trent and All That: Renaming Catholicism in the Early Modern Era*. Cambridge, Mass., 2000.

———, ed. *Catholicism in Early Modern History: A Guide to Research*. Reformation Guides to Research. Vol. 2 of 2. St. Louis, 1988.

O'Meara, Thomas F. "The Dominican School of Salamanca and the Spanish Conquest of America: Some Bibliographic Notes." *The Thomist* 56 (1992).

O'Reilly, Terence. "Melchor Cano and the Spirituality of St. Ignatius Loyola." In *Ignacio de Loyola y su tiempo*. Edited by Juan Plazaola. Bilbao, 1992.

Ortega, Sergio, ed. *De la santidad a la perversión: O de por qué no se cumplía la ley de Diós en la sociedad novohispana.* Mexico, 1986.

Ortega y Pérez Gallando, Ricardo, ed. *Historia genealógica de las familias más antiguas de México.* Mexico, 1908.

Osorio Romero, Ignacio. *La enseñanza del latín a los indios.* Mexico, 1990.

Ots y Capdequí, José María. *El estado español en las Indias.* Mexico, 1941.

——. *Manual de historia de derecho español en las Indias y del derecho propiamente indiano.* Foreword by Ricardo Levene. Buenos Aires, 1945.

Padden, Robert C. "The Ordenanza del Patronazgo of 1574: An Interpretive Essay." In *The Church in Colonial Latin America.* Edited by John W. Schwaller. Wilmington, Del., 2000.

Pagden, Anthony. *The Fall of Natural Man: The American Indian and the Origins of Comparative Ethnology.* Cambridge, 1982.

——. *Spanish Imperialism and the Political Imagination.* New Haven, 1990.

Palacios Alcalde, María. "Legislación inquisitorial (1478–1504)." Tesis de licenciatura, Universidad de Granada, 1987.

Palau y Dulcet, Antonio. *Manual del librero hispano-americano: Bibliografía general española e hispano-americana desde la invención de la imprenta hasta nuestros tiempos.* 28 vols. Barcelona and Oxford, 1948–77.

Pardo, Osvaldo F. *The Origins of Mexican Catholicism: Nahua Rituals and Christian Sacraments in Sixteenth-Century Mexico.* Ann Arbor, 2004.

Pardo Tomás, José. *Ciencia y censura: La Inquisición Española y los libros científicos en los siglos XVI y XVII.* Madrid, 1991.

Parker, Geoffrey. *The Grand Strategy of Phillip II.* New Haven, 1998.

Pasamar Lázaro, José Enrique. *La cofradía de San Pedro Mártir de Verona en el distrito inquisitorial de Aragón.* Zaragoza, 1997.

Pastore, Stephania. *Un'eresia spagnola: Spiritualità conversa, alumbradismo e inquisizione (1449–1559).* Florence, 2004.

——. *Il vangelo e la spada: L'Inquisizione di Castiglia e i suoi critici (1460–1598).* Rome, 2003.

Pavia, Mario N. *Drama of the Siglo de Oro: A Study of Magic, Witchcraft and Other Occult Beliefs.* New York, 1959.

Pavón Romero, Armando. "Doctores en la Universidad de México en el siglo XVI." In *Colegios y universidades I: Del antiguo régimen al liberalismo.* Edited by Enrique González González and Leticia Pérez Puente. Mexico, 2001.

Pennington, Kenneth. *Pope and Bishops: The Papal Monarchy in the Twelfth and Thirteenth Centuries.* Philadelphia, 1984.

Peña, Margarita, ed. *La palabra amordazada: Literatura censurada por la Inquisición.* Mexico, 2000.

Pérez, Antonio Roldán. "Reflexiones sobre la producción literaria de los funcionarios inquisitoriales." In *Perfiles jurídicos de la inquisición española.* Edited by José Antonio Escudero. Madrid, 1989.

Pérez Fernández, Isacio. *El derecho hispano-indiano: Dinámica social de su proceso histórico constituyente.* Salamanca, 2001.

Pérez Martín, Antonio. "La doctrina jurídica y el proceso inquisitorial." In *Perfiles jurídicos de la inquisición española.* Edited by José Antonio Escudero. Madrid, 1989.

Pérez Villanueva, Joaquín. "El colegio de los españoles en Bolonia, ¿Jurisdicción exenta?, y algo de inquisición." *Annuario dell'istituto storico italiano per l'età moderna e contemporanea* 35–36 (1983–84).

———, ed. *La Inquisición española: Nueva visión, nuevos horizontes.* Madrid, 1980.

Pérez Villanueva, Joaquín, and Bartolomé Escandell Bonet, eds. *Historia de la Inquisición en España y América.* 3 vols. Madrid, c. 1984.

Peters, E. M. "Francisco Peña and the 'Directorium Inquisitorum' of Nicholas Eymerich." *The Library Chronicle* 1975.

———. *Inquisition.* New York, 1988.

———. *Torture.* New York, 1985.

Phelan, John Leddy. *The Millennial Kingdom of the Franciscans in the New World.* 2d ed., rev. Berkeley, 1970.

Pinto Crespo, Virgilio. "La censura: Sistemas de control e instrumentos de acción." In *Inquisición española y mentalidad inquisitorial.* Edited by Ángel Alcalá. Barcelona, 1984.

———. *Inquisición y control ideológico en la España del siglo XVI.* Madrid, 1983.

———. "Thought Control in Spain." In *Inquisition and Society in Early Modern Europe.* Edited by Stephen Haliczer. London, 1986.

Poole, Stafford. *Our Lady of Guadalupe: The Origins and Sources of a Mexican National Symbol, 1531–1797.* Tucson, 1997.

———. *Pedro Moya de Contreras: Catholic Reform and Royal Power in New Spain, 1571–1591.* Berkeley, 1987.

Powell, James M. *Innocent III: Vicar of Christ or Emperor of the World?* Washington, D.C., 1994.

Prado Moura, Ángel de. *Inquisición e inquisidores en Castilla: El tribunal de Valladolid durante la crisis del antiguo régimen.* Valladolid, 1995.

Prosperi, Adriano. "L'Arsenale degli inquisitori." In *Inquisizione e Indice nei secoli XVI–XVIII: Testi e immagini nelle raccolte casanatensi.* Edited by Angela Adriana Cavarra. Rome, 1998.

———. *L'Inquisizione romana: Letture e richerche.* Rome, 2003.

———. *Tribunali della coscienza: Inquisitori, confessori, missionari.* Turin, 1996.

Putnam, George Haven. *The Censorship of the Church of Rome.* 2 vols. New York, 1906–1907.

Quezada, Noemí. *Enfermedad y maleficio: El curandero en el México colonial.* Mexico, 1989.

———. *Sexualidad, amor y erotismo: México prehispánico y México colonial.* Mexico, 1996.

Quezada, Noemí, Martha Eugenia Rodríguez, and Marcela Suárez, eds. *Inquisición novohispana.* 2 vols. Mexico, 2000.

Rábade Romeo, Sergio. *Francisco Suárez (1548–1617).* Madrid, 1997.

Ramírez Flores, José. "Prologue." In *Descripción de la provincia de San Pedro y San Pablo de Michoacán, en las Indias de la Nueva España.* Diego Muñoz. Guadalajara, 1965.

Ramírez González, Clara Inés. *Grupos de poder clerical de las universidades hispánicas: Los regulares en Salamanca y México durante el siglo XVI.* 2 vols. Mexico, 2001.

Ramírez Leyva, Elsa M. *El libro y la lectura en el proceso de occidentalización de México.* Mexico, 2001.

Ramírez Montes, Mina. *La catedral de Vasco de Quiroga.* Zamora, 1986.

Ramos, Demetrio, et al. *Francisco de Vitoria y la escuela de Salamanca: La ética en la conquista de América.* Madrid, 1984.

Ramos Soriano, José Abel. "Criterios inquisitoriales en la prohibición de literatura relacionada con la comunidad doméstica en la Nueva España." In *El placer de pecar y el afán de normar.* Seminario de Historia de las Mentalidades. Mexico, 1988.

Ricard, Robert. *Études et documents pour l'histoire missionnaire de l'Espagne et du Portugal.* Louvain, 1930.

——. "Notes sur la biographie de Fr. Alonso de Montúfar, second archevêque de Mexico (1551–1572)." *Bulletin Hispanique* 27 (1925).

——. *The Spiritual Conquest of Mexico.* Translated by Leslie Byrd Simpson. Berkeley, 1982.

Rodríguez, Pedro. *El Catecismo Romano ante Felipe II y la Inquisición española: Los problemas de la introducción en España del catecismo del Concilio de Trento.* Madrid, 1998.

Rodríguez Cruz, Águeda María. *Salmantica docet: La proyección de la Universidad de Salamanca en Hispanoamérica.* 2 vols. Salamanca, 1977.

Rodríguez Molinero, Marcelino. *Origen español de la ciencia del derecho penal: Alfonso de Castro y su sistema penal.* Madrid, 1959.

Rodríguez-Vigil Rubio, Juan Luis. *Bruxas [sic], lobos e inquisición: El proceso de Ana María García, la Lobera.* Oviedo, 1996

Rojas Garcidueñas, José. *El teatro de Nueva España en el siglo XVI.* Mexico, 1935.

Roldán Pérez, Antonio. "Reflexiones sobre la producción literaria de los funcionarios inquisitoriales." In *Perfiles jurídicos de la inquisición española.* Edited by José Antonio Escudero. Madrid, 1989.

Roth, Cecil. *The Spanish Inquisition.* New York, 1964.

Rubial García, Antonio. *La santidad controvertida: Hagiografía y conciencia criolla alrededor de los venerables no canonizados de Nueva España.* Mexico, 1999.

Rueda Ramírez, Pedro. *Negocio e intercambio cultural: El comercio de libros con América en la carrera de Indias (siglo XVII).* Seville, 2005.

Ruiz Fidalgo, Lorenzo. *La imprenta en Salamanca (1501–1600).* 3 vols. Madrid, 1994.

Ruiz Medrano, Ethelia. "Los negocios de un arzobispo: El caso de fray Alonso de Montúfar." *Estudios de Historia Novohispana* 12 (1992).

Ruiz y Torres, Josefina Edith. "A puerta cerrada: Lectura e inquisición en el siglo XVI novohispano." Tesis de licenciatura, Escuela Nacional de Antropología e Historia [Mexico], 1998.

Rundine, Angelo. *Inquisizione spagnola: Censura e libri proibiti in Sardegna nel '500 e '600.* Sassari, 1996.

Sacristán, María Cristina. *Locura e Inquisición en Nueva España, 1571–1760.* Mexico, 1992.

Salaverri de la Torre, Joaquín. "La noción de Iglesia del Padre Luis de Molina." *Revista Española de Teología* 20 (1960).

Sanchiz, Javier. "Funcionarios inquisitoriales en el tribunal, siglo XVI." In *Inquisición novohispana*. Edited by Noemí Quezada, Martha Eugenia Rodríguez, and Marcela Suárez. Mexico, 2000.

Sánchez Bella, Ismael, et al. *Historia del derecho indiano*. Madrid, 1992.

Santonja, Pedro. *La herejía de los alumbrados y la espiritualidad en la España del siglo XVI: Inquisición y sociedad*. Valencia, 2001.

Saranyana, Josep Ignasi. "La eucaristía en la teología sacramentaria Americana del siglo XVI." In *Eucaristía y nueva evangelización: Actas del IV Simposio la Iglesia en España y América: Siglos XVI–XX*. Córdoba, c. 1994.

Sarrión Mora, Adelina. *Beatas y endemoniadas: Mujeres heterodoxas ante la Inquisición, siglos XVI a XIX*. Madrid, 2003.

Schons, Dorothy. *Book Censorship in New Spain*. Austin, 1949.

Scott, James Brown. *Catholic Conception of International Law: Francisco de Vitoria, Founder of the Modern Law of Nations; Francisco Suárez, Founder of the Modern Philosophy of Law in General and in Particular of the Law of Nations*. Washington, D.C., 1934.

Schwaller, John F. *The Church and Clergy in Sixteenth-Century Mexico*. Albuquerque, 1987.

——. *Origins of Church Wealth: Ecclesiastical Revenues and Church Finances, 1523–1600*. Albuquerque, 1985.

——, ed. *The Church in Colonial Latin America*. Wilmington, Del., 2000.

Schwartz, Stuart B. *All Can Be Saved: Religious Tolerance and Salvation in the Iberian Atlantic World*. New Haven, 2008.

——. "Pecar en las colonias: Mentalidades populares, Inquisición y actitudes hacia la fornicación simple en España, Portugal y las colonias americanas." *Cuadernos de Historia Moderna* 18 (1997).

——, ed. *Implicit Understandings: Observing, Reporting, and Reflecting on the Encounters Between Europeans and Other Peoples in the Early Modern Era*. Cambridge, 1994.

Scribner, Robert W. *For the Sake of Simple Folk: Popular Propaganda for the German Reformation*. Cambridge, 1981.

Seminario de Historia de las Mentalidades. *El placer de pecar y el afán de normar*. Mexico, 1988.

Serrano y Sanz, Manuel. "Pedro Ruiz de Alcaraz, iluminado alcarreño del siglo XVI." *Revista de Archivos, Bibliotecas y Museos* 8 (1903).

Sharrer, Harvey L. "Juan de Burgos: Impresor y refundidor de libros caballerescos." In *El libro antiguo español*. 5 vols. General eds. María Luisa López-Vidriero and Peter M. Cátedra. Salamanca, 1988–99.

Simpson, Leslie Byrd. *The Encomienda in New Spain: The Beginning of Spanish Mexico*. Berkeley, 1950.

——. *Many Mexicos*. Berkeley, 1963.

Smith, Gerard. *Freedom in Molina*. Chicago, 1966.

Socolow, Susan Migden. *The Women of Colonial Latin America*. Cambridge, 2000.

Starr-LeBeau, Gretchen D. *In the Shadow of the Virgin: Inquisitors, Friars, and Conversos in Guadalupe, Spain*. Princeton, 2002.

Stump, Philip H. *Reforms of the Council of Constance (1414–1418)*. London, 1994.

Tau Anzoátegui, Víctor. *La ley en América hispana: Del descubrimiento a la emancipación*. Buenos Aires, 1992.

Tavárez, David. "Autonomy, Honor, and the Ancestors: Native Local Religion in Seventeenth-Century Oaxaca." In *Local Religion in Colonial Mexico*. Edited by Martin Austin Nesvig. Albuquerque, 2006.

——. "La idolatría letrada: Un análisis comparativo de textos clandestinos rituales y devocionales en comunidades nahuas y zapotecas, 1613–1654." *Historia Mexicana* 49 (1999).

——. "Idolatry as an Ontological Question: Native Consciousness and Juridical Proof in Colonial Mexico." *Journal of Early Modern History* 6 (2002).

Taylor, William B. *Magistrates of the Sacred: Priests and Parishioners in Eighteenth-Century Mexico*. Stanford, 1996.

Tedeschi, John. "The Dispersed Archives of the Roman Inquisition." In *The Inquisition in Early Modern Europe: Studies on Sources and Methods*. Edited by Gustav Henningsen and John Tedeschi in assoc. with Charles Amiel. De Kalb, Ill., 1986.

——. *The Prosecution of Heresy: Collected Studies of the Inquisition in Early Modern Italy*. Binghampton, 1991.

Tellechea Idígoras, José Ignacio. *El arzobispo Carranza y su tiempo*. 2 vols. Madrid, 1968.

——. "Biblias publicadas fuera de España y secuestradads por la inquisición de Sevilla." *Bulletin Hispanique* 64 (1962).

——. *El proceso romano del Arzobispo Carranza: Las audiencias en Sant'Angelo, 1568–1569*. Rome, 1994.

Tentler, Thomas N. *Sin and Confession on the Eve of the Reformation*. Princeton, 1977.

TePaske, John J., and Herbert S. Klein. "The Seventeenth-Century Crisis in New Spain: Myth or Reality?" *Past and Present* 90 (1981).

Tierney, Brian. *Foundations of the Conciliar Theory: The Contribution of the Medieval Canonists from Gratian to the Great Schism*. Cambridge, 1955.

Terraciano, Kevin. *The Mixtecs of Colonial Oaxaca: Ñudzahui History, Sixteenth through Eighteenth Centuries*. Stanford, 2001.

Thomas, Hugh. *Who's Who of the Conquistadors*. London, 2000.

Tomás y Valiente, Francisco. "El crimen y el pecado contra natura." In *Sexo barroco y otras transgresiones premodernas*. Madrid, 1990.

——. *El derecho penal de la Monarquía absoluta, Siglos XVI–XVII*. Madrid, 1969.

——. *Gobierno e instituciones en la España del antiguo régimen*. Madrid, 1982.

——. *La tortura judicial en España*. Barcelona, 1994.

——, et al. *Sexo barroco y otras transgresiones premodernas*. Madrid, 1990.

Torquemada, María Jesús. "Censura de libros y barreras aduaneras." In *Perfiles jurídicos de la inquisición española*. Edited by José Antonio Escudero. Madrid, 1989.

Torre, Esteban. "Introducción." In *Examen de ingenios para las ciencias*. Juan Huarte de San Juan. Edited by Esteban Torre. Barcelona, 1988.

Torre Revello, José. *El libro, la imprenta, y el periodismo en América durante la dominación española*. Buenos Aires, 1940.

Torres Puga, Gabriel. *Los últimos años de la Inquisición en la Nueva España*. Mexico, 2004.

Tortorici, Zeb. " 'Heran Todos Putos': Sodomitical Subcultures and Disordered Desire in Early Colonial Mexico." *Ethnohistory* 54 (2007).

Ullmann, Walter. "The Significance of Innocent III's *Vergentis.*" In *The Papacy and Political Ideas in the Middle Ages.* London, 1978.

Vainfas, Ronaldo. *Trópico dos pecados: Moral, sexualidade e Inquisição no Brasil.* Rio de Janeiro, 1989.

van der Vekene, Emil. *Biblioteca bibliographica historiae sanctae inquisitionis.* 2 vols. Vaduz, 1982.

Vera, Fortino Hipólito. *Concilios provinciales mexicanos y privilegios de América.* Mexico, 1893.

Villa-Flores, Javier. *Dangerous Speech: A Social History of Blasphemy in Colonial Mexico.* Tucson, 2006.

———. "Voices from a Living Hell: Slavery, Death, and Salvation in a Mexican Obraje." In *Local Religion in Colonial Mexico.* Edited by Martin Austin Nesvig. Albuquerque, 2006.

Vovelle, Michel. *Ideologies and Mentalities.* Translated by Eamon O'Flaherty. Chicago, 1990.

Wagner, Klaus. *El doctor Constantino Ponce de la Fuente: El hombre y su biblioteca.* Seville, 1979.

———. "¿Qué costaron los estudios universitarios en Salamanca a principios del siglo XVI?" *Archivo hispalense* 59 (1976).

Wakefield, Walter L. "Notes on Some Antiheretical Writings of the Thirteenth Century." *Franciscan Studies* 27 (1967).

Ward, Ken. " 'Estos cuentos son sin cuenta': The Inquisition Trials of Pedro Ocharte and Juan Ortiz." M.A. thesis, University of Texas, Austin, c. 2001.

Weckmann, Luis. *La herencia medieval de México.* Mexico, 1984.

Weis, René. *The Yellow Cross: The Story of the Last Cathars, 1290–1309.* London, 2000.

Weruaga Prieto, Ángel. *Libros y lectura en Salamanca: Del barroco a la ilustración 1650–1725.* Salamanca, 1993.

Wicks, Jared. "Doctrine and Theology." In *Catholicism in Early Modern Europe: A Guide to Research.* Reformation Guides to Research. Vol. 2. Edited by John O'Malley. St. Louis, 1988.

Winroth, Anders. *The Making of Gratian's Decretum.* Cambridge, 2000.

Wood, Charles T., ed. *Philip the Fair and Boniface VIII: State vs. Papacy.* New York, 1967.

Zaballa Beascoechea, Ana de, and Josep-Ignasi Sarayana. "Bartolomé de Ledesma y su doctrina sobre los justos títulos." In *Actas del III Congreso Internacional sobre los Dominicos y el nuevo mundo.* Madrid, 1991.

Zambrano, Francisco, ed. *Diccionario bio-bibliográfico de la Compañía de Jesús en México.* 16 vols. Mexico, 1967.

Zavala, Silvio. *Filosofía política en la conquista de América.* Mexico, 1947.

Zawart, Anscar. *The History of Franciscan Preaching and of Franciscan Preachers (1209–1927): A Bio-Bibliographical Study.* Franciscan Studies, series 1, no. 7. New York, 1928.

Zúñiga y Ontiveros, Mariano Joseph de. *Catálogo de los Colegiales del Insigne Viejo y Mayor de Santa María de Todos Santos.* Mexico, 1796.

Index